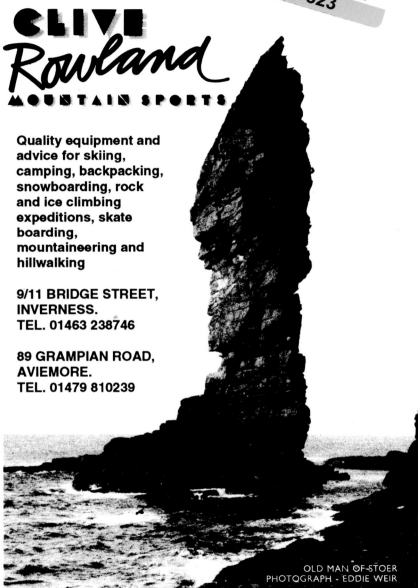

All aboard the S.Y. Erne during the SMC Yacht Meet – Easter 1887.

THE SCOTTISH
MOUNTAINEERING
CLUB JOURNAL

| Vol. XXXVI | 1997 | No. 188 |

HOOKS, TORQUES AND CHICKEN HEADS

A Collection of Winter Climbs

Scottish winter climbing is increasing in popularity every year, and has never had so many devotees. Despite the wide interest, the precise nature of the sport is often misunderstood. Over the last 20 years or so, techniques have evolved, attitudes have changed, and the definition of what makes a good winter route has been transformed. Climbers are fitter and stronger than before, and the emphasis has moved away from ice to more technically demanding mixed routes. The following tales of derring-do, by some of those at the forefront of the sport, capture the flavour of today's top-level winter climbs.

The collection starts with Andy Nisbet's inspiring account of The Rat-Trap (VIII,8) on Creag an Dubh Loch. Ten years on, perhaps no other winter route has equalled this for commitment and sustained difficulty. Compare this with Robin McAllister's description of the first winter ascent of Direct Direct (VII,9) on The Cobbler. Here it is the pure technical difficulty of the climbing which shines through, especially when you consider that it took all day to climb the 35m-long route.

Winter climbing is more than about just physical skill however, and Rab Anderson describes the mental resources required to climb the crux of Raven's Edge (VIII,7) on the Buachaille. In a similar vein, Chris Cartwright recounts Dave Hesleden's inspirational lead of the thinly-iced Foobarbundee (VIII,7) on Liathach, a route that is generally recognised to be one of the most serious ice routes in the country.

In an age of pushing limits, repeats are important too, and Dave McGimpsey takes us up the second ascent of Inclination (VIII,8) on Stob Coire nan Lochan in Glen Coe. For some climbers though, the key challenge is to venture onto terrain which would be unthinkable in summer. Roger Everett gives us a perfect example as he describes the first ascent of The Screaming (VIII,8), a wickedly steep and futuristic line on Beinn an Dothaidh.

The collection finishes with an account of Cornucopia (VII,9), a difficult mixed climb on Ben Nevis. These routes are at the vanguard of today's developments, but given the pace of today's winter scene, they will almost certainly be eclipsed soon. The next few years are likely to be very exciting indeed!

Simon Richardson.

THE RAT-TRAP

By Andy Nisbet

IN THE early Eighties, I thought that Creag an Dubh Loch was the place for the future. In summer, the big open faces with their raking cracklines offer routes of the highest technical difficulty for pitch after pitch. Surely, this is where Scottish winter climbing would go? I was wrong. The cliff has only seen limited activity over the past 10 years. Why? Is it perhaps the epics that have accompanied most of the big Dubh Loch winter routes? Labyrinth Direct and its non-existent belay below the crux, and Norman Keir and Dave Wright's enforced bivvy on White Elephant have passed into Cairngorm climbing folklore. Other tales still remain to be told. How about Alfie Robertson fighting up the top pitch of Vertigo Wall with a failing torch at midnight on the second day, or the occasion when I contracted hypothermia after belaying Phil Thornhill for five hours in a blizzard halfway up Black Mamba?

So what is wrong with the place? There's too much ice maybe, but then only rarely. There's certainly too much temptation to wait for ice, and it's too far from the road to find out if there is any. If there's no ice, there could be snow on the faces instead, but then there could always be too much. And, of course, there is always work on Monday. Back then I didn't work, I climbed on the Dubh Loch instead. Now I work and don't climb big Dubh Loch routes, and life is a little less exciting as a result. Lochnagar is too short, Coire Mhic Fhearchair too well protected, and the Shelter Stone is too escapable.

That's the problem with the Dubh Loch, it's easy to get side-tracked into thinking about other places, so back to The Rat-Trap. It was 1986, and I had turned down the offer of a first season at Glenmore Lodge to leave the winter free for climbing. I knew I couldn't turn down a similar opportunity again, so I was focused on the Dubh Loch. Sandy Allan was focused too, but the season is short. The bivouacs are too long in January and from mid-February onwards, the Central Gully Wall is stripped by the sun. Suddenly, at the end of January, we had a good forecast for two calm and cold days. It was a bit early, but the full moon tempted us out. And not just us, for we met Dougie Dinwoodie at the Glas Allt bothy all set to do Mousetrap. It was a relief to know we weren't competing for the same climb. Mousetrap was the only winter route on the front face of Central Gully Wall, but it takes the obvious easy line (I was cocky in those days). We would start up Dubh Loch Monster and climb the non-obvious easy line on the face to the right. I'd climbed Dubh Loch Monster in summer, and knew that the crux roof low down on the route was split by a thin crack, so it had to be 'possible'. The rest was less immediate and would probably follow after a bivouac. So a hauling rope, stove, food, sleeping bags etc. were added to the normal climbing gear, and we set off at 5am to reach the crag at first light.

The first pitch proved to be a lot easier than expected, but the roof was a different story. Placing gear was incredibly strenuous, but after some protracted climbing up and down I was eventually in a position to pull over the lip. My hammer pick then lost its top inch (the only time it's happened to me torquing), and my feeling of total confidence was reduced to one of imminent failure. I dangled beside the belay with exhausted arms and minus one tool for the long traverse above. Sandy comes to the fore in these situations: 'You take mine,' and the traverse 'inshallah.' With two tools the traverse was sustained but never desperate, and it was the same for the next pitch to below the Red Wall fault. Sandy seemed happy enough with one-and-a-half axes, but my memory of these pitches was aching arms from the roof. The sack-hauling was time consuming. The bag caught on every knobble, and it was now dark. I say dark, but the cliff faces the rising moon, so it was gloomy rather than pitch black. After the haul-sack took some monster swings on the traverse, it finally had enough and refused to come past an overlap. The decision was made for us – we wouldn't bivouac. It only took one second to let go of the rope. . .

The fault was tricky but had good ledges for rests. Now everything was veneered with thin ice – a bizarre transition between the powdered slabs below and the huge sheet of ice covering the top 120m of the cliff. My energy had dwindled by the time I reached the crackline above. I was close to being hypoglycaemic (maybe one bar of chocolate in 14 hours wasn't enough), and had reached a transitional state when the hours drift by. Retreat was not an option, but upward progress also seemed unlikely. The zombie would find a peg placement, aid up, stand on it, make another move into thicker ice, find a worse peg etc. I continued up towards a roof dominating the gloom above, without the energy to consider how to get past it. After three pegs for aid, I reached the overhang and pulled over onto thick ice. A quick couple of steps led to the icefield and it was all over. Sandy was still awake, and had never encouraged me to come down. He knew I was beyond resisting. Sandy seconded as quickly as ever while the moon slunk behind the hillside. This was well timed since our head torches were in the haul sack. The way above was summer 4c and 5a slabs, but submerged under snow-ice they were a doddle. We emerged on the top at 3am with a mixture of relief and pleasure. Dougie had finished somewhere around midnight. We collected an undamaged sack from the cliff base, and by the time we reached the bothy it was daylight. We had been lucky – the next day it thawed.

DIRECT DIRECT

By Robin McAllister

THE VIEW from the col between The Cobbler's North and Centre Peaks is non existent. There is just an eerie silence, occasionally punctuated by the croaking of a raven. As Dave McGimpsey and I had hoped, the South Face of the North Peak is in full winter garb. The recent cloudy weather has allowed a heavy build-up of rime, and everything is coated in a thick covering of hoar frost.

The previous week, we'd had an extended bouldering session on the initial overhanging crack of Direct Direct. The first sequence had been worked out. It is now time to put theory into practice.

I start up the crack. Steep torquing with front points teetering on tiny footholds, enable a good hook to be reached. Locking off on my hammer, I place a nut at full stretch, reverse the top moves and jump off. Breathing heavily, I notice that I've bent a pick.

Belayed now, I move up again to the hook, and clip the nut. I rock up on my left foot to get a higher torque for the axe, reach through awkwardly, and place a good wire. Instead of pulling up the free rope, I stupidly take the one with the first runner. The torque pulls, and before I know it, I'm lying on the ground, sprawled out in the soft snow.

A cigarette is called for. After a wee break, I climb back up and clip the runner. A high torque allows me to step up and precariously lean my shoulder against the right edge of the groove. After much clearing a poor hook enables me to get my left knee, then my right foot, into the base of the groove. At last I can get some gear and a breather. The groove is good and turfy in places, and yields to bridging and a lot of clearing. A bold step left at the top of the groove, followed by an awkward mantel and I'm at the belay. Dave follows and we sit on the stance. The next pitch looks hard.

The crack above is guarded by an overhang. Hand jamming seems the only way. I work my feet up high, praying the jam doesn't pop or I'll go flying off backwards into space. I find a rest of sorts above the roof with my feet on the slab and shoulders pressed onto the right wall. My back is in agony, so I can't stop there for long. I shove a Friend into the crack and carry on. The wall on the left looks possible, but thin. As I move up and left, I wake up to the fact that there's no gear and retreat is now impossible.

I consider jumping off, but then I find the key. A tiny foothold allows me to reach the upper crack and the security of good foot and hand jams. There's still no gear, but after the next move a ledge materialises on the left. I grab a block and collapse onto the ledge. I'm in luck, for there's a good nut placement here as well. A couple more moves and I gratefully mantel over the top.

It's dark now, and Dave follows by headtorch. I stare into the night. It's going to be very late by the time we get home, but it hardly matters. I'm too happy and tired to care.

RAVEN'S EDGE

By Rab Anderson

THE FLOG up to the foot of Raven's Gully had been quite unpleasant. In fact, it had been really unpleasant, with the snow alternating between unstable hard crust on a soft base, and a soft crust on a hard base. Still, once firmly secured to the foot of Slime Wall it was time to relax while Rob got to grips

Rob Milne on 'Raven's Edge' VIII,7, Buachaille Etive Mor during the first complete winter ascent. Photo: Rab Anderson.

with the initial groove just right of the crest. Rob had tried the route the week before with Robin McAllister and Dave McGimpsey. Their attempt failed at the foot of the big 'open book corner' which soars above Raven's Gully.

Information gleaned from Rob led me to believe that the first pitch was okay, and that the next was a traverse which was 'quite hard'. My game plan had been to get Rob to lead the first two pitches since he had seconded them before, then I would take over for the main challenge of the 'open book corner'. This was soon abandoned at the foot of the route when Rob said that he could lead the first pitch, but that he didn't think he could do the 'quite hard' traverse. Shit, it must be 'quite hard'.

Rob belays some 60m up on stretch and it's time to find out. Some 10m above Raven's I wobble around the edge and see how horrendous a 'quite hard' traverse looks. Seeking information, I ask Rob what gear Robin had got the week before. 'Oh, a tied-off peg in the middle.' 'Quite hard' now sounds quite hard and quite serious. Calves straining I teeter in the middle on balance only. A peg goes in, then another, both tied off. Quite crap.

Nothing else materialises and soon my arms ache as much as my calves did 15 minutes ago. Time passes as do a few tentative attempts. The wall leans beneath an evil ramp forcing me onto my arms and onto the non-existent footholds below. Mind you, a small sod of turf leers at me from beneath the snow near the end of the traverse. Something to go for. I scuttle back to the middle and ask for more information. 'Did Robin get any more gear?'

'No' comes back the reply. 'He just went for it, I think he was quite gripped.' Shit, that's all I need to know. I'm too old to be that bold so I dither again. All I get for wasting more time and strength is a sling over a small notch on the ramp. Whether it's ice or friction holding it on I'm not quite sure, but it looks nice just sat there, so I leave it. Whether Rob has been trying not to psyche me out by keeping the full story from me, I don't quite know. From the titbits I have gleaned I am now quite psyched out, and this is more 'quite hard' than I thought it would be.

I go for it. Arms screaming, I reach up and fire a tool into the mouth of that leering sod of turf, and lock-off on one arm. I momentarily feel fine, and wonder why didn't I just go for it earlier when I was fresh? I try my next tool and it simply rips bits of turf out and bounces off rock. Well-aimed placements are replaced by a wild thrashing action, then the lactic burn of a fast-approaching pump. No way back, one armed pull, lock-off, high heel-hook, try not to kick the sling off, flag the left foot, roll over onto the front points of the right, then the knee, face pressed against snow, try to stand. Just as I think 'I'm there', I suddenly catapult off backwards. 'Mmmh, so that's what Raven's Gully looks like as you drop head first towards it.' A stomach wrenching jerk accompanied by much clattering of gear and I stop with my head a few feet above the gully. I wonder why my right arm feels so heavy, and just as I am turned upright I see the sod of turf detach itself from my axe and disappear down Raven's, laughing at me. 'Am I hurt? . . . don't think so . . . good. How far? . . . 20ft perhaps . . . not far. What stopped me? . . . the useless sling on the notch . . . amazing!'

Praying that the gear continues to hold, I haul on one rope while Rob takes in on the other and I scrabble back to the start of the traverse, let the heartbeat and breathing return from 200 rpm, then teeter out into the middle again. I'm not psyched any more, just psycho. I launch out onto the ramp and manage to hang there on one arm to chop out some crap and arrange a sling, hung off something which seems okay. At my high point, where there was some turf, there is now none and I have to continue left for another few moves. Arms burning, sweat running into my eyes, I bridge a corner at the end, haul up on poor placements and get myself together before making the final few moves to the belay. Quite hard indeed.

Others might find the traverse quite hard, or it might be quite easy but it is dependant on a number of factors. They might say that the 'open book corner' above is quite hard, but it could be quite straight-forward, since you are warmed into it by then. The final pitch could quite well be the crux, but it might quite not be. What is a fact by then, is that you are quite tired and quite committed. It's a lot more cut and dried at the top of the route. Failure is not an option, you quite simply switch the brain off and go for it.

I've given quite enough away now, so no more, and you can figure it out for yourself. I'm sure that you too will have been in a situation quite like it yourself at sometime. That's climbing, quite different. Raven's Edge might not be quite Grade VIII but it could quite well be. Who quite cares anyway, it's quite hard and it's definitely quite good.

FOOBARBUNDEE

By Chris Cartwright

AN OVERWHELMING sense of foreboding lent a leaden aspect to the rhythm of my walk. The ghostly stillness of the early morning, while breaking trail into Coireag Dubh Mor on Liathach, only served to enhance my mood. On my first visit to the cliff seven years before, I was swept away by a thin layer of windslab from just below the foot of the cliff. On another occasion I suffered a broken bone from a lump of falling ice. I had now climbed many of the routes in the coire, but like several other climbers, I had become fascinated by the unclimbed thin sliver of ice that sometimes trickles down the hanging slab to the right of Poacher's Fall. I was now heading into the coire with a partner who had never been there before, and was not carrying the same emotional baggage as myself. Added to that Dave Hesleden was strong and fit, and keen to add another route to our free ascent of Great Overhanging Gully on Beinn Bhan the previous day.

Voices drifted up from below, and Dave broke into my reverie to impel a sense of urgency. As we gained height the mist slowly lessened allowing

Dave his first view of the route. With typical confidence he assured me that there was enough ice and névé on the slab to make it feasible, and quickly set off up the initial series of icy grooves. A short traverse right gained a recessed belay, of the slightly dubious variety, under a large left-facing corner. As I took the gear from Dave I couldn't help repeatedly glancing over to the slab. Although the ice build-up appeared to increase with height, it was impossible to ignore the transparent nature of the first 10m. A tied-off knife blade at thigh level provided some respite, but as I stepped onto the slab I was immediately aware that any untoward movement would deposit me below the peg. A small vertical overlap on the right looked hopeful, but cautious investigation revealed this to be blind. I stepped down and pondered the likelihood of sticking to the slab long enough to reach the thicker ice above. Dave's obvious impatience, generated by the level of self-belief that us mere mortals probably should not even aspire to, crystallised my decision to retreat. I climbed back down and we changed over the belay.

Dave quickly established himself on the slab, and soon came to the same conclusion as myself – it was unclimbable. I had already started to ponder the best abseil point, when Dave suggested another option. While I had been grappling with the slab he had been examining the left-facing corner above our heads. He believed that he could climb the corner to a point level with the better ice, and then step across the intervening rock wall to reach the slab. With a scrabbling surge he got himself established in the corner, and quickly climbed to a potential traverse point. The opening of the crack in the back of the corner allowed a good Hex placement and a more leisurely examination of the traverse. In contrast to the power climbing of the corner, Dave gingerly stepped out left, front points skating off downward sloping edges, until a reach to the left allowed a shallow placement in the iced slab.

It was obvious that the next move, transferring body weight from rock to ice, was going to be the crunch. Gently, Dave placed his left points in the ice, and started to pull through to allow his right tool to be brought into play. With a sudden roar he was off. He swung wildly, all arms and legs, across the intervening rock wall before slamming into the corner. With an adrenaline-fed rush he was quickly established in the corner again, confident both in his gear and in his ability to make the move onto the slab. The delicate step left was controlled and positive this time, but the left tool placement was barely in the ice before he was off again. A rational assessment of the problem concluded that the ice on the slab was just not strong enough to allow the transfer of his body weight. The third attempt was successful, with a little tension from the rope just at the point where Dave brought his right tool and foot onto the slab.

Now all that was required was for Dave to negotiate about 20m of dubious thin ice up the uniformly steep slab to reach a hoped-for belay point beneath an obvious overhang. Without any possibility of gear at all, he tentatively set off. I was scared for Dave, feeling helpless, knowing that he was now totally committed. I watched each move with bated breath, trying to gauge where he would stop if he fell. Was the belay good enough? Could I do anything about it? I concentrated totally on my leader, willing his placements to stay in, and praying that he could hold it all together to reach safety. Up above, Dave was in a world of his own, focused only on his tools and points, and not uttering a sound. Imperceptibly, he gained height through tiny steps, no more than six inches at a time. The ice was so thin that he had to search carefully for the each placement, and gently hook his picks as opposed to swinging them in. Time appeared to stand still until Dave eventually reached the overhang. After some silent work, I eventually received a slightly tremulous 'Safe'.

What more is there to say? Some smart rope work allowed me to use the Hex in the corner for tension to get established on the slab, and then pull it out from above. A strange calm overcame me climbing the slab. It was as though there was a transfer of thought directly to my tools, assessing the relative merits of each placement and then encouraging them to stay in as I made each move. The process was nearly mathematical in its exactitude. The calm was wiped away on reaching Dave when an uncontrolled adrenaline rush took control of our systems. The rest of the route passed in a blur, with steep, but solid ice, leading us ever higher. The echoing voices from earlier in the morning turned out to be acquaintances, and insults were exchanged. Control was re-asserted as we trended right to stay on a broken buttress to avoid the upper avalanche-prone slopes before topping out on the final ridge leading to Spidean a' Choire Leith.

Walking back down the Allt a' Choire Dhuibh Mhor we pondered the consequences of a fall high on the slab. All in all, I estimated a fall of 50m. And in case you're wondering about the name – you'll have to figure that one out for yourself!

INCLINATION

By Dave McGimpsey

LAST SEASON was an awkward one. Good conditions rarely coincided with days off work, and flu bugs and lack of driving licences for one reason or another, were not conducive to getting a lot done. So, when Robin McAllister and I walked up into Stob Coire nan Lochan and arrived at the base of Inclination at a rather late hour with only one headtorch, it appeared another wasted day was on the cards. Mindful that persistence often reaps rewards however, we quickly started up the route, which looked in very good condition.

The climb began with a steep ramp which was guarded by a short, bulging corner. Exiting this, I was unable to retrieve my hammer from a nasty crack, which refused to give up the pick it had just swallowed. At least it offered some welcome protection, so I clipped it, and continued upwards with Robin's hammer instead. He soon joined me at the belay, and began gearing up for the crux. We were already in an impressive position, with the corner of Unicorn soaring upwards to our right, and very steep ground above and below. Standing tip-toe on a block, Robin launched onto the wall above. He hooked up a small corner, but soon returned, perplexed at not being able to find a way of reaching the thin turf ledge at the top. The next go revealed a hidden hook at the top of the corner under a thick covering of rime. I watched nervously as Robin gained the ledge – a fall from here would have hurt both of us.

It was now my turn. Although the hooks were good, the smooth andesite offered nothing in the way of footholds, so much pedalling was needed to gain the only foothold high on the left. The crucial hook turned out to be just a silly button of frozen moss wedged in the crack, and I fell off soon after, when my picks ripped out of the thin turf ledge above. Altogether, it was not an impressive performance!

The next pitch was described as the 'unlikely wall on the left'. It was my lead, but I concluded that it really did look unlikely, and offered Robin the pitch. Being an understanding fellow, he accepted, but soon regretted it when a wrong turn led to no protection and some very unenticing down-climbing. Watching Robin extending himself like this is always exciting, but also nerve-wracking. He slowly talked himself back down to safety, incoherently muttering, and was soon back on line. My chain-smoking subsided as Robin made a long series of wild moves, which hurt my neck to watch, and was up the pitch in double-quick time.

By the time I had seconded the pitch it was getting dark. We exchanged gear quickly in the gathering gloom and I climbed up into the series of chimneys that form the upper half of the route. These were easier than the climbing below, but still very steep in places. With only one headtorch, the climbing was time-consuming, and it was a relief when the route was finished. We staggered back down, and arrived at our friend's car the wrong side of midnight. Our late return had not gone unnoticed, for in our absence, the local constabulary had been chastising us as irresponsible idiots.

THE SCREAMING

By Roger Everett

THE NORTH-EAST Coire of Beinn an Dothaidh presents an escarpment of easily accessible schistose cliffs, riven by deep gullies and compelling crack systems. The steeper buttresses are an excellent place to learn the art of mixed turf climbing, and the cliff also has a number of high-quality gully lines. When I was first getting into this winter game, long ago, I climbed several of the gullies, and well remember the sight of the buttress bounding the left edge of Cirrus. Its hanging walls were interspersed with small turf ledges, which drooped frozen vegetation and hanging icicles in a series of discontinuous lines. How exciting, I thought, would it be to try to link the howking placements in the turf and forge a route up such steep ground? But such ideas were purely theoretical for me, and I was very impressed when Graham Little started his development of the steeper lines and climbed Pas de Deux up the great barrel-fronted buttress just left of Cirrus.

Time passed and I became more competent and confident. Careful appraisal of the buttress revealed that the lower part, at least, was much less steep if viewed side on from higher in the coire. I was still under the impression that Pas de Deux took the upper, extremely steep section direct, until one day I summoned up the courage to follow its line. I found that it cunningly weaved from side to side to avoid the steeper sections, and then completely outflanked the final overhanging tier. But again my curiosity was raised, since was there not a crack system that went straight up that final leaning wall? On each subsequent visit that crack beckoned, only for my timidity to rule it out as too steep. Anyway, if it were possible, it was so obvious that surely someone would have done it by now?

As so often, the impetus was provided by Simon Richardson, who had also characteristically spotted the line. He too had ideas about a very direct alternative to the lower section, which took those walls that I had admired so long ago from the safe confines of Cirrus. With a settled forecast and a suitable history of weather and conditions, we found that our ideas for the day coincided exactly. We would give it a try.

Arriving at the gearing-up boulder under a blue sky, we gazed up at that final buttress to discover that, now the theory was ominously close to being tested, from all vantage points the wall really did overhang. Even worse, there was clearly a capping beak of overhangs. Such impressions are never very good for one's confidence (moral – never look up too closely!) so we meandered up towards the foot of the climb, zigzagging here and there, looking up, debating and all the time feeling that really, this is silly. But somehow the courage to call the whole thing off didn't materialise and we found ourselves gearing-up at the foot of Cirrus.

The close-up view of the lower section was intimidating, but not hopeless, and with the bravado that comes from knowing that it's not my lead, I arranged a belay while Simon scouted around. The first section was quite bold, on poor hooks and crumbling turf to scrabble into a small niche, from which a very exposed and narrow ramp led out to the hanging arete. Once there, Simon arranged bomb-proof gear and made a few steep pulls on spaced hooks to reach an easy turf line which led up to a fine ledge on the very edge of the buttress. With ever-increasing exposure, it was a great pitch to second. Getting into the swing of things, I took over the lead to tackle (perhaps unnecessarily) all the obstacles on the next pitch as directly as possible. A few steep walls led to the traverse line of Pas de Deux, then more short walls straight up opened the way to a fine open groove which gave delightful climbing to a commodious ledge below that final hanging wall. First sights were very encouraging – there was indeed a crack, interrupted by small niches, and the whole pitch was draped with frosted turf and moss. Surely this would go at a reasonable standard?

Somehow it had been decided that this was my crack, so Simon anchored himself firmly to the huge boulder belay and wished me luck. Instantly, it became clear that I should have known better. With my first few attempted placements it was obvious that the wall really did overhang, and soon afterwards I learned that the turf was thin, mossy and full of air. But in a few minutes I had got into the first of the niches with the route ahead clear. After a good deal of effort – hanging out from a single tool on a weird undercut – I managed to arrange some protection and launched into battle. Two moves later I was thoroughly pumped, hanging from one poor tool trying to place a Friend in a choked crack. Perhaps I could (or should) have carried on, but no respite was in sight, and linking hard moves while doubtful protection recedes from view is not my *forte*. I clipped into the axe in the slowly disintegrating turf, and somehow it held. A period of recuperation followed, then I set off again, only for history to repeat itself a few moves higher. Even though I had been going very well (for me) on the climbing wall, such fitness just didn't translate to the extended one arm lock-offs required to both climb the route free and protect it. It would have been easier if the placements had been good, but the cracks weren't well suited for torques and the thin turf kept ripping. I just got used to the idea that I was continuously on the point of flying.

I began to think that I really should leave it for someone stronger, bolder and better, but encouraging noises were wafting up from below and I thought I could see some good turf within reasonable striking distance. I arrived at a wider bit of crack, where at least I could get partially wedged and arrange gear in conventional fashion, even if the piece in question was one of Simon's home-made specials, an approximate Hex 15. After a few steep moves I was right under the final roof and launching rightwards on hooks across the overhanging wall to the beckoning turf, but the pump in my arms had drained my brain of the ability to communicate with my feet. For a moment I thought I'd fall out of my wrist loops, but such ignominy was avoided when suddenly both tools ripped and I became, not before time, well and truly airborne.

This unplanned tactic at least gave me the opportunity for an extended rest. On the next attempt, armed with experience and a careful mental rehearsal of the exact sequence of moves, I got myself firmly fixed to the turf which had so spectacularly ejected me, arranged another runner, and then swung out above the void over an overhang and onto a short poised arete. Then it was just a question of avoiding my speciality of grabbing defeat from the arms of success.

So what of the route? It's an excellent direct line, with much fine climbing. Despite our flawed ascent, even allowing for the axe rests, the grade must be in the higher numbers. While it may be argued that we should have left it for another day, or even not claimed the route, I'm happy to be honest and leave it as a marker for someone to better. I've no doubt that an on-sight free ascent is possible by the talented and strong, but perhaps it may become an example of, I suspect, an increasingly common form of winter climb – a target for a 'red point' ascent with sports climbing ethics.

CORNUCOPIA

By Simon Richardson

EARLY ONE Sunday morning last April, Chris Cartwright and I trailed up through the wind and rain to Ben Nevis. The prospect of a winter climb looked slim, but as we plodded through deep wet snow up into Coire na Ciste, the rain turned to sleet, and at the foot of The Comb it was snowing. At the base of No. 3 Gully it was freezing. We were in luck, for conditions were perfect for what we had in mind – an unclimbed clean-cut corner on the right flank of the gully. After a couple of entry pitches, Chris launched out on to a bold arête. A difficult step left led to a steep wall below the main corner. The climbing was steep and the best line was not obvious, so after an hour on the sharp end, Chris came down and offered me the lead. We pulled the ropes through and I set off.

Chris had set the groundwork. I now knew the correct sequence of moves to reach his highpoint. A good Rock gave me the confidence to lurch up the next few moves to a narrow ledge on the left of the corner. Appearances in winter are often deceptive, and the ledge turned out to be a smooth, sloping shelf coated with loose snow. Struggling to hold on, I torqued an axe in a crack and stepped left. Standing on one foot I wasn't in balance, but at least I was able to rest my left arm. After an age I gingerly placed a wire above my axe, and then hammered home a good angle.

I was now in a position to consider the corner proper, which reared up to my right. Undercut at its base, it had a vertical right wall and a slightly overhanging left face. It looked hard, but the first move over the initial overlap was obvious enough. I stepped right and jammed my right Koflach hard into the wide crack. There was a good ice placement for my hammer and I pulled up. The corner now soared above, with blank hoar-frosted walls to either side. The crack was parallel-sided and too wide to torque. To progress any farther, I needed a foothold, but there was nothing. For perhaps the first time when climbing a winter route I couldn't figure out how to climb it. Sure, I'd backed off many pitches in the past, but always I'd known it was possible for someone who was stronger or bolder than I. This corner looked impossible.

I hung there with my right foot jammed beneath me and the hammer in

Dave Hesleden on Foobarbundee, Liathach. Photo: Chris Cartwright.

the trickle of ice for what must have been nearly an hour. I cursed the rock. I cursed the corner. I cursed the mountain. Surely, there must be a way? In frustration I started to meticulously clear the left wall with my adze. Underneath the layer of frost all I found was smooth rock with no hint of a crack, edge or ripple. About 3m above me I could just make out a dimple under the hoar. If only I could get that high, perhaps I could bridge across to some small holds high up on the right wall?

I carried on scraping until at shoulder height I found a tiny chicken head. The knobble was perfectly formed, shallow and round, and about the size of my thumbnail. I brushed the hoar off with my glove and then used the heat of my bare hand to melt it free. It was slightly rough to the touch. Perhaps this was the key? I kept my glove off and held it between my thumb and forefinger. It wasn't big enough to pull up on, but by leaning away to the right on my pick I could move my foot farther up the crack below me. As I slowly inched up I found myself in a mantelshelf position with the chicken head pushing into the flesh on the outside of my left hand. I was about to fall, and needed something for my left foot, but the chicken head was too rounded and shallow to take a crampon point.

In desperation I had to think of something quick. I moved my left foot above the chicken head and gently placed the vertical outside edge of the crampon frame onto it. I held my breath as I transferred my weight onto my left foot. It held! Slowly, ever so slowly, I stretched my left leg and stood up. I had to get a runner in quick. I grabbed the first piece of gear that came to hand, and pushed it into the crack. Rarely have I been so lucky. The crack was parallel-sided and slightly icy. Too icy for a Friend and not flared enough for a nut, but it was the perfect size for a No. 8 Hexcentric. A millimetre too small it wouldn't have fitted, and a millimetre too large it wouldn't have cammed. I breathed again, and continued up, one point precision front-pointing on the ripples on either side of the wall. Another first-time Rock placement in an icy crack and I pulled over into an overhung shelf a few inches wide. A step right to a niche and the pitch was over.

By the time Chris came up it had taken five hours to climb the corner. It was to take us another four hours to battle up the flared cracks above, and then work out a way through the final steep wall to the top. As Chris fought his way up the off-width, I reflected on the pitch. It had been a personal revelation that it was possible to link a long series of unseen technical moves on a winter route. I knew it was unlikely that I would ever be able to repeat such a performance again, but for the new breed of winter climbers, fit from climbing walls and honed with finer technical skills, a vast world of possibilities awaits.

Roger Everett on The Screaming, Beinn and Dothaidh. Photo: Simon Richardson.

THE CENTENARY YACHT MEET OF THE SMC, 1897-1997

By the time the present issue of the Journal is published, the 1997 SMC Centenary Yacht Meet, planned for May, should also be history.

SAILING and Mountaineering were considered complementary activities by the Founding Fathers of the Early Club. In 1903 Raeburn wrote: 'To beat to windward against a strong wind and heavy sea, has something akin to the feeling of fighting one's way up the ice pitches in a snow gully, or difficult traverses on a steep rock face.' After a yachting race in the Firth of Forth he had rushed up to Ben Nevis and soloed Observatory Buttress. On the summit he met his friends, the Clarks and shared in their afternoon tea with bread, butter and jam. His account continues: 'The weather, that Coronation week, had been glorious. The air was dry and crisp, with a "life" in it that fairly lifted the climber out of himself, and made him feel, as he affectionately grasped the warm rocks of the old Ben, "Nothing is impossible to-day".'

A physical, aesthetic and intellectual polymath, Raeburn had what today we would call a 'holistic' approach. The rocks were part of a larger world. He describes the flora and fauna in detail; fox and vole tracks, croak of raven and song of snow bunting, the gleam of golden saxifrage, and the rose-pink cushions of moss campion all find a place in his world view. On the summit he concludes: 'Of the rest of that glorious evening, I shall not write. I for one shall never forget it.' This admirable holistic tradition continues today. The tigers and tigresses of the present Club, bolts and drills notwithstanding, are no doubt also sensitive to the total ambience of their surroundings.

But what of the 1897 Meet? A report of this Easter Meet, held in April 1897, appeared in the May 1897 issue of the Journal (SMCJ IX, 23, 288-293 and *ibid*, 299-302). The cruise began at Oban and ended at Rothesay. The weather was bad with wind and rain for the first part making the preferred anchorage at Loch Scavaig untenable but better for the second. Climbs were made from anchorages at Rum, Loch Hourn, Loch Nevis, Ballachulish and the Isle of Jura. There was good conversation and songs in the evening and music from the flute of the President (H. T. Munro, no less). There was a considerable amount of photography ('almost every member was an amateur photographer') and this included on-board development of film. In this issue you will find a Munro print of the assembled company on board the *S.S. Erne*. To celebrate the centenary of the Yacht Meet this year's Journal presents some of the mountaineering/sailing exploits of our present members and shows that the holistic approach is still healthily with us.

MOONLIGHTING

By John Peden

FOR SOME reason which escapes me, the vast majority of boat owners go into a frenzy as soon as the first birch leaves turn yellow. Cranes are hired and cosseted craft are removed from their natural element, to spend the winter huddled in some draughty boatyard or shored up uncomfortably in the front garden.

Their loss is immeasurable, for it is no less magical to ride the waves by winter moonlight than to crunch along a snowy mountain ridge; and no harder to weigh anchor on an unpromising January morning than to open the door of the CIC and head off up the Allt a' Mhuilinn. Moreover, a warm saloon is as good a place as any mountain hut to spend a long winter evening in convivial conversation over a glass or two of malt. Perhaps the compulsion to haul out in the autumn is due simply to collective memory of a time when wooden boats needed months of hard graft each winter to keep them serviceable. Technology has its benefits.

The weather at the tail end of 1995 was memorably cold, which suited our purpose well. We had taken the bunkhouse at Doune at the western tip of Knoydart for a week of family entertainment over New Year, and we had brought *Hecla,* our trusty 30ft sloop, to join in the fun.

The passage from Oban to Mallaig on the weekend before Christmas had itself been quite special. Accompanied by a former President of the Club, his French teacher and my wife's brother, I slipped our mooring in Saulmore Bay at 10 o'clock on the Friday evening and headed for the Sound of Mull. It mattered not that the moon had set with the sun. It was a night of startling clarity and the Earth was awash with starlight, punctuated by the silent slash of meteorites. In the north, far from any civilisation, there was a shimmering light which could only be the Aurora. While our ship bowled along before the south-easterly tradewinds, I lay on deck enchanted, watching the masthead brushing the diamond-dusted velvet of the sky. A simple flight of the imagination transported me south to coral seas and coconut trees.

Tobermory was weel-happit and sound asleep as we tip-toed in about half past two. We dropped anchor in Acairseid Mhor on Calve Island: much more snug than the bumpy visitor moorings.

Despite a predictably late start on Saturday we were round Ardnamurchan in good time to watch the sun setting extravagantly into the sea beyond Muck, and we used the last embers of its light to pick our way into the perfect natural harbour of Loch nan Ceall. A ceilidh in the Arisaig Hotel that evening was an unexpected bonus, enlivened by the spectacle of Iain Smart explaining to the local lass he was dancing with that he was indeed the Flying Dutchman (an entirely plausible claim), and by Veronique winning a fresh lobster in the raffle. Sadly, the organisers had not anticipated visitors: the creature was still at home on Eigg, and no amount of VHF transmission next morning could raise its keeper.

After Christmas the main party assembled on the pier at Mallaig, complete with assorted small persons. The low afternoon sun could make no impression on the penetrating cold. It was as well the weather was fine, for *Hecla's* cabin was packed, quite literally, full with all the multifarious equipment, cases of whisky, musical instruments, food and so on that are essential for a good New Year bash. (Travellin' light? Ha!) The dozen or so crew clung on where they could and *Hecla* settled sluggishly by the stern as I opened the throttle. Sailing was a physical impossibility. The few citizens who had yet emerged from their Yuletide excesses raised a communal eyebrow as we sallied forth to cross the four miles of placid sea to Doune. Knoydart will rarely be seen so Arctic. Deep snow lay down to sea level and the views up Loch Nevis and out to the Small Isles were stunning. The next few days saw intense activity as all and sundry sought to capitalise on such beneficence before the spell broke and normality was restored on the weather front. In these conditions the lower hills at the western end of the peninsula provided excellent Nordic touring, and the slopes behind the bunkhouse were ideal sledging country for babies and small children (of all ages!)

On the eve of Hogmanay, as the first subtle hint of light suffused the eastern sky, four of our party rowed out to *Hecla* with rucksacks and skis balanced precariously over the black water. This uncharacteristically early start was essential if we were to achieve our aim: an ascent of Sgurr na Ciche. There was an over-arching imperative to be back for the start of the banquet at 8 o'clock.

An insidious easterly breeze spoke of the cold clear weather continuing. As we left the anchorage Bla Bheinn and the Cuillin Ridge glowed in the strengthening light, rising provocatively above the indistinct white shape of Sleat. In the half-light we resisted the temptation to take the short-cut through the reefs and islets off Sandaig and motored south awhile before turning east into the entrance to Loch Nevis. This fine fjord, second only to Loch Hourn in its grandeur, was enhanced this morning by the uncompromising whiteness rising from its dark waters, giving the scene a most un-Scottish feel.

Off Inverie, where the loch turns south, the wind freshened and we hoisted sail for an exhilarating fetch towards Tarbet. Before long, however, we were sailing close-hauled, and with pressure of time stifling purist thoughts of beating through the narrows into the inner loch, the engine was restarted. Approaching the narrows at Kylesmorar requires care, for a shallow spit extends a fair distance from the northern shore and we had no

Graham Little on the first ascent of 'Morning Glory' E1 5a, 5b, Sloc Chiasigeo, Mingulay. Photo: Cath Pyke.

wish to spend precious time waiting for the tide to lift us off. The flood tide runs strongly through the narrows. As it drew us in we could see disturbed water ahead where it met the waves driving down the inner loch, setting up a stretch of very steep seas. Romping through this at 10 knots over the ground was more akin to white water rafting than yachting.

The shapely cone of Sgurr na Ciche, glistening now in the sunshine, lured us on up to the head of the loch with all speed. We anchored where we ran out of water, a little way short of Camusrory, and sprachled ashore in the inflatable which was left tied to a tree, along with our wellies. Skiing from the high water mark was a novel experience, (very purist), and we quickly got into a rhythm gliding along the track. The barking of the dogs at Camusrory, outraged by this impertinence, brought forth the keeper who inquired our business. The explanation of our simple plan for the day produced an indignant, 'Ye're all aff yer f . . . . . . heids! It'll still be there in the summer!' Somehow I felt he had missed the point.

Undeterred, we skated across the frozen Carnach River and skimmed over the peat hags and normally boggy flats to the foot of our mountain. Alas we were quickly to discover that an ascent on skis was out of the question. Although respectably deep, the snow was baseless and unconsolidated, and the *Malinia* tussocks hereabouts are man-sized. Climbing to the crest of the ridge was laborious and time-consuming. The sun had already passed its zenith by the time we reached easier ground where we paused to rest and refuel. There now seemed little prospect of getting to the top and back to Doune in good time, but it would have been criminal not to make the most of such a day. We gathered ourselves up and headed along the gently undulating crest of Druim a' Ghoirtein, absorbing breathtaking views of the Rough Bounds.

Persistent easterly winds had scoured the right-hand side of the ridge and dumped the snow in deep drifts in the hollows and on the west flank. As we picked our way from knoll to knoll I became aware that my subconscious had not yet relinquished the summit. I was evidently not alone in this, for the party was steadily accelerating. At last Will and Julie saw sense and opted for a less breathless appreciation of the views. Bob's laid-back demeanour conceals a driven man, however, and the two of us raced on towards the subsidiary top which marks the end of the long ridge. This we reached at a quarter to three, only 15 minutes before our 'absolute latest' turnback time. Over half-a-mile and 1000ft of ascent still separated us from the summit, but by now, of course, we were firmly in the mountain's thrall. Without discussion we dropped our sacks and ran. Forty minutes later, after a delightful scramble up the steep upper slopes, we were looking down to Loch Quoich, sucking in the freezing air which greeted us from over by Glen Kingie. There were no other footprints in the snow.

Despite the keen wind and the lateness of the hour, the spectacle

'Hecla II' anchored at Galmisdale with the Sgurr of Eigg in the background. Photo: John Peden.

commanded our attention. We were surrounded by peaks near and far, glinting in the late afternoon sunshine and looking as fine as ever I have seen them. To the west, beyond Morar, the islands of Eigg and Rum were surreal white silhouettes against a dark, sparkling sea, and over Meall Buidhe, far out beyond the Sea of the Hebrides, sailed the Uist hills: Beinn Mhor and Hecla. Or was it perhaps Tir nan Og?

The reverie broke. Night's approaching shadow was stalking the eastern sky and on the loch far below us we saw *Hecla* tugging impatiently at her anchor. While we cartwheeled down the mountainside the sinking sun painted the snow orange and purple and green. Wind-etched sastrugi cast intricate azure shadows, while myriad golden hoar crystals coruscated underfoot. We glissaded and ran and danced over the freeze-dried rocks in a joyous daze.

A big half moon was already high over the hills to the south and a fierce frost was crackling along the shore when we reached the boat, 75 minutes after leaving the top. There was not a moment to lose: all hands to the anchor! With the wind astern and the tide under us we surged through the narrows by the last glimmer of daylight. We gave the engine wellie as we turned the end of the spit, and the off-duty watch hurried below. In the warmth of the Tilley lamp a dram never tasted so good.

We made it to the banquet with 10 minutes to spare; the ceilidh which followed lasted long into the night.

Bogha-cloiche

ROCK JOCKS AND SEA DOGS

By Graham E. Little

A grey-green swell lifts our inflatable, pushing it forcibly towards the shore. The outboard propeller crunches onto foam-hidden rocks. The engine stalls; the next wave swings the rubber craft around and rasps it across the barnacled reef. Norman, our boatman, sits transfixed. I grab the painter and leap out onto a wave-washed platform, the surf creaming high around my legs. Rock hopping, I pull the inflatable into a deeper channel, jump back in, then scream at Norman to start the outboard. He does and we limp back to our boat. The next attempt at landing is less eventful and we say a silent prayer.

ROCK-CLIMBING trips to remote Hebridean islands are challenging affairs with the logistics of boat hire and coastal access often the key to success. Add to this the challenge of new routing on storm-lashed sea cliffs and a planned outing quickly turns into an adventure, with marine activity vying with cragging for its share of the thrills and spills. The whole experience is, of course, enhanced by the characterful, not to say eccentric, personalities that are inclined to join one on such jaunts.

I've sailed to and climbed on the lonely island of Mingulay on three occasions. A few personal cameos from these trips perhaps best illustrate the richness and unpredictability of remote island access and cragging.

The first was in 1993 when I was joined by an all-star cast of Chris Bonington, Mick Fowler and Kev Howett.

Rather than endure a slow sea crossing from Oban the four of us fly from Glasgow, and land on the hard sand airfield of Traigh Mhor on Barra. After piling mountains of kit (mostly CBs) into the Post Bus we climb in. Our driver turns in a slow and deliberate manner to observe his passengers. 'Well, well, well, and what brings Mr Bonington to this part of the world?' It is a good question.

Peter Daynes's 30ft yacht, *Liverbird,* slices through the gentle oily swell of the ocean, long trailing vapours still clinging to the Outer Isles. We sit on deck soaking in the rays. The sky is a fresh blue after a spell of unseasonably bad weather. Mick, the inheritor of Tom Patey's stack-climbing credentials, and seasoned sea cliff aficionado, turns a pale shade and then, to our amazement, vomits violently overboard. The rest of the team exchange shocked and sympathetic glances then, after a short, but decent interval, reach for their cameras to record this momentous occasion.

The Biulacraig, our first objective, is certainly steep, but even Mick's appetite for less than pristine rock is dulled by this great, green, guano-splashed vision. Chris is visibly relieved, although Mick's alternative of swimming out to the big stack of Lianamul causes a temporary relapse.

My first full abseil down the central section of Dun Mingulay casts very serious doubts upon my judgment and upon the sanity of Kev Howett, my partner. The Atlantic licks its lips, I spiral down a free hanging bit of string, the rock stares blankly out at me. So OK, it is the best bit of rock in the World and we did climb two superb routes (The Silkie, E4 and Voyage of Faith, E3) but those moments of fear are with me forever,

☆ ☆ ☆

Our planned return trip in the spring of 1994 had to be aborted due to the serious storms lashing the Outer Hebrides, but in 1995 all systems were go. We sailed from Oban, in the afterswell of a Force 8 on an ex-lifeboat, *Poplar Diver,* (named after a line of poplar trees next to the skipper's garage somewhere in The Midlands). On this occasion it was nearly an SMC meet with Kev and I being joined by Bob Reid, Grahame Nicoll and Andy Cunningham. We dubbed it the Big Nosed Expedition (with Bob Reid as honorary member).

Bob, armed with a tape recorder and a large furry (sea) dog, did his best to imitate a combined Alan Wicker and David Attenborough. His attempts to record the climber in its natural habitat resulted in some entertaining sequences, with the low-wing rush of the great skua and the booming and sucking of the sea adding to the 'on location' atmosphere.

We discovered the delights of Guarsay Mor under a scorching hot sun. An immaculate 50m high wall of clean gneiss rising above a non-tidal rock ledge is just a Rock Jock's paradise. We put up nine routes from HVS to E5, all in the two and three-star category. Kev and I struggled up our own routes but stopped to admire the cool of Andy as he made steady progress up the magnificent A Word with the Bill (E3) – a razor sharp name if there ever was.

On the subject of route names, I get to use Children of Tempest for our third route on Dun Mingulay's main wall (which goes, amazingly, at El). It is the title of a novel by Neil Munro that has, as its climax, the climb out of a great sea cave on Mingulay.

Our return to Oban on the *Poplar Diver* again tested our sea legs and we were not found wanting. The sinking sun burnished the wave tops then slid below the long trail of the outer islands. We arrived at night on a wet and windy pier to discover that the weather had been foul on the mainland for the duration of our trip. Oh! joy.

☆ ☆ ☆

1996 sees a seriously motley crew, packed on to a chartered launch, heading out from Castlebay on a cold, grey, May day. The age range of the 11-strong team is from 17 to 47 – our youngest member, Lawrence Hughes, quickly being nick-named Roof Warrior, after his strange affinity for massive overhangs.

A landing on the beach is out of the question due to the wild sea so we damply decant onto the rocks to the south. What the hell is this place like in winter?

Cath Pyke and I spend an enjoyable afternoon exploring the cliffs of Rubha Liath in the far south of the island, delighting in the rock and the language that gives us Rubha Soul (E2), although she is too young to remember the album, and The Power of the Sea (E3), and who needs an explanation?

George Ridge's tent is ripped to shreds by the wind and he joins Cath for the night (every cloud . . .). Jim Lowther entertains Kev and I with tales of Eton and Arctic exploration. As the wind howls and the rain lashes down, the newly-married Grahame and Mel Nicoll drink a box of red wine and practice bird songs – at least that's their story. Ropes blow vertically in the roughly teasing wind, the sea explodes from the ocean, we speculate on what can be done and decide to photograph puffins. Crawling back across the island for a well-earned brew, we debate the likelihood of the launch picking us up tomorrow. Despite the continuing foul weather, our boat arrives. As we ferry our wet gear across the slippy coastal rocks and load it into the malevolently bobbing dingy, I reflect upon the need for a new set of criteria to define the success of island rock-climbing expeditions.

Three trips to the wonderful island of Mingulay, memories that are more than the rock, the pitch, the route. An island of magic where all experiences are memorable and transcend the climb; where rock jocks and sea dogs strike a pact so as to relish the touch, the taste and the time. Where we sail but never quite return, for in spirit we have never left.

ASCENSION

Again the flick and twirl and quiver
as he probed and picked, then climbed
a runnel of blue ice. Shards and slivers
tinkled, rattled down the chute
between legs, beneath the balance of his feet.
I watched the axe's steel dull gleam,
its adze and curving pick
strike hard and strike again
the solid cold of comfort.
All blade, point and deterrent.
Even borne lashed to his sac
its message was intimidate.

Donald M. Orr.

THE CIRCUMNAVIGATION

Anon

THIS IS a tale of lang syne, before the SMC abroad had become the SMC at sea; when members who sailed yachts kept quiet about it, lest it were bruited in the Journal. It relates to two ex-Presidents, an ex-Secretary, and a pregnant woman. The event was long before one of these ex-Presidents made nasty remarks in the Journal about the other; in fact in the days when the Journal was a record of climbing achievement or enjoyment, and not for venting inner thoughts or streams of consciousness. We were then perhaps half our present ages, at the peak of our climbing form.

My tale relates to a circumnavigation, now a feature of the Journal, but in a more modest boat, to wit a 16ft open clinker-built dinghy. We had no charts, but the OS maps. In our planning we did not consider this a serious factor, as we expected to keep close to the coast, the males on board being well known for a timidity bordering on cowardice. Indeed, it was this character defect that enabled two of them to evolve as Presidents during a period when the Club had a distinctly salvationist hue, now to be abandoned under the leadership of President Richardson.

Now the rules of circumnavigation are simple, but quite strict. At some point in the voyage one must cross the outgoing trajectory without doing so by turning back. This is a feature rarely encountered in mountaineering. Imagine extending the crab crawl on Meagaidh right round the hill on the same contour.

Our objective was Mull, which according to the Club guidebook of the time, 'is 25 miles from north to south' (and, I can affirm, as a result of my voyage, that it is also 25 miles from south to north) and, 'between 3 and 20 miles wide', according to one's latitude. (The mountaineers in the club can rest assured that I shall not be trotting out many arcane nautical terms. I know how irritating they can be. This one seems inevitable). What the guide book failed to inform us was that it is surrounded by sea. I mean not just salty water, but sea, real sea with big waves and remorseless currents. But to that in due course.

The boat had a nice beamy front end (naut: 'bow'), and flat back end (naut: 'transom') and was called the *Tippa too*. This is an insider joke, too complex to explain here. There was considerable competition to sit at the back end. In the first place it was drier, but also it meant you had grasp of the tiller (the thing that steers the boat) AND the throttle control on the outboard engine. This meant you had total power over the others, and could head fast for the shore if a walrus or other sea monster popped up, or you desperately needed a pee. Unlike being in a yacht, peeing from the side of a small dingy tossing about in a Force 5 with a lady aboard is not something that can be done with gentlemanly discretion. This fact alone distinguishes our voyage from other recent narratives.

A glance at the world atlas will inform the reader that off west of Mull lies America, some 3000 miles away. In case we lost sight of land, or were blown off course, we resolved, like Jerome K. Jerome's characters, to take ample food. Thus when we left on a September Friday evening from the Argyll shore we were heavily loaded. We nosed over to the east coast of Lismore, and in high spirits, headed south. There were excited discussions of the potential for rock routes on its short but extensive dolomite cliffs. We had planned to camp the night at Eilean Musdail, the lighthouse on the south tip but the swell was breaking heavily on the shore. We should have turned back, of course, but as all had gone so well, and believing ourselves already seasoned sailors, we were seduced by the distant calm of the bay to the north of Duart Castle. Thus we entered the Sound of Mull quite unprepared, ignorant of the fact that the entire volume of the Sound of Mull and the Lynn of Morven were in the process of emptying into Loch Linnhe. This is a period of the tidal cycle known to sailors as 'the flood'. Somewhere in the middle of this, turbulent water, wind and tide came into opposition creating standing waves 6ft high. Anyone who has schussed into 6ft sastrugi will know what it is like. The boat's front end soared into the sky, a body came tumbling towards the back, the boat then plunged into the water, and much water came aboard. After about two such episodes we retreated. However, I am pleased to be able to say that my diary records 'the crew behaved admirably'. Thus were two putative Presidents preserved for future glory. More importantly, the Club was able to profit from the continued labours of an excellent Secretary

The Saturday dawned still and perfect, and armed with experience of 'the flood', we picked our time, and whistled across the Sound towards the south shore of Mull at slack water. A call for coffee brought us ashore at Grass Point where we strutted importantly in front of the tourists brought over from Oban to see the seals. Then on, intrepidly. Beyond the mouth of Loch Spelve great cliffs rose above us. We were a little disquieted by a surging sea that, as it hit the shore, projected sea foam to their very crests. This observation put paid to a theory upon which the entire expedition was predicated; namely, that three strong men and one pregnant women could anywhere pull the boat out of the sea onto the shore, from which vantage we could relax till the sea improved.

The boat weighed down by weeks of food, bottles of whisky, a pregnant woman and three hulking Club members was, even to the landlubbers, obviously overloaded. Desperate measures were called for. Volunteers were sought and found. The boat was nosed towards a small escarpment while the volunteer balanced on the prow (the top part of the front end). At the right moment he leapt for the rocks shouting 'long live the SMC', and successfully found holds that allowed him to climb up to the raised beach below the cliffs. Another followed in more modest fashion: a victory for mountaineers. The remaining sailors now forged on westwards, while the climbers had an interesting rock traverse along several miles of coast. We all foregathered in a little inlet with a storm beach of polished pebbles, hauled the boat out and camped on a delightful piece of sloping greensward to the caress of a fine driftwood fire. Across the loch the lights of Easdale twinkled mischievously.

Next day, since it was too rough, we snorkelled into a salmon net, but it was empty. By early afternoon the sea was down, and off we headed for Loch Buie with two members ashore, working under the high cliffs, still virtually unclimbed, that form the inaccessible hinterland of this part of Mull. The sea, though calm, was graced by a vast undulating, awe-inspiring swell. And thus we reached Carsaig. Here we faced the paradox of small boating. There are plenty of small boat havens, and plenty of super camping places. There is a great paucity of the two together. At Carsaig there were none. With a gale forecast on our transistor, we moored the *Tippa* with climbing ropes to two reefs that embraced a narrow gut of water. A driftwood fire eased the misery of a drizzle. Shortly, a lady arrived from the 'big house', patronisingly anxious for our welfare. No doubt we looked like ship-wrecked mariners. Rather than go in for complicated explanations we told her that we had lost daddy's yacht, but that daddy's helicopter would soon be here. This being quite normal in her circles she then offered us blankets and eggs. We took the eggs.

Next day was wild, and we watched helplessly as our craft tossed and turned, but our belaying was sound (another explanation for our survival to the age of gerontocracy). The boat survived without a scratch. And so the day after we set off towards the Ross of Mull. The shore was more inviting now, and past Ardalanish point we came upon on that sublime combination of steep rocks, sheltering headlands and shell sand. It was called Traigh nan Gael. What perfection! Greensward, running burn, driftwood, shelter: the closest this crew would ever get to paradise. Our trip to Iona next day, threading between the reefs of the Ross of Mull, was such fun. It was not a serious matter to bump into a sunken rock, and so we could take risks going close inshore, and slaloming through the islets and reefs.

I have to tell readers that there was one constant irritation on this voyage. Once a day, in eight hours, the MV King George V circumnavigated Mull, bearing its load of tourists. It was an affront to our daring, making our voyage of exploration seem as pointless as Ranulph Fiennes crossing the Antarctic plateau. Never mind, we saw bits of Mull no tourist ever sees. We put-putted through the yacht anchorage known as the Bull Hole, and out into Loch Scridain, and along the wilderness of Ardmeanach, putting ashore at Doire a Gabhaig opposite Little Colonsay. A good 30 miles, this day. There was just time before dark to get up Ben More. One President-to-be did it in 1 hour 30 minutes.

What excitement the next day. We went through the sound of Ulva, something only small yachts can do, and then under ideal conditions. Wonderful terrain, Ulva, Gometra and the Dutchman's Hat the obscene spice islands of the west, and identified as the future location for the Institute for Theoretical Biology once the Nobel Prize had been duly awarded. Such is youthful hope and speculation! And so to Loch Tuath, and coming up was the crux: Calliach Point. Lacking the 'Admiralty sailing instructions' we depended for warning on Alaistair Dunnet's book on canoeing the west coast. His description of rounding Calliach Point had us shivering in our wellies, indeed so much so that we put the pregnant woman ashore at Calgary Bay, crossed ourselves, and said we hoped to see her at Langamull on the north coast. Wiser from our experiences in the Sound of Mull, we attended slack water, and round we went no bother. The anti-climax was intolerable in the face of sustained female teasing.

The north shore of Mull is not a nice place for yachties. However, the *Tippa* nosed effortlessly through the reefs of Loch Chuchain and went right to the head of the loch at Dervaig, where we pulled her out of the water. At the pub we solemnly inscribed her in the yacht book.

Once into the Sound of Mull, the voyage took on an effete character. No danger (except from McBrayne's charging steamers). But the sea was not yet finished with us. Working up the Lynn of Morvern in a strong westerly we experienced the odd and terrifying sensation of the *jabble,* a sea full of standing waves which tossed about as so much chaff in a gale. The effect is created by the reflected wave from shore cliffs. And so to home, round the North end of Lismore.

Thirty three years later I feel able to admit to this adventure, and of course it was an *adventure* because at our level of experience every moment was new and unexpected, a learning experience. How lucky we were to have lived in that age.

SCOTLAND'S LAST MOUNTAIN

By Ken MacTaggart

LAST AUTUMN saw a little-known anniversary in Scottish mountaineering, an important centenary which passed uncommemorated and almost entirely unrecognised. It was an event which deserved better.

In the autumn of 1896 a party of four gentlemen made a long rock-climb to the summit of a minor Skye peak. That in itself was not remarkable in a period when, over several decades, enthusiastic Victorian mountain explorers had scrambled into every corrie and over almost every crest in the Cuillin range.

What made the party's ascent of Sgurr Coir'an Lochain significant was not the intrinsic merit of this little-repeated route, but what they encountered as they reached the mountain's north summit. They looked around and saw no cairn, no track, no sign of any prior visitation. From all sides the peak was inaccessible to anyone but a rock-climber, and they correctly concluded that they had made the first ascent. For the last time in the British Isles, climbers had reached an untrodden mountain summit.

The group was made up of SMC founder William W. Naismith, Professor John Norman Collie, local Skye guide, John Mackenzie, and a friend of Collie, E. B. Howell. The date of their historic ascent was September 12, 1896.

A century on, when almost any hill in the country over 2000ft receives multiple ascents every weekend, both summer and winter, it is hard to imagine the experience of climbing a virgin Scottish mountain. But in the mid to late-1800s, a small band of devotees regularly enjoyed the novelty of making the first ascents, not just of classic rock climbs, but of the mountain peaks.

At the start of the 19th century there were probably 10 unclimbed mountains in Skye which would become Munros when Sir Hugh published his tables at the century's end. Numerous other lesser peaks had never been reached. Skye was remote, and in those pre-Ordnance Survey days was little known to the active British mountaineers of the time, most of whom lived in the south of England. For them, Chamonix and the Alps were an easy trip compared with a long journey by stage coach to Glasgow, then steamer from the Clyde to a distant, barely-mapped Hebridean island.

Today, it seems incongruous that even in the early 1830s, when intimidating Alpine peaks such as Mont Blanc, the Jungfrau and the Finsteraarhorn had already been climbed, Sgurr nan Gillean, Bruach na Frithe, Sgurr Alasdair and Sgurr Thearlaich still awaited their first ascents. Skye mountain fever only took off when the adventurous Professor James D.

Forbes and local man, Duncan Macintyre, climbed Sgurr nan Gillean in 1836.

Each subsequent decade saw further slow exploration, but the arrival of the railway to Strome in 1870, with a connecting ferry to Portree, finally ended Skye's long centuries of isolation. A sustained assault on the Cuillin started that year and continued through the 1870s and 1880s. The last Munro to be climbed, still undesignated, was Sgurr Mhic Coinnich in 1887.

The golden age of Scottish mountaineering, which had seen one Cuillin peak after another fall to a sustained assault by the period's best climbers over 60 years, was almost at an end – but not quite. Out on a spur overlooking Loch Coruisk, a neglected summit was set to become, by default, the country's last mountain prize.

Sgurr Coir'an Lochain is not usually ranked among Skye's most impressive peaks. It lies off the main Cuillin ridge, a twin-topped summit on a side ridge curling north from Sgurr Thearlaich and Sgurr Mhic Choinnich. Its location is almost exactly one kilometre east of Sgurr Dearg's Inaccessible Pinnacle, where it stands astride Coireachan Ruadha and the small hollow of Coir'an Lochain.

Most climbers passing by on the main ridge hardly notice this minor summit in the Coruisk basin. At 729m (2392ft), it is dwarfed by the greatly more impressive Coire Lagan Munros. Although it fades into obscurity when seen from the ridge, it shows a radically contrasting aspect to the east. From Coir'uisg, the flat glen at the head of Loch Coruisk, it is an altogether different sight, with steep rock faces on three sides. Massive boiler-plate slabs rear up to a prominent peak more than 2000ft above the glen. This is undoubtedly the reason why it merited a *sgurr* appellation by the native Skyemen in the pre-mountaineering era, at a time when many greater, but less accessible peaks, were still unnamed.

In those days it was known to the climbers by the subtly different name Sgurr a'Choire Lochain. Linguistic purists subsequently advised the Ordnance Survey to inscribe it on their maps as the Sgurr Coir'an Lochain used today. In whatever form, it means the peak of the corrie of the little loch, named after the tiny rocky pool lying to its south, 1900ft up in Coir'an Lochain.

By summer 1896 neither of Sgurr Coir'an Lochain's two tops, the north one at the apex of the main cliff, and the higher main top, from which it is separated by a pronounced cleft crossing the ridge, appears to have received an ascent.

That summer season had been an active one in Skye, and the date 1896 is regularly encountered in the first ascent details in today's guidebooks. The Scottish Mountaineering Club was then just seven years old, but already very active. Many of its notable personalities of the time were based at Sligachan that year, among them Collie, Naismith, James Parker, Dr. James Collier, and Charles Inglis Clark. Several parties were on the ridge during June, July and August, but the exploration of new rock climbs did not get fully under way until September, which turned out to be a month of unusually good weather.

On September 1, Collie and Howell completed the 2000ft south-east ridge of Sgurr a'Ghreadaidh. Two days later, with Naismith, they climbed Sgurr Alasdair direct from Coire Lagan on the classic route now known as Collie's Climb. On the fourth, Naismith and James Parker scaled the south face of Sgurr na h-Uamha from Harta Corrie, and on the fifth the pair joined Collie and Howell to claim the north-west buttress of Sgurr a'Mhadaidh. September the sixth was a Sunday, so no-one climbed.

Naismith and Collie resumed on the seventh, with a new route on the Sligachan face of Sgurr nan Gillean. More followed in the subsequent days, among them Naismith's Route on Clach Glas. It was a remarkable fortnight in Scottish mountaineering, but it was not over. The night of September 11 found a party of four – Collie, Naismith, Howell and local guide John Mackenzie – camped by Loch Coruisk, having traversed Sgurr Dubh. It was just a day after Collie's 37th birthday.

With a little extrapolation from the scant, business-like notes left by the taciturn explorers, it is possible to construct a fairly accurate picture of the events of the historic next day, Saturday, September 12, 1896.

That morning the party set off from their camp site, 1400ft up the steep slopes to the bottom of the cliffs which form the northern prow of Sgurr Coir'an Lochain. In the style of the time, they wore tweed jackets, breeches, long wool socks and hob-nailed boots. Mackenzie, a Skyeman from the village of Sconser, also habitually wore a flat tweed cap, as photographs of the period show.

Here, in Coireachan Ruadha, the area gets its name from the reddish peridotite which replaces the usual Skye gabbro. The face above them was ominously marked with damp black streaks, and the climbers found the rocks treacherously wet and slippery. They toiled on steeply-inclined slabs, roped together with a sodden hemp line.

They left no precise description of their route, but they did provide a rough sketch of the mountain showing their approximate route zigzagging up the prow. The climbers' notes are not much help – Collie simply recorded the ascent, a brief note of the conditions encountered, and the date in the Sligachan Hotel Climbing Book covering 1893-1911[1]. Naismith carefully wrote down the day's summits, and indeed all those from that summer in Skye, in his minute hand-writing in the small black notebook which records the list of his life's climbs[2]. He then submitted a paragraph on the climb to the SMC Journal for publication the subsequent year[3].

Finally, after two-and-a-half hours' climbing, the four heaved themselves to the top of the enormous rock face, then scrambled up the easier slopes to Sgurr Coir'an Lochain's north summit. They had reached the last unclimbed mountain in the British Isles.

The summit overlooks the minuscule patch of water after which it is named. The view east extends to the north end of Loch Coruisk and Druim nan Ramh, but westwards is blocked by the great peaks of the main ridge towering 1000ft higher, all having received their first ascents in the preceding 25 years. The climbers particularly admired the view of the Inaccessible Pinnacle from here. Collie got out his aneroid and judged the top to be 'about 2450ft in height', an estimate which compares well with today's surveyed height of 2392ft.

We can only speculate on any feelings of achievement they might have had, although new ascents of long routes on virgin rock were no novelty to them. Collie's brief notes do acknowledge that they looked for but failed to find any evidence of a prior ascent, and Naismith records that they built a small cairn. Whether they felt the significance of the historic event or not, the day was far from over for Collie and his companions.

First they crossed the awkward rocky gap on the south-west side, 60ft deep, which separates the north top from the main peak of Sgurr Coir'an Lochain. They followed the ridge running towards Sgurr Mhic Choinnich for some distance, then left it to cross 'some horrid stone slopes' over to Sgurr Dearg, where they climbed the Inaccessible Pinnacle on its summit.

From here they followed the main Cuillin ridge north over Sgurr na Banachdich, its north top which would later be named Sgurr Thormaid in Collie's honour, and Sgurr a'Ghreadaidh. Finally, they left the main ridge at Sgurr a'Mhadaidh, dropping down the Thuilm ridge into Glen Brittle. Even by today's standards, it was a fairly strenuous outing.

Sgurr Coir'an Lochain's north face had to wait 17 years to receive a second ascent, and a fuller account of the route taken[4]. In 1913 Harold Raeburn, J. B. Meldrum and the Wallwork brothers started up the steep edge facing Bidean Druim nan Ramh, but were forced to traverse east on steep slabs under a large overhang. This barred the way to the upper layer of slabs, and was not breached until they reached the left-hand corner overlooking Coruisk. Belays were poor.

Today, the route remains remote and rarely climbed. It has been joined by just a handful of newer routes on the north and north-east faces, and the mountain's west face is apparently still untouched. But some of the personalities who made that inaugural climb have left more memorable legacies than that little known climb on Sgurr Coir'an Lochain.

William Naismith, aged 40 when he climbed Sgurr Coir'an Lochain, is best remembered for 'Naismith's Rule', which estimates how much time should be allowed for hill-walking, and of course, as one of the founders of the SMC.

John Mackenzie is immortalised in the 3100ft Sgurr Mhic Choinnich (Mackenzie's Peak), being a member of the party which made the first ascent in 1887. He continued guiding in the Cuillin and working as a ghillie, and died in July 1933 aged 76. He is buried in the quiet, Free Presbyterian churchyard at Struan on Skye's west coast, under an unusual headstone, irregularly shaped from several small boulders of gabbro. Despite his undoubted contribution to Scottish mountaineering, he was never a member of the SMC. But perhaps that was not surprising for the time, in an era when a London gentleman would hardly expect his butler to join him at the Reform Club.

The least-known climber in the party that day, E. B. Howell, remains a mysterious figure. He is said to have been a friend of Collie, and was probably English. His name seems not to be recorded against any climbs other than those of that memorable summer in Skye, and he was not a member of The Alpine Club[5].

Norman Collie, born in Cheshire but with a Scottish father, has become the best-known climber of the group, and went on to make many more notable climbs in the Alps, the Himalaya and the Canadian Rockies. Already a renowned chemist, he made an important contribution to organic chemistry and took the first X-rays of a metal object inside a human body. His professional achievements earned him a Fellowship of the Royal Society. Later, he lived out his bachelor retirement in the Sligachan Hotel, where he would sit gazing on summer evenings at his beloved Cuillin. A solitary figure at his reserved table in the hotel's dining room, he attracted the curious whispers of other guests.

Collie died in 1942, aged 83, some weeks after being drenched in a fishing mishap at the Storr Lochs. At his own request, he was buried close by his guide, John Mackenzie, at Struan. The length of his grave is marked out not by grass or a stone slab, but by a line of roughly laid stones, in symbolic imitation of the rocks over which he climbed. He lies at Mackenzie's feet, some say in deference to the man who was his constant guide and companion, not infrequently his leader, and on whose incomparable knowledge of the Skye mountains he was so regularly reliant.

Collie's grave lies in an enclosed hollow by the Voaker Burn. However, travel a half-mile or so up the loop road to Coillemor, or to the headland west of Struan, or any of a dozen points on this coast, and the view opens out. From these spots on a clear day, a more permanent reminder to Collie is visible. The southward horizon is dominated by the Black Cuillin, stretching between the sharp peaks of Sgurr nan Gillean on the left, and Sgurr na Banachdich on the far right. Just to the left of Banachdich, and slightly lower, the similarly-shaped north summit nestles against it. Probably named by Naismith, the map now records it as Sgurr Thormaid, the Gaelic for Norman's Peak.

Personal Postscript: The precise date of the first ascent of Sgurr Coir'an Lochain was realised only a few weeks before the anniversary date. The author had intended to make a centenary ascent with a small party by the easy route on September 12, 1996, but having recently had his abdomen rearranged by the National Health Service, was judged unfit to do so. SMC office-bearers seemed unaware of the anniversary, and to the best of the author's knowledge, it passed unmarked.

References

[1] Anonymous notes in the Sligachan Hotel's climbing book for 1893-1911, now deposited in the National Library of Scotland by the SMC, were confirmed as Collie's by comparing with known hand-writing samples held by The Alpine Club of London.

[2] Naismith's Notebook of Climbs, SMC Deposit, National Library of Scotland.

[3] W. Brown, *The Coolins in '96*, SMC Journal, Vol. IV, No. 22, January 1897.

[4] E. W. Steeple et al, *Island of Skye*, SMC, 1935.

[5] Howell is unknown to the historian of English and Welsh rock-climbing Alan Hankinson, author of *The First Tigers*, Dent, 1972, etc.

Other Sources

B. H. Humble, *The Cuillin of Skye*, 1952 (Robert Hale), reprinted Ernest Press, 1986.

K. MacTaggart, *Challenging Summits*, in Discover Scotland, 1990, Vol. 3, Part 30, p. 832.

Christine Mill, *Norman Collie: A Life in Two Worlds*, Aberdeen University Press, 1987.

J. W. Simpson, SMC Climbers' Guide: *Cuillin of Skye*, Vol. II, SMC, 1969.

William C. Taylor, *The Snows of Yesteryear: J. Norman Collie, Mountaineer*, Holt Reinhart and Winston, Toronto, 1973.

AN EXPERT CRAGSMAN
John Buchan Articles in the SMC Journal.

By Donald M. Orr

THE FACT that only three articles by John Buchan were submitted to editors of the SMC Journal is at once strange and yet acceptable. It is odd that one so dedicated to mountaineering generally, and rock-climbing specifically, and also who had such a talent for descriptive, well-observed prose did not leave more than a couple of fine essays, a vague reminiscence, and some shimmering chapters about a favourite pastime.

However, reviewing the demands of his editors and publishers, politics and the law, and of his family and friends, there must have been few quiet moments when he could reflect on the climbs and summits he had achieved or plan any new ventures.

Buchan's interest in mountaineering is seen as a minor, youthful aspect of the man. His fondness of wild places and wandering through them, coupled with his love of angling are seen as mainstays of his holiday periods and the delights of his spare time. He has never been viewed as a serious mountaineer.

Yet contrary to the popular notion two aspects stand out:

1. John Buchan never did anything by halves, nor did he maintain casual interests in topics he touched upon. The period of his greatest activity as a climber was as planned and structured as his time at Oxford, or in Parliament, or in Canada.

2. The climbs he ascended, and the summits he attained, are still valid exploits for the contemporary mountaineer. Time, technique and modern equipment have not devalued them. The Cuillin is still one of the most rugged ranges in Britain and a stern testing ground for any aspirant mountaineer.

Buchan, over a period of years, climbed with the best of the Skye guides – John Mackenzie*, and at the same time as many areas of the Cuillin were being initially explored. His dedication in returning year after year to Skye and interspersing his work in the Cuillin with expeditions to the Alps put him among a small, elite band of men whose exploits set them apart from other sportsmen.

Buchan joined the Scottish Mountaineering Club in 1904. Among the routes listed on his application are climbs on Buachaille Etive Mor and Bidean nam Bian in Glen Coe; three major routes on Ben Nevis; 14 ascents on Arran, and various peaks in the north of Scotland.

While in South Africa from 1900-1903 Buchan made many climbs in the Drakensberg Range of Natal, the Zoutpansberg of the Northern Transvaal, and an ascent of Mont-aux-Sources which, at over 10,500ft, was the highest mountain in what was then called Basutoland.

From 1903-1907 he climbed in the Dolomites and around Zermatt and Chamonix in the Alps making ascents of the Untergletschorn, the Riftelhorn and the Matterhorn, among others. These activities were recognised in his election to the Alpine Club in 1906. With this background of technical expertise and wealth of Alpine experience he was well poised to comment on the developments of any aspect of mountaineering.

In 1907 the *SMC Journal* published *The Knees of the Gods*. Set in a future dreamscape, where mountains are full of lifts and elevators, glass-enclosed cafes dominate the summits of most alpine peaks. The mountaineer has become as streamlined and intense as some of our current rock athletes – non-smoking, non-drinking and dedicated to the extreme. In many ways aspects of his comic fantasy of the 1900s have become part of the reality of the 1990s. Writing with a great deal of humour and whimsy, he sets his dream sequence in the Sligachan Hotel. This at once stamps the hallmark of his work; his ability to fictionalise incidents in a factual context and/or setting. Here his well-observed notes about the interior of the Sligachan Hotel and his awareness of the difficulties of the Cuillin, including the then untried, but talked of, continuous traverse of the Cuillin Ridge from Sgurr nan Gillean to Garsbheinn, set the tale on a solid structure that will easily support the fantasy he describes. The Cuillin is seen as the last true mountains worthy of consideration in a tourist world of cossetted 'adventure'.

The stark grandeur of the range must have impressed him when he first saw it in 1903, fresh from South Africa and in need of some excitement in another corner of the world, and this time in the company of his sister, Anna (who also went on to become a novelist under the name O. Douglas). He spent the following two summers on Skye, in partnership with John Mackenzie, opening up new routes. This in many respects was as remote and frontier-like as climbing in South Africa must have been. It should be remembered that the last unclimbed peak in Britain was Sgurr Coir'an Lochain on Skye, which had only been ascended a few years earlier in 1896 by John Mackenzie and party. (*See article by MacTaggart. Ed.*)

Another point of interest is that both Buchan and Norman Collie were climbing in Skye in the summer of 1904, both using the services of Mackenzie and both, presumably, staying at the Sligachan Hotel. While both were professional men and greatly interested in travel and mountaineering, and must have been aware of each other through Mackenzie, it would appear they never met. I can find no reference to either in their fairly extensive respective writings and one is left wondering what kind of team they might have made if their trips to Skye had overlapped.

These experiences developed a deep respect for the mountain environment that later allowed him to write so authoritatively on climbing episodes in books like *Mr Standfast* and *The Three Hostages*. By 1907, when his first article for the Journal appeared, he was a member of both the SMC and The Alpine Club, had started working for Nelson's the publishers, and had married Susan Grosvenor.

In 1913 the Journal published a review by Buchan under the title *Half Hours in the Club Library*. His study was *A Journey to the Western Isles of Scotland* by Dr. Samuel Johnson, in two volumes, and published in 1775. It is not really surprising to find Buchan in a reflective mood in 1913 and involved in researches into Scottish literature. This was the year his biography of *The Marquis of Montrose* was published and the event must have given him much personal satisfaction as its martial hero was a stalwart of individual freedoms and the good of the Commonwealth. A considerable amount of his research would later be woven into the intricate strands of his great novel *Witch Wood* (1927).

Buchan finds Johnson's work 'an accurate but colourless itinerary' and finds that it, 'compares ill with Boswell's *Tour to the Hebrides* '. He is, however, commended for leaving the tea shops and coffee houses of London to go and see what was 'the nearest approach to the free and barbaric natural existence about which 18th-century literati talked wisely and knew nothing'. Over all, Buchan feels that at the age of 64 the Doctor was perhaps too set in his ways to appreciate the starkness and grandeur of the Highlands. His intellectual tastes were depressed by the 'wide extent of hopeless sterility'. What appealed to Buchan, and indeed to most mountaineers, was that sense of wilderness whereas the Doctor displays the complete antithesis, typified by this comment on Loch Lomond: 'The islets, which court the gazer at a distance, disgust him at his approach, when he finds, instead of soft lawns, and shady thickets, nothing more than uncultivated ruggedness.'

While acknowledging the dignity and beauty of the work, and Johnson's place among our great literary figures, he feels that the book is 'scarcely a work that calls for frequent re-reading'.

His final contribution to the *SMC Journal* was in 1939 with an article entitled *Pan*. This mirrors an episode in the section, *The Middle Years* of his autobiography, *Memory Hold the Door* published in 1940, the year of his death. Interestingly, the incident published in the Journal is a slightly different version and is dated 1911, whereas in his autobiography he quotes the event as occurring in 1910. Small matter, after all the years, as Buchan's stamp endorses the narrative.

He attempts here to deal with an aspect of the supernatural, an area that had always fascinated him. There are many places in the mountains of Scotland that can be held in awe, especially with the right climatic conditions and a raking light. There are the disturbing effects of avalanche, lightning, mists and Brocken spectres, and in climbing there are countless tales of falling rocks, loose holds and the trundles and tumbles whose timing may be strange but are generally accepted as part of the game. The unexpected and the bizarre are always memorable and often disconcerting. (The personal experience of being almost knocked off a slim stance by an incensed owl, exploding at head height from the narrow chimney we were unwittingly sharing comes to mind.)

Buchan's short narrative is set on the descent of the Alpspitze near Partenkirchen in Bavaria. His guide at one point falls silent and Buchan notices that he is white with terror and staring straight in front of him. They set off running downhill in panic with no real knowledge as to why. On reaching the highway they collapse exhausted and, on recovering he acknowledges their embarrassment on the way home: 'We did not speak; we did not even look at each other.'

While one appreciates Buchan's treatment of the uncanny in *The Gap in the Curtain*, and in his short story *The Wind in the Portico* this little article does seem weak, but as a small note in an autobiography of a very full life, I suppose it gets by with its hint of the goat-footed god and a strangeness in the landscape that somehow can encourage a more primeval awareness within us.

In *The Three Hostages* (1924), Buchan relates a vivid account of chimney, crack and wall climbing, under dangerous circumstances, on the fictitious 'Machray' estate in Wester Ross. The hero's negotiations and appreciation of rock structures and formations clearly reveal the author's capacity on Skye and in the Alps. Many aspects of his novels deal with varying details of hillcraft related to stalking and fishing, and again display his love of rugged landscape and mountain atmosphere, an influence that was to remain with him throughout his life.

* See SMC Journal No. 179, 1988. *Desperate Rock Mountains.*

A VISIT TO SKYE FIFTY YEARS AGO

By W. D. Brooker

I HAD become interested in mountains after climbing Mount Keen as a 12-year-old Boy Scout, and began to explore some of the Deeside hills on outings from Aberdeen. A couple of years later I discovered some of the magnetism of the West Coast by making an Easter cycle tour to Fort William and Ben Nevis with two classmates. One of my companions was keen to continue the experience, so during the school summer holidays Ken and I set off for a two-week holiday to Skye. I kept a diary of this trip and wrote a full description so that the details were reliably preserved. Some of these will no doubt evoke memories of similar experiences in the minds of others whose activities go back to those early post-war years.

The train took us to Inverness and we cycled 26 miles along Loch Ness to the Youth Hostel at Alltsaigh. The next day we pedalled up Glen Moriston, along Loch Cluanie and crossed the divide to reach Glen Shiel. At that time the road was still narrow, and although tarred, occasional tufts of grass grew through a central ridge, well scraped by the undercarriages of passing vehicles. However, this did not detract from the thrill of descending Glen Shiel, swooping down, down, and still on downward, while the mountain walls rose higher and higher on either side. And these mountains were quite different to the broad, plateau-topped hills of the eastern Grampians to which we were accustomed. These were sharp, pointed peaks, rising from precipitous slopes, buttressed with irregular ranks of rock outcrops. To our eyes they looked like mountains, not just hills, and very exciting. Crossing Shiel Bridge I remember looking across at the orange seaweed fringing the tidal shores of Loch Duich and feeling that this was the real West Coast and that we had truly crossed the divide to a different world. It is difficult to convey the sense of remoteness we felt, when modern motoring can make the same journey between breakfast and a morning coffee break.

The road began to climb to the notorious Mam Ratagan, but apart from having to push the bikes up the steepest part I don't recall any problems and we had soon left the gravelled surface of the pass and were spinning down Glen More to Glenelg Youth Hostel at the Kyle Rhea narrows. It had been a long, tiring day and was followed by a rest day during which we visited the ruined brochs in Glen Beag, Dun Telve and Dun Troddan. These kindled an interest in prehistoric features which I have still.

The following day started with the ferry to Skye. The fare was a shilling each, with an additional sixpence for each of the bicycles. The swift current and the course taken by the boat was interesting enough, but the scene was enhanced at one stage by the water boiling with fish leaping and splashing all around in a feeding frenzy. We were told they were saithe. It was only 26 miles to Sligachan but it was hilly and we had to pedal hard against a stiff breeze. However, our minds were soon taken up by the scene before us as we stopped on the Sligachan bridge.

Our first view of the Cuillin was impressive as Sgurr nan Gillean stood out jet black against a leaden sky, its sides patched with grey screes from which darker gullies and chimneys sprang upward. It was obviously a mountain for real climbers and not for boy cyclists. Six miles of easy going followed and then the tarmac ended. We had been warned that the crossing to Glenbrittle was by one of the worst roads in Scotland and it certainly fulfilled this expectation, writhing over the pass with a surface strewn with stones and pocked with wheel-jarring potholes. It must have been bad enough for cars but on a heavily-laden bicycle it was bone-shattering. We were well down on the Glenbrittle side but still had about three miles to go when there was a sharp report as my rear tyre burst. The attempt to repair it only lasted five minutes before a ravening horde of midges drove us headlong down the road, wheeling my bike along the verge. At dusk we reached the Youth Hostel, a large wooden building, Norwegian we were told, and capable of sleeping 80 people. Our first impression was that all 80 had dumped their wet boots in the porch, and were now competing for cooking space on the stove and for seats at the long wooden common room tables.

Next morning the mist was clearing from the peaks and we consulted Alex Sutherland, the Hostel Warden, who lent us a map and told us the appropriate route up Sgurr Alasdair, the highest of the Cuillin. At that time the height was given as 3251ft above sea level but it was to change to 3309ft on later maps and is currently at 3258ft (993m). Such Ordnance Survey orogenetic frenzies have affected a good number of Scottish summits and occasionally create minor positional changes as well. Anyway, we set off across the wet, grassy moorland, passed through the rocky portal of Coire Lagan and found the feature which had made me both curious and apprehensive when I read its name, The Great Stone Shoot. I think I had envisaged a kind of giant rock chimney and indeed we found a huge open gully curving upward with vertical sides, but its bed was sloping and filled with scree, easy to ascend although very laborious, as it continually slipped away underfoot. In an hour-and-a-half we had reached the cleft at the top and were able to scramble up the ridge to the right and reach the summit.

Here we met two young men sitting astride the ridge on either side of the cairn. The mist was coming down and we just had time to take in an impressive view of sharp, rocky peaks and a narrow ridge disappearing down into the mist along which the two told us they had come from Sgurr Sgumain. They intended to continue to Sgurr Thearlaich and invited us to join them, so we all returned down the arête to the head of the Great Stone Shoot. Here the way ahead was barred by a vertical wall until I found a crack leading to a ledge from where the top was easily reached. The ridge continued, so narrow that at times it was a knife-edge with a steep drop on either side. It was our first encounter with what we were told was 'exposure' and we were shown how to cope by straddling the ridge at these places. Soon the ridge widened, but then dropped so steeply that we had some difficulty, until our new friends produced a couple of slings which allowed us additional handholds. Ahead towered the dark bulk of Sgurr Mhic Choinnich but by now it was drizzling, so we descended from the ridge by a loose gully which eventually took us into the lower part of the Great Stone Shoot, only a scree slither from the floor of Coire Lagan. The rain stopped and we were fairly dry by the time we had parted with our companions in Glenbrittle after what for us had been a very exciting introduction to the Cuillin.

That evening we went for a walk down to Loch Brittle and when we returned to the Hostel there was a singsong under way. Such occasions were a fairly usual and very enjoyable communal feature of camp and hostel life, in the days before folk singing became established as a commercially-based entertainment, and the availability of recorded material reduced the need to memorise the words of songs. Anyway, here were songs to learn which featured climbing and crags and ropes and abandoned maidens. It was all new and exciting. We listened avidly to snippets of conversation between tough-looking men in check shirts; some even had rope slings secured around their waists by metal snaplinks to prove (as if that were needed) their status as real climbers. One exchange I overheard was about an 'Inaccessible Pinnacle', and afterwards I asked the Warden where it was. He told us. 'And is it really inaccessible?', I asked. 'It is to the likes of you' was the unequivocal reply. Even if this was not taken as a challenge, The Pinnacle obviously required investigation to satisfy our curiosity.

The following day the weather looked promising, and we set off up the path used the previous day, leaving the road beside Glenbrittle House and climbing up grassy slopes to pass along the brink of the dramatic canyon which houses Eas Mor. Leaving the path, which continues to Coire Lagan, we struck up the screes leading to the western spur of Sgurr Dearg. The screes gave way to broken rock and we reached the cairn of Sron Dearg, beyond which was a narrow, but easy, arête leading upward to the summit of Sgurr Dearg. 'The Inaccessible' (not yet undignified by the term 'Inn Pinn') rose unmistakably above the top of the mountain from the slope on the other side. It was a great fin of gabbro rock, its far edge sweeping up in a blade of 125ft and the near side dropping almost vertically for 50ft to the slope below the summit cairn of the mountain. Ken's curiosity had been satisfied, so he stayed at the cairn while I descended to the foot of the long knife edge, changed into gym shoes, secured the beret firmly on my head and had a look.

There were plenty of holds and at first it seemed easy, but I became increasingly aware of the exposure. Yesterday's ridge on Sgurr Thearlaich was nothing to this. Later, I was to read this arête described as having 'an infinite and vertical drop on one side and an even longer and steeper one on the other'. Fanciful perhaps, but it was beginning to seem like this to me and I was growing nervous when I came to a stop less than half-way up. The good holds had petered out and there was no alternative to making a couple of balance moves on very smooth rock which must have been polished over the years by the anxious scrabbling of thousands of bootnails. The standard, of course, was only Moderate, but the exposure was considerable and it all seemed very precarious. It was the kind of decision point with which all climbers become familiar, but to a callow 14-year-old it was so unnerving that I still remember it vividly. Once past the critical point the rest went without any problem until I reached the haven of the summit block. Then the reality of my position had to be faced. There was no alternative but to descend and do it all again – in reverse. I was so frightened that I said my prayers and promised God that if I were allowed to get down safely I would never do anything like this again! Thus reinforced with Divine Support I got a grip of myself and very carefully climbed back down. Presumably, I was becoming accustomed to the exposure because this time it all seemed easier – even the crux, which had frightened me so much on the ascent.

With a sense of elation surging through me I rejoined Ken and we set off northward along a ridge leading down to Bealach Coire na Banachdich, the easiest pass between Glen Brittle and the Loch Coruisk basin. The ridge continued easily over two subsidiary tops to the main summit of Sgurr na Banachdich. It was now a perfect day and my diary records: 'The finest view I have ever had, from the Islands in the south to the Outer Hebrides in the west and all the north of Skye itself, the blue sky and sea contrasting with green grass and yellow sands.'

After a last look at range after range of rugged hills fading into the distance in the east, we turned west along the spur leading to Glen Brittle. This terminated in the easy peak of Sgurr nan Gobhar. From its cairn we scrambled down a gully and then by screes and grassy slopes to the Hostel. Tired after a wonderful day we sought our beds earlier than usual that night.

Glenbrittle Hostel was not run on the usual strictly regulated basis, so the next morning we were able to have a long lie and potter about the hostel all day, writing letters, and doing odd chores for the Warden. We also fitted the new cycle tube brought from Portree by the kindly bus driver and were ready to continue our cycle tour the next day. This time we took no chances with the Glenbrittle road and used the bus as far as the main road. At Bracadale we stopped at the shop/Post Office and after penetrating a barricade of scythes, fence wire and other crofting materials reached the counter. It was manned by a very aged and somewhat deaf greybeard with only a smattering of English, so it took us some time to obtain the items we wanted, pay for them, and extract the right change. A stiff headwind made the second half of our journey to the hostel at Harlosh something of a trial. The famous Dunvegan Castle was the main object for the following day and my contemporary account of this visit to Skye contains all the usual information about it. Perhaps even more enthusiasm was contained in the reference to 'a huge tea' we enjoyed in a cottage for only one shilling and ninepence!

Rha Youth Hostel at Uig was our next destination and was reached by cycling to the shore of one of the arms of Loch Snizort, and boarding a small boat along with two other hostellers who crowded up to let us pile our bikes on board. It was only a small boat, and because the sea was rough I helped the elderly ferryman to row. The hostel was 'delightfully dirty and haunted by rats', which gave us lots of sport in unsuccessfully hunting them in the evening. Our main reason for visiting this part of Skye had been to see the Quiraing, a feature on the great lava escarpment which extends past Portree northward throughout the length of Trotternish. On a day of continuous sunshine we cycled up the gravel road to Staffin, and leaving our bikes at the point where it breaches the scarp, we walked round to explore the bizarre collection of fairy towers, crevasses and basins formed by erosion and landslip of the basaltic lavas. We were impressed by this remarkable rock scenery, and the ease with which it could be reached.

It was time to start our return journey, and on the following forenoon we left for Kyle of Lochalsh together with two lads from Preston. Strong headwinds made for very hard going until past Sligachan, and we only just made the last ferry from Kyleakin at 9.30pm. At Kyle the hostel was a group of unsightly old army huts, but in a magnificent situation. Our companions arrived the following morning, having been delayed by a succession of punctures and forced to spend the night at a B and B near Broadford. It was a fine day, so we hired a boat very cheaply and all went rowing about in the Sound of Sleat. We even visited Skye again under our own steam but the tidal currents were strong and demanded caution. In the evening we enjoyed a magnificent orange sunset and as we watched the last vivid glow reflected on the water, the sound of pipes came drifting over from Skye. It has the ring of a tourist brochure cliché, but it actually did happen like that as a fitting end to a first visit to Skye.

Editor's note: William (Bill) Brooker, the new Honorary President of the Club, was conferred with another honour on Friday, November 29, 1996, when he was made a Master of the University by Aberdeen University. The Laureation Address detailed the mountaineering highlights of my forerunner, including the invention of the pseudo-medical terminology for those suffering from the Munro-bagging disease and perhaps more healthy deeds such as editing the *Century of Scottish Mountaineering*.

THE MAIDS HAVE ALL GONE FROM GLEN BRITTLE

By Ian Walton

'WHAT DO you mean they've moved the phone box ?'

You do expect some changes when you've been gone for 23 years, but moving the phone box a couple of hundred yards down the road really seemed like sacrilege. How many times had I walked over from the campsite to phone home and let everyone know that we were all still alive? How often had we crammed six people into that small red box, to shelter from the pouring rain that always started right after we put down the receiver? That phone box was an icon. But I suppose it honestly did make more sense to put the only phone beside the Youth Hostel, rather than beside the farmhouse that always seemed totally deserted.

It has been more than 20 years since I camped in Glen Brittle with St. Andrews University Mountaineering Club. That end-of-spring-term meet was an annual celebration after final exams. We had celebrated my 21st birthday right there in the campground; somehow I don't remember too many of the details. But, 'where's that bottle of . . . CRASH!' still brings back vivid memories of someone falling flat over the club tent – and it didn't even have guy lines to trap the unwary. We called it the 'Nalley' because it was shaped like an alley and held 'n' people, where 'n' is the traditional large whole number, beloved of mathematicians.

Now I was back for a quick reunion visit with my climbing partner, Andrew. He and his family have conveniently settled in Inverness, albeit with several year-long detours to Finland, Afghanistan and Holland. I have lived in the northern California beach paradise of Santa Cruz (earthquakes excluded), for the last 23 years, so we've moved apart in some ways.

I have developed a fondness for the great Alaskan wilderness; just a hop, skip and jump up the west coast from Santa Cruz (or at most a short flight on the exquisite Alaska Airlines). This story was written as I sat on a curving mussel bar below McBryde Glacier, in Glacier Bay National Park. The others in my group were off watching for chunks of ice calving from the glacier face into the lagoon. I had stayed behind to ferry the six double kayaks up the channel on the incoming tide. Otherwise there was a nasty choice between the quarter-mile walk across (or rather through . . .) the glacial silt, at low tide, or playing dodgem kayaks with the icebergs barrelling out of the channel from the lagoon.

Andrew and I thought a short reunion on the Skye ridge would be fun – a reality check on the changes in the last few years. Some things change in 23 years and some things don't. The phone box has changed. The Glen Brittle road game has not, despite a few largely cosmetic changes to the road itself. The rules of play still seem to be approximately: 10 points if the other car has to slow down, 50 points if they have to reverse, and 500 points if they go into the ditch. Of course, even in its original incarnation, the game felt much safer than the more recent time that I was driven down to Glen Brittle by an American friend, who insisted on trying to drive on the left side of the single-track road.

So how about the campsite itself? The bathrooms have actually improved – but then that wouldn't be hard. However, the wee footbridge still threatens to slide the unwary reveller into the burn on a dark and stormy night. The campsite is remarkably unchanged even though the musical wake-up call of 'Campsite fees, please' has been replaced by a boring, pay-in-advance system. Most of the tents have changed, but ours hasn't. The old Black's 'Good Companion' stands out like a sore orange thumb, and is somewhat less than weather proof. But it does have character which is entirely missing from the uniform advance of the nylon domes. On the other hand, I certainly wouldn't want to take it with me to Alaska.

The journey to the west from Inverness had already shown some interesting changes. The imminent opening of the bridge seemed like a monumentally bad idea – at least from the folk-song point of view. 'Take the boat over to Skye', and, 'If you've never been kissed in that isle of the mist' seems to lose all of its romance if you can just drive over a bridge to get there. I suppose the National Trust took that important idea into account in its deliberations on the project!

The Sligachan Hotel had changed enormously for the better. The bar was better, the beer was better, the food was better and the staff actually appeared to be pleased to serve climbers. Perhaps the large campsite is taking it a little too far though.

So how about the ridge itself? Has the climbing changed? A lot of the answer to that has to lie in your perspective. The first time I saw them as a teenager, the cliffs of Coire Lagan looked so enormous, and the bogs on the Loch Coruisk path felt interminable. But now I've climbed in Yosemite Valley with its 3000ft sweeps of unbroken granite, and I've slogged over the tussocks of the Arctic National Wildlife Refuge's north slope. And I've spent a lot of time paddling beneath the tidewater glaciers of South-east Alaska – or just sitting writing stories beside them. So things look different to me.

Andrew had put it another way one year when we were debating whether I could live with a girlfriend in Scotland, the same way I had in California. It would have been unthinkable when I left Scotland in the Sixties. 'You could do it now – Scotland may not have changed much, but you have,' was Andrew's verdict. It's all in your viewpoint.

So, back on the ridge, there do seem to be more people scurrying along the rock than I remember. The advent of guided parties produces some entertaining moments: there are, count them, the eight people in identical blue crash hats lined up at the foot of the Inn Pin. And there is that chance encounter with Andrew's neighbour from Inverness, as we round a less well remembered pinnacle. We are trying to decide which way to go when two tentative figures appear from the opposite direction. When we ask them which way they have come they respond: 'Oh, we don't know anything – you'll have to ask our guide on the end of the rope.' And then the neighbour appears. It does make for a good conversation until the clients start getting restless.

Strangely, route finding needs more effort than it used to – I'm sure I never used to abseil going off Sgurr Alasdair in that direction! And my GPS receiver insists that walking over the cliff is the correct way to go, and offers to record how fast I'm moving on the long way down. But the rays of evening light from Garsbheinn are as beautiful as ever. And the islands still float on a magical mystery carpet. My knees, however, just aren't what they used to be. After that descent to the Loch Coruisk path the boggy stretches are quite a struggle in the gathering gloom. It's really hard to negotiate all those tussocks without bending my left knee. In fact, they really are comparable to those Alaskan North Slope tussocks that only a caribou can cross with any semblance of elegance. But at least it isn't as bad as that dreadful night when we carried a stretcher across those same tussocks in the pouring rain, descending from the ridge above Coir a' Grunndha. The bad news then was a rockfall on White Slab and a badly-broken ankle. But the good news is that, thanks to the skill of the surgeon at Raigmore, the victim can still walk today, and lives happily in Oregon.

And, of course, the final comparison is the weather. It has clearly changed for the worse – perhaps we can blame it on global warming. I remember the good old days of lying in the morning sun in the campsite before wandering up to Coire Lagan for an afternoon of climbing. The top of the Cioch had always seemed like it would be a grand spot for a 'bring your own rope' party. (And there weren't any midges in those days either. If you believe that statement, I have a bridge for sale in Arizona . . .) This year we spent four days in Skye and three days prior to that, waiting for clear weather in Inverness. All told there has been one dry spell of 12 hours during my week's visit. So we only did half the ridge. But it was still very satisfying.

To add final insult to injury though, everyone I met in Scotland a year later apologised for the bad weather that summer, and reminisced about how wonderful the weather had been the previous summer. It's amazing what just one year will do to the memory cells, let alone 23 . . . Were there really maids in Glen Brittle?

> *Lay me out on the pitiless Nordwand*
> *Where the bivouac sites are few –*
> *Alone – with a stone for a pillow*
> *And an uninterrupted view.*

(Tom Patey, *The Last of the Grand Old Masters*).

THE CLASSIFICATION OF MOUNTAINS

By David Purchase

1. Introduction:

Of making many lists there is no end, and the climbing of all the hills therein is a weariness of the flesh.

MANY have been the comments that the number of Munroists grows at an ever-increasing rate. What was once a trickle is now a flood. I note, for example, that a compleation year as recent as 1989 puts me firmly in the first half of the list. Less frequently noted is that the *publication* of lists of mountains appears to be following the same pattern. What used to occur about once a decade now seems to happen at least once each year, with no sign of abating. The frustration is that each author devises his or her own criteria for entry, in order that the resulting list may differ from all others. And then, when the list is published, there is often no information which would enable the user to check the validity of the entries or test for omissions.

There are two main objectives for the current work. One is to propose a set of criteria which could be used for the listing and classification of hills; and the other to suggest what should, and should not, be changed in the currently published lists. In doing this I would emphasise firstly that I think historical precedent is as important as the use of criteria based on topographical data, and secondly, that I think it is highly desirable that a basis is adopted which can be consistently applied not only in the Highlands but also in the Scottish Lowlands and the rest of the British Isles. In order to address these objectives the paper will start, after a few points of definition, with a brief description of the more important published lists.

It is natural that an exercise of this type should concentrate on the Munros. The basis to be proposed divides those current Tops which might be worthy of promotion into two quite distinct groups – one group of eight hills which only just qualify, and another of nine hills which are far more clear-cut cases. The former group are neatly balanced by 12 Munros which just fail to qualify, and I shall propose that all these marginal examples are left unchanged, with only the Group of Nine becoming eligible for full Munro status.

2. A few definitions:

It is hardly surprising that different writers have used different terminology in their tables and lists. However the current discussion will be eased by a consistent usage throughout, and so I adopt the following definitions:

mountain – Any point which is regarded, on the criteria being considered, as a 'separate mountain' (e.g. a Munro). For clarity 'separate mountain' is sometimes used but the meaning is unchanged.

top   Any point which does *not* qualify as a mountain but which is regarded, on the criteria being considered, as a 'subsidiary top'.

minor top Any local high point which does not qualify as a mountain or top.

hill   Any local high point; that is, mountains, tops and minor tops are all hills.

summit   When it is necessary to refer explicitly to the location of the highest point of a hill, the word 'summit' is used. Summit can apply whatever the status of the hill in question. But in context the words 'mountain', 'top' and 'hill' will often be used to describe the highest point.

separation The separation between two points is defined in distance and height, with a time derived from them. As this concept is used throughout the paper, it is described more fully in the next section.

the Tables Unless otherwise stated, 'the Tables' refers to *Munro's Tables*, but excludes the 'Other Tables of Lesser Heights'.

For consistency with modern Ordnance Survey (OS) mapping, distances and heights are given in metric units. When referring to the Imperial units in earlier works, conversions are accurate when this is critical to the discussion (for example, the minimum altitude for a Munro is 914.4m) and are then shown in square brackets [ ]. Frequently, precision is not of the essence; for example, 150m and 500ft will often be regarded as equivalent (and then the converted value will be in normal parentheses). Note that horizontal distances are always quoted in kilometres or miles, whereas heights are in metres or feet.

3. A note on separation:

The concept of the 'separation' between two points is used throughout the paper, and so a short description follows. Some more detailed matters are deferred until a later section. In describing separation, horizontal (map) distances are given in kilometres ('km'), normally to one decimal place, and heights are in metres ('m'). Times are calculated from these distances and heights using a walking speed of four kilometres per hour, plus one minute per 10 metres of ascent; these calculations take no account of terrain. The result is taken to the nearer minute.

In considering the separation of a hill from its neighbour, it is convenient to start from the *lower* summit. The distance to any other (higher) point is measured *along the connecting ridge* even if a shorter route is available which involves little extra loss of height. The 'reascent' or the 'drop' (the terms are used interchangeably) is defined as the altitude of the hill, *minus* the altitude of the lowest bealach traversed along that connecting ridge. Determining a required distance from the OS map to 0.1km (the normal accuracy of a grid reference) is difficult in only a few cases. However, the drop is less easy, as although there is often a height given for the summit of even minor hills it is quite rare to have a value at the bealach. But in practice I have found that a careful interpretation of the contour lines near the bealach enables a value for the drop to be derived which is usually accurate, to 5m or so. For the purposes of classification this is quite adequate, especially if (as in the case of the system to be proposed) small errors cannot lead to the total exclusion of the summit under consideration.

Historically, separations were measured from one summit to another. In his important contribution to the subject, Bonsall[1] introduced in 1973 the concept of measurement to the 'nearest higher ground'; that is, in practice, to the first point reached along a connecting ridge that has the same altitude as the summit in question. Using nearest higher ground has, of course, no effect on the drop but will always reduce the distance – sometimes trivially, but often by a substantial amount. Figure 1 should make this clear. So far as I can tell, the concept has not been used in any published lists, even recent ones, but I shall use it in my own proposals.

4. Some traditional approaches:

Munro's Tables

Any discussion of mountain classification must start with *Munro's Tables*[11]. Munro himself gave no definitions of separate mountains or subsidiary tops, stating only that each decision, 'although arrived at after careful consideration, cannot be finally insisted on'. However, there is strong evidence (see, for example, Campbell[4]) that an important influence was whether the hill was separately named on the OS maps published in the late 19th century. Indeed in eight cases this was taken, in the first publication in 1891, to the extreme of identifying a named point as the Munro and a nearby, *higher* but unnamed point as a top; these anomalies were among a number of corrections planned by Munro but implemented posthumously in the first revision in 1921. (Though the Tables have passed through several new editions and reprints, the editions of 1921 and 1981 were the only ones in which significant changes occurred. It should be noted that, though the words 'mountain' and 'top' are sometimes used in the Tables in the same sense as in this paper, often 'top' is used for 'hill', that is, for any listed point including separate mountains.)

Interestingly, the editor of the 1933 edition, J. Gall Inglis, though making only one change (other than to names) to the 1921 Tables, included a note 'for the next revision' with a description of the conditions that he deemed appropriate for deciding whether a point is a 'top'. He proposed a drop of 75–100ft (say 25m) 'of decided gradient' and with 'some kind of individuality'. He added that three classes required special consideration even if not quite meeting these conditions: the rising ends of long, fairly level ridges; spur tops; and plateau tops.

In his second paper[2], Bonsall demonstrated that the limit for a Munro was in practice equivalent to a separation in time to the nearest higher ground of 30 minutes or more (using Naismith's original formula; at the standard

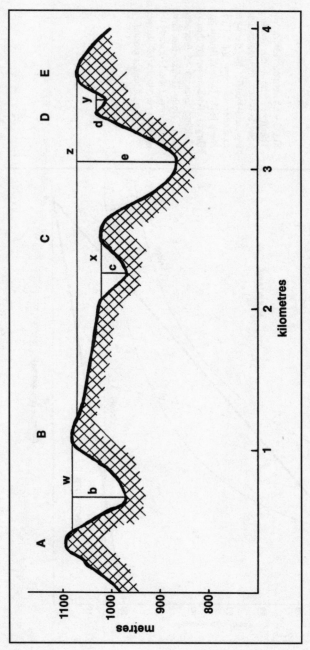

Fig. 1 – Mountains, Tops and Minor Tops

The figure shows an outline of the elevation of a ridge comprising five hills, A to E, with A being assumed to be the highest in the neighbourhood. The 'reascent' components of the separations for B to E are indicated by b, c, d and e. The separations in distance to the nearest higher ground are shown as w, x, y and z. It can be seen that, while the separation of B is almost unaffected by using 'nearest higher ground', that of E is significantly reduced and that of C is very greatly reduced. In this hypothetical instance A and E would be mountains, B and C tops and D a minor top. But if separations were measured to the summit of a nearby mountain then C might well qualify as a third mountain since its separation from A would be large in distance, and from E large in reascent.

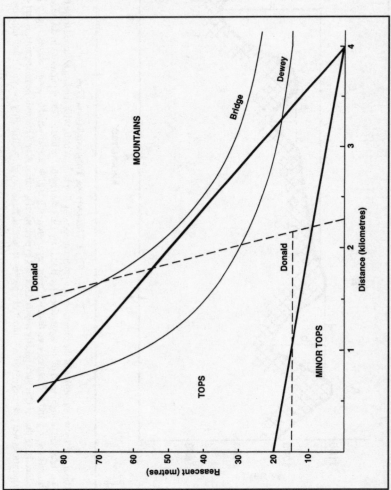

Fig. 2 – Classification Zones
The figure shows the dividing lines between mountains and tops, and (Donalds only) between tops and minor tops, for the lists compiled by Donald, Bridge and Dewey. Also shown are the two dividing lines to be proposed later. Note: Unlike the three named lists, I shall be using the more severe criterion of 'distance to nearest higher ground'.

pace used herein that time is about 35 minutes). However, there were, and are, plenty of anomalies in both directions.

In logical sequence I should next consider Corbett's Tables[5], though they were published (posthumously) later than those by Donald. However, the Corbett list, with its strict requirement for a 500ft [152.4m] drop, does not assist in the development of a classification system, and it is to Donald that I now turn.

Donald's Tables

Donald's Tables[10] of hills in the Scottish Lowlands were published in 1935. They showed all hills in Scotland south of the Highland Line and over 2000ft [609.6m] high. His list is divided into mountains and tops, though he uses the word 'hill' to mean a separate mountain, and the word 'top' to include all listed hills including mountains. Donald also listed 15 'minor tops' which were, originally, 2000ft contour rings which did not qualify even as tops; subsequent editors have added higher so-called minor tops to his list.

Donald's is the first list we consider with a 2000ft limit. Figure 2 shows the dividing lines between mountains and tops, and if appropriate between tops and minor tops, for his and several other such lists. The dividing lines to be proposed later for these lists are also marked.

Donald's classification rules, which have never been altered, are as follows. He defines a 'unit' as one-12th of a mile or one 50ft contour of ascent. He then states that a mountain must be at least 17 units from other mountains, and that any hill with a reascent of more than 100ft that is not a mountain is a top, adding that a hill may be a top with a reascent as little as 50ft if it is of 'sufficient topographical merit'. He states that, in general: 'While the rules . . . rather lack mathematical precision [sic; a remarkable statement], the actual result of their application is that . . . an 80ft drop determines a 'top' and the 17-unit rule a 'hill'.' For our purposes these rules must be metricated. A 'unit' is 134m of distance or 15.25m of height; hence 17 units (2.25km or 260m or some combination) corresponds to a time between 34 and 26 minutes. It is not unreasonable to say that, as an equivalent rule, a mountain requires a separation of 30 minutes. So far as tops are concerned, Donald implies that any hill with a 25m drop qualifies and that some with lesser drops are included so long as this is 15m or more.

However, Donald measures separation, as already indicated, from one summit to another. This has produced anomalies of such degree that it is surprising that no editor has emended his classification. I take just one example – the ridge of the Ettrick Hills (Section 7) running north-east from Andrewhinney Hill. Trowgrain Middle is near enough to Andrewhinney Hill to be classified as a top. But Herman Law, which is lower than Trowgrain Middle and only a kilometre from it, is classified as a separate mountain – presumably because it is 2.4km (hence more than 17 units) from Andrewhinney Hill. Measured from the nearest higher ground, Herman Law has barely enough separation to qualify as a top!

Bridge's Tables

Although this paper is primarily about Scottish hills, any basis that is satisfactory for the Donalds should also be appropriate throughout the rest of the British Isles. Some early writers merely extended the Tables to include the 3000ft hills 'Furth of Scotland' and, as the number of hills was quite small, added a comment to the effect that 'we do not know how to distinguish between mountains and tops consistently with Munro's Tables, so if you want to claim the Furths you had better climb them all' – though much more elegantly expressed, of course! Between 1929 and 1962 several lists of hills down to 2500ft or 2000ft, including the fascinating volumes by Docharty[8,9], were published, but they used no new principles. But in 1973 George Bridge published his *Mountains of England and Wales*[3], and his classification method must be described. Like Donald, he used 2000ft (610m) as the height criterion, and evolved a system of classification into mountains and tops which depended on both the distance and the drop in height. (In fact, Bridge uses both 'mountain' *and* 'top' in the sense of 'hill'; the distinction is conveyed by the phrases 'separate mountain' and 'subsidiary mountain'.)

Bridge has a graphical approach to classification. Hills must have a drop of at least 50ft (15m), and *any* separation between summits of more than 500ft, or more than 4 miles, will qualify a hill as a separate mountain. Intermediate points include a drop of 250ft at 1 mile, and 100ft at two miles. Arithmetically, the rule is almost '*distance* x *drop* = *constant*' (200 to 250 in Imperial units). In metric units the equivalent product of kilometres and metres is, in the important region of the graph, about 100. The calculated separation in time is exactly 27 minutes at 150m of height and also at 1 km of distance, and is about 35 minutes at 2 km. Thus a separation of about 30 minutes defines a mountain consistently with Bridge as well as Donald. (Bridge's rule produces greater times for more distant hills with smaller drops, but then the refinement of measuring to the nearest higher ground becomes even more necessary.)

A recent list is that by Dewey[7]. This will not be described in detail, but the separation, shown on Figure 2, is also of the same '*distance* x *drop* = *constant*' form as Bridge's, though with the significantly lower metric value of 60 instead of 100 or so.

5. What are we seeking in a classification system?

Consideration of the historical precedents, experience of the hills throughout the British Isles, and a mathematical background lead me to put forward the following criteria that a good classification system should meet. I regard them all as important, and they are not listed in any particular order. They are hereafter referred to as C1 to C6.

C1. The system should be simple to apply. It should not require data that is not readily available, and it should be as insensitive as possible to any lack of precision (e.g. on OS maps) in that data.

C2. The system should achieve consistency throughout the British Isles.

C3. The results should match currently accepted lists as closely as possible.

C4. The system should classify hills as 'mountains', 'tops' and 'minor tops'

C5. The system should produce a clear and unambiguous result for every hill. That result should not depend on result for any other hill. But . . .

C6. Editorial discretion must be preserved.

Some of these criteria may require elaboration or explanation. For example, it seems to me important (C5) that the classification of any particular 'local high point' should not depend upon whether its neighbouring higher hill is a mountain, top or minor top. (Donald, as we have seen, based his classification on separation from the nearest *mountain*, not even the nearest higher hill, and this is one reason for the anomalies already described.)

There are several reasons why it is essential that some discretion remains with the compiler of the list (C6). Firstly, the terrain can justify a higher ranking than the raw data suggest (though in practice this may apply only in the Cuillin of Skye). Next, there may be local features which affect the classification. For example, in the south-east Grampians (Section 7 of the Tables) there are eight hills with separations all quite close to 2 km and 75m. A strict application of the basis to be proposed would split these into four Munros (Tom Buidhe, Cairn Bannoch, White Mount and Cairn an t-Sagairt Mor) and four tops (Creag Leacach, Carn an Tuirc, Tolmount and Broad Cairn), but this would be a quite unjustifiable differentiation between very similar hills and the compiler of the Tables would rightly retain them all as Munros. Then there is the matter of historical precedent. This may not be significant for lists other than the Munros and Corbetts, but for them it is of great importance. Overall, a system based on physical parameters should not be regarded as definitive, but as a guide to the compiler. Decisions to override its results being taken for good reasons rather than by accident or oversight.

More surprising may be C4, the suggestion that the classification should allow for minor tops as well as mountains and tops. This calls for some justification.

• The division into mountains and tops, however it may be achieved, reflects a natural and well-accepted concept. Lists which have only one grade of hill invariably have merely a minimum drop for inclusion: this is either large (as with the Corbetts) excluding many fine hills, or small (15m or 30m is often used) which leaves the feeling of many unworthy points being classed as mountains.

- If there is no *minimum* criterion for a top, then it is impossible both in theory and practice to produce a complete list. (Even a list including every point defined by a separate contour ring will not do; for a smaller contour interval on the map would produce more points to record. In the extreme the compiler would need to include every minor undulation, even every rock, if it is above the minimum altitude.)

- Thus it is useful to allow the classification of 'minor top'. This can include all those points which seem important to the compiler, for example, because they are conspicuous on the ground or close to qualifying, even though they do not meet the criteria for a 'top'. The class will also include all such points which are 'tops' in existing lists such as *Munro's Tables* (and should, in my view, extend to those which have ever been tops, now removed). The list of minor tops is, of course, always subjective and can never be complete; but because it enables us to have a minimum criterion for tops it ensures that it is possible to include all *true* tops in any list.

The requirement in C3 to match current lists is also important for the acceptability of any new approach. It leads us, I suggest, to conclude *inter alia* that classification purely by distance apart, or purely by drop, is inadequate to reflect the almost instinctive belief that the closer two hills are, the deeper the intervening drop needs to be to justify both as mountains. This is an explicit feature of the Donald and Bridge lists and was clearly implied in *Munro's Tables*.

Lastly, I suggest that any list should include the data that justify the classification; in practice this will be the separation from the nearest higher ground in kilometres of distance and metres of reascent. This has a number of advantages. It will enable others to check the classifications if desired, highlight cases where editorial discretion has been exercised, and allow swift correction of errors. It will render it easy to give effect to any changes when new information is made available by the OS. And it also allows users to draw up their own lists on other criteria should they so wish.

6. A proposed system of classification:

The system of classification to be put forward here has evolved over the best part of a decade of consideration of the principles and details. Approaches for the Highlands (with a 900m lower height limit) and the rest of the British Isles (with a 600m limit) were for a long time independent but it was heartening to find, towards the end of the work, that they could be combined. An initial approach was based directly on Bonsall[1], ranking hills purely in order of their separation in time, but this soon proved unsatisfactory. The reason is that this method gives too much weight to distance and not enough to drop; for example a drop of 150m is equivalent to a distance of a kilometre, whereas in classification terms the former is a good deal more significant than the latter. Bonsall's separation of 30 minutes is in practice close to saying that the separation must be 1.5km of distance. (On Figure 2, a dividing line based on time would be close to, and even nearer the vertical than that for the Donalds, which already suffer from inadequate emphasis on the drop, especially having regard to the Lowland terrain.)

One early move was to plot the separations (to the nearest higher ground) of all the hills in each region. The results for the Munros and Donalds are in Figures 3 and 4. These plots, and those for England and Wales, led quickly to the realisation that, as might be expected on physical grounds, the reascent is correlated with the distance apart, and hills are clustered around an imaginary line (call it the 'centre line') rising 'NE from the origin' of the graph. For example, looking at the Munros and Tops, the centre line is approximately *reascent in metres = 60 × distance in kilometres* – and no hill has a reascent significantly less than 20 times the distance. Of course, I am here referring only to smaller reascents, say up to 100m. For much larger reascents the separation in distance can be as great as you wish.

It follows that the critical decision is the point on this 'centre line' at which a hill might qualify as a mountain. The way in which outlying points are dealt with is then less important, as relatively few classifications will depend on this. In particular it was realised that, however intellectually appealing was a curved dividing line using a formula similar to Bridge's, to do this was complex and unsatisfactory. Look at Figures 2 and 4 together. Such a formula is either too generous near the centre line (as is Dewey[7]), or too severe for close hills with larger drops (as is Bridge[3]). In accordance with C1, the simplicity of dividing lines which are straight was to be preferred.

The two bases for classification, one for the Highlands and the other for use elsewhere in the British Isles, are now defined. In doing this the graphical approach is used. I emphasise that all separations in distance are to the nearest higher ground.

The Highlands

Draw a line connecting the two points 'zero distance, 150m drop' and '4 km distance, zero drop'. Then any hill on or above this line is a mountain (a Munro).

Draw a further line connecting 'zero distance, 30m drop' and '4 km distance, zero drop'. (The second point is the same as before.) Any hill below this second line is a minor top, while hills between the two lines (or on the lower line) are tops.

The end points defining these lines are selected both to match the current Tables as closely as possible (C3), and to use values which have gained widespread acceptability. 150m (500ft) and 30m (100ft) seem far and away the best values for height. There is no similarly obvious value to use

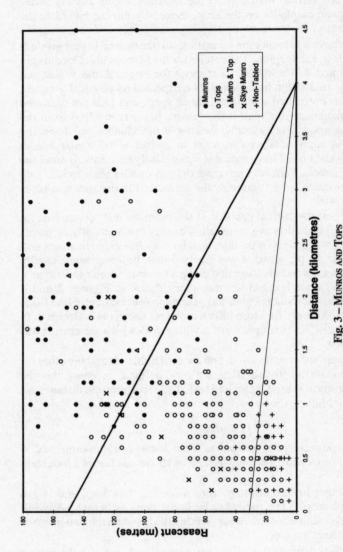

Fig. 3 – MUNROS AND TOPS

The figure shows all Munros and Tops with a reascent of 180m (600ft) or less and a separation in distance to the nearest higher ground of less than 4.5km (nearly 3 miles), plotted by their separation in distance and drop. The symbol indicates whether the hill is listed in the current Tables as a mountain or a top; Skye Munros are distinguished. A few hills not in the Tables are also shown, together with the proposed dividing lines. No attempt is made in this figure (or Fig. 4) to indicate that two or more hills should be plotted at the same point *unless they have different classifications in the current Tables.*

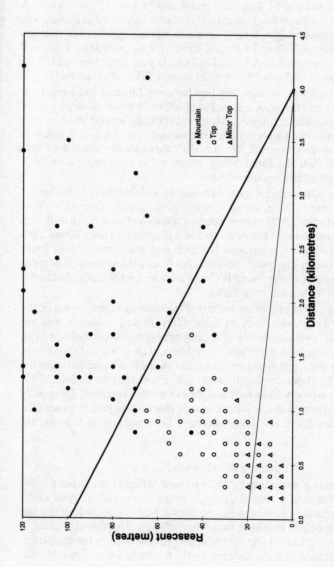

Fig. 4 – The Donalds

The figure shows all Donalds with a reascent of 90m (300ft) or less, plotted by their separation in distance and drop. The symbols indicate whether they are listed in Donald's Tables as mountains, tops or 'minor tops' (Section 13). The proposed dividing lines are also shown. Note that the separations are taken to the nearer 0.1 km in distance and nearly always to the nearer 5m of drop. There is thus no physical significance in the horizontal or vertical alignments. However it is clear that in only a handful of cases could more accurate measures affect the resulting classification.

for distance, so I have chosen the convenient one of 4 km (equivalent to 1 hour) – but this is the less critical parameter anyway. The upper line goes through points such as '2 km, 75m drop' and '1 km, 112.5m drop'. A 'typical' hill (i.e. one on the 'centre line' described above) that qualifies as a Munro by a small margin, would have a separation of 1.5km in distance and 100m of reascent (about 1 mile and 350ft). Beinn Liath Mhor Fannaich and Conival are examples. A typical hill that is just a true top will have a reascent of 30m (100ft), or 25m with at least 0.75km of distance.

To clarify the proposed dividing line between Munros and tops, I am suggesting that *any* hill with a reascent of 150m or more, or at a distance of 4 km or more, *must* qualify as a Munro. It could be argued that two very close hills should need a higher reascent, or that even 4 km of distance is not enough if the drop is small. But in real life there are no such hills! There is only one hill (Garbh Chioch Mhor, promoted in 1981) with a distance below 1 km and a reascent over 150m.

There are six hills with distances between 1 and 1.25km (up to 0.75mile) and reascents over 150m, all of which (except Ruadh Stac Mor) have always been Munros. At the other extreme, there is also only one hill with a distance separation of 4 km or more and a drop of less than 100m. That hill is Beinn Bhreac; its separation is 4.5km and 80m, and I would doubt that it has ever been suggested for demotion from Munro status. The most extreme outlier that I have found is Geal Charn in the Monadh Liath, with a separation of 10 km but only 100m.

The true test of the proposals is their effectiveness in the region of the graph where there *are* plenty of hills. Here Figure 3 shows that the proposed line is fairly close to the boundary between Munros and tops, with 12 current Munros falling just below the line and only two so far below as to be embarrassing. (For obvious reasons the Skye Munros are not included in this analysis.) There are slightly more tops above the line – a total of 17, of which eight are very close to it and should not be promoted. It is hardly to be wondered at that this leaves nine tops that clearly justify promotion to Munro status. There are those who have been arguing such a case for years.

South of the Highland Line

In the Highlands a minimum height of about 900m is used, but for the Donalds and Furth of Scotland the appropriate limit is 600m (just under 2000ft). A natural adjustment to the above rules is to reduce all the parameters relating to height to two-thirds of their 'Highlands' values; it was most pleasing to find that this matched almost exactly the classification system already derived independently for these hills. Thus the rule now becomes:

• Draw a line connecting 'zero distance, 100m drop' to '4 km, zero drop', and a further line connecting 'zero distance, 20m drop' to '4 km, zero drop'. Then, as before, the lines divide the graph into three regions, of mountains, tops and minor tops.

There are two observations to make. Firstly, some might think that the distance parameters should also be two-thirds of those in the Highlands, leading to either (say) $2^1/_2$km in this rule, or 6 km for the Highlands. The latter would significantly worsen the match with Munro's Tables, and cannot be seriously considered. The former would allow some more current Donald's to remain as mountains, but is seems far too lenient – at 2km it would demand a reascent of only 20m. After all, the 50m of the proposed rule is hardly severe. Hence it was felt better and simpler to use 4km (1 hour) of separation throughout. Secondly, it may be thought that the lower limit for tops, which allows all hills with a drop of 20m to qualify, is rather generous. However the rule as proposed is a better match for the Donalds than 30m would be, and Bridge has many tops which do not qualify even using a 20m drop. Hence I concluded that it was better, on a matter in itself of little importance, to maintain the 'two-thirds' consistency with the Highland rules.

7. Some consequences:

It may be of interest to summarise the changes to the three lists in *Munro's Tables*[11] that could follow from the adoption of the proposed classification rules. It is useful to have a simple 'measure' of the amount by which a hill meets, or fails to meet, the minimum requirement, and for this purpose I use a value in metres. This is the difference between the *actual* reascent, and the reascent at the point on the dividing line with the *same separation in distance*. It is worth noting also that the likely error in estimating this measure is typically 5m or less (very rarely up to 10m) whereas in all cases where a change of status is proposed the value is much greater than this. Similarly, an error of 0.1 km in the distance estimate would alter the measure by less than 4m.

As already stated, most significant would be the promotion of nine tops to Munros. These are listed in Table 1 in descending order of 'merit' for promotion. The table also shows the eight tops which marginally qualify, but which I do not recommend for promotion. It is interesting (and convenient!) that there is such a large gap between the two groups of hills. Comment could be made about each hill, but I will confine myself to a mention of two. Firstly, the Affric Sgurr na Lapaich is often said to be the most worthy of Munro status, yet it ranks only fourth in the list. Secondly, the separation quoted in Table 1 for Cairn Lochan is measured from Ben Macdui. The separation from Cairn Gorm is 2.8 km and 116m, and the corresponding excess is 71m; Cairn Lochan is even more worthy of promotion when compared with the hill of which it is currently deemed to be a top.

Next would be the Munros that could be demoted to tops. There is one clear candidate: Carn Ghluasaid, which falls short by over 50m. Next is the interesting case of Sgor an Iubhair, which falls short by nearly 30m. If a case is to be made for its retention as a Munro (a status it was only granted in 1981), it is presumably either because there are *two* drops (one of 77m and one of about 70m) between it and Sgurr a'Mhaim, or because of its location where an important spur meets the main ridge. As will emerge later I do not regard the first reason as adequate, but the second is a clear instance of a situation where editorial discretion may be appropriate. (All the other 1981 changes are quite clear-cut and their current status are consistent with these proposed rules.)

Other Munros which fall below the dividing line are Creag Leacach, Carn an Tuirc, Tolmount, Broad Cairn, Na Gruagaichean, Aonach Beag (Alder), Creag Pitridh, The Devil's Point, Creag a'Mhaim, Sgurr an Lochain, Saileag and Sail Chaorainn. The first four of these, as already mentioned, are part of a compact group of eight hills, all of which should retain the same status. Nearly all the rest have reascents of 90m or more, are close to the line and should not, I feel, be demoted. It is interesting that

Table 1.

Top	Munro	Sect.	Separation			Excess
			km.	m.	min.	m.
Stob Coire Raineach	Buachaille Etive Beag	3	1.7	177	43	91
Glas Leathad Beag	Ben Wyvis	15	2.9	130	57	89
Spidean Coire nan Clach	Beinn Eighe	13	2.2	151	48	84
Sgurr na Lapaich*	Mam Sodhail	11	2.9	109	54	68
Sail Mhor	Beinn Eighe	13	2.6	120	51	67
Stob na Doire	Buachaille Etive Mor	3	1.9	145	43	66
Tom na Gruagaich	Beinn Alligin	13	1.4	155	37	58
Stob na Broige	Buachaille Etive Mor	3	1.8	135	41	53
Cairn Lochan	Ben Macdui *(see text)*	8	2.8	90	51	45
Stob Coire Sgreamhach	Bidean nam Bian	3	1.0	128	28	16
Beinn Iutharn Bheag*	Beinn Iutharn Mhor	6	1.5	105	33	11
Sgurr na Carnach	Sgurr Fhuaran	11	0.7	135	24	11
Creag Dubh*	Cam nan Gobhar	12	1.7	96	35	10
Sgor Choinnich*	Sgor Gaibhre	4	0.9	125	26	9
Sgor an Lochain Uaine*	Cairn Toul	8	1.0	118	27	5
An Stuc	Meall Garbh (Lawers)	2	0.7	127	23	3
Coinneach Mhor	Beinn Eighe	13	1.0	115	27	2

TOPS THAT QUALIFY AS MUNROS

The 'excess' in the right-hand column indicates the difference – expressed as a time in minutes – between the actual separation and the nearest point on the proposed dividing line between Munros and tops. The nine tops in the upper half of the table are recommended for promotion but not the eight tops in the lower half. However, the hills marked with an asterisk (*) were Munros in the original (1891) Tables which were demoted in 1921. Consideration should therefore be given to promoting the four such hills in the lower half of the table as well.

although the South Glen Shiel Ridge is often regarded as having far more Munros than can be justified, only two of its seven mountains fail to qualify and one of those (Sgurr an Lochain) is extremely marginal. (Although Skye Munros cannot be assessed by the standard rules, I should mention Am Basteir and Sgurr Mhic Choinnich. Both have a reascent of less than 60m, below any other Munro apart from Carn Ghluasaid. However in each case the separation by the 'easy' route is much greater.)

As I have said, there are eight tops that 'just' qualify as Munros, and 12 Munros that could 'just' be demoted. The closeness of these two numbers is an indication that the dividing line is in the right place. It would be possible to move it slightly to reduce one of the numbers, or to ensure that all hills in the cluster in Section 7 fall in the same region of the graph; but if this were done then the corollary is that the other number would become larger. Such a change would also result in less memorable end points for the dividing line, and inconsistencies with the basis outwith the Highlands, and so I would prefer to let the inevitable 'fuzziness' at the boundary fall exactly as shown in Figure 3.

Lastly, affecting *Munro's Tables* are hills that justify inclusion as tops. (My proposals would not require the removal of *any* current tops, as they will all qualify for retention in the 'minor top' category, however small the reascent). I have found only three clear candidates: the SE top of Meall nan Tarmachan, the W top of Druim Shionnach, and Stob Coire Dhomhnuill near Carn Eighe. (For the second of these I am indebted to recent Tables by Alan Dawson[6]). These have reascents between 30m and 40m. There are a few more with a reascent of 25m or so that just qualify, and a few which may have recently been recognised as reaching the 914.4m level, but I

Table 2.

Donald Mountain	Section	Separation		Shortfall
		km.	m.	m.
Herman Law	7	0.8	31	49
Bell Craig	7	0.8	47	33
Swatte Fell	6	1.7	35	22.5
Lowther Hill	8	1.6	40	20
Hillshaw Head	4	1.3	55	12.5
Stob Law	5	0.8	70	10
Talla Cleuch Head	5	1.2	62	8
Tarfessock	10	1.0	69	6
Middle Hill	5	2.2	41	4
(SW of Pykestone Hill)				
Birkscairn Hill	5	1.4	62	3

DONALD MOUNTAINS TO BE DEMOTED TO TOPS
The 10 hills shown would be demoted to tops under the proposals herein. The 'shortfall' in the right hand column indicates the difference, expressed as a time in minutes, between the actual separation and the nearest point on the proposed dividing line between mountains and tops.

would not put them forward until more accurate measurements have been made.

As all Corbetts have a drop of over 150m, and will clearly all continue to rank as mountains whatever the precise criteria adopted, I now turn to the Donalds. There would be no promotions, and Table 2 shows the 10 mountains which would be demoted to tops under the proposed rules. At least half of these are demoted because the use of nearest higher ground gives separations significantly less than those measured to a mountain summit. Only the last four in the table, with shortfalls below 10m, could perhaps be retained at their current status on grounds of historical precedent. I have also identified six points not in the list which justify the status of top – Shiel Dod in the Lowther Hills is the most deserving example – but further work is needed to be certain that this list is complete.

8. Some points of detail:
It may be as well to cover a few less important matters, mostly of definition, relating to the proposed classification system.

When measuring the separation of a hill from the nearest higher ground, the distance should be measured along the connecting ridge. But in some terrain (Section 7 of the Tables, the south-east Grampians, provides excellent examples) 'the connecting ridge' is not clearly defined. In this case, and subject to the requirement that the route passes through the bealach (i.e. has minimum reascent) any natural route may be chosen. It is most unlikely that the choice will affect the emerging classification, but if there is doubt the lesser status should be selected.

The reascent or drop is simply the hill's height minus the height of the lowest bealach traversed. This definition stands even if there are intervening undulations (e.g., as in going from E to B in Figure 1); the extra height gain thereby incurred 'on the ground' is ignored. This is necessary as otherwise that extra height could lead to a status much greater than the topography justifies. (In theory, if not always in practice, the extra height can be avoided by contouring round the intervening bumps).

There is a potential problem if a hill is connected to higher ground along two high ridges. (I have not found any instance of a hill where it is necessary to consider seriously three or more ridges.) In determining the hill's status, clearly the lower must be chosen if they are different. If both separations lead to the same status, then the separation to be recorded is that nearer to the dividing line. Here 'nearer' is used in the same sense as the 'measure' of the excess or shortfall described at the start of the previous section. For an example, imagine the two separations given earlier for Cairn Lochan, plotted on Figure 3. This will usually result in the separation with the smaller reascent being chosen, but there are a handful of exceptions. Even in these cases a study of the actual topography confirms that the mountain to which the top 'belongs' should be determined by the 'nearer' separation.

One factor that does not enter into the proposed classification process is the difference in altitude of the two summits being considered. To do so would infringe C1, and perhaps C5 as well. However, in marginal cases I can imagine that editorial discretion might demote the lower hill. Consider, as an example, the range comprising Beinn Eibhinn, Aonach Beag and Geal Charn, north-west of Ben Alder. The centre hill, in fact, has a separation of 1.1 km and 105m and just fails to meet the criteria for Munro status, but should certainly be retained as such on historical and other grounds. However, if it were only 950m high instead of 1114m, even with the same separation (i.e. the same drop), there is no doubt that 'top' would be the right status. This instance is purely imaginary. In fact, there are so few cases where a large difference between the heights of the hills might influence the allotted status that a formal rule would be overkill; the matter should be left for editorial judgment.

My final comment relates to the view that 'we should not promote Stob Coire Raineach [or Glas Leathad Beag, etc. – the equivalent point arose with the 1981 promotion of Mullach an Rathain] because Sir Hugh allowed only one mountain in cases like this'. I would have no quarrel with this if it were consistently applied, but it would mean that many small groups or ranges of hills would have only one Munro. Examples include Ben Cruachan, the two pairs adjacent to Loch Treig, Carn Aosda and Cairnwell, Sgurr Choinnich and Sgurr a'Chaorachain, Ruadh Stac Mhor and A'Mhaighdean, and Conival and Ben More Assynt. If you insist rigorously on a large drop between mountains a coherent list can be derived; but it is not the Munros. (A minimum drop of as little as 150m would leave Lochnagar, Glas Maol and Mount Keen as the *only* Munros in Section 7. If the intervening bealach had to be below 600m in height Glas Maol and Mount Keen would disappear as well). It seems to me that the argument that a complex hill should have but one Munro, whereas a range can have several, is forcing the classification to be driven by the naming practice of the OS in the 19th century. Since the OS still, a 100 years later, seem reluctant to accept that walkers and climbers are among the major users and determiners of hill names, I refuse to concede that names shown on current maps, let alone early ones, should dictate the content of mountain lists.

9. Conclusion:
Many readers, if they are still with me, will be saying: 'What is all this about? Why should we not retain Munro's Tables, and the Corbett and Donald lists, as an historical record, rather than try to evolve any sort of formal classification rules? Let others, if they wish, produce tables of hills on whatever basis they choose.'

This is a perfectly valid approach, and one with which I have some lingering sympathy. However, there are two reasons why I suggest that it is not the right one. Firstly, the pass has already been sold; many changes have been made to the Tables that have not resulted purely from resurveys. The tension between modernisers and traditionalists has meant that those changes have often been an unsatisfactory compromise. Secondly, there is clearly now a demand for hill lists covering all of the British Isles to a limit of 600m if not lower. To this sympathetic observer, it would be unfortunate if the SMC, by maintaining the 'historical' attitude, allowed its rôle to be taken over by others. One consequence is bound to be a plethora of systems; whereas if the Club took the lead I believe that its views would command respect. Accordingly I conclude with a set of recommendations for the Club to consider. After the first, they are in what I expect to be the order of increasing sensitivity. It will be interesting to look back in five or 10 years to see just how far down this list we have proceeded!

1. The SMC should endorse a system of classification. Of course I should like it to be the one put forward here; but the detail is less important than the endorsement. It would also be useful if a standard usage of 'mountain' and 'top' could be adopted and given effect to consistently throughout the introductions to Munro's and Donald's Tables. At the same time

Table 3.

Hills	Current			Proposed				Proposed with lower limit			
	M	T	Total	M	T	N	Total	M	T	N	Total
Munros	277	240	517	285	175	122	582	311	204	142	657
'Furths'	20	14	34	16	18	5	39	18	19	6	43
Corbetts	221	–	221	221	–	–	221	210	–	–	210
Donalds	87	51 +28	166	77	66	26	169	86	81	40	207
Totals	598	333	931	592	259	153	1004	618	304	188	1110

SUMMARY OF THE EFFECTS OF THE PROPOSALS

The Table shows the numbers of Mountains (M), Tops (T) and Minor tops (N) in each of the regions under consideration on three bases. First, the current version of the published tables (using Hamish Brown's classification of the Furths). Secondly, using the classification basis proposed herein (with discretion used as suggested in Table 1, and retaining all current Skye Munros as such). And lastly, using that basis and *also* lower height limits of 900m, 750m or 600m as appropriate (and with 150m as the Corbett reascent qualification). The middle set of figures shows an increase of 8 in the number of Munros (i.e. 9, less 1 for Carn Ghluasaid). The final set includes a further 21 mountains of 900m or more which are currently Corbetts, and 5 hills which would qualify as mountains despite *not* meeting the Corbett criterion. It is notable that the Corbetts would gain only 10 hills in the 750m-761m range which is fewer than they would lose to the Munroes. It should be added that I have not found any hills with reascents of 150m but not 152m, but there could be one or two such, not yet identified. The totals in the final row of the table differ slightly from the preceding rows, as an adjustment has been made for the 7 Corbetts which are also Donalds. These overall totals in the final row are shown purely for interest, as it is not suggested that the lists are comparable (even without the Furths, the total of *all* 600m hills in Scotland would be much larger). In order to produce a fair comparison, minor tops are included above only if they are or have been tops in the published list or if they are fairly close to qualifying as tops. My own lists include a few more Munro 'minor tops', and considerably more in the Donald region.

the description of Donald 'minor tops' should be brought into line with the actual practice.

2. The classification of the Donalds should be changed as described.
3. The hills that justify 'top' status should be included in Munro's Tables.
4. The nine tops recommended in Table 1 should be promoted to Munro, and Carn Ghluasaid (at least) should be demoted.
5. Eventually, the minimum altitude for a Donald should be taken as 600m and that for Munro's Tables should be 900m. For Corbetts the minimum altitude should be reduced to 750m, the maximum to 900m and the minimum reascent taken as 150m.

By way of a summary, Table 3 shows the number of mountains and tops (and my own count of minor tops) on three bases: the current published Tables; the Tables as modified by the rules proposed herein (with discretion exercised as suggested earlier); and the Tables with the addition of hills down to 900m or 600m as appropriate. (Interestingly, this last change would allow the inclusion of every hill that has *ever* been listed in the Tables – bar one. That one is Sgurr na Creige, north of The Saddle. And the number of Corbetts would actually be reduced, to the benefit of the Munros.) I suggest that the numbers on the third basis support my view that all the above changes could be made without in any way detracting from the quality and authenticity of *Munro's Tables* and the other *Tables of Lesser Heights*.

Finally, I should like to acknowledge the help given by the librarians of the SMC and the Alpine Club, without whose willing grant of access to their collections this paper could hardly have been written.

References:

1. **Bonsall, F. F.** *The Separation of Mountains* SMCJ **30**, 1973, pp153-156
2. **Bonsall, F. F.** *The Separation of Munros* SMCJ **30**, 1974, pp254-256
3. **Bridge, George.** *The Mountains of England and Wales – Tables of Mountains of Two Thousand Feet and more in Altitude* West Bealach Publications 1973
4. **Campbell, Robin.** *Munro's Tables, 1891-1991* SMCJ **35**, 1992, pp 21-27
5. **Corbett, J Rooke.** *List of Scottish Mountains 2000ft and under 3000ft in height* SMCJ **25**, 1952, pp45-52 *(Subsequently included in* Munro's Tables*)*
6. **Dawson, Alan.** *The Murdos* TACit Press 1995
7. **Dewey, Michael.** *Mountain Tables* Constable 1995
8. **Docharty, W. McK.** *A Selection of some 900 British and Irish Mountain Tops* 1954 *(privately printed)*
9. **Docharty, W. McK.** *The Supplement to A Selection of some 900 British and Irish Mountain Tops, and a Selection of 1000 Tops under 2500ft* 1962 *(privately printed, in two volumes)*
10. **Donald, Percy.** *Tables giving all hills in the Scottish Lowlands 2000ft in height and above* SMCJ **20**, 1935, pp415-438 *(Subsequently included in* Munro's Tables*)*
11. **Munro, Sir Hugh T.** *Munro's Tables:* First published as *Tables giving all the Scottish Mountains exceeding 3000ft in height* SMCJ **1**, 1891, pp276-314. Second edition published as part of the *SMC General Guide, Vol. 1, Section A* 1921 (ppA109-144) First published separately in 1953 Latest edition *Munro's Tables and Other Tables of Lesser Heights* SMC 1990

SCOTTISH HILL-NAMES – THE IRISH CONNECTION

By Peter Drummond

THE SCOTS and Irish share a common Gaelic heritage, and many hill-names are mutually understandable. This can sometimes lead to a little confusion. Like the Irish climber we met on the windy summit of Croaghan (Cruachan, naturally) on Achill Island, 500m above the Atlantic surf – where else to engage in talk of place-names? – who was puzzled on his recent visit to Ben Nevis to spot signs to Aonach Mor. He came from the town of Nenagh, in Irish An Aonach, the word there meaning a fair, market or assembly. In Lochaber no more is aonach a fair, but a ridge-shaped mountain: in exchange for this information he confirmed to me that the seeming paucity of names of hills on the Irish OS maps was a reflection of the map-makers, not the locals for whom every cnoc had a name.

Our own party could get confused too. We were savouring the prospect of the huge horseshoe culminating in Ireland's highest, Carrauntoohil, from the outflow of Lough Chom Luachra (loch of the rushy Corrie). An Irish father and his son were nearby, the boy excited and chatty: as they left, Ian, normally the party's sage, said – in a serendipitous manner – that they had pronounced the hill's name just as we would of Cairn Toul in the Cairngorms. I had to warn him of the risk of bringing Irish place-name study into disrepute, for the map clearly showed the Irish original of Corran Tuathail – certainly not cairn of the barn – and usually translated as inverted reaping hook. The Irish dictionary gives corran as a hook or sickle, and tuathail as left-handed, wrong, or widdershins: though interestingly, cor tuathail is given as kink.

The summit, two hours later, was a stunning viewpoint, and – befitting its position on the edge of the Atlantic – had echoes of Europe. The huge crucifix of black iron girders was Alpine, the distant views of blue hills and yellow sandy estuaries were Welsh, the close patchwork of hedged fields in the northern view was quintessentially English, but the names to south and east were Scottish – bens and mullachs, bruachs and cruachs, and as many cnocs as you could take. The team that day (for cognoscenti) were Beenkeragh, Mullaghanattin, Broaghnabinnia, Cruach Mhor, and Knockmoyle representing a crowded subs' bench of cnocs. There is even a Buachaille, mapped as Boughil.

The connection between the two Gaelics on either side of the Irish Sea was made not by the Scots, who were 'planted' in Ulster from the early 17th century, but by the Irish tribe known to the Romans as the Scotii who settled in Argyll from the 5th century, and gained territory and influence, political and linguistic, throughout the first millennium and beyond. But the two Gaelics, like British and American English, may have sprung from the same watershed but found different glens to follow, and became distinctive. This is particularly true of hill-names. After all, Irish Gaelic was the language of a people whose territory was mainly lowland – until the Cromwellian evictions to the west in the 17th century: while Scottish Gaelic territory was mainly highland. The Scots therefore had more practical need of a fuller range of hill-words.

One language, two vocabularies:

One difference that emerges from a study of the two sets of hill-names is that the Irish stock is smaller, not surprising in view of the much greater mountain mass of Scotland. Of some 60 Scottish hill-name elements that occur several times here, only about 20 have exemplars in the Auld Sod. Some others – like ceann (head), dun (fort), sail (heel), sgor (rock pinnacle), sidh (fairy hill), sron (nose) and stuc – are found in the Irish dictionary, but didn't take on flesh in a hill-name: while others still, even though common in Caledonia, seem unknown to Irish Gaelic altogether – such as bidean, monadh, sgurr, stob, and stuchd.

Of course, if Gaelic in Scotland invested its Irish talents well, as youth often does when liberated from the bounds of the parental home, it also forgot a thing or two – or, possibly, in the parental home new tricks were learned after the brood had left. For Irish Gaelic has hill-words like ceide (for a flat-topped hill, as in Keadeen Mountain), screig (rocky place, Skreigmore being on the Carrauntoohil horseshoe), mas (a thigh or a long low hill, Masatiompain on Dingle peninsula), and the splendid obvious stumpa (Stumpa Dulaigh, 784m) – none of these seemed to have sailed with the south-westerlies across the Irish Sea.

But even among those hill-names that are found in both countries, often one word in common contains two quite different descriptions. Consider the four most common Scottish hill-names: beinn, meall, sgurr and carn. Carn exists in Irish Gaelic too, but is almost exclusively used for a pile of stones, usually a burial marker, and not as a hill as in Scotland: the apparent one exception is Carnaween (carn uaine?) in Donegal, standing above an old graveyard on its southern flanks. Sgurr does not exist at all in Ireland, being probably of Norse origin. Meall, with the same 'lump' meaning, is confined entirely to hills in Munster, south-west Ireland, and has no significant representation in the higher hill-names – while in Scotland there are 1000 examples, some of them Munros.

And beinn, chief of the Highland hill-clan, while its roots lie in the Irish beann or binn, a horn or antler, there are few in Ireland, perhaps a 10th of the large number in Scotland: and in further contrast to Scotland they are not the highest hills but the middle-sized ones. The largest grouping are in the west, in the range known as The Twelve Bens of Connemara (The Twelve Pins to those English ears who mistake the soft consonant of the gael). We climbed the highest, Benbaun (binn bhan, white – from its limestone upper mass), leaving 11 for a day with less Scotch mist: the Gaelic name is Beanna Beola, lips mountains.

Irish emigrants' fortunes:

There are three hill-names that dominate in the higher Irish hills, as listed, 200-strong, in Paddy Dillon's guidebook; cnoc, ben and slieve. Cnoc dominates the higher hills in the south and south-west, including the MacGillycuddy Reeks (properly Na Cruacha Dubha). It is common in Scotland too, but only for lower hills. Ben dominates the west in and around The Twelve Bens and Connaught. Sliabh – usually anglicised to slieve – is the main Irish mountain name in the north and especially in the north-eastern Mourne Mountains: there are more than 100 occurrences of slieve in Bartholomew's Gazetteer, thrice the number of bens, and nearly as many as cnocs.

All three of these main Irish hill-names crossed to Scotland. Like all emigrants they had varying fortune. Cnoc flourished, but only numerically: from being one of the elite in Ireland naming many high hills, in Scotland it sank to a much lower social level, being applied generally to knolls. Ben (or beann) was the great success story, becoming the main Scottish mountain word and marrying into the top families, from Ben Nevis (Beinn Nibheis) downwards.

But what of poor sliabh? Logically, it should have been the front-runner in colonising the Caledonian world, from its heartland in the north-eastern Mountains of Mourne, running down to the sea, in sight of the Scottish coast. There are several on Islay and a few in Argyll like Sliabh Ghaoil, mountain of love – where a nasty fate caught up with eloping Diarmaid and Grainne. There are a few sliabh names on Speyside, but the word there means a moor or slope of a hill, not a summit. In western Galloway there are a number of hills called slew, a name suggestive of sliabh bending to a foreign tongue like grass in a gale, forced down onto minor hills of under 400m. Flattened thus, it failed to disperse its seed from these slender Scottish beachheads to the broad sunny uplands beyond.

But many other seeds fell on fruitful ground in Scotland, blossoming in new forms in fertile upland territory. Cruach (or cruachan) means, in both countries, a rick of hay or peat, and by transference a hill, usually with steepish sides: Ireland has the high Cruach Mor and the holy Croagh Patrick (respectively an O'Munro and an O'Corbett), Scotland has Cruachan itself and Cruach Ardrain. The latter also contains the element ard (height), which in Scotland is usually found in mere settlement names (Ardrossan, for instance) while across the water it is often a substantial hill like Ardnageer at 644m in the Blue Stacks.

Dun is another hill-name element that changed a bit in the crossing. In Ireland it means a fort, usually a prestigious one, home and castle to a prince or king: but there are no excavated authentic examples of a hill-fort on a dun. In Scotland dun (sometimes spelt dum) does mean a hill-fort, and is found everywhere, from Edinburgh's Castle Rock (dun-eidinn), Dumyat (the hill-fort of the Maetii), Dumbarton Rock (hill-fort of the Britons), to Dun Cana on Raasay and hundreds of others, many with legends of battle attached. Two other Irish words for fort or castle are caiseal and cathair, and the last of these is the source of Caher, the bold peak on the Carrauntoohil horseshoe: perhaps the concept of hilltop as castle was the inspiration of Scotland's several caisteal peaks, like the shapely granite tor of Arran's Caisteal Abhail. Most caisteals – figuratively not historically named – lie in the south-west, many in sight of Ireland.

Shedding light on Scottish names:

Knowing the Irish genetic inheritance of some names can help us under-stand them better. Take cul, which in Scottish Gaelic translates as 'back of (anything)' – which leaves Cul Mor and Cul Beag a little short on explanation. In Irish, the word originally referred to the back of the head and was then transferred to hills of that shape, like Coolmore in Donegal. Inverpolly's Cul Mor now makes more sense, as a steep-sided close-cropped hill! Or take Conival – several – and cognates Cona Mheall, an elusive name in the North West. There is a Convalla in the Wicklows, which Paddy Dillon's book *The Mountains of Ireland*'translates as ceann an bhealach, head above the pass: a plausible interpretation, certainly, shedding light over here.

Further daylight can be cast on the common name-element suidhe, the individual hills Ladhar Bheinn (Knoydart) and Vinegar Hill (where?), and the uncommon but distinctive names with adjective preceding noun. Sui means seat and in Ireland is often used for the reputed resting places of saints and figures of legend, for instance Seadavog for St Davog in Donegal and the several Seefin hills – one of them just west of Carrauntoohil – from Suidhe Fionn (the legendary hunter). He had a seat in Skye too on Suidh' Fhinn above Portree: and other suidhes often have personal connections in the Irish style – Suidhe Fheargais on Arran (Fergus – first king of the Scots), or Suidhe Chatain on nearby Bute (St Chatan).

Ladhar Bheinn of Knoydart is usually translated as hoof or claw mountain, aptly enough. In Ireland ladhar is a place-name element indicat-ing a convergence of rivers or hill-ridges – quite thought-provoking in a Scottish context, too. Vinegar Hill is less well known: it lies east of the dreary Drumochters, and is said by early 20th century toponymist, Alex-ander MacKenzie, to be a corruption of a'mhin-choiseachd, the easy-walking one. But for such a corruption to stick must surely have been due to the fame of Vinegar Hill in Ireland, which is anglicised from (Cnoc) Fiodh na cGaor (field of the berries), but was given real fame as the site of a major battle. Perhaps someone passing along the Mounth had heard of it in Ireland and made the Scottish parallel, which stuck.

In Gaelic, adjectives usually follow the noun, as in Beinn Mhor. In older Scottish Gaelic the order is sometimes reversed, usually with adjectives of colour, size or age, especially in the west. (See my argument, SMCJ, XXXV, 1993, 351-352). We find this pattern in Ireland in places, confirming its origin in their Gaelic – hills like Seanleeve (Sean shliabh, old hill), Glasdrumman (glas dromainn, grey-green ridge) and Beglieve (beag shliabh, small hill): but curiously, no big hills as in Scotland's several Morvens, while we in turn have no beagbheinn.

There is another Irish place-name element worth holding up to the Scottish scene – cuilleann meaning a steep slope. We look anew with raised eyebrows at our Cuillin hills (Rum and Skye). Their name has been the subject of considerable speculation, with one uniquely Irish connection proposed, by the eternal romantic Walter Scott, suggesting a link from Cuchullin, Ossianic hero. Others – present author included – have argued for a Norse connection from kiolen. Now cuilleann, steep slope, is certainly apt: but two facts stand ranged against it; that almost every high hill-name in Rum and in Skye are Norse (the individual Skye sgurrs were later names within the Cuillin cirque); and the absence of cuillean names leapfrogging from Ireland up the south-west and the southern islands, as might have been expected – with the possible exception of Gualachulain at the foot of steep Beinn Trilleachan.

And what can the connection be between the devil mountains? In Scotland we have The Devil's Point in the Cairngorms, a Victorian figleaf for the original Bod an Deamnain, devil's penis. Over in County Mayo stands the hill Devil's Mother at 645m. Its original name appears on the bilingual Irish OS map as Magairli an Deamhain, literally the devil's testicles. The Gaels clearly shared the earthiness of many peoples before organised religion pulled faces at the practice. Iceland, for instance, whose Vikings had linked Scotland and. Ireland too, has a mountain called Uptyppingur, which appears to mean erect penis – without the Gaels' devilment! But I digress from the Irish connection

An Irish legend echoed:

But one of the most striking gems of our 1996 Irish expedition, an emerald of a hill, is Ben Bulben (Beann Ghulbain) near Sligo. Not very high at 525m – not even an O'Graham – and indeed really a subsidiary top of Truskmore. But who could failed to be moved by its dramatic appearance, a flat plateau top of considerable depth suddenly rounding over 90° to drop vertically down in the western cliffs, rough-seamed by gullies, to a steep, but easing, slope running down to the coastal plain. In plan like a ship's bow, in profile like the prow of a Phoenician warship. Now gulban in Irish (and Scots) Gaelic can mean beaked, or more specifically the curlew. But authoritative Irish work links it to Irish hero Conal Guiban: and the mountain is home to the legend of Diarmaid, Grainne and Fionn. Told in one sentence, the former, lover of the second (which made the third jealous) died at the tusk of a fourth, the hill's wild boar, but only after Fionn had spitefully denied him a sip of the hill's life-saving water. The legend clearly had Arthurian

Evening light on MacGillycuddy's Reeks and Carrauntoohil, Ireland. Photo: Niall Ritchie.
Early evening at Lagangarbh with 20° frost in prospect! Photo: Matthew Baker.

dimensions, for the tale seized the contemporary imagination among the 'exiled' Gaels in Scotland. And there are five or six hills of this name – in addition to many places linked to one or other characters in the soap legend – chief among them being Ben Gulabin in Glenshee. In almost all of these cases, nearby features – lochans, rocks, hill shoulders – usually carry the name torc, the boar. Ben Gulabin is also – perhaps coincidentally – a flattish-topped, steep-sided, and prow-nosed hill.

Cloud and drizzle restricted our appreciation of Ben Bulben on 1996's Hibernian trip to the view from below, from the church graveyard of a different hero, W. B. Yeats. The ascent is straight-forward from the north, the back-door route, as I had found a few years earlier on my first exploration of the island. It took me less than an hour. As I approached the trig point, louping over the boggy pools, two curlews flew up from the rough moor.

MOVE

A lark above the quarry,
beyond the sheep cropped turf, piping
a march across the summer light
and a climber trembling in silhouette.

Hand, shaken out to ease the tension,
cancel the heat effects,
dismiss the bird's distraction,
floats back to the sharp edge of the
moment.

Eyes scan for flake or fissure,
memory holds, hard facts issue
no second chance, no rehearsal.
The lark rises on a summer thermal.

Donald M. Orr.

The Coire Lair approach to Sgorr Ruadh. Photo: Alastair Matthewson.
Aerial view into the crater of the erupting Mount Ruapehu, New Zealand. Photo: Iain Young.

A PARTIAL HUT ROUTE

By Bob Richardson

THE ARTICLE by Alec Keith (SMCJ, XXXV, 1995, 625-628) on his athletic cross-country traverse of all the SMC Huts in four days prompts me to add some comments. The idea of an SMC Hut Route had been floating around for a year or two before Alec's trip in 1994. The geographical location of the huts offered the opportunity to carry out a lightweight and, for SMC members, cheap route through a large sector of the Highlands. There was also the physical challenge of covering the distance in the minimum number of days. Hamish Irvine and I had talked about it briefly and, learning of his schedule, I timed a maintenance trip to CIC so that I could watch him limp in at the end of the second day of his successful four-day trip. I myself had contemplated the idea for some years but had never (as usual) done anything about it. Anyway, now the thing has been done, I feel free to add my bawbee's worth of comment and record my efforts in the genre. Either in whole or in part, a Hut Route is potentially the best extended hillwalking (or running) expedition in Scotland.

The route as followed by Alec and Hamish is a Hut Route, but it isn't a Haute Route. I had always felt that, to be ethically satisfactory, such a trip must involve a significant number of summits in a logical progression. This implies either taking more than four days or being very fit. The geographical situations of Lagangarbh, CIC, Raeburn and Ling are tempting, and form the apices of a considerable range of hill country, but the distance involved in getting to Ling from either Raeburn or CIC turn that leg into either a rapid and exhausting exercise in the horizontal, or a multi-day epic with a long stretch between interesting hills. The legs of a route between the Central Highland huts are all accomplishable in one day. Also, by starting from Raeburn and going across country to Lagangarbh, Alec and Hamish had (a) taken the easy option, (b) left out the most interesting leg – that between CIC and Raeburn. My preferred route would have been Lagangarbh, CIC, Raeburn, Ling. This offers the best opportunities to use the run of the ridges in a more or less high-level route. I had jokingly suggested to Hamish that a handicap system be established with a 'par' time of 70 hours and a reduction of one hour for every Munro climbed from the actual time taken. This would encourage some interesting tactics to record a minimum handicap time.

My initial interest came from a suggestion of John Gillespie's some years ago for a weekend trip from Lagangarbh to CIC and back. This seemed like a good idea, but the weekend chosen was wet and the most memorable aspects of the trip were the mist, cold, and a number of hazardous stream crossings. We went over the old road to Kinlochleven and then round the back of Sgor Eilde Beag, and then along over Na

Gruagaichean to the col before Stob Coire a' Chairn before dropping down to cross the Nevis Water and eventually cross the CMD arête to reach the CIC. The next day we took a more direct route back along the track from Achriabhach to cross the Mamore ridge at the col east of Stob Ban. That weekend was an educational experience in survival but convinced me that, given a reasonable state of fitness and decent weather, such trips could be fun. On a later occasion, heading for Lagangarbh from Tyndrum via Ben Alder Cottage, I spent a glorious sun-soaked day from CIC traversing from Mullach nan Coireachan to Na Gruagaichean en route to the Devil's Staircase and Lagangarbh. This leg, in either direction, is highly recommended in itself. Of course, Ben Nevis and Tower Ridge should be included by the non-geriatric.

In July 1995, I was due to go up to CIC to paint the interior. It is one of the Custodian's privileges to have the opportunity to have the Hut to himself for a few days and spend them washing down walls and throwing paint about. Over the years, I have been remarkably lucky in the weather on these trips and have usually managed a ridge or two in the lunchbreak or in the evening. With the Hut Route in mind and aware of the need to test out my ideas about the CIC to Raeburn leg, I negotiated an open ticket with my wife, packed my bivouac bag and took a single ticket on the Fort William bus.

I arrived at CIC on a dreich, damp Sunday evening. There were two Grampian Club members in residence but they decided to flee the next day (whether this was due to my painting activities or the weather is open to discussion). Monday it drizzled and there was nothing to tempt me from my labours. By contrast, Tuesday dawned bright and clear (it was in fact, the first day of the glorious late summer of 1995). By three o'clock the main room had received a single coat of paint and, unable to resist the temptation, I set out for my annual canter up Observatory Ridge. This is a great route to do solo on a good day, although it is at its best on a late June evening with the sunlight streaming up the Allt. The climbing is sufficiently exposed to keep the attention from straying but not so technically demanding as to discourage one from admiring the rock scenery around. I reckon it to be the best solo scramble on the Ben.

The top was reached in 65 minutes from the Hut for the second year in succession, proving that the days of sub-60-minute ascents were behind me. Passing quickly through the throng on the summit, I headed for the top of Tower Ridge and descended to the Hut. On the way down I had the malicious pleasure of meeting, just above the Little Tower, two lads I had passed at the foot of the Douglas Boulder on the way up. Leaving them suitably impressed, I continued down to the original descent route into Observatory Gully and arrived back at the Hut in 2 hours and 10 minutes from starting out. I was obviously not sufficiently unfit and decision time was upon me.

The prospect was not altogether pleasing. I was far from my previous fitness levels, had a decrepitating knee, inadequate food, and would be carrying more weight than ideal. The plan was to go over Aonach Beag and the Grey Corries and then continue eastwards in two days, climbing as many summits as appeared sensible. I had a bivouac bag, sleeping bag and mat, but no stove. My food supply was mainly decomposing cheese, raisins and trail mix with a couple of packets of noodles to be consumed at Raeburn. Some semi-respectable clothing also had to be carried for the bus journey back to Glasgow. Altogether, some serious effort would be called for. With any luck it would be raining in the morning.

At half-past five the next morning the sun was warm, the sky was cloudless and the Bullroar slab was bone dry. I had no excuse. Shortly after half-past-six I started up the long drag to the summit of Carn Mor Dearg, keeping the pace down and stopping frequently to gaze across at the Ben. The sun was high enough to illuminate everything but the Orion Face and it was an impressive and rare sight to see so much of the north face picked out in detail (no camera of course). An uplifting start to what was going to be a long day.

The drop down the other side to the bealach took me out of the sun and then I went reluctantly up the dreary slog to the Aonach Mor – Aonach Beag ridge. Dehydration was one of my main concerns and I took care to fill a litre bottle at the stream off Aonach Mor as I knew there was likely to be no good water until beyond Stob Choire Claurigh. The replenishing of the water bottle was to be a constant concern over the next two days as, although never running, I was constantly pressing on. Passing over Aonach Beag, there was a dramatic contrast between the bare, wind-scarred earth on the summit and the lush growth of grasses just a few hundred metres farther east and at only a slightly lower altitude. A remarkable example of the effect of a change in micro-climate. From previous experience on an afternoon ramble from CIC, I knew that the direct route to the east col from the end of the ridge was an interesting example of high-angle grass and once was quite enough, thank you. The safer route is to go south along the ridge towards Sgurr a'Bhuic until just past the top of the slabby buttress (the one with an interesting overhanging wall on its north face) and then drop eastwards to pick up the line of the old march dyke and fence across the bealach to Sgurr Choinnich Beag.

The next section over Sgurr Choinnichs Beag and Mor and along to Stob Choire Claurigh was delightful; the legs still fresh, the sun warm but with a cooling breeze, the visibility good – a total contrast to the last time I had been on this ridge on the back half of a mist-enshrouded Tranter round and pushing to get it finished by dim daylight. This time I had the opportunity to enjoy the views and, at closer hand, examine the curious patterns made by the slow-growing lichens on the quartzite, their intersecting circles making designs reminiscent of Pictish patterns. The rock was also decorated with crampon scratches; reminding me that, one February many years ago, Jimmy Marshall and Robin Smith had come this way, taking a day off from their legendary week step-cutting new routes on the Ben. When I got home I dug out my copy of the entry in the old SMC Hut Book and it is worth setting out in full (spelling and punctuation as in original):

11th Feb. Carn Mor Dearg, Aonach Beg, Sgurr Coinnich Beg, Sgurr Coinnich Mor, Stob Coirie nan Easain, Stob Coirie na Claurigh, Beinn Bhan.

R. C. Smith, J. R. Marshall (Through leads).

Timetable: 1200 HOURS: Left CIC.

1835 HOURS: Entered Spean Bridge (Bar).

1920 HOURS: Entered Bus to Fort W.

1945 HOURS: Repulsed from Hell's Kitchen.

1946 HOURS: Entered Rendez-vous.

2000 HOURS: Left (Nae Juke Box) for Jacobite Arms.

2030 HOURS: Entered Argyll Bar, Dominoes.

2100 HOURS: Left Argyll Bar.

2110 HOURS: Arrrested.

2115 HOURS: Police station: Interrogation, Confession, Humiliation

2155 HOURS: Dismissal.

2200 HOURS: Further reiving.

2205 HOURS: Peaing Session.

2215 HOURS: Entered last Corpach Bus.

2225 HOURS: Distillery.

2350 HOURS: Re-Entered CIC.

Now, that's what you call a rest day.

From Stob Choire Claurigh my logical route would have been over Stob Ban and down the south ridge to pick up the track to Creaguineach Lodge, but I had never climbed the Easains so I headed for the Lairig Leacach bothy. Coming down the corrie I came across a burn running in a little gorge. Two small waterfalls, a rowan tree, a patch of grass – a little Xanadu among the peat and heather. I stopped to eat the rest of my rapidly-decomposing cheese and a rotting banana. If it had been later in the day I would have been sorely tempted to bivouac there. As I sat beside the burn I reflected how many of my epiphanic moments among the hills were connected with this combination of water, rock, surrounding hills and sky.

However, the Easains and distance called and I went down to pass the bothy to cross the headwaters of the Allt na Lairig. As I approached the bothy, I saw a male and a female standing down at the stream and another male outside the bothy. Passing the couple, I wished them 'Good Day'. No word in reply, only vacant stares and a half-grin from the man. Up at the bothy the other male was urinating beside the gable end. Leaving these couthy bothy folk to their Highland idyll, I crossed the Allt na Lairig and headed for Stob Coire Easain.

If you are going for distance, even lightweight hill-walking boots will become heavy on the feet after a while. I was wearing a pair of hill running shoes with high ankles which are ideal for summer hill-bashing but with these on my feet and about 12 kilos on my back, the screes on the north-east ridge of Stob Coire Easain did not look inviting. To avoid them, and stay on grass as much as possible, I dog-legged right and left across the west side of the hill. This delivered me almost to the summit without setting foot on rock and had the additional advantage of taking me past a number of springs of cold water which issued from between the prominent bedding planes of the rock. On the summit it was a relief to drop my sack and trot across to Stob a' Choire Mheadoin.

As I was ascending the slope to the summit I saw a file of men coming down. Evenly spaced, wearing T-shirts and long trousers, with uniform style of rucksacks, they signalled the military. As I passed about 20m away, no-one as much as looked at me. After this and my encounter at the bothy I began to wonder if I was invisible or was already a ghost. Coming back from the summit of Stob a' Choire Mheadoin it was my turn to think them ghosts for they were nowhere in sight. Now, I am not yet too slow on my feet and only a few minutes had elapsed, but they must have ascended from the col to the summit of Stob Coirie Easain at some pace. Resuming my now noticeable load and glad to have the last summit of the day behind me, I wandered down along the south ridge. This is a magnificent stroll, good going underfoot, gently undulating downwards with wide vistas to east and west. Highly recommended.

Eventually, as the ridge began to rise again, I dropped diagonally down to cross the river. (It was running low but this could be a difficult crossing after heavy rain.) As I approached the Allt, I heard whistles blowing and could see figures running about in the heather about 100m up the opposite slope. Obviously, military games were in progress. Their rucksacks were neatly lined up beside the path. Impressed again by their fitness and reassured about the expenditure of taxpayers' money, I strolled on.

This is a lovely strath. The alder trees beside the water are huge in girth, there are wide meadows of good grass, the stream flows over rock slabs and through deep pools. It invited stay, but I was locked into my immediate goals and continued on. This glen, and it's neighbour of the Aimhann Rath, seem to convey an atmosphere of times long past, of people's presence and the passage of cattle along these old ways through the hills. Few places in the Highlands have given me such an impression of an old landscape and former way of life.

After the pleasures of the last miles, the huge expanse of mud and rubble exposed by sorely shrunken waters of Loch Treig and the sad debris and dereliction of the Lodge changed the mood. The first time I had passed the Lodge (back in the Fifties) there had been children's toys outside and a swing in the trees. Now it was only a store for the recent clip of wool. Across the bridge and on along the track to Corrour I began to relearn the discipline of marching on the level. It was now after six o'clock and I was somewhat surprised to see a girl of about 10-years-old come towards me on a mountain bike. She was followed by her father, also on a bike, wearing a Panama hat and with a fishing rod strapped to his bike. They reassured me of my corporality by greeting me, but where they were going at that time of day and where they had come from I was left to wonder. I followed their tyre tracks all the way through the boggy bits up to Corrour Station.

Beinn na Lap had been on my mind since the Grey Corries. It was a logical part of my 'high level' plan but to get from there to Beinn Eibhinn looked unamusing from my study of the map. The alternatives from the summit were to go north-east across some probably boggy ground towards Strath Ossian House and then slog up the steep east side of the glacial trough, or to take a longer but easier line eastwards towards Corrour Lodge and skirt above the forest. Altogether, Beinn na Lap had lost attraction as the day wore on and, anyway, I had to leave some room for improvement on my route for the younger generation. To avoid any last-minute temptation, I took the road along the south side of the loch.

It was now well into the evening and I reckoned I had done enough to justify stopping for the night. About two-thirds of the way along the loch I saw what I was looking for. Down at the shore there were the remains of a fire and a pile of dead wood alongside a fairly level patch of grass. Obviously, a spot where anglers had come ashore from a boat. I unrolled my mat, unpacked my bivouac bag and sleeping bag and lit a fire. Being able to cook some noodles and brew coffee was an unexpected bonus and as I lay in my bag with the little waves lapping on the shore, the embers of my fire still glowing, and the mass of Beinn na Lap bulking against the still luminescent sky it seemed like a damn good day.

Of course, the wind dropped at midnight and the inevitable ensued. The next five hours were spent buried deep in my bag dividing my time between dozing and killing midges. Shortly after five in the morning I carefully planned the exact sequence of rapidly-executed movements which would be required to get me dressed, shod, packed and on my way with minimum torment. These executed, but not rapidly enough, I went on my breakfastless way through the silent woods at the beginning of what promised to be another fine day. Once on the move the midges were not a problem and I padded along the edge of the road to the foot of the loch. Not a dog barked as I passed the houses.

I stopped to eat at the bridge over the Uisge Labhair. The sun was already

warm and it was pleasant to sit on a rock slab at the side of the stream
enjoying the sight of the rushing water coming down over the slabs with
the hills rising up on either side of the broad glen. There was a feeling of
light, space and the promise of another fine day on the summits. At my back
there were planted trees, estate roads and houses but, facing to the east, I
could only see the open strath and the hills. The planned route lay over
Beinn Eibhinn and the summits to Loch Pattack, so I turned off the track
leading east to the Bealach Dubh and headed northwards over the rising
moor to Glas Choire.

Undoubtedly, the best way to do long cross-country trips is solo. You
have the advantages of being able to make your own pace, shout, curse,
sing, and generally achieve an appropriate state of mind. If you are
travelling hard, the falling glycogen levels and rising endorphins can
generate a state of elated weariness which is not unpleasant and is best
enjoyed in solitude. Solitary travel satisfies a basic human need and to do
it in fine weather over remote hills is a rare pleasure. The problems arise
if you do something stupid, but risk-free enterprises are boring by nature.
The foregoing philosophy did suffer a temporary dent when I put a leg into
a heather-obscured hole in the ground heading up to Glas Choire and
pitched forward to wrench my decrepit knee. Waiting for the pain to
subside, I had the opportunity to estimate the time required to limp back to
Corrour. However, subside it did and I limped on. (Incidentally, a tel-
escopic ski stick is strongly recommended for this game. Invaluable for
stream crossings, emergency crutch and general flourishing to celebrate
the joy of being.)

The isolated range of summits from Beinn Eibhinn to Carn Dearg form
a gently undulating, mainly grassy, ridge with wide prospects. They cry out
to be run on a sunny day. My years and condition, and the now noticeable
heat kept me to a walk and, once again I regretted not having tried this trip
years ago. Second-day fatigue and the heat kept my pace down and the heat
had generated a haze that reduced visibility, but it was fine to stroll
eastwards on this high broad ridge looking down into the broad corries on
the north side and over towards the hills between me and Loch Laggan.
(Another possible variant to the route?) The going was good. In some
places, especially the plateau east of Geal Charn, the grass was like a hay
meadow and yet (pace the comments in the Central Highlands Guide) I saw
no deer or any other sign of life along this whole ridge. This plateau also
held the remnants of a snow field and I was glad to refill my water bottle
where the stream fed by it plunged over the lip down to Loch an Sgoir.

East of Carn Dearg, I was disinclined to follow the rise of the ground over
the last top and turned north-eastwards to descend to the obvious track in
the glen below. Besides, my water bottle was empty again. Even on the
ridge the heat was now uncomfortable. On the way down I passed through
considerable numbers of deer – the only ones I saw on the whole trip. The

track led me easily down to Loch Pattack where the heat was now really oppressive. The sight of cultivated grass, fences and the general air of human presence brought about a need for mental re-orientation. Solitary hill travel can change your perceptions. This feeling of unreality was reinforced as I approached the junction of the estate roads at the east side of the loch. A man and a woman on mountain bikes appeared from the east and disappeared down the grassy road towards Laggan. They were dressed as for a cycle run in a city park, carried no packs, not even a cycle pump. Their casual approach to this 'wilderness' through which I was laboriously walking was unsettling. I felt cheated.

Beyond Loch Pattack my route took me up the side of the wood and over the long stretch of gradually-rising moorland to the southern end of the ridge leading to The Fara. Glycogen levels were now running low, the heat was uncomfortable and there was no water. As I wearily slogged up to the distant ridge over the dried-up moor I thought enviously of Hamish jogging down this ideally-angled descent. (Alec had opted for the low-level route along the Loch Ericht track.) At last, the broad swell of the ridge top was reached and I went more easily along with the expectation of a gentle stroll to my last top. Having walked off my map somewhere east of Geal Charn, the considerable drop and re-ascent came as an unpleasant surprise. However, progress continued and somewhere in the haze ahead lay The Fara and a (presumably) downhill finish.

Now I was walking along wearing running shorts, with a salt-stained Lifa vest rolled up to cool the costals and a bandanna tied round my skull to protect the back of my neck; a bumbag slung to the front, a rucksack on the back and a pair of sunglasses on an unshaven face completed the ensemble. The three neatly-dressed hillwalkers – long trousers, sleeves rolled down against the sun, neat sun hats, map case at the dangle – appeared up a dip in the ground so fast that I did not have time to even whip off my impromptu keffiyeh. They were polite although obviously startled and allowed me to look at their map in order to check my route intentions. Leaving them to continue southwards, I went on to reach the little stone hut that marked my last summit.

When planning my route I had decided that the aesthetic finish was to strike north from the summit of The Fara and head across to Loch Caoldair from where there is a path down to the road close to the Raeburn. This looks alright on the map and avoids the long tarmac plod along the road but I should have known that going across the grain of moorland is never a good idea. This last stretch involved knee-high dead heather, bogs, positive thickets of bog myrtle and three deer fences unequipped with stiles. Not recommended to the weary. (Hamish by contrast, starting off fit and frisky on his Hut Route, had found this line quite acceptable.) At last, I came under the crags and down to the loch. I had previously walked up this way from the Raeburn a couple of times and remembered it as a pleasant stroll along clearly-defined paths. Either through my weariness or rampant growth of the local vegetation, I now had difficulty finding the path and fought through the undergrowth until a more evident path was found at the little boat house. After that, the way was relatively easy down past the lochan to reach the road and the final 100m or so of tarmac along to the Hut.

Twenty-seven hours of travelling and just over 5000m of ascent (the distance is unmeasured and is fractal anyway). This route could be run in the daylight of a summer day and would be one of the finest mountain runs in Scotland.

All the way along The Faras I had been looking forward to reaching the Hut and having a shower. As the ground was dry and frequently cracked I should have known this was a delusion. True enough, the water pump spat out about a pint and then coughed to dryness. I managed, with difficulty, to get enough water out of the burn for a wash down and to cook a packet of noodles. Later, I hitched down to the phone box at Catlodge to report my survival. Naturally, it wasn't working and I was so disgruntled that I walked the whole way back without trying for a lift. Truly, it is better to travel than to arrive. The next morning I walked over to Dalwhinnie and through stopping for a coffee and a bacon roll, missed a bus by five minutes. Two hours of lying in the sun beside the A9 passed pleasantly enough before the next one arrived and took me south. I am told that I was quite quiet for a few days.

Further Thoughts and Suggestions:

There is obviously no one Hut Route and that is one of the beauties of the concept. Every traveller can design his own and do it in one grand sweep or in discontinuous sections. A good challenge would be to run between Lagangarbh, CIC and Raeburn in a weekend. With a support party at the huts, this should be within the capabilities of a fit mountaineer or the average hill runner.

Having argued the case for a CIC to Raeburn (or reverse leg), and executed it, I have left the problem of connecting Raeburn and Ling at the theoretical stage. The most logical route north from Raeburn would involve a long road and track section over the Corrieyairick Pass to Fort Augustus. From there the path over to Glen Moriston could be followed and then it would be back on the road up to Loch Cluanie. Then it's Munros *a la carte* all the way to Achnashellach. Depending on the number of summits, this could take two or three days. I suppose I had better try it some time. The complete trip would occupy a week, but I may leave that to someone else.

A MERRY DANCE

By Malcolm Slesser

I FIRST noticed it out of the corner of my eye. It worried me like some irritating piece of dirt. It was May and crisply clear, a day when breathing air was like the first sip of a good claret after a hors d'oevre of vinaigrette. It was way back when Smart was still a frisky acolyte doing solos on Salisbury crags. It was early in the day, and when I at last took in this distant dark speck there were few shadows to bring it into relief; nor could I tell if it was steep. Nor was I sure upon which hill it lay – I was relatively new to the Highlands then. But it looked interesting. Well you all know the feeling. You file it away for future reference; only I forgot.

Years later, I think, I saw it again, only I didn't know it at first. This time it was nearer and more in profile. Wallace and I were skiing the south Cluanie ridge at the Easter meet in 1983. It was just a glimpse between blatters of hail. Even as one-time general editor of SMC guides I couldn't recall this crag. Bill was ahead isolated by the screaming wind so I couldn't ask him. Bennet, who has edited the latest guide would know (he has a memory like a CD-ROM), but then you know what guide book editors are like. They're never going to tell anyone about a new crag until they've had first crack at it, are they? Think of Lurg Mhor and Roger Everett.

But with Bill ahead, and some exacting slopes to deal with, the whole matter slipped my mind till I got home.

It took some time with the maps to place it. There was nothing in the *SMCJ* to say Bennet had got there first. The thought of a sizeable unclimbed crag raises in a climber a sort of naked desire that makes sex seem trivial. My chance came one lovely June day when, having an Indian climber to entertain, we headed north. It is quite a responsibility showing off our native hills to a Himalayan veteran. Fortunately Scotland, the fickle mistress that she is, was decked out in all her beguiling loveliness. Not a hint of the foul mood she occasionally puts on. We had tent, gear and food. A perfect prospect, and my friend was game for a carry in.

Actually, we couldn't see the crag from where we camped, a tiny patch of greensward alongside a nascent burn, with a gnarled old birch guarding us. I warned my friend that the crag might turn out to be that usual thing of some rock bulges interspersed with grassy ledges; no belays and no drama and no route. As we came round the hillside on a rising traverse the first vision was of an upper bulge that looked distinctly out of my class. At the foot, there were happily no cairns, no arrows or 'I LOVE DB' scratched on the rock, no fossilised human droppings, not so much as a sweetie paper. Could this really be virgin territory? The urge to climb overcame my natural timidity. The impending crag looked rather severe. I briefly wondered whether I should wait for a larger, more competent party with a block and tackle. No-one would ever find us here if we ran into trouble. But my friend was enthused. The rock, I was glad to see, was not quartzite – a rock I tend to distrust, but rough and holdworthy.

A rowan stuck out of a crack 6ft up, and I rapidly belayed to it, thus, as politeness demanded, giving the first lead to my guest. The crack petered out some 30ft above, but seemed, anyway, to reach beyond the immediate bulge. Anja, for it was he, grabbed the rowan, stood on it, and surveyed the wall, his brown hands delicately exploring the texture of the rock. Suddenly he was off, moving in smooth *pas de bas,* hooching a little (it seemed appropriate), and had gained the top of the crack at the crest of the bulge before he came to a prolonged stop. I dozed in the glorious morning sun, watching the light flicker on the lochan below. It was then I heard a sound not heard for many a year. The ping-ping-ping of a piton being driven in. No wonder the man's sack had been heavy. Anyway, it reached that delicious note of high C, and two hoochs later six more feet of rope had left my hands. Pause. No scraping, no remarks, not even heavy breathing. And then as if a decision had been made, the rope slowly left my hands – 40, 50, 60ft. 'I'm at a belay,' he shouted down, with an undoubted note of jubilation in his voice, but it could have been the nervous shout of someone who wanted to share his predicament. I didn't spoil it by asking.

It was nice, and after the piton (which I had to leave in place, having no hammer), it was without any possibility of runner, rather like the top pitch of Ardverikie Wall. The next pitch was mine, and I was happy to see that we were tied on to a massive chock embedded in a V-crack. There wasn't much of a stance, but the way ahead looked just my speed, slabby, if thin, but with nice sideways over-lapping rock that would surely take nuts. And so it proved – just like the first pitch of Spartan Slab. The rock, getting warm by now, lured me on and on, from runner to runner, until just when I felt the weight of 130ft of rope proving too much there was the ledge, commodious with a massive boulder behind. To my satisfaction it was not a ledge one could walk off. This really was a route. I sat on a heather couch and could scarcely pull it in as fast as Anja climbed. 'That was just a dance,' said he. And so it was. We called it the fox-trot pitch.

Above, things seemed a trifle more strenuous, but my leader was unabashed. Now girt with some of my nuts he struck off to the right and into shadow, searching for weakness. I had already schooled him, given my cowardly nature, of the need to put in plenty of runners. After running out half the rope the only sign of life was an occasional twitch and a continuous avalanche of tufts of heather and moss. Anja is a Buddhist. For him to destroy nature thus must mean something desperate was going on. This was emphasised by the whirr of a passing stone. I shrank into the rock face.

This third pitch, when it came to my turn offered an explanation. After the steep slab there was a short wall, whose top surface had an hour before been covered with moss and heather. It was succeeded by yet another short wall. And no placements, either. My struggle to the top was quite a tarantella. 'Mine too,' he said.

Pitch 4 legitimately fell to me. I viewed it with a mixture of awe and apprehension, wondering whether the time had come to mention my advancing age, number of dependents etc. etc. Frankly, I'm not now too good 10ft beyond a decent runner.

Well 10ft up, there was such a runner, and though the crag was now more holdworthy, it was also steeper. A chimney broke the face above, offering the comfort of the womb as I perched with my back on one side and feet on the other, searching for that essential belay. Ahead was one of those interesting moves where the rock is overhanging, but within the chimney one could actually rest. Good thing. My power to weight ratio is not what it was. With two tiny nuts in place I forced an unwilling mind into the next upward movement. Surely soon I could honourably give up and pass the lead to my friend, but as I looked down, my confidence in being able to retreat was undermined by being able to see the whole of the face beneath. Upwards it would have to be. Actually, the holds were not bad, and with a set of movements reminiscent of a Strathspey step (I was humming an auld Scots air to keep my cool) I ascended what proved to be no more than severe. A jug presented itself, to which I gratefully looped a long sling, and whooped with joy at seeing a line of holds for the next 20ft. Then life came to a stop. The rest looked distinctly for the new breed of climbers reared on exercise machines and climbing walls. I settled for an excellent nut belay, for I had one decent foot hold, and called up Anja, who wafted up effortlessly. 'The waltz pitch,' he said.

He was now like the bull fighter honed for the finally rapier thrust. I could sense his excitement, his belief in himself. With a glint in his eyes he relieved me of the gear and went forth. The chimney had given way to a crack, disappearing out of sight. Anja moved as only one with a superbly fit body and trained mind can move. Delicately, without hesitation, from minuscule hold to sloping edge and on again. I was quite certain I did not want him to fall off. I tried to reinforce my confidence by re-examining my belay, but it seemed increasingly inadequate. By now he had topped the crack, and I saw his hands move out of sight. Then a mantelshelf, a grunt, a pause and call for me to come.

I would never have done it without a rope from above. It took me back to some terrifying moments on the Campanile Basso. 'What shall we call this pitch,' I remarked 'fandango?' He shook his head: 'Just a merry dance.'

My turn, pitch 6. The fact that I was still alive and well encouraged me to reflect on the wisdom of proceeding farther. We were on a commodious shelf, ideal for a bivouac, enlivened by a garden of roseroot and saxifrage. The sun beat down, creating in me a drowsy enjoyment of my situation, with no desire to alter it. The wall above overhung. It was perfectly clear to both of us that I could never lead such a pitch. The good news, as far as I was concerned, was that after several sorties up a few feet and back again, Anja came to the same conclusion. With the smugness that comes from climbing mountains rather than mere crags, we opined that this pitch was definitely for the new breed of crag rats, and that wise old (and middle-aged) mountaineers should now retreat. And this we did.

You may wonder just where is this crag. I leave this mystery as a bequest not to my generation, or even the one after that, but to the new generation, who now make the rules. But when the climb is finally completed, may I suggest it be called – The Merry Dance.

SGURR AN FHEADAIN

BEN NEVIS – THE TOUGH WAY

By Alec Keith

There was an obscure exchange of FAX and E-mail messages on p.744 of the 1995 SMC Journal for which an explanation has been requested.

THE 1990s offer some great opportunities to celebrate the achievements of the pioneers by making a few sporting centenary ascents. You can get a strange sense of satisfaction from pulling on shabby, moth-eaten old clothes and, armed with little more than a few conversational gambits, spending the day clinging to some mossy classic, secretly longing for your rock-boots and a rack of Friends. You too can savour the situation, as a union of porphyry and Harris tweed interposes the most slender obstacle to an airy slide into the glen. And this sub-sport is growing in popularity, with no less than two separate teams being reported on the North East Ridge of Aonach Beag in April 1995 – although there are lingering doubts about the then President's ethics in choosing to use the gondola for access.

While the pioneers put up many fine climbs, I've always been more impressed by the lengths they had to go to to get to the hills, something easily overlooked by today's motorised mountaineers. But few measures can have been as extreme as those adopted by William Brown and William Tough to climb the North East Buttress of Ben Nevis on May 25, 1895. As centenary climbs go this was an obvious plum, even if it was only to commemorate a second ascent. And so it was that in the early months of 1995 the buttress became an object of ambition to a large circle of climbers, the chief topic of the smoke-room at night and the focus of many critical glances during the day.

Tough and Brown's efforts involved a 45-hour marathon effort from Edinburgh by a bewildering variety of transport, and recreating their journey was obviously going to be far more bother than getting up the North East Buttress. That was one of the idea's main attractions, but speedier forms of rail travel (Scotrail's efforts notwithstanding) meant that the trip would have to be done much more quickly. Preferring others to do my planning, I looked around for an open-minded logistician for company, but found only Derek Bearhop. Bearhop showed initial promise, his administrative skills honed at the cutting edge of the Civil Service. But it was either Bearhop or the West Highland Railway that refused to fit in – the point is still in dispute – as it was soon clear that, for Derek to take part, Tough and Brown would have had to have done the whole thing by car at the weekend. Only a little persuasion was needed to enlist Matthew Shaw in his place. A climber of impeccable historical pedigree and the grandson of G. G. Macphee, Shaw exhibits many of his forebear's habits, having a natural affinity for grass and an obsession with the collection of the obscure. (Is there anyone else whose *Munro Tables* show that their owner, having bagged all the hills in the book, has then made a start on ticking the list of Compleaters, both alive and dead?) Moreover, he was already a veteran of other re-enactments such as the notorious Black Shoot and a gondola-free visit to Aonach Beag's North East Ridge. But for every plan he hatches he has a clutch of sub-plans incubating, and I lived in fear of being dumped.

The amount of travel, the expense, and the general lack of sleep which our plans entailed would have been utterly repulsive as applied to anything but the North East Buttress, but it just had to be done. In the week leading up to the big day we were faced with a couple of minor crises, both caused by what passes in this country for a rail network. The first difficulty, Scotrail's policy of only allowing one bicycle on each train on many services, even on the main line from Edinburgh to Inverness, was overcome by renovating an old folding shopper bike which could be passed off as hand-luggage. The second obstacle was more serious; having run/ cycled from Kingussie we would need to catch a train which passed through Tulloch at 8am, but this was the infamous Deerstalker express, due for the chop the very next day and, as it was a dozer service from London, you were not allowed to get on anywhere between Glasgow and the Fort in case you woke somebody up. It seemed that you could get off anywhere if you really insisted. Scotrail were quite certain that they wouldn't be stopping for us.

There seemed little we could do in the face of such customer-hostility. Perhaps we could hold up a sign on the platform to tell the driver that the wrong sort of leaves were on the track and jump on when he stopped? But even if that happened the train would probably still be packed with anorak-clad types savouring the thrill of the last ride of the Deerstalker. The alternative was to jog an extra 10 miles to Spean Bridge then hitch to the Fort. Again this was utterly repulsive, but there was a certain gloomy satisfaction that we were doing something quite out of the common, which deepened in gloom as our arrangements waxed in originality. We decided just to turn up at Tulloch and see what happened. We also sensed a perverse symmetry in our dilemma as it was due to time-tabling difficulties with the then recently opened West Highland line that Tough and Brown were forced to adopt their convoluted approach to the Ben in the first place.

To my relief, and mild surprise, Shaw appeared on time at my central Edinburgh flat on the Wednesday evening, and we made our way to Waverley with an assortment of bikes, sacks, a hawser-laid rope and a

ove: Matthew Shaw (left) and Alec Keith outside the Alexandra Hotel, Fort William before setting off on their centenary climb of the North East Buttress of Ben Nevis.

Below: The intrepid pair on the summit. Photos: Keith Collection.

couple of G. G.'s old axes, our outfits causing a few raised eyebrows among the capital's more fashion-conscious citizens. The train ride proceeded without incident and we got off at about 10.30 or so. Very grey and miserable was Kingussie when we reached it, rain was falling dismally, and a dense white mist hung low upon the hillsides. We pedalled west for a few miles in the dark to Laggan, and here made a minor departure from the original itinerary to join in at a party to celebrate the 10th anniversary of the Laggan pottery coffee shop. Luckily, the revellers were already sufficiently well oiled to not need too many explanations about us or what we were doing; we were made welcome, wine flowed freely, and an ethnic clothes seller took a keen interest in Shaw's plus-fours. Some time well after one we were put in an office and rested fitfully until four when it was time to crawl down to the kitchen to have breakfast and sneak away without waking the pottery's dogs.

The morning was heavy and dull as we cycled for three miles or so to a spot just before the Falls of Pattack where the road used to contain a hump on which it was possible to get a university minibus, its passengers and a trailer airborne. No such fun today, however, as the spot is even more famous as the place where Brown tells us that there was 'a sudden report, resembling the simultaneous opening of six bottles of Bouvier' . . . followed by Tough's despairing cry: 'Your tyre's punctured.'

Planning for this incident had given us many hours of innocent amusement. Inquiries at off-licences for Bouvier had produced no more than blank looks; we compromised on Taittinger but only bought one bottle as our livers were less absorbent and our finances decidedly more limited than those of Tough and Brown. The bottle made a pleasingly loud report, but we were uncertain as to how to dispose of the contents. We drank most of it while wrestling with this dilemma, then put the last bit in a cycling drinks bottle. I hid the shopper in a ditch, Shaw unsteadily mounted the remaining bicycle with a pyramid of ropes, axes and rucksacks piled up on his shoulders, and I started jogging along behind in my boots. You may not have tried running in boots before – my advice would be not to. My knees' advice would probably be to not bother with the running either.

We operated in three-mile shuttles, Shaw choosing some ethically more relaxed footwear for his share of the running, and we leap-frogged each other from time to time, each suspicious that he was doing less cycling and more running than the other. The sun was making a feeble demonstration, but its rays passed almost unnoticed in the moral gloom which now fell upon the expedition. Soon we had settled into a distrustful rhythm and knocked off the 16 miles to Tulloch in a couple of hours. Here we abandoned the remaining bicycle and sat down to have a rest and nervously wait for the arrival of the Deerstalker.

Guy Lacelle high on 'Terminator' V,6+, Mount Rundle, Alberta, Canada. Photo: Alan Kerr.

Our fears about the train proved unjustified; it stopped, we got on without waking anyone except the guard who said we shouldn't but that we could, and we completed our journey to Fort William in comfort on a mattress unaccountably located in the guard's van. This success put us in the Fort at 8.30, so we reckoned we now had time for a full breakfast in the Alexandra Hotel – justifiable, of course, as this was the base used by the pioneers 100 years before, albeit for lunch.

An hour or so later we were sweating off an uneasy mixture of bacon, tea, eggs, toast and sausages as we flogged up the grass slopes of painful memory that lead up by the tourist track from Achintee past the Halfway Lochan and round into the deep cleft of the Allt a' Mhuillinn. A few bodily disorders developed – our ageing trousers itched, we were pretty shattered after our early start, and my own system was still suffering from a bad sailing experience a few days earlier. We staggered over the bouldery path under the dark and dripping crags of Carn Dearg and the weather began to cheer up, the sun shone occasionally and a blustery wind helped dry the rocks. The CIC came into view and the winter snow gleamed cold and ghastly out of the gloom as we skirted round the steep frowning basement of the North East Buttress into the foot of Coire Leis. Clouds were moving rapidly across the summit as we followed what must be the original line rightwards up grotty loose ledges and moss to gain the buttress. It was most exasperating to find, wherever a friction grip was necessary, how persistently one's sodden knickers and boots kept slipping on the wet mossy surface, and how unreliable was the hold thus obtained.

On reaching the First Platform we rested by a small stone man, our climb towering, crag over crag, above us – an inspiring sight. After a while Shaw woke me and we made rapid progress up the ridge, pleasant scrambling over slightly greasy rocks with a few more awkward steps blocking our way from time to time. I wobbled around, still mentally and physically at sea, and took my time while Shaw prospected the route ahead and tried not to get too impatient with me.

Eventually, we found our way barred by a steep little bastion. Though this is now known as the Mantrap, it seems from Brown's description that it was to the slabby rocks on the left that the pioneers were referring. Shaw was keen to avoid the historically correct line and tackle the pitch direct so I had to remind him of the ethics of his situation and drove him at the point of my axe to explore the rocks on the right. This was the original line, nowadays justifiably avoided, but we were soon standing at the base of the Forty-foot Corner. A soggy rope lay strewn on the rocks beneath us, witness no doubt to someone's recent winter epic. We roped up for this pitch which Shaw led in fine style by a series of ape-like lunges from polished ledge to polished ledge until there was nothing more to climb and we raced up the last few feet of the ridge into sunshine on the top of the Ben. No overflowing hospitality in the Observatory for us though, not even a mug of steaming coffee. We had a bite to eat and knocked back the last of the Taittinger, but then some very noisy trippers were approaching so we turned and fled the summit, enjoying a glissade down the Red Burn before the usual body-mashing back down the track to Achintee.

We reached the Nevisbank Hotel at five, in good time for the next stage of the journey. Being the less wasted of the pair of us, Shaw headed off to the Alexandra to send the appropriate fax to the Journal Editor to advise him of our success while I lay in the sunshine and looked out for our driver. Tough and Brown had taken the mail-gig back to Kingussie, an option not available to us. However, Hamish Irvine has a red Post-Office type van and had allowed himself to be persuaded by offers of whisky to return from his Inverness work to his Aviemore home via Fort William. He turned up more or less on time though we were a little disappointed by the casual approach he had taken in dressing for his cameo role in the proceedings.

We headed back east to Kingussie, stopping on the way to pick up our abandoned bicycles and the empty champagne bottle, and to collect our stuff from Laggan, arriving with five minutes to spare before the Edinburgh train left. As the bike space was already taken, only the shopper came with us, the other being left with Hamish to sort out another day. The Editor, however, was not there to welcome us on our return to Waverley at 10.10 that night, after 27 hours of (almost) continuous travelling.

As we get older, so the noteworthy centenary ascents will start getting harder, and it'll be time to look for other objectives . . . such as bicentenary ascents. See you in the queue at the foot of the Dee waterfall on Braeriach on July 17, 2010.

I must acknowledge heavy reliance on William Brown's excellent article, *The N.E. Buttress of Ben Nevis.* SMCJ vol 3, p. 323 et seq, used both for inspiration and for quotation but left unacknowledged in the text for an easier read. A bottle of Taittinger is offered to the first Club member to correctly identify all 19 borrowed snippets – entries by December 1, 1997. The Editor's contribution in the last Journal should be attributed to Gilbert Thomson. Thanks also to Matthew Shaw for his helpful suggestions on what should be done with this article.

Editor's note: Mr Keith and his various press-ganged companions are to be congratulated for their sustained efforts to return to the energetic and inspired times when the Club was young and every route was new. This may be a time for those who sniff at new-routing to take stock and remember what it's all about. For those without access to the original Brown article, it is reprinted in *A Century of Scottish Mountaineering.* I have no doubt that the bottle of Taittinger will be won. Finally, to remind interested readers, Tough was apparently pronounced *Tooch.*

NEW CLIMBS SECTION

OUTER ISLES

LEWIS, Mungarstadh Sands area (Map Ref. 008 309):
Two routes on the obvious triangular pillar seen on the north side of the beach. Care
is needed with loose rock near the top. The belay is on a rope from boulders well
back.
Ocean Drive – 18m E1 5b. K. Archer, A. Norton. 28th July, 1996.
Takes the crackline on the front face. Folow this to a niche, then follow the diagonal
crack to ledges.
Body Surfin' in a Body Bag – 16m VS 4c. A. Norton, K. Archer. 28th July, 1996.
The pillar forms a corner 3m to the right at its junction with the face. Follow the
corner passing a bulge at two-thirds height.

Painted Geo area (Map Ref. 005 334):
The Seventh Wave – 80m HVS. K. Archer, A. Norton (alt.). 1st August, 1996.
Traverses the south-facing wall that forms a seaward extension of the north wall of
Painted Geo. From the top of the latter, walk westwards and descend slightly to gain
the neck of land that joins the geo to this wall. The wall can be identified by a central
gully and a rising band of pink quartz in its right-hand section. Walk to the seaward
end of the wall and abseil down to a ledge on the left arête, the start of the route.
1. 35m 5a From the ledge descend to a line of flakes that leads to the break and
follow this to cross a section of rounded holds. Regain the break, now less
continuous, and follow it to black ledges that lead into the gully. Descend slightly
to a stance.
2. 45m 5a From the stance cross the gully, traverse below a block overhang.
Continue traversing rightwards to a short corner, passing this to gain the right-
wards-rising pink band; follow this to belay on the arête.

MULL, Balmeanach:
Is it Safe was climbed by J. Fisher and C. Moody on 18th July, 1996 (missed out
of FA list in new guide).

Scoor, Dune Wall:
The Crystal Ship – 10m E4 6a*. T. Charles-Edwards. 1996.
The blind groove just right of Troglodite.

Creag Eilean an Duilisg:
Calluna Cornice – 12m VS 5a. D. Brooks, L. Gordon-Canning, C. Moody. 12th
September, 1996.
Well left of Nest Trundling, climb a juggy arête. Runners are in the shallow corner
on the right. Move right across the corner for the last section.
Eye of Toad – 15m E2 5b**. C.Moody, L. Gordon-Canning. 29th September, 1996.
Round left of Nest Trundling are twin cracks. Climb the left-hand crack with a little
help from the right-hand crack high up.
Screech Owl – 15m HVS 5a*. C. Moody, L. Gordon-Canning. 10th September,
1996.
A jam crack. Belay as for Golden Eye.
Goldeneye – 15m VS 4c*. A. Moody, L. Gordon-Canning. 10th September, 1996.
A jam crack with a block at its base. A belay stake is 8m back.

Bloody Louse-Bird – 15m E1 5b*. C. Moody, D. Brooks, L. Gordon-Canning. 12th September, 1996.
The corner-crack right of Golden Eye runs up left of a nose high up; a finger crack just right is also used. Belay as for Golden Eye.

Take me to the River – 20m E2 5c**. C. Moody, L. Gordon-Canning. 25th September, 1996.
The line of the waterfall is sometimes dry. Climb twin cracks, then awkward bulges. Belay as for Donald Duck.

Feathers McGraw – 20m E2 5b**. C. Moody, L. Gordon-Canning. 29th September, 1996.
Right of the waterfall is an overhang; start below this. Good varied climbing. Climb up, then hand traverse right to a jam crack which leads to the top of a pillar. Step left, climb a finger crack, then finish up a shallow chimney. Belay as for Donald Duck.

IONA, Aoineadh nan Struth:
Gully Wall – 20m E1 5b**. D.Brooks, C. Moody, L. Gordon-Canning. 22nd September, 1996.
Scramble into the gully until under the chockstone. Follow the crack which slants out left below it.

Blood Donor – 20m VS 4b*. C. Moody, L. Gordon-Canning, D. Brooks. 22nd September, 1996.
Start at a puddle in the gully, gained either by scrambling past the start of the previous route or abseil. Climb straight up.

Haemoglobin – 20m VS 4c *. D. Brooks, C. Moody, L. Gordon-Canning. 22nd September, 1996.
Start at the puddle, move farther into the gully, easily past the chockstone. Climb straight up.

SKYE

AM BASTEIR, North-West Face:
Hung, Drawn and Quartered – 75m E4. I. S. Dring, M. E. Moran. 16th September, 1996.
A classic struggle up the striking chimney line starting 10m left of King's Cave Chimney.
1. 15m 6a. Climb the slanting slot just right of the main chimney. Belay 6m higher at a cave.
2. 17m 5c. Swing up left, climb a ladder dyke, then follow the chimney to a grassy break.
3. 18m 5c. An impressive chimney pitch.
4. 25m 4c. Up the dyke above to finish over a chockstone just west of the summit.

SGURR DEARG, South Buttress:
The following route was recorded in 1995 but the cliff was uncertain. Sgurr Dearg, South Buttress seems a possibility. 'The central chimney on the west shoulder (W-SW) of Sgurr Dearg (IV, mixed), exit via mixed ground on the right.' Perhaps the chimney between South Buttress and East Corner? C. Givannel, R. Page, P. Maurichon, Y. Astier. 27th March, 1995.

SGURR SGUMAIN, West Buttress:
Blazing Saddles – 185m Severe. D. Hanna, S. Kennedy. July, 1996.
Follows a line between West Trap Route and Sunset Slab to the right of the 'white blaze', aiming for a conspicuous groove near the top. Start up West Trap Route. Climb the small chimney at 27m until below the open slabs on the right (passing two old pegs). Pull on to a narrow ledge on the left wall and follow this round to a wide ledge above the vertical section of the buttress (45m). Climb grooves and walls to the base of the conspicuous groove (45m). Struggle up the back of the groove, then move out and up a slabby wall to reach an obvious trap dyke (45m). Finish up the dyke and broken rocks above (50m).

BLA BHEINN: NORTH-EAST WALL OF THE EAST RIDGE:
The new guidebook descriptions of routes in this complex area are rather confused. Access Gully, as described and as located in the diagram, shares the same start as the winter line, The Crucifix – climbing the deep gully below a huge chockstone to an 'X' shaped junction. The continuation of Access Gully leads to a col, which A1 Gully reaches from the SE side, and directly above the col on the R is the short hard step by which A1 Gully reached easier ground.
The other half of the 'X' formation is almost certainly the line of Serious Picnic which comes over a small col from the left, stays on the NE side and crosses diagonally up to the right, sharing its last two pitches up the ramp with The Crucifix. To the R of the 'X' and above this upper ramp is a chockstoned gully.
Teddy Bears' Gulch –70m III,4. M. E. Moran and M. Welch. 10th January 1997. Start up Access Gully/Crucifix, and climb to the 'X' junction; go right for 10m on to the ramp of Serious Picnic to a short step, then leave the ramp and climb directly up the obvious chockstoned gully in two interesting pitches, exiting R on to the top of the East Ridge.

SGURR NAN GILLEAN: KNIGHT'S PEAK:
West Ridge of Knight's Peak –150m III,4. P. Franzen, M. E. Moran, S. Potter. 26th February, 1997.
A good mountaineering route, gaining the ridge by the obvious ramp trending up right from the foot of 3/4 Gully, then weaving up grooves just left of the crest and finishing by two steep mixed pitches, the first on the crest and the second a chimney 1m right of it, which lead to the summit arête.

SGURR NAN GILLEAN: THE BHASTEIR FACE:
Flutings Climb – 90m IV,6. P. Franzen, M. E. Moran, S. Potter. 26th February, 1997
Right of Forked Chimney there are three further lines, a roofed chimney, a left-slanting chimney with bulging chockstone at its foot, and a longer chimney, shallow at start and with a leftward kink at half-height. Whether this last chimney is Flutings Climb is not certain, but it gave an excellent winter climb at the top end of its grade.
1. 40m. Climb steepening and poorly protected mixed ground into the shallow chimney. At its top move left across the kink and go up the deeper upper chimney for 5m to a chockstone belay.
2. 50m. Climb the iced chimney to a steep exit, then the continuing snow gully to block belays just below the West Ridge.

NEIST, The Upper Crag, The Financial Sector:
Worm's Eye View – 40m HVS 5a*. C. Moody, B. Taylor. 17th August, 1996.
Well left of Earthbound, a dyke forms a flake/chimney. Start left of the left side of
the flake and climb the fault, taking the flake at mid height on the left.

Earthbound – 35m HVS 5a*. C.Moody, M. Tweedley. 13th June, 1996.
The groove left of Terminal Bonus. Start round left of Terminal Bonus, climb an
easy slab, two steep cracks, then the groove.

STAFFIN, Staffin Slip South:
Babe –13m E2 5b*. B. Taylor, C. Moody. 18th September, 1996.
The wide crack right of Lateral Thinking. Chockstones will take a downward but
not an outward pull.

Jugs of Deception – 18m E4 6a**. M. Tweedley, C. Moody. 10th June, 1996.
The pillar left of Hand Jive using thin cracks. The final bulge is climbed by a
layaway off the edge to reach a hidden hold on the right.

Glorious Five-Year Plan – 35m E2 5c**. C. Moody, M. Tweedley. 10th June,
1996.
The corner right of The Latvian, starting between a birch tree and an ivy.

Sgeir Bhan (Map Ref. 497 676):
Approaching from Staffin slipway, walk up to the foot of the obvious north-facing
buttress, then about 50m farther on the east side where there are two pinnacles. The
right-hand pinnacle is nearly the height of the cliff; the left-hand one is about 20m
high. The crag is a dolerite sill.
Loose Woman – 30m Severe. R. Ascroft, Z. Parkin, G. shcroft. 4th June, 1996.
Climbs the large pinnacle. Start on the NW side of the chimney between pinnacle
and main cliff. Bridge up following an obvious off-width crack which divides the
pinnacle in two, until the gap widens and it is necessary to commit oneself to the
pinnacle alone. Continue to the top. A few metres of old rope round the top is
recommended as a better abseil anchor.

Persistent Vegetated State – 30m E1 5a. R. Ascroft, G. Ashcroft. 4th June, 1996.
About 8m right of the short pinnacle and 3m left of the taller one are two parallel
cracks which rise vertically up the face providing excellent climbing to about half
height. From here on it is vegetated and loose and the top is particularly nasty,
taking the right-hand of three possible exit lines as the least obnoxious.

NORTHERN HIGHLANDS

SOUTH AND WEST (VOLUME ONE)

KNOYDART, Sourlies Bothy Crag:
A Good Day Spoilt – 40m E3 5c. M. Harris, M. Ballance. 26th June, 1996.
The climb is on a large slab/wall situated low on the hillside a few hundred metres
east of the bothy. It is prominent on the approach to Sourlies but not visible from
it and lies just below and right of an obvious pillar with a horizontal roof. The lower
slab is very smooth; the climb starts 5m farther left and thrashes rightwards up
jungle. From the top tree, move right in a wide diagonal crack, then up to a thinner
break a few feet higher. Move left in this for about 3m, then up a flake-crack to a
cleaned jug in the next break. Go left again to another excellent flake-crack and up
this past a good spike, finishing up a blunt arête to trees and abseil descent.

CLUANIE DAM SLABS (Sheet 34, GR 177 094):

These slabs can be clearly seen across the loch from the road at the north end of the dam. They are bigger than they look and offer good climbing on rough granite with the occasional quartz seam. The slabs face north and require a day or two to dry after rain. Cross the dam and follow a faint path west to the foot of the slabs (approx. 20 min). From the path the slabs present a steep north-east face with two obvious cracklines. Around to the north the angle eases and the slab runs into a short upper north-east face forming a long corner, an excellent climb.

Persistent Reward – 55m VS. R. Simpson, D. Morrison. 14th May, 1996.

Start at the foot of the north slab, next to a blackened corner and below a roof.

1. 10m. Climb up to and over the first overlap, follow a groove over the second overlap and move right to a peg belay.

2. 45m 4c. Go up the corner (peg runner) to a roof. Move left into the main corner and up this to a small stance. Continue up to a short overhanging crack, move down and pull up into the upper corner (strenuous). Follow cleaned cracks to the top.

The small slab with a huge boulder at its foot and about 50m east of the above gives a 10m climb of V. Diff.

CREAG LUNDIE (Sheet 34, GR 152 110):

Just below the summit are some clean slabby crags, best seen from the road at GR 144 100. The crags and slabs face south and extend well to the east, becoming less steep and more discontinuous the further east one goes. Quick drying rough granite. At the west end of the first crag there is a prominent tree at mid height with a large heather patch to its right. Right of the heather is a conspicuous white slab with a short V-chimney and crack running up its left side. Above the slab is a deep vertical crack. These features give the following route.

The Lost Knuckle – 40m MVS 4b. D. Morrison, R. Simpson. 2nd June, 1996.

Start at the lowest rocks directly below the white slab (small cairn). Climb a short overhanging crack on to a small slab. Go up this and left along a heather terrace to the V-chimney. Go up the chimney and cracks to a good ledge. Climb the deep crack above to heather.

CREAG COIRE AN T-SLUGAIN:

Ploughshare Groove – 130m V,5. A. Nisbet, G. Nisbet. 15th February, 1997.

Start at the base of Rowaling and climb the first groove (left-facing corner/ chimney) on the left (25m). Continue left to reach and climb a steep turfy groove (45m). Move right to a wide slot; climb this, then more easily to the top (60m).

Rowaling – 135m V,6. A. Clapperton, A. Nisbet. 3rd January, 1997.

Climbs the most prominent groove towards the left side of the crag and a regular ice forming line. The groove is right of a slab with wide crack set against a vertical wall. Climb the groove, on this occasion on thin ice to a ledge on the right (45m). Return to the groove, pull over a bulge and climb the next wall by a turfy pull-up on the left. The final section of groove may be possible with more ice. Instead, a short overhanging chimney on the right led to an easier turfy fault, climbed to easier ground (45m). Easier turfy climbing to the top (45m).

Rose Garden – 120m IV,4. J.Gillman, A. Nisbet, D. Roberts. 20th February, 1997.

Climbs an ice line between the deeper grooves of Rowaling and Ridge and Furrow. Continuous ice; perhaps a grade harder if mixed. Start 5m right of Rowaling and climb direct to a barrier wall, taken at its top left corner. Move right on to a big inset

slab above Ridge and Furrow and obvious from below (45m). From the top of the
slab a short iced rib led into a long groove, the source of the ice. The angle slowly
eased (40m, 35m).

The Ridge Direct – 130m III. J. Ashby, J. Hubbard, A. Nisbet. 2nd February, 1997.
A fairly continuous line of shallow grooves just right of the crest of the blunt ridge
in the centre of the crag, sharing about 10m with Ridge and Furrow (after its easy
traverse).

Right End Buttress – 130m II. A. Nisbet. 31st December, 1996.
The crest immediately right of the Grade I gully at the right end of the cliff.

Hidden Gully – 120m I. A. Nisbet, G. Nisbet. 15th February, 1997.
On the right side of Right End Buttress and well hidden is this deep, narrow but easy
gully.

AONACH AIR CHRITH, North-West Face:
Boa Constrictor – 270m IV,4. A. Nisbet, G. Nisbet. 30th November, 1996.
Takes a constricting line up the tower at the top left of the crag. Start at the base of
the left buttress, left of the 'Mother' routes. Climb the shallow gully which splits
the lower buttress and leads to the central snowfield, followed to its top and a belay
below the big left-facing corner on the left of the crest of the tower (120m). Start
up the corner until forced left by a big bulge. Climb a line of cracks parallel to and
about 6m left of the corner to a flake (40m). Continue up the crackline until one can
go easily back into the corner. Go up this into a wide slot, an apparent *cul-de-sac*.
An unexpected chimney splits the steep wall on the right and involves wriggling
behind a chockstone leading to the crest (40m). The crest is unhelpful, so traverse
a ledge rightwards with an awkward step down and climb the first sensible option,
a thin crack filled with turf and leading to a big spike (40m). Easy to the top.
Note 1: The rib on the left has been climbed in summer followed by a traverse right
to the unexpected chimney and a finish up Boa Constrictor (Severe and vegetated)
– A. and G. Nisbet, 6th May, 1995.
2. J. Burton, S. Collins and J. Preston climbed Mummy Knows Best finishing direct
with a belay in a cave under the final capstone and passing it by ice on the left (20th,
February, 1997). Grade III,4.

CISTE DUBH, South-East Face:
Rest in Peace – 80m IV,6. J. Lyall, A. Nisbet, G. Nisbet. 20th November, 1996.
Climbs the left-hand parallel fault, the right being The Undertaker (SMCJ, 1996).
Start 10m right of the fault.
1. 25m. Gain a left-slanting ramp which leads into the fault. Climb this until close
to an overhang and belay out right.
2. 25m. Climb through the overhang (excellent runners) and up another hard step.
3. 30m. Continue up the fault passing through a short chimney to finish past a big
spike on the right.

SGURR A' BHEALAICH DEARG:
Solution Gully – 200m III. A. Nisbet, N. Smith, R. Storm. 20th March, 1997.
The 'left branch' of Resolution Gully, but really a separate route since the fork is
at the start. Climbed in poor conditions; might be Grade II when iced. Two steeper
pitches, then two easier leading to the crest of the north-east ridge which makes a
fine easy finish to the summit.

Beinn Gunn's Buttress – 150m III. R. Cooke, C. Darwin, A. Nisbet. 25th February, 1996.
The buttress between the branches of Resolution Gully. Start just inside the left branch and climb a steepening groove followed by a right-sloping ramp to the crest (50m). Follow the crest in two long pitches to reach scrambling up the north-east ridge.

CREAG AN DUISILG: PLOCKTON (GR: 836336):

The imposing face of Creag an Duisilg was first explored in 1971 and several routes recorded in the SMCJ, all of which have fallen into disuse and are overgrown. Later in the 1970's, Ginger Cain and friends climbed here but their routes are not recorded. In the 1980's Jim Kerr is reported to have climbed on the crag but, again, did not record what he did. A lower crag next to the Plockton-Stromeferry road at GR 838338 was equipped with a few bolts some years ago and has been used by local climbers.

The upper crag is so luxuriantly vegetated and it's base so well defended by near-vertical woodland that further exploration has been deterred until 1996, when an easy approach was discovered from Fearnaig Cottage to the east (GR 846336), where there is parking space for two or three vehicles. By climbing the brackened slopes diagonally right up and over an obvious knoll, a broad terrace is gained which runs below the crags for 600m to a deep gully.

Just beyond the knoll, a vile and grossly overhanging section of crag is passed, the Left Wing. This peters out into a broken and slimy tier of crag, but 300m farther along the terrace a more compact and continuous section of cliff is reached, first a black-streaked section of wall, the Black Walls, then an impressive slim wall with a square-cut overhang and ivy at its base, the Animal Farm Wall. Beyond is a shorter overhanging section with a big terrace at third height, then a fine white-lichened wall, the 007 Wall, a tree-filled bay and a large verdently vegetated ramp which gives access to a much higher section of cliff some 100m high. Right of this ramp is another steep 35m wall, the Brigadier's Redoubt, then a stone-filled diagonal ramp.

The terrace can be followed for another 150m to the big gully, beyond which it peters out.

All the recorded routes, from both 1971 and 1996, are in these zones of the cliffs. Despite the prevailing vegetation, the quality of some routes is considerable, and the situation and beauty of the crag are exceptional. The rock is of a slaty texture with plenty of flat holds and, despite some loose flakes and superficial debris, is surprisingly solid. The crag doesn't get any sunshine until mid-afternoon even in midsummer, and takes a few days to dry out after a really wet spell. Once dry the rock will not be affected by light rain or showers because of its overhanging angle. The midge rating is extreme! All of the new routes required gardening, but are graded for on-sight leads. Descents should be made by abseil from the many birch and rowan trees at the top of the routes. A few slings have been left in place for this, but extras should be carried.

The 1996 ascensionists were Ian Dring (I.D.), Martin Moran (M.E.M.), Andy Nisbet (A.D.) and Martin Welch (M.W.)

LEFT WING:

Bungle in the Jungle – 50m E2 5b. M.E.M. and A.N. 27th June, 1996.
At the left end of this section, just left of a big bay festooned with trees, is a bulging

grey wall. Gain the ledge below the wall, move slimily right to the left edge of the big bay, then climb up left on to the wall and up to a sloping break. Go right along the break for 5m and up a flake crack on to a long narrow ledge (possible belay here). From 3m along the ledge climb a bulge on big pockets then move right and finish into the trees. Abseil quickly off. Can only improve with traffic.

THE BLACK WALLS:

Crocodile Shoes – 40m E2 5b. M.E.M. and A.N. 26th June, 1996.
At the right hand end of this section, just right of the area of black rock, is a steeper tower with a ledge at a quarter height. Climb on to the ledge, then up the face of the tower, moving R through bulges to a finishing slab (tree belay).

ANIMAL FARM WALL:

This lies 8m right of Crocodile Shoes and is easily identified by the block overhang at third height with ivy beneath it. The wall is steep and imposing and bounded on the left by a tree-filled corner line.

My Sex Romp with Llama Sid – 40m E5 6a/b. M.E.M. and A.N. 26th June, 1996.
Climb the left bounding corner for 8m to a holly, then follow the seams and thin cracks direct up the wall of black rock on the right (sustained, Friend No. 0.5 useful). Finish up right to trees or, better, go slightly L through final bulges of sooty rock.

Seals Guaranteed or your Money Back – 40m E2 5c. I.D. and M.E.M. 26th May, 1996.
Start at a tree just left of the square-cut roof. Pull up into the bay beneath the roof, then make thin moves left and up alongside the overhang and a delicate crux step on to a hold on the lip. Follow a good break up right, go up the side of a flake then back left and finish up a massive flake in the final wall. A good route, probably at the top end of its grade.

Hamish Quick-Death –30m E4 5c. I.D. and M.E.M. 25th May, 1996.
Right of the Animal Farm Wall there is a shorter wall with a terrace at 8m. In the centre of this is an obvious bulging crack. Climb this to a gripping finish; prior arrangement of a rope loop from the top is recommended to avoid an exit on vertical heather.

THE 007 WALL:

The next obvious feature is a fine white wall with an overhang split by a groove at its top. The two routes are cross-diagonals, described as such for consistency of grade, and finish on a wooded terrace just left of the main section of crag.

Jim Kerr Knew My Father – 35m E2 5b. M.E.M. and A.N. 11th May, 1996.
Start up the corner on the left, then break out steeply up cracks in the wall. Traverse right at two-thirds height and pull through the roof into the obvious groove to finish. (J.K. may have done this in the 1980s).

James Bond is Alive and Well and Living in Plockton – 35m E4 6a. I.D. and M.E.M. 26th May, 1996.
Start at the right-hand side of the wall at a blunt rib. Go up the rib trending left (runners out right), then utilise hidden slots to climb the bulging wall above, mantleshelfing on to a small ledge to easier ground. Move left, crossing JK Knew My Father, and go up into a niche below a bulging roof. Swing strenuously over this and exit left to the terrace.

THE MAIN CRAG:

Cypress Avenue Direct – 100m E1 5a, 5a, 4c. M.E.M. and A.N. 11th May, 1996.
Just right of the 007 Wall is a black bay with a tree directly below an open groove
in the upper section of the crag. This direct version of a 1971 route climbs a bulging
flake in the lower wall to gain the groove direct.
1. 40m 5a. From the top of the bay go up right and ascend the flake line to a ledge,
then up a delicate lichenous wall to gain a ledge at the foot of the main groove (the
original route climbs vegetated corners to the left to gain the wooded terrace, then
went back right to the lichened wall).
2. 20m 5a. Climb the corner groove to a wide crack and belay behind a detached
monolith.
3. 40m 4c. Go left and up a steep wall and corner, finishing on good holds (belays
20m on top of crag).
The Original Route was climbed by S. Docherty and N. Muir. 29th May, 1971.
From all routes finishing at the top of the Main Crag the easiest descent is to abseil
off trees at the left-hand side down heathery outcrops to the wooded terrace, and
then down the Animal Farm Wall to the base of the cliff.
To the right of Cypress Avenue is a steep ramp of luscious vegetation, just beyond
which the full height of the Main Crag can be viewed. There are three obvious
corner crack lines. The left-hand line, Shenaval (Schipper and Chambers 1971),
takes the prominent crack in the middle of the crag leading to the detached monolith
common with Cypress Avenue and was repeated at HVS 4c, 5b, 4c. Unfortunately,
this line can only be accessed by scrambling 50m up the ramp and, due to the fragile
and possibly precious vegetation here, the start is not recommended.
Chanter (Muir and Schipper 1971) crosses Shenaval from the left to gain an obvious
overhanging chimney corner, then aids up the final overhanging tier. This was not
repeated, but since it starts from the bottom of the ramp it offers an alternative way
of getting on to Shenaval.
The highest and rightmost of the three lines is Easy Rider (Crymble and Schipper
1971), which takes the corner starting at the top of the ramp beneath the overhangs
at the top of the crag. This was accessed by climbing It Ne'er Rains but it Pours,
and traversing across the top of the ramp. On repeat it was considered to be a
worthwhile HVS 5a, 5a, 4c.
The impressively overhanging headwall of the Main Crag has a right diagonal
break sandwiched between roofs which is best gained by climbing a route on the
Brigadier's Redoubt and the first pitch of Easy Rider.

The Hanging Traverse of Babylon – 40m E4 6a. M.E.M. and M.W. 24th June, 1996
From the finely-poised stance at the top of the corner climb the 'hairy' wall on the
left and pull out on to the ledge, as for Easy Rider. Then, go straight up the brown
wall above to gain a break, which leads rightwards into a corner directly above the
belay. Move out along the top of a hanging flake, then swing across the impending
wall and follow the fault for 5m to a break in the final overhangs. Pull through this
to the top. An impressive pitch.

THE BRIGADIER'S REDOUBT:

This is the wall to the right of the vegetated ramp which terminates in a diagonal
stone-shoot. The routes here are worthwhile in themselves, but are equally useful
for getting to the top section of the Main Crag
Brigadier Braggart's Little Secret – 35m E3 5c. I.D. and M.E.M. 27th May, 1996

Takes the central line. Pull through a flake overhang at the right-hand end of the wall, then traverse left until below a hanging groove. Go up this to a roof (peg runner), and then launch out left with conviction to gain a ledge. Step left, then go straight up with continuous interest to finish at a tree belay.

The Queen's Garden Party – 30m E1 5b. I.D. and M.E.M. 27th May, 1996.
Start as for Brigadier Braggart. Pull through the roof, then go up the arête on the right edge of the wall to gain big sloping ledges out right. Finish up the corner above and go left at the top to tree belays.

It Ne'er Rains but it Pours 35m VS 4c. I.D. and M.E.M. 28th May, 1996.
Start 10m up the diagonal stone-shoot and step out left onto the face. Go up a short corner to roofs, then traverse left to sloping ledges and finish up the corner above, as for The Queen's Garden Party. Climbed during a deluge. A good warm up for the upper Main Crag.R

MORUISG, Coire nam Mang, The Great Grey Slab of Moruisg:
A large reasonably-angled grey schistose slab lies above Loch Cnoc na Mointeich at approx. 800m about 1hr 30min from a layby off the A890 at M. Ref. 125 542. The slab is of a remarkably smooth undulating appearance with steeper sections. Despite the rock being onion-layered into flags which precludes heavy-footed climbers, the slab and its setting and scale give it more than a passing attraction.

The slab is approx. 140m high on the easier-angled right to about 90m on the left near a grassy corner. Above this corner lie further corners and inset slabs, diminishing in height leftwards. A remarkable property about the rock is the friction which is relatively unaffected in the wet owing to a lack of lichen. It is perfectly possible to ascend the easier routes in the rain with little change in grade. The rock is very clean but protection is almost entirely lacking and when found, often worthless due to the layering which easily splits from the slab underneath. Short thin blade pegs and smallish Friends and wires can be satisfactory if placed with precision and care. Taken in the right spirit, it is all rather exhilarating.

The slab has certainly seen some ascents before, an ancient peg near Disposable Slab pointing to either a summer or a winter line, but nothing is known.
Disposable Slab – 100m Moderate. J.R. Mackenzie. 27th June, 1996.
Climbs the right edge of the main slab, starting above broken rocks. Follow the best line just left of the edge.

Close to the Edge – 140m V. Diff. J. R. Mackenzie. 27th June, 1996.
Probably the best of the easier lines, this follows the left edge of the dirty groove which cuts up the slab left of Disposable Slab. Start to the left of a large flake above the broken rocks and climb a steep slab to gain the edge overlooking the groove. Follow the edge all the way to a terrace, move left to the edge above and follow this either up the edge, or easier, up a crack to step back right below the edge at a dirty chimney-crack (good flake belays). Step right and climb the sandwiched groove to the top. A pleasant excursion with a fair amount of disposable rock and some easy friction, but quite seriously unprotected.
Variation: – Diff. W. McKerrow, J. R. Mackenzie. 31st August, 1996.
From the terrace, instead of moving left to the edge, continue up the slab on the left between two corners and climb the dirty chimney to the flake belays. Less good but a more obvious line.

The President's Men – 95m VS. J. R. Mackenzie, W. McKerrow. 31st August, 1996.

Walk left below the main slab up a rake to a steeper narrow slab near the left where the terrace descends to the rake, cairn.

1. 25m 4c. Climb the smooth slab right of loose flakes and left of a small corner on friction to an overlap. Step over the overlap and continue straight up to the terrace.

2. 45m 4a. Continue straight up on the slab, easy at first then steepening, to belay below a double overlapped right-trending corner.

3. 25m 4c. The slab above steepens with good friction to the crackless corner, which is climbed to the next overlap. Step right and climb the next corner through an overlap and better holds and protection to the top. A fine pitch.

FUAR THOLL, Mainreachan Buttress:

Enigma – 240m VII,7. S. Richardson, C. Cartwright. 4th January, 1997.

A sustained mixed route up the front face of the buttress. There appears to be some confusion as to the whereabouts of the original winter line on the face. The Northern Highlands I Guide suggests the 1969 Fyffe/Macinnes/Spence ascent followed the first pitch of Enigma and then traversed left to enter the groove of Nimrod (clearly possible and a natural way to go). MacInnes's description and diagram in his selected winter guide states that after the first pitch of Enigma they joined Sleuth on the right (the next guide will describe it as such, probably VII,7, and notable as the hardest route in Scotland at the time). The route described below is loosely based on the summer route of Enigma, and lies between the above two lines. Above the Great Terrace, the 1969 route was followed which is the natural winter way. Start just left of the first tier below a short gully (about 5m right of Nimrod).

1. 20m. Climb the gully to a terrace.

2. 15m. Continue up the prominent V-groove to ledge.

3. 20m. Move up and right along a narrow slabby ramp to below a steep wall (junction with Sleuth, which traverses left to reach this point and then goes back right along a horizontal ledge). Move left below a big square flake and continue up and left to niche overlooking the corner of Nimrod.

4. 15m. Climb the groove just left of the niche to a bay.

5. 15m. Nimrod takes the corner up and left. Instead, traverse horizontally right for 3m below an overlap, and move up to a small ledge. Climb the short groove above to flat ledge.

6. 20m. Climb the bulging groove just right of the left edge to reach the Great Terrace which girdles the cliff at two-thirds height. Move up to belay below a steep pillar.

7. 45m. Traverse right along the dwindling ledge for 20m, then trend diagonally right on mixed ground to reach a right to left diagonal line of weakness where the angle eases.

8. 30m. Climb up diagonally left for 15m to below a steep tower. Traverse horizontally left along a ledge for 10m, then move up to the left edge of the buttress.

9 and 10. 60m. Straightforward mixed ground leads to the top.

SGORR RUADH:

Spanner in the Works – 240m V,6. A. Nisbet, J. Preston. 21st December, 1996.

Climbs the buttress between the Superdirect and Tophet Gully. Start midway between the two at a 5m icefall at the base of V-shaped diverging faults. Climb the icefall to a ledge, then traverse left into the left fault, almost a shallow chimney. Follow this to a bulging section which forces a 6m traverse left to a large flake against the wall. Climb steep cracks above the flake to a terrace (45m, could be split). The fault continues left to join the Superdirect, so traverse easily right and up to the right-hand of parallel grooves (35m). Climb the right-hand groove to a notch on the skyline and easier ground (70m). Follow the easy buttress to the crest.

Gopher's Gully – 200m IV,4. M. E. Moran, A. Nisbet. 28th November, 1996.
Takes a shallow gully starting below First Blood and just outside North Gully. It has the very obvious feature of a large chockstone on the first pitch underneath which one must chimney. The second pitch continues up the gully, also steep and leads to an easy broad rib and the crest of Raeburn's Buttress.

The Sandstone Virgin – 130m V,7. J. Lyall, A. Nisbet, J. Preston. 26th November, 1996.
Climbs the line which is erroneously described in the Northern Highlands Guide as being Tango in the Night. Tango climbs the very impressive fault 'formidable *cul-de-sac*' which is the right branch of the starting gully of Splintery Edge. This route is the next gully down, between Highland Scottische and Ruadh Awakening. It was climbed in four pitches, the second being steep but helpful (and crucial that many blocks are frozen in place) while the third involved a big chockstone with a very hard exit on to scree which would be a lot easier with a little ice. Arguably VI,6.

The Last Waltz – 110m V,6. A. Nisbet, J. Preston. 21st December, 1996.
Takes an unexpected easing in angle between Tango in the Night and steep walls higher up the gully. Start as for Tango but at the start of its difficulties, traverse right along a narrow grass ledge above a steep wall to a spike (30m). Take a line of cracks slanting slightly right and leading to a right-facing slabby corner with a fine crack. A belay was taken in a niche above the corner (45m). A strenuous pull out of the niche, then a right-trending line via a groove to an easier finish (35m).

BEINN BHAN, Coire na Poite:
Consolation Buttress – 130m IV,5. G. Ettle, P. Munford, A. Nisbet. 24th November, 1996.
Climbs the buttress left of North Gully, taking a line of weakness which forms intermittent chimneys and corners about 30m left of the gully. In better conditions of fully frozen turf and taking an easier finishing pitch farther left, the route might be Grade III.

North Buttress – 375m IV,4. A. and G. Nisbet. 28th December, 1996.
The crest right of North Gully, close to the summer route initially. Start just inside North Gully on the right wall. Traverse easily round to the front, then climb the crest through four tiers to below the clearly steepest tier (100m). Climb the steep tier by a turfy corner just left of a small tree on a ledge (25m). Traverse away right until possible to breach the next tier by a short steep wall (100m). Return left diagonally through the next tier and continue trending left until an easy chimney on the crest leads to A' Chioch.

SGURR A' CHAORACHAIN, North Buttresses:
Tomahawk – 170m IV,6. J. Lyall, M. Sclater, D. Williamson. 31st December, 1996.
Climbs the right side of Totem Buttress. Start midway between the 5m chimney of Totem and No. 4 Gully. Climb a shallow gully line until easy ground leads to a deep wide chimney. Move left below the chimney to climb a steep left-facing corner with a wide crack and helpful chockstones. Follow the continuation fault to the top.

High Domain – 110m III,6 (?). S. Allan, J. Lyall. 3rd January, 1997.
A big groove line running straight up the buttress between the forks of No. 5 Gully,

which can be descended for access to this route. The first pitch leads to a terrace, then the upper groove gives superb climbing with the crux near the top.

Summit Buttress:
Wanda Lust – 80m IV,6. S. Allan, J. Lyall. 3rd January, 1997.
A mixed line slanting left up the buttress, starting 50m right of Blade Runner. A short easy pitch leads to a terrace. Gain a ledge leading left to a short chimney/crack. Climb it and move right on another ledge until the diagonal fault is followed back left to a terrace. The final steep wall is climbed by a tricky move to gain an icy recess.

South Face:
Roadhog's Wall – 20m E3 5c. M. E. Moran (unsec). 14th June, 1996
Close to the gullies just right of the main section of crag (with Sword of Gideon) is a steep clean wall split by a thin crackline, clearly seen from the road below. Well worth the 150m approach scramble. Enter the crack from the right and climb it direct to the top. Sustained and well protected.

MEALL GORM, Cobalt Buttress:
The Lamppost – 90m HVS. A. Nisbet, G. Nisbet. 6th September, 1996.
Scramble up vegetation through the easy lower tiers to the big ledge below the steep upper wall. At the right edge of the wall is slightly slabbier ground bounded on the left by the first right-facing corner which is about 20m left of Rattlesnake. Start left of the corner.
1. 10m. Climb vegetation rightwards to the base of the corner.
2. 40m 5a. Climb the slabs right of the corner to a long roof with a fine crack splitting it and the clean wall above its left side. Climb the roof and crack, then move left past some unpleasant large jammed spikes, and further left to a large flat block sitting on a ledge.
3. 40m 5a. Climb the crack above, initially offwidth and awkward, until a step left is made into a shallow chimney with wedged blocks (not a bigger one further left). Climb the chimney back into the crack and continue until it is easier to trend right to finish close to Rattlesnake's left arête.

Blue Velvet – 275m V,6. R. and C.Anderson. 27th December, 1996.
A direct line on the crest between Rattlesnake and Cobalt Butress, joining Cobalt Buttress for the last tier but taking a more direct line. Start 10m left of the lowest rocks at the right side of the crag. Above the initial turf field are three corners, the central and most obvious having a wide crack in it; head directly towards this for two easy pitches to steepening ground (100m).
3. 25m. Climb to a short corner and wide crack, then pull out left and continue to beneath the main central corner.
4. 15m. Climb the corner and the crack in its right wall to gain a terrace and belay on the left beneath the most obvious corner in the crest.
5. 15m. Climb the corner to reach a terrace beside a huge block.
6. 30m. An obvious fault line slants up rightwards in the crest. Start just to the right of this and climb up left into it, then traverse left around the edge to find easier ground and climb this to gain another terrace.
7. 50m. Find the easiest line to another terrace below the final tier (joining Cobalt Buttress at some point?).
8. 20m. Above is a huge poised block just left of the crest. Climb up and left to reach

the block, then pull carefully around beneath this and climb easily to a ledge.
9. 20m. Move right, then climb up to the crest and easier ground.

Note: The gully immediately right of Cobalt Buttress, between it and Wedge
Buttress, was climbed at Christmas, 1996. It has been climbed several times before
by parties thinking they were climbing The Six Track Mono Blues and has been
named Turquoise Gully. The grade was given as III, but it has often been climbed
at II by bypassing the first pitch on the right.

B*oulder Problem Buttress* – 130m III. R. Cooke, A. Nisbet. 27th February, 1997.
The buttress between the broad easy gully and The Six Track Mono Blues, climbed
by grooves and turfy walls generally on the left side of the crest and finished by
a boulder problem wall.

BEINN DAMH:
Aquila Gully – 370m VI,7. A. Nisbet, J. Preston. 8th January, 1997.
Aquila Gully (Northern Highlands Vol. 1) and Boundary Gully (SMCJ 1995) are
almost certainly the same route. Although Aquila Gully was the first ascent (1979),
the name Boundary Gully is more descriptive, particularly since there is a big gully
immediately right of the summer route Aquila, taken by the following route.

The gully contained some very awkward chockstones (easier with some build-
up?) leading to a big pitch (100m). The sharp crest of Aquila on the left was climbed
with difficulty to bypass the pitch (which might have been easier?) – 40m. The gully
was regained above and climbed past a right-angle right turn to a chimney pitch
(70m). The buttress on the right was climbed (60m) to easier ground leading to the
quartzite (100m).

BEINN ALLIGIN:
Wall of the Outcry – 105m VI,8. M. E. Moran, A. Nisbet. 5th December, 1996.
Climbs the steep right wall of upper Eag Dubh, aiming for a big right-facing corner
which forms high up at the right side of a shield of rock, the left side being a left-
facing corner and well seen from the main ridge at the top of Eag Dubh. Start on
the immediate right of the entrance to the narrow upper gully between Sgurr Mhor
and Sgurr na Tuaigh (flake belay close against the wall).
1. 30m. Bridge past a good spike and awkwardly up grooves to the left. Go up to
a steeper rock tier and traverse 5m left to a flake belay.
2. 25m. Just right of the stance pull into a vertical corner with a large flake on its
right-hand side and climb it strenuously to a terrace. Move out right on turf ledges
and make thin moves back left to a bay directly beneath the big corner.
3. 35m. Make hard moves off the right side of the stance to an easement, then move
into the corner. Bridge up to a roof and from a spike, use tension to swing down to
a ledge on the right. Make a hairy mantleshelf up right again to a thin footledge.
Traverse this right for 6m and pull into a ramp which leads back left to a terrace.
4. 15m. Traverse 6m left and climb a left-trending line of flakes to the top.

LIATHACH, South Side, Coire Liath Mor:
The Tight One – 60m IV,5. I. Grimshaw, T. Hawkins. 2nd January, 1997.
Climbs the narrow cleft 20m left of Spidean's Sting, starting with an offwidth
crack, then into the fault, starting up its left side, then traversing right and ending
up a narrow chimney topped with a chockstone.

Coire na Caime:
WPC Gully – 120m II. A. Lockley, J. Moore, A. Nisbet. 11th February, 1997.

The shallow gully that runs from Gully 7 up the left side of PC Buttress to reach its crest at the final col.

BEINN EIGHE, Coire Mhic Fhearchair, Far East Wall:
Sting – VII,7. M. E. Moran, A. Nisbet. 6th January, 1997.
A sustained route by the summer line.

Eastern Ramparts:
Samurai – VII,7. A. Nisbet, J. Preston. 9th January, 1997.
Sensational and helpful as ever, perhaps VI,7. Start about 6m left of the summer route at a shallow right-facing corner with the first move gaining the top of an awkward block (same as Forgotten Warrior).
1. 20m. Climb the corner and traverse right to the cave of Samurai.
2. 30m. Climb directly out of the cave and up its fault to a steep wall below the Upper Girdle. Go up and traverse a flake on the left to gain the Girdle. Walk along the Girdle to regain the summer line.
3. 35m. The 'overhanging chimney' was climbed direct followed by the move under the 'perched block'.
4. 35m. As for summer, finishing at the square-cut notch.

Central Wall:
East-Central Ribs – V,6. J. Hubbard, A. Nisbet. 4th February, 1997.
Following the summer route except that the second tower was climbed direct but the third less direct; after the overhanging chimney, a ledge was traversed right into the top of another chimney which led up and left back to the crest.

Central Buttress:
Dusk – 65m E1. G. Latter, A. Clapperton. 17th July, 1996.
A fine finale up the final tower. Start round right of the large detached flake, beneath a smaller such feature a short way up the wall.
1 25m 5b. Climb up to just right of the flake, then head up rightwards on good edges into a slim left-facing groove. Ascend this by a fine finger-crack to belay on the ledge just above.
2 40m 5b. Continue up the open chimney/corner above, with difficult moves above a large ledge near the top. Belay a long way back on the right.
Note: The Ed. is unsure how much of this is new. The final tower is very confusing in the guide and other lines have been climbed recently. Probably Parker's and Piggott's Routes are different descriptions of the same line; Parker's may well have originally finished up Collie's Route as there seems only to be one obvious line up the crest at a suitable grade. The next guide will clarify.

West Buttress:
Junior Direct Start – 10m E3 5c. C. French, T. Prentice. 25th July, 1996.
A desperate and badly-protected start which avoids the green slime. Start left of the corner and climb steep rock to gain a prominent jutting horn of rock. Hard and unprotected moves lead right into the Junior corner.

Maelstrom – 90m HVS. A. Nisbet, G. Nisbet. 5th September, 1996.
A summer ascent of the winter route with a direct start. Start about 15m left of the mossy groove of Blood, Sweat and Frozen Tears at the next but shallower groove left.
1. 25m 4c. Climb the groove which splits into two. Take the right-hand which leads to the lower of the Girdle ledges.

2, 3. On the left is the mossy groove of winter. Much more pleasant is to go 5m right to a clean arête, climb it and return right to join the winter route at its chimney. Continue up the winter route to the top.
Grade opinions (T. Prentice): Sumo – E3 4b 6a 5b and at least **. Junior – second pitch 20m 5a. Shoot the Breeze – 5b 5a 5c ***. Turkish Delight – second pitch 5b, *.

Spidean Lochans (M. Ref. 964 600):
Two lochans are located on a shoulder on the north west side of Spidean Coire nan Clach, Beinn Eighe. The outlet from the northern one flow over a rock band and offer two 80m icefalls; Christmas Day Special III (25. 12. 96) climbs the left-hand of the pair and has a large ledge and block after about 30m. The right-hand one Whiteout, IV,4 is slightly steeper with poor rock belay potential (27. 12. 96).
    Above these is a rock band leading to open slopes and to two craggy areas leading to the summit. The right hand crag is split by a narrow gully which trend left near its top at II (25. 12. 96). A start was made up a chimney at the right end of the lower rock band though its easy to walk round it. The best gully on the left-hand section cuts up its centre and has a few rock steps in it, III (27. 12. 96). The four routes described above were soloed by B. Davison.

Sgurr nan Fhir Duibhe, North-West Face:
Approached by the Coire an Laoigh footpath, diverging to the col between Sgurr Ban and Sgurr an Fhir Duibhe. An easy traverse leads to the base of the cliffs. Well seen from the col is a smooth steep wall at the base of a ridge. Left of this ridge but hidden from the col is an easier angled but very pinnacled ridge, Ragged Muffin Ridge. This was climbed by Tom Patey at Diff. in August, 1957.

Rockhoppers Ridge – 130m III,4. C. Kempster, J. Preston, S. Snowden. 3rd March, 1997.
The ridge left of Ragged Muffin Ridge, starting with a steep wall (crux), then a chimney, huge square-topped block and easier to the top.
Note: The gully at the right end of the cliff, right of the smooth wall, finishing by the right branch, gave the above team a 100m Grade I.

Ragged Muffin Ridge – 110m IV,4. R. Callard, S. Hinshelwood, A. Nisbet. 3rd March, 1997.
Follows the crest of the ridge over several pinnacles including chimneying behind an alarmingly slender tower on pitch 3.

TORRIDON CRAGS, Creag nan Leumnach:
Cross Dressing – 20m E3 5c. I. Taylor, T. Fryer. 26th May, 1996.
Climbs the bold wall left of Warmer, Cleaner, Drier. Five metres from the top, traverse right and finish up Warmer, Cleaner, Drier.

The Vanishing Frog – 30m E5 6b. I. Taylor (unsec). 8th August, 1996.
Climbs the streaked rounded nose in the centre of the wall right of Squeezin' yer Heid. Bold and not obvious. Start up the second groove right of a wide flake-crack to gain a break. Climb the shattered wall to the next break and using hidden holds above, make a hard move rightwards round the nose. Climb the right-hand side of the noise until a move left at the top gains a ledge.

DIABAIG, The Main Cliff:
The Dominie – 35m E1 5b. G. Latter, A. Clapperton. 15th July, 1996.
On the upper right side of the wall, above the gully is an orange-coloured wall with

three vague discontinuous cracks. Approach by climbing out of the flat upper gully bed, or by one of the routes on the right side of the wall. Follow the central crack. Only the middle section presents any difficulty, with the lower section about Severe and the upper crack easing back to about Diff.

Evasion and Bogie, extended finish – HVS. G. Latter, A. Clapperton. 15th July, 1996.
2. 12m 5a. From the belay, traverse the lip of the roof above the ledge leftwards to reach an easier crack. Follow this to tree belay on the spacious grassy ledge above. (This would be best run together with pitch 1).
3. 10m 4c. Climb the short awkward corner above, moving out right to finish easily up the rib.
Note: Instead of moving out right on Evasion, the top crack of Bogie was gained by traversing left along the prominent horizontal break – E1 5b.

The Domes:
Glandular Problems – 30m E2 5b. T. Fryer, I. Taylor. April, 1996.
Climbs a pitch right of Boab's Corner pitch 2. Start 5m right of Boab's Corner and climb a thinly-cracked black wall to gain a short hanging corner. Go up the corner, then follow a curving ramp on the right. At the top of this, go right to another crack, climb this for a couple of moves, then go straight up to finish.

CREAG RUADH (Kinlochewe, M. Ref. NH 037 631):
This small crag lies on the skyline above the Slioch car park at Kinlochewe. At the first gate across the path ascend the hillside beside a fence, then up and left to the crag – 20 mins. This route takes a central line on the right-hand buttress.
Watch Ma Sheep – 10m E1 5b. C. French, F. Wolfenden. Spring, 1996.
Start at a shallow corner and swing up onto the wall to a diagonal crack. Follow this to finish left.

BEINN A' MHUINIDH, The Bonaid Dhonn:
All routes get the afternoon sun and dry very quickly. Approach from the bottom is tedious. However, approaching from the top by fixing an abseil rope to the excellent first belay on Vertigo allows a number of routes to be climbed in a day.
Dream Ticket – 70m E3***. T. Prentice, C. French. 17th July, 1996.
Fine climbing up the immaculate wall right of Vertigo (see photo Northern Highlands Vol. 1). The rock is the finest quartzite in Torridon, the climbing pleasantly sustained and quite intimidating, and the position superb. Protection is good, but spaced, and a double set of Friends up to 2 useful. Start at a large block at the base of the wall.
1. 50m 5c. Climb ledges to a prominent pair of thin cracks, then move up and right to the left end of a long overlap. Return back left into the centre of the wall and continue to a small overlap level with the top of the Vertigo flake. Pull over this, climb the crack above and follow the scoop right to belay on the right edge of the wall.
2. 20m 5b. Move back left and follow the right edge of the wall and easier ground to the top.

Balances of Fate – 70m E2**. C. French, T. Prentice. 17th July, 1996.
Another excellent route starting up the wall left of Vertigo and finishing up the steep crack directly above. Start as for Dream Ticket.
1. 30m 5b. Climb up and left below the flake crack of Vertigo. A small overlap

guards access to the wall. Pull over at the narrowest point, continue straight up the wall and follow a small slab to belay on top of the flake as for Vertigo.

2. 40m 5c. Traverse right and climb a steep, undercut crack to slabbier ground above. Follow the prominent diagonal crack through a steep bulge to an awkward exit. Follow the groove and easier ground to belay right of a large block.

Grades of Shey – 50m E1*. C. French, T. Prentice. 17th July, 1996.

Two pleasant pitches on the wall right of Safari, lead to a fine finishing corner in the left arête of the prominent recess. Start under the overhang at the end of pitch 1 of the Tallon (reached by a 50m abseil).

1. 25m 5b. Pull over the overhang 2m left of The Tallon and climb the crack and rib above to a stance.

2. 10m 5b. Move left along a large projecting block and step off on to the wall which leads to a stance in the large recess, below the corner.

3. 15m 5b. The prominent hanging corner in the arete is steeper and harder than expected.

Note: The first two pitches are similar to a line climbed by Roger Everett and Kim Kaiser in the late 1970s, but not recorded.

MEALL LOCHAN A' CHLEIRICH, Stone Valley Crags, Rum Doodle Crag:

Juniper Slab – 25m Severe 4a. R. Brown, J. R. Mackenzie. 24th July, 1996.

Immediately left of Rum Doodle Arête is a narrow red slab. Start left of the central crack and climb directly up the slab keeping left of Rum Doodle Arête.

Roman Wall – 35m Severe. J. R. Mackenzie, R. Brown. 24th July, 1996.

To the right of Rum Doodle Arête is a clean slabby wall with a central rib leading to a small tree, all on superlative rock.

1. 10m. Climb the central rib.

2. 20m. Step left on to the wall and climb upwards to a right-slanting ramp. Follow this to below a vertical wall with thin cracks and step left to take the final few metres of the arete direct (crux) to the ledge.

3. 5m. Climb the optional central crack (4b).

Chleirichal Error – 25m VS 4c/5a. R. Brown, J. R. Mackenzie. 11th August, 1996.

To the right of Roman Wall lies a gully/groove with a steep right wall. To the left of a pair of short cracks is a groove. A steep entry gains the base of a thin grass-filled groove. Step right on to the wall and climb this to step back left above the grass. Excellent rough rock to the top.

Red Wall Crag:

Bold as Brass – 25m E3 6a. J. R. Mackenzie, R. Brown. 9th May, 1996.

This is the red-coloured left bounding pillar of the wall. It gives a sustained and technical climb with the crux near the top. Gain a small ledge just left of Flaming June, step up right to below the flange, then climb it stepping left to below a thin curved crack. The crux section continues up the wall just right of the crack, then follows it to the top.

Lucky Strike – 25m HVS 5a. R. Brown, J. R. Mackenzie. 3rd May, 1996.

The most enjoyable steep route on the crag, sustained and varied. Start at a pronounced groove right of Flaming June and climb up it on smooth rock to a large spike. Stand on this and climb the seemingly blank wall up and right on hidden holds to the ledge.

Short Sharp Shock – 8m E1 5c. J. R. Mackenzie, R. Brown. 3rd May, 1996.
A steep shallow corner above the finish of Bold as Brass.

Gas Bubble Wall – 30m V. Diff. J. R. Mackenzie, R. Brown. 3rd May, 1996.
At the top of the heather rake right of Bold as Brass is a black vesicular wall. Climb
it and up a corner on the left, then step back right and climb tiered slabs to the top.
Pleasant but a bit artificial.

Stone Valley Crag:

The Beer Bottle Dilemma – 30m E3 5c. I. Taylor (unsec). August, 1996.
Start a few metres right of the second pitch of Melting Pot. Climb cracks trending
slightly rightwards to gain a ledge. Easier pleasant climbing to the top.

The Domes:

Controlled Steering – 20m VS 4c. J. R. Mackenzie, R. Brown, D. Wilby. 18th June,
1996.
Left of the thin red slab is a lower wall, increasing in height leftwards before tailing
off into the hillside. Near the left end of this wall and left of the highest point is a
pronounced V-groove above a slanting heather rake. Surmount the rake and enter
the groove via an overhang with some loose blocks. Continue to the capping roof
and move left to another groove and finish up this.

Demon Razor – 20m E3 6a. R. Brown, J. R. Mackenzie (both led). 24th July, 1996.
To the right of Controlled Steering is an overhanging wall split by a thin flake crack.
This is an excellent exercise in positive thinking! Start in the 'cave' and burn to the
ledge. Continue up the pleasant arête above.

Mellow Ambler – 30m VS 4c. D. Wilby, R. Brown, J. R. Mackenzie. 18th June,
1996.
To the right of Demon Razor there are some boulders with a grooved arete above.
Climb the groove on the left of the arete to exit right by a small tree. Continue up
the edge to rough rock and climb the right side of the topmost arete via cracks to
the crest.

The Thug – 35m E2 5c. R. Brown, J. R. Mackenzie. 9th May, 1996.
To the right of The Thin Red Line is an overhanging wall, the top of which is split
by a striking crack. Start left of the crack at a curved groove.
1. 15m 4c. Climb the groove and ease back right to a small ledge below the crack
to a semi-hanging belay.
2. 10m 5c. The crack yields to a no-frills approach and has plenty of gear with the
crux at the top.
3. 10m. Finish up the straight-forward arête.

The Lum – 70m V. Diff. R. Brown, J. R. Mackenzie. 9th June, 1996.
To the right of The Thug the crag turns a right angle which contains a vertical
chimney. Climb the fine chimney to a stance on the right below a shallow red corner
(25m). Left of the corner is an overhung crack. Surmount the bulge and follow the
crack around to the front face and follow to a terrace (20m). Either walk off
leftwards or continue up easy but pleasant rocks to the summit of the dome (25m).

Lumside Phew – 40m E2 5c. J. R. Mackenzie, R. Brown. 24th July, 1996.
To the right of The Lum is a red wall. Start directly below a shallow groove near
the left-hand end.
1. 10m 5c. Climb up the wall and groove to make the crux moves (thin) left into a
scoop. Continue to a ledge.

2. 30m 4c. Climb straight up, then left across The Lum to surmount some poised blocks, then straight up the slab to the terrace.

Questionable Crack – 65m H. Severe 4b. J. R. Mackenzie, R. Brown. 9th June, 1996.

To the right of The Lum is a red wall split by a crack at its right-hand end.

1. 25m 4b. Climb the crack to an awkward landing and then more easily to the stance below the shallow red corner.

2. 15m 4a. Climb the steep corner to the terrace.

3. 25m. Either walk off left or continue up easy but pleasant rock to the summit of the dome.

Pink Wall – 25m Diff. R. Brown, J. R. Mackenzie. 3rd May, 1996.

The upper right wall of the right-hand dome offers numerous routes up to Diff. in standard, the best line being approximately central.

RAVENS CRAG:

N. Hodgson and B. Williamson climbed four routes at V. Diff and Severe on a 10m crag about 500m north-west of Ravens Crag (sheet 19, M. Ref. 793 716). A photo was supplied.

LOCH TOLLAIDH CRAGS, Creagan Dubha (sheet 19):

This is the collection of gneiss crags overlooking Loch Tollaidh, just off the road on the south side of the Gairloch to Poolewe road a short way before the turn-off to Tollaidh Crags at Tollie Bay on Loch Maree. The hillside is named on the OS Map as Creagan Dubha but the crags are best referred to collectively as Loch Tollaidh Crags. They are reached by a 10-15 minute walk across boggy ground passing the northern end of Loch Tollaidh where there are stepping stones across the outflow, the Tollie Burn. There are a number of places to park just off the road at the northern end of the loch – don't try the track which leads down to the boats at the lochside unless you fancy grounding your car.

From the road, four main bands/escarpments can be seen running diagonally south westwards (left to right) up the slope, away from the road. The Main Band is closest to the road, with Bands 2 and 3 lying just behind. To the right of The Main Band, there is a collection of crags, The Inlet Area, most of which face the road, grouped close to a narrow inlet on the loch, the lowest of these lies just to the right of the inlet. A few routes showed signs of others having pottered about here.

THE MAIN BAND:

Closest to the road, this is the main band of crags, running from the first crag, the Eyrie Wall, away up rightwards to The Laraig Wall on the skyline, identifiable by the large block just out from its base.

THE EYRIE WALL (M. Ref. NG 8495 7828):

This is the first crag reached after crossing the outflow from the loch and walking across the flat, boggy ground. Unfortunately, there is a large eyrie sitting in the middle of the crag blocking one of the main lines and thereby preventing development of the central section. The right edge of the crag is formed by a fine 40m slab – a metal stake at the top of the slab would tend to indicate that the slab has been climbed.

The following four routes are tightly packed together at the left-hand end of the crag, up the slope, left of the eyrie.

Rushed-up – 20m HVS/E1 5a. R. and C. Anderson. 21st July, 1996.
The flaky groove at the left side of the wall.

Slowed-down – 20m E2/3 5b. R. and C. Anderson. 21st July, 1996.
Immediately right of the groove, climb the edge and continue up this to some protection before pulling round right and continuing to a thin crack which leads to the top.

Squeezed-in – 20m E4 5c. R. and C. Anderson. 22nd July, 1996.
Eliminate in the upper part and bold in the lower section. Start in a shallow recess with a crack, climb up, step right, then go up a thin crack (RP1 and Stopper1) to the jug on Boldered-out. Climb directly up a vague crackline between the routes on either side with good gear in Slowed-down.

Boldered-out – 20m E4 6a**. R. and C. Anderson. 22nd July, 1996.
The thin crack up the right side of the wall. Boulder directly to the crack at 5m, then climb this to the top.

On the section of cliff right of the eyrie there are two short, right to left-slanting cracks starting at ground level, then two grooves just before the fine 40m slab marking the right end of the cliff. Stake belay at the top of the slab.

Super Sleuth – 40m E2 5b. R. and C. Anderson. 8th August, 1996.
Climb the short left-hand crack, then step right and follow the ramp-cum-groove of Semi-Automatic all the way up right onto the edge of the crag. A slim groove on the crest leads to heathery ground, then the top.

Semi-Automatic – 40m E4 6b**. R. Anderson, D. Cuthbertson, C. Anderson. 8th August, 1996.
The right-hand crack. Start at the base of the left-hand crack and climb boldly up to the right-hand crack. Follow the crack to a ramp cum-groove and go up this to near its top. Move left to breach the bulge and continue directly above to reach heathery ground on the crest which leads to the top.

Feathering The Nest – 40m E5 6a**. R. and C. Anderson. 16th August, 1996.
This route climbs the groove just left of a short groove leading onto the slab marking the right side of the crag. Climb to the bulge (nut in dubious rock in groove – back-up Friend or large nut, high on left in obvious crack), pull up onto the right wall, then move up into the groove. Step left and climb the groove to the slab, which leads easily to the top.

THE EWE WALLS (M. Ref NG 8493 7824):
An area of slabs and walls just to the right of the Eyrie Wall, before the slope rises to The Gairloch Wall. From the top of the routes a heathery ramp leads back down rightwards to the base of The Gairloch Wall.

Ewephoria – 30m VS 4c**. R. and C. Anderson. 8th June, 1996.
The fine, dark coloured, narrow slab at the left side of the crag is climbed by a central line, protection is scant but there when required.

Ewereka – 25m E1 5c*. R. and C. Anderson. 8th June, 1996.
Around to the right is a corner with a small holly tree part way up it. This route climbs the thin crack which springs from above a small roof at the start, passing just left of the holly tree.

THE GAIRLOCH WALL (M. Ref. NG 8491 7820):
Lying just to the right, this wall is located above a slight rise in the slope, just above

some large boulders. Undercut at its base, the cliff has a vertical wall at its left side and a ramp slanting up rightwards from beneath the undercut section. The base of the crag is sheltered from the elements.

Balding Oldie – E6 6b 35m**. R. and C. Anderson. 19th May, 1996.
The left-hand line on the vertical wall at the left side of the cliff. A flake-line springs from a slanting break at half height. Stopper 1s and small wires essential. Stand on an embedded flake and climb to a good but hollow sounding hold (good RP1 deep in slot to right). Stand on the hold (sideways RP3 on left – bombproof Stopper1 in slot on right) and continue directly to the break. Gain the flakeline and a poor, tied-off PR, then make a hard move to reach a crucial nut placement in the base of a small undercut directly above, similar sized placement in horizontal slot just on right. Continue directly up the thin crack, small wires, to pull over onto easier ground leading to a belay just below the top.

El Passe – 35m E5 6a**. D. Cuthbertson, R. Anderson. 12th May, 1996.
The obvious crackline up the right side of the vertical wall, a slime streak springs from a niche at the start. Swing right into the niche, from good holds, PR and back-up nut in hold in niche, and continue up, then left to reach the break. Step right and climb the crack to easier ground leading to a belay just short of the top.

Old El Pastits – 35m E6 6b***. R. Anderson, D. Cuthbertson (both led). 11th May, 1996.
The obvious undercut crackline up the middle of the leaning wall. Pull into the crack and awkwardly place a crucial Rock 6 above the obvious slot, then continue to a point at mid-height where a span across left gains a jug and a good nut placement just above. Pull up right, then climb the crack to the top and pull over onto easy ground. Either belay here, or continue easily up left to the belay of the previous routes.

Conquistador – 35m E7 6c/7a***. D. Cuthbertson. September, 1996.
The crackline immediately to the right of Old El Pastits. Stickclip the peg and try to climb to it, then past it to a breather before tackling the vague crack in the leaning headwall.

Aging Bull – 35m E4 6b**. R. and C. Anderson. 26th May, 1996.
The thin crack which cuts through the bulge above the start of the slanting ramp. Gain the crack after a bouldery start, then follow this through the bulge and on up the groove to easy ground.

The Imposter – 35m E3 5c/6a*. R. Anderson. 26th May, 1996.
Just right of Aging Bull is a short hanging groove in the lower wall leading to the ramp and a thin crack in the headwall. Bouldery moves gain the groove and then the ramp. A good wire on the right protects the first pull onto the rock, after which each of the moves can be protected with small wires. Move up the ramp a short way, step left onto the wall and climb to easy ground. The thin crack provides some protection but the holds are on the wall to the right.

Avoidance – 35m E1 5b. R. And C. Anderson. 18th May, 1996.
Start immediately to the right of The Imposter below some jugs. Gain the jugs by bouldery moves, then move up right into the niche of Zig-Zag. Move up and left around the roof, then go right onto the edge, avoiding the block above, and climb directly to the top.

Zig-Zag – 35m HVS 5a. R. and C. Anderson. 18th September, 1995.
The right end of the crag is formed by a pleasant-looking rough slab, this route takes a line immediately to the left. Climb a short corner up left to a niche, move right and surmount the roof, then move left onto the edge and climb to the top.

Rough Slab – 35m VS 4c*. R. and C. Anderson. 18th September, 1995.
The slab at the right-hand end of the crag via a central line.

THE CURRA WALL (M. Ref. NG 8490 7815):
The extension of The Gairloch Wall is a low band of steep rock which is useful for bouldering on. There is a slabby upper tier.

RED ROCKS (M. Ref. NG 8490 7810):
Immediately right of the Curra Wall is an area of fine reddish rock, beyond which the crag merges into the hillside before rising up towards the Laraig Wall. The base of the crag is a bit boggy in places.

Crack Bush Chimney Route – 30m VS 4c. R. and C. Anderson. 17th September, 1995.
Crack and chimney at the left end of the crag, passing a holly.

Scarlatina – 30m E2/3 5b*. R. and C. Anderson. 17th September, 1995.
Bouldery moves lead directly onto a ledge just right of Crack Bush Chimney Route. Move right, then up and left to the roof. Continue up the crack above.

In The Pink – 30m E1 5b**. R. and C. Anderson. 17th September, 1995.
The obvious crack in the middle of the crag, awkward to start.

Red Faced – 30m E2 5b. R. and C. Anderson. 17th September, 1995.
The next crack just around the edge to the right leads to a finish, either up the easy wide groove, or the arête and slab.

Rouged-up – 30m E3 5c*. R. and C.Anderson. 17th September, 1995.
Line up the wall immediately right of the crack.

Flushed-out - 30m E1 5b**. R. and C.Anderson. 17th September, 1995.
The crack, groove and slab at the right end of the crag

THE LARAIG WALL (M. Ref. NG 8482 7785):
This crag, visible in profile from the road, lies higher up at the far right end of The Main Band, beyond where Red Rocks merges into the hillside. A huge shattered block lies just out from the base of the crag. Opposite this block is a small alcove, occupied by a split boulder. Routes are described from here. The left side of the small alcove forms a blunt rib with a steep slab leading to a roof on its left. There are two routes on this side wall.

Brush-Off – 25m E2 5b*. R. and C. Anderson. 13th August, 1995.
Climb up the left edge of the slab, close to heathery ledges on the left, then up a slim corner and out onto the wall to make an awkward finishing move to reach easier ground leading to the top.

Rain Drain – 25m E2 5b*. R. and C. Anderson. 13th August, 1995.
Climb the centre of the slab to the roof, move right, then out left and up to the next roof. Move out right and climb cracks to the top.

The following routes lie just to the right of the alcove.

Heave-ho – 25m E4 6a*. R. and C. Anderson. 12th August, 1995.
Climb the thin crack just right of the split block, pull through the roof and continue up the crack to the top.

Lean-to – 25m E3 5c. R. and C. Anderson. 13th August, 1995.
The leaning, cracked groove immediately right of Heave-ho is climbed steeply to easier ground and a deep crack leading to the top.

Push Over – 25m E1 5b. R. and C. Anderson. 12th August, 1995.
Just right of Lean-to is a short leaning crack whose right side forms a pedestal. Climb a short crack on the right to a holly bush, pull out left onto the pedestal and climb the groove above. Easier cracks lead to the top.

The following routes lie a short way further right. Just beyond some roofs is an attractive smooth bulging wall. The first route climbs the right side of the smooth wall.

Peek Practice – 25m E4/5 6b**. R. and C.Anderson. 13th August, 1995.
Just above ground level at the right side of the smooth wall is a small overlap, on the right of which is a short groove with a small boulder at its base. Climb the groove, then move right to an alcove and go up left with difficulty to easier ground. Go a short way up a slabby groove, climb to a recess under a roof, then pull out left through the top of this and continue to the top.

Intrusion Zone – 25m E1 5b**. R. and C. Anderson. 13th August, 1995.
Immediately to the right of Peek Practice is a reddish coloured intrusion running up the wall. Climb this, pull out left and continue above by a short groove and easier slabby ground.

The next route lies along at the right-hand end of the cliff just before some slabs where the rock merges into the hillside.

Reddy Ribbed – 25m VS 4c**. R. and C.Anderson. 13th August, 1995.
Just right of a heathery crack is a short V-groove. From the top of the groove pull out left and climb the rib to easier ground and the top.

BAND 2:
The line of crags running parallel to and about 100m behind the main band of crags, overlooking a flat boggy area – The Meadow. They can either be reached from the left side of the Eyrie Wall, or from the right side of Red Rocks. The crags and the routes are described from left to right.

SIREN SLAB (M. Ref. NG 8515 7820):
This is the obvious large, steep slab which lies at the left-hand side of this band, set back and a little higher than the rest of the crags. Buttock Buttress on Band 4 lies just behind it.

Lorelei – 35m E4 5c*. R. and C. Anderson. 16th June, 1996.
A line up the middle of the slab. Good climbing but somewhat marred by having to dodge about a bit to get gear. Start at the lowest rocks and climb up, then left to a heathery ledge beneath a short groove in the middle of the wall. Climb the groove to a good hold, small wires right and left, then run it out, up, then left and back up right to a thin break, good small wire (RP3 sized) just below break. Move across left to a break with fail-safe gear. Now, either move straight up to a diagonal crack, or go back right and up to another thin break for gear, before coming back left and up to the crack. Move up left along the crack and finish straight up.

Alternate Finish: – 5c. From the start of the diagonal crack near the top, step right and climb straight up passing some thin horizontal breaks which take gear, including a Rock 4 on its side and an RP3 in the top one.

Strip-teaser – 35m E4 5c**. R. and C. Anderson. 15th June, 1996.
The very thin right-slanting crack, right of centre on the slab. Start at the lowest rocks and climb straight up to a heathery ledge below a shallow groove/flakeline just right of Lorelei. Climb this, stepping right for gear, then go up and around the leftside of the obvious overlap to reach the thin crack which leads to a bulge just below the top. Pull out, up left to finish more easily.

Temptress – 35m HVS/E1 5b. R. and C. Anderson. 15th June, 1996.
The right-slanting crackline which leads to the right edge of the slab. Start as for Temptress and climb up and slightly right to pull into a short groove with a crack in it. Continue to the overlap, go around the right side of this and climb the crack to a finish up the easy edge of the slab.

THE CLOICHE WALL (M. Ref. NG 8510 782):
The wall some 50m to the right of Siren Slab, from which it is set slightly farther forward and lower down. The crag appears to incline to the right with slanting faults either side of it.

Pump Action – 40m E3 5c**. R. and C. Anderson. 8th June, 1996.
The obvious groove and crack which slants up rightwards.

White Fright – 40m E4 5c*. R. and C. Anderson. 8th June, 1996.
The shallow quartzy groove just to the right. Move up and boldly right into the base of the groove which leads with interest to easier ground.

BOOR BUTTRESSES (M. Ref. NG 8509 7815):
Two small but steep buttresses down the slope a short way right.

FEOIR BUTTRESS (M. Ref. NG 8508 7810):
The bigger buttress a little farther right, steep at the bottom and slabby above. The steep lower face is split by two obvious cracklines which finish beside each other.

Rock Bottom – 40m E3 5c**. R. and C. Anderson. 17th August, 1996.
The left-hand crack which springs from above a wet streak. Either finish up the slabby rib of Zeazy Top or find another easy line to the top.

Zeazy Top – 40m E3 6a**. R. and C. Anderson. 17th August, 1996.
The right-hand, z-shaped crack, then the slabby rib above.

THE THOLL WALL (M. Ref. NG 8504 7802):
This crag sits at the right-hand end of this line of crags. It lies just behind Red Rocks and is best reached by crossing the slope just beyond that crag and cutting across The Meadow to it. A tall, reddish coloured wall is cut by a number of prominent cracklines.

Buena Vista – 40m E2 5b**. R. and C. Anderson. 18th September, 1995.
The prominent vertical crackline which lies immediately right of a crackline springing from a series of soggy sods of turf.

Malpasso – 40m E3 5b**. R. and C. Anderson. 18th September, 1995.
Move up onto the ledge just to the right of Buena Vista and boldly climb the short initial wall to better holds and protection. Climb the vague crack in the wall, step right to another crack and continue to the top.

BAND 3:
This is the highest level of crags, on the left. Viewed from the road, the tops of the crags form the left-hand skyline. The crags are described from right to left.

BUTTOCK BUTTRESS (M. Ref. NG 8528 7820):

This is the right-most crag on this band, lying just below the highest point on the left-hand skyline (208m). It is best reached from Siren Slab, which it lies just above and behind. Smallish looking but clean, the crag is split into two halves by a diagonal fault, a steeper left half and a less steep right half.

The Drying Game – 20m E2 5b*. R. and C. Anderson. 25th May, 1996.
The shallow, chocolate coloured groove at the left side of the crag.

Inclement Proposal – 20m E1 5a*. R. and C. Anderson. 25th May, 1996.
The thin cracks in the wall immediately right of Fair Enough, leading to a thin slanting crack, passed on the left, at the top of the crag.

Dangerous Lesions – 20m E5 6a**. R. and C. Anderson. 25th May, 1996.
A line straight up the middle of the wall. Start at the foot of the fault. Pull left onto the wall, then gain a break beneath the left side of a small roof and pull around this to enter a shallow groove. From the top of the groove a Black Diamond Steel 5, or possibly an RP5 and then a good RP2 can be awkwardly placed on the right. Continue up, then right to good but hollow sounding holds. Above is a small triangular feature with a thin crack taking a good Stopper 1, or similar. Place this, then reach holds from where a more satisfying nut can be placed high in the crack up on the right to protect the moves up to easier ground.

CHEEKY SLAB:

Just left of Buttock Buttress is a small slab of clean rock split into two parts by a central crack. A few lines were soloed on this slab by unknown climbers on 24th July, 1996.

THE INLET AREA:

These are the crags grouped around the head of a narrow inlet on the loch. Most of the crags face directly toward the road.

THE RECESSED WALL (M. Ref. NG 8472 7796):

This wall is located just to the right of the Inlet Wall from which it is a little higher and set back a bit. Although it can be reached by scrambling rightwards up heather from beneath that crag it is best reached by following the path up from Red Rocks towards the Laraig Wall, then cutting across right and climbing up past the level section at the top of the Inlet Wall to a level section above slopes which descend to the top of the wall. Just to the west a shallow gully/ramp descends between slabby ribs to meet heathery slopes cutting back right to beneath the wall. The first route lies on the slabby rib running up the left side of the descent gully, facing up.

Descent Gully Rib – 20m Severe. R. Anderson. 24th July, 1996.
Climb a shallow groove in the lower buttress, then climb the slabby rib to the top.

The next three routes take lines up the centre of the fine wall and are described from left to right. A large boulder lies at the base of the wall.

Hollow Heart – 25m E3 5c**. R. and C. Anderson. 24th July, 1996.
The obvious central line, starting at the boulder. Make a move up a thin crack, then pull out left to flake holds and continue up to reach the left side of a ledge girdling the wall at one third height. Move up, then right to the base of a line of flaky holds and follow these to the top.

Simple Mind – 25m E3 5c**. R. and C. Anderson. 26th July, 1996.
Start as for Hollow Heart and climb straight up the thin crack to a good hold and good protection with a poor RP 3 just above. Gain the girdling ledge, move right,

then up to a junction with Hollow Heart. Move up right and climb the obvious line just right of Hollow Heart.

Tortured Soul – 25m E2/3 5c *. R. and C. Anderson. 26th July, 1996.
Start to the right of Simple Mind where a diagonal crack slants up right at the base of the crag, a black streak comes out of a small hole above. Climb to the hole, good protection, and climb the wall just to its right to reach the girdling ledge. Step left, then pull up right and climb up to the right side of a block type feature at the top of the wall just right of Simple Mind. Finish up the edge of the wall.

WEE LOCHAN CRAG (M. Ref. NG 8450 7800):
This small crag lies low down, just beyond the small inlet on Loch Tollaidh. It lies in front of the Recessed Wall and slants in the same direction as the crags in the other bands. After crossing the river, go a short way towards The Eyrie Wall, then rightwards across boggy ground and around the head of the small inlet. A short slope leads up right to where the crag becomes visible around the corner. The rocks are low to start and increase in height rightwards. The crag is in two sections, with the right portion set back a little. The start of this right section is denoted by a corner with embedded blocks at its base. A tiny lochan lies out from the base of the crag.

Left-hand Section:
Solo – 10m VS 5a. R. Anderson. 20th May, 1996.
In the centre is an obvious flakeline. Pull out right onto this and climb it to where it goes heathery, then climb thin cracks straight to top.

Duet – 10m HVS 5a*. R. Anderson, 1996.
Climb the centre of the steep wall just to the right of the flakeline.

Trio – 12m Severe. R. Anderson. 20th May, 1996.
Just right of another flakeline, easy rock slants up right, before the crag turns the corner. Climb this a short way then go straight to the top.

Right-hand Section:
This is in two parts, a left and a right, with the central area being heathery and less high. The first four routes lie on the left side of this section, all climbing to the highest point.

First Amendment – 20m VS 4c. R. and C. Anderson. 20th May, 1996.
Start just right of the embedded boulders at the foot of the corner. Climb thin cracks just right of the corner, then slant up and right to the top.

Second Charge – 20m E2 5b**. R. and C. Anderson. 20th May, 1996.
Start in the centre of the wall beneath a small curving overlap. Climb to the overlap and gain a short left slanting crack. Move left up the crack a short way, then climb directly to the top.

Third Degree – 20m E1 5a. R. and C. Anderson. 20th May, 1996.
Just right of the previous route, climb past the left side of a right slanting crack to a blunt spike, then up a thin crack. Move up left to a jutting block type feature and climb straight to the top.

Fourth Dimension – 20m HVS 5a*. R. and C. Anderson. 20th May, 1996.
Climb the right slanting crack to gain a spike, then up a short, shallow right-facing corner and on directly to the top.

The following three lines lie on the highest piece of rock on the right side of the crag.
One Up – 20m HVS 4c. R. and C. Anderson. 20th May, 1996.

Start in line with the crack in the headwall. Climb a dark streak with flaky holds for 3m, step right and continue over a small overlap and on directly to the top using the crack.

Two Down – 20m HVS 4c*. R. and C. Anderson. 20th May, 1996.
Climb straight up the middle of the wall.

Three Across – 20m HVS 4c. R. and C. Anderson. 20th May, 1996.
Gain a small overlap, pull left around this, then up and slightly left and on directly to the top.

CREAGH MHOR THOLLAIDH, Farm Crag (sheet 19, M. Ref. 859 785):
Go about 200m down the Tollie farm track (park here) and walk up the stream for about 300m to the crag, which overlooks the stream and is nice and clean, particularly Spider Corner.

Spider Corner – 30m VS 4c. N. Hodgson, B. Williamson. 15th June, 1996.
Follows the main corner system half way along the crag. Go straight up the corner passing a couple of overlaps.

Westie – 30m H. Severe 4b. N. Hodgson, B. Williamson. 15th June, 1996.
Follow the crackline left of Spider Corner round an overhang and up to slabs, which are followed to the top.

BEN LAIR:
Bat's Gash – 220m V,6. F. Bennet, J. Fisher. 2nd January, 1997.
Follow the summer route throughout. Two through-routes not described in the guide were used, the first requiring a partial undressing. Passing the chockstones on the third pitch constituted the crux (well protected). Some of the sections are so recessed they hold little snow, however a route of great character.

Dragon's Lair – 240m V,6. F. Bennet, J. Fisher. 3rd January, 1997.
The first obvious line right of Wisdom Buttress. Climb Cavity Chimney to the large snow bay – Wisdom Buttress takes the left fork. Climb the right fork in three sustained pitches, a narrow off-width section and an overhanging chockstone were avoided by moves on the right wall. Exit right at the chimney's conclusion finishing up an easy snow ridge. A good winter climb.

BEINN DEARG MOR:
Central Buttress – 240m V,5. C. Cartwright, I. Stevens. February, 1995.
A winter ascent of the summer line. Enjoyable climbing with amazing ambience, coming out virtually on the summit of Beinn Dearg Mor. The crux may be crossing from Shenavall over the burns at the head of Loch na Selga, the level of which can rise and fall rapidly later in the season.

AN TEALLACH, Glas Mheall Liath:
Rhoddies Fault – 150m III. E. W. Brunskill, H. Ellen. 28th January, 1995.
The route is situated on a north-facing crag at the bottom of the eastern spur of Glas Mheall Liath and takes the obvious icy fault line up its centre. Poor protection and belays.

LOCH BROOM (West):
The following two routes gave roadside ice, five-minute walk-in and unique views.
Dutch Courage – 150m II/III. D. Whalley, McPherson, Holland. 7th January, 1996.
GR on Sheet 20, 169 860.

1. 30m. Steep ice to ledge below ice pillar.
2. 35m. Climb pillar and up to bay.
3. 25m Scramble up the river bed, then a short pitch.
4. 35m. Two steep steps and a ramp.
5. 25m. Scramble to top and descend by the left-hand side.

Heavy Handed – 90m III. D. Whalley, Holland. 8th January, 1996.
GR on Sheet 20, 162 874. Just visible from the road, this icefall is hidden by the village of Letters. A black garage marks the starting point to walk in. Walk up to the left shoulder and traverse in via a faint path to a bay.
1. 30m. Start up thin ice and tree belay on the right.
2. 25m. Climb up more thin ice to the left of 'The Icicle', traverse past this (quite tricky) to a fallen tree belay on the right.
3. 35m. Climb 'The Icicle' direct, short-lived fun, warthog runner in turf. Continue up another short steep icefall to the top.

NORTHERN HIGHLANDS NORTH AND EAST (VOLUME TWO)

SGURR NA MUICE, North-East Face:
Swine Fever – 150m III,4. J. R. Mackenzie, G. Cullen. 24th November, 1996.
This is the leftmost of the lines on the North-East Face, being a well-pronounced gully/groove blocked by a vertical wall. It lies to the right of Piglet and can be approached either as for that route or (as on this ascent) via the lower snow ramp of Sty in the Eye. Interesting climbing which is not sustained; excellent belays.
1. 15m. Climb over a short bulge.
2. 25m. Continue up the gully/groove to the blockage.
3. 20m. Step down and traverse across the smooth left wall (crux). Continue up the groove in the arête to a flake belay.
4. 45m. Above are two grooves. Climb the left one to an inset stance.
5. 45m. Step left and climb up to a snow ramp, cross this and trend right to climb steeply up a rib which forms the left edge of a very narrow slot which runs straight up the crag.

Sty High – 190m III. G. Cullen, J. R. Mackenzie (alt.). 29th December, 1996.
A direct line up the left side of the face taking a line between Swine Fever and Sty in the Eye. Follow the left-hand couloir to the lower barrier and take the left-trending ramp as for Sty in the Eye (40m). Climb the ice bulge on the left and gain the snow ramp above. Belay at the base of the left-hand of two grooves about 12m right of the wider entrance of Swine Fever (30m). Climb up this groove, up an interesting slot and step right to belays higher up (45m). Continue up the groove to a small overhang, turned on the left to another which is turned on the right via a spike. Continue up another steepening with chockstones (45m). On the left is the final slot of Swine Fever; instead take the interesting rib to the right which has an awkward bulge (crux) and continue more easily to the top (30m). Pleasant and varied climbing which is not sustained.

Gammon Gully – 100m II. G. Cullen, J. R. Mackenzie (alt.). 29th December, 1996.
This narrow gully lies on the right of the face and well left of Pigsty Gully. Either climb up the right-hand couloir and traverse right or descend from the little col below the summit and descend the slopes to trend right across a ramp to gain a bay with short, steep groove lines. The gully lies on the left of the bay and is sometimes

bottomed by a sheet of blue ice. It can also bank up in full conditions. On this occasion the ice sheet led to the gully which gave copious ice.

STRATHCONON, Scatwell River Slabs:
Note: A. Matthewson notes that he considered The Joust (SMCJ 1994) to be nearer E1 5b, and the best route on the crag (the older routes seem to have reverted to their natural state).

Creag Dubh (Map Ref. 280 515):
This steep north-west facing valley slope has four burns that in periods of frost form discontinuous icefalls of more than 150m. A sustained moderate frost produces the most ice.
Allt Mhairi – III.
This is the burn to the left (north-east) of Creag Dubh and usually sports one good 30m ice pitch. It forms much less readily than the burns on Creag Dubh itself.

Centrefall – IV. J. Burns, S. Travers. 1986 or 1987.
In the middle of the face there are two prominent narrow streams. Centrefall takes the less prominent left-hand one over ice pitches to below the top icefall which can be seen from the road falling from the summit rocks and facing right. This gives 50m of ice with three near vertical sections, providing the crux of the route and offering excellent climbing.

Rightfall – III.
This lies just to the right and usually forms more readily. A series of icefalls of between 10m and 20m leads to the summit. A short traverse left then leads to the top icefall of Centrefall.

CREAG GLAS, West Face:
The pitch gradings for Salamander (SMCJ 1996, p79) should have read 4c 5a 4c/5a (5b) 4a 4c 4b.

FANNICHS, Carn na Criche:
Blood on the Tracks – 200m IV,6. F. Bennet, J. Fisher. 28th December, 1996.
Start between The Boundary and the left end of the crag at an obvious open chimney. Climb the chimney in two sustained pitches, mixed, to a snow bay on the left. Climb up to an overhang and climb it direct (crux) exiting right on to easier ground. Follow open slopes to the upper finishing gully.

BEINN DEARG, West Buttress:
West Buttress – IV,5. J. Currie, E. Lawson. 10th February, 1996.
Based on the summer route. Start at the base of the rib which separates the two starts of Penguin Gully, below a crack bounded on its left by a curious curl of rock.
1. 45m. Climb the crack steeply to gain the rib. Follow it to belay below an overhanging corner-crack.
2. 25m. Climb the corner-crack and crest above to below a concave wall.
3. 45m. Climb the wall just right of centre (crux), then follow the rib to its finish where the dog-leg start of Penguin Gully comes in from the right. Move right along an obvious diagonal ramp to gain the buttress proper.
4 etc. Thereafter follow the crest of the rounded buttress. 50m from the top the buttress levels and a short tower bars the way. Climb the tower by an obvious corner/groove, then continue easily to the top. The tower can also be bypassed on the right.

Windpipe – 55m V,6. J. Currie, A. Crofton. 19th February, 1996.
This route climbs the obvious chimney-fault tucked into the right-hand side of the bay where Vanishing Shelf starts. Rucksacks should not be worn.
1. 20m. Climb the fault easily until it steepens.
2. 35m. Continue up the fault and climb the squeeze chimney (crux) until below an impressive roofed niche. Exit easily out right. Abseil, move into Penguin Gully on the right, or scramble to the top.

Coire Lair:
Troubled Waters – 70m III. A. Nisbet. 27th December, 1996.
The frozen waterfall above Loch na Still at Map Ref. 292 812.

Note: The gully on the crag below Loch Prille at Map Ref. 287 813 was climbed by A. Nisbet on 27th December, 1996 but contained only one short pitch, Grade II.

Cadha Dearg:
The following routes are situated on the North West facing cliffs opposite Meall Glac an Ruighe, encountered on the right side whilst descending into Gleann a' Chadha Dheirg from the head of Coire an Lochain Sgeirich.
The following two routes are situated on the continuation cliff (Map Ref. 272 862) round the corner from the north-facing cliff containing Geddes's Gully and Captain Patience. The cliff is then split by a broad gully/slope before commencing to taper off to the right.
The Mercy Seat – 130m VII,6.
C. Cartwright, S. Campbell. 29th December, 1996.
The left hand of the two obvious ramps trending right to left, the apex of which forces a swing onto the face containing Geddes's Gully.
1. 25m. Climb the ramp on steepening turf, trending left, to belay at a short groove.
2. 25m Continue up the ramp, staying to the left, then trend right back to the main corner line leading up to a ledge cutting the right wall and an inconspicuous but good belay. The corner above and to the right is a tempting belay point but not recommended.
3. 20m. The corner above curves left to become a capping roof. Climb the ramp trending left to its apex. Make hard, airy, committing moves up and around the cap, pulling on the North face, and then up steep heathery ground before gaining a spacious ledge.
4. 30m. Climb the deep groove above, choosing the right hand option where the groove splits. Where this peters out surmount perched blocks on the edge of the buttress, pulling back on to the North West face. Easier climbing leads to a belay below the final short wall, overlooking Ruighe Ramp.
5. 30m. A series of short, turfy steps leads to the top.

Ruighe Ramp – 120m IV 4.
B. Goodlad, C. Cartwright R. Clothier. February, 1995.
The right hand of the two obvious, broad turfy ramps dominating the North West facing cliff of Cadha Dearg.
1. 2, 3 – 90m. Climb the obvious ramp in three meandering pitches to belay on the headwall overlooking the ramp.
4. Surmount headwall by devious, airy, but reasonable rocky ramps.

The next two routes are situated on the cliff (Map Ref 271 860) to the right of the broad gully/slope.

Looking Glace Gully – 50m II.
D. Harvey, A. Faulk. 29th December, 1996.
Obvious, second easiest gully right of centre of crag.

Judas Gully – 50m III.
D. Harvey, A. Faulk. 29th December, 1996.
Less obvious gully just to the right of Looking Glace Gully.

ALLADALE, Meall nam Fhuaran, NE Face:
Parasol Route – 100m III. D. J. Allan, A. Todd. 9th February, 1991.
The short right-hand icefall at the north end of the crag.

The Fhuaran Shroud – 270m V,5. D. J. Allan, B. MacKenzie. 27th December, 1993.
The obvious steep icefall and shallow gully above, up and right of Campsite Cleft and below and left of Parasol Route.

An Socach:
Summit Gully – 200m II. D. J.Allan. 7th April, 1990.
The prominent gully in the corner of the corrie and leading to the hill's summit with three ice pitches.
Smear Test – 150m VS 4c. D. J. Allan, B. Mackenzie. 23rd May, 1993.
Takes the left-hand of the two left-facing corners right of Snowdrop. Start right of Snowdrop and climb into the corner. Go up this halfway, then traverse right to the arête and on to a slabby wall. Continue above by thin slabs. Four pitches.

RHUE SEA CLIFFS:
Rhue-Rhapsody – 25m E4 6a. W. Moir, G. Latter (on sight). 21st September, 1996.
Climb grooves up the left side of the prow. Pull over an overhang and go rightwards under the massive roof, finishing up a crack on the right side of the prow.

The following routes were received, but have been climbed many times by locals, hence the names are omitted. 200m inland from the first climbing area is a clean compact crag with several obvious lines. This provides a good alternative to the sea cliffs when a high tide is running, and offers a number of routes in the easier grades. The outcrop catches the sun and has generally excellent protection. Routes are 8m long and described from left to right.
1. V. Diff. The obvious corner-crack.
2. V. Diff. Starting 1m right of Crack Wun, follow the crack past a small ledge.
3. V. Diff. The blunt arête, easier than it looks.
4. HVS 5a. Climb the centre of the wall just right of Rhue Arête.
5. VS 4c. The chossy-looking wide crack with an awkward exit.
6. VS 4c. The obvious right-slanting crackline.
7. H. Severe. Climb the slightly grubby crack right of the last route, with an exit left at the top.
8. M. Severe. Just right again, the crack and triangular pod on the broken arête.
9. E2 5c. On the right-hand side of the buttress is an obvious hanging groove above a crack, taken by Groovy. Start at the crack and follow it up and left over the arête.
10. HVS 5a. The hanging groove is easy after an awkward start.
11. HVS 5a. Follow the right-hand shallow groove, starting from the right end of the block.

BEN MOR COIGACH, Sgurr an Fhidhleir:

Castro – 180m VS. D. J. Allan, B. MacKenzie. 13th June, 1993.
The right-facing corner 70m left of The Magic Bow. Follow the obvious fault to the bottom of the corner which is mid way up the face. Climb the layback corner, 25m, 4c, crux. Continue right below overlaps. Continue up the corner via a layback up a flake etc.

Nero Gully – 250m II. D. J. Allan. 18th February, 1994.
This climb is in the small corrie one mile SE of Sgurr an Fhidhleir and is the second from the left of the four gully lines. 60m of water ice, then snow.
Note: I. Taylor sends a revised description for Nose Direct Route. There are a number of variations in the middle section which have been taken both summer and winter and it seems an unsuitable route for a pitch-by-pitch description.

STAC POLLAIDH, West Buttress:

Fear of Flying – 40m E6 6a. G. Latter, W. Moir. 22nd September, 1996.
A direct line breaking through the apex of the prominent roof at the right side of the wall. Start at the same point as Expecting to Fly, at a vertical tongue of heather. Move up to follow a flake and shallow grooves over a bulge to a small ledge beneath the roof. Follow the tiny groove using a good edge on the lip on the right to reach a good hold, then slightly right to a good flake and reasonable rest (2 PRs at foot level in diagonal break on left). Shuffle left and climb direct above the PR's past small sidepulls (RP #3 3m above PRs) to good rounded holds. Traverse diagonally left on rounded holds to finish up an easy crack.

No. 2 Buttress, Upper Buttress:

Pretty Pollaidh – 35m HVS 5a. R. McAllister, D. McGimpsey, A. Fraser. 14th May, 1996.
At the left side of this buttress is a wide chimney, the route. It is better than it looks, with some good, if thrutchy climbing.

REIFF, Stone Pig Cliff:

Clatterbridge – 20m E5 6b. P. Tattersall. 17th May,1996.
The smooth black concave wall right of Strongbow. Start right of centre of the wall below a ragged crack. Climb easily to a large ledge (which can be reached by abseil at high tide). Climb the ragged crack to a horizontal break, move up and left to the next horizontal break. Tricky moves gain the right-hand end of a higher break, move slightly left (small Friends), then direct past two more breaks to reach the top.

POINT OF STOER (Map Ref. NC 023 356):

The prominent cliff clearly visible 600m north of the Old Man. The cliff and more particular its neighbours are inhabited by a thriving seabird population. The Great Corner is less affected (by fulmars), but Haramosh is only really climbable outwith the nesting season.
Descent: Make a 45m abseil from block at top of The Great Corner to large platform just above the high tide mark.

The Great Corner – 50m Severe. P. and M. Ross. 1995.
Gain the main corner by the obvious diagonal left-slanting line of small corners on the right (25m). The corner (25m).

Direct Start – 25m E1 5b. G. Latter, C. Murray. 14th June, 1996.
Start under the prominent left-slanting V-groove left of the original start, (halfway down the slabby ramp leading to the base of Haramosh). Awkwardly up the groove

to exit left onto ledge by a diagonal crack. More easily up rightwards to belay at the base of the main corner. Useful to avoid fulmars on the lower pitch.

Haramosh – 55m MVS P. and M. Ross. 1995.
A great little route taking the slabby left-trending corner 12m left of The Great Corner. Descend the slabby ramp to a lower platform at the base of the corner.
1 35m 4b. Follow the corner to a ledge below some roofs.
2 20m 4c. Make 'a very exposed scary looking traverse' right under the roof. Right of the roof go up a little groove and traverse back left above the belay, then direct for 3m (past fulmar's nest) to finish.

BEN KLIBRECK, North-East Face of Creag an Lochain:
Crampon Cleft – 200m II. D. J. Allan. 4th February, 1996.
The right branch of the Y-shaped cleft on the left side of the corrie. 150m of water ice, then snow.

The Breck – 200m III,4. D. J. Allan, B. MacKenzie. 31st December, 1992.
The prominent gully in the corrie centre and with a cave halfway up.

Don's Downfall – 250m IV,4. D. J.Allan, G. Cumming. 24th February, 1994.
The steep left-facing corner and icefall right of The Breck.

Route 3 – 250m III. B. MacKenzie, G. Cumming. 3rd January, 1994.
The shallow right-facing corner and buttress right of Don's Downfall and left of Anniversary Gully.

Anniversary Gully – 250m II. D. J. Allan, B. MacKenzie. 31st December, 1993.
The obvious gully at the right side of the corrie.

West Face:
The Fox – 100m III,5. N. Stevenson, N. Wilson. 3rd February, 1996.
A winter line on Eyrie Buttress. Start at an obvious stepped chimney in the centre of the lowest rocks. Climb the chimney (crux). Follow the crest above in three pitches to the top.

CREAG AN SGRIODAIN (Sheet 15 Map Ref. 351 341):
This interesting crag lies close to the east end of Loch More in Sutherland and a five-minute walk north from the A838, which has limited parking in laybys opposite the crag. Despite a rather vegetated air the crag is both bigger and better than it looks, having much clean rock lower down with heather ledges higher up but clean rock in between. Some of the routes are well worth climbing being in the sun for most of the day and very quick drying. It is composed of a very compact schist which is curiously eroded into shallow pockets and horizontal breaks. The climbing is mostly on flat or incut holds giving routes which are much easier than their appearance from below would suggest. Protection is often scanty or well spaced and mostly limited to camming devices. Descents are to the right. The routes are described from left to right.

Western Front – 100m HVS*. J. R. Mackenzie, R. Brown (alt.). 17th September, 1996.
The crag is highest to the left and presents an apparent edge. To the right is a tree-filled gully/groove. Between the two a slim ramp cuts up the lower rocks. Start at a vertical wall with a prominent hold below the ramp and beneath a clean sweep of slabs above.
1. 40m 5b. The problem start is to get established on the slab above the prominent

hold (crux). Continue straight up the fine slab which gives good delicate climbing to gain the ramp. Climb this to the top and then up more vegetated rock to belay just right of a bay with small trees.

2. 25m 5a. Continue into the bay and take the thin slabby ramp up right to gain the tree-filled gully and tree belay. A serious pitch.

3. 35m 4a. Traverse out on to the right wall from the gully and climb the clean rippled slab heading straight up to a headwall. The headwall is taken steeply and slightly to the left in an exposed position on good holds.

Friends Essential – 85m E1*. J. R. Mackenzie, R. Brown (alt.). 29th August, 1996.
The best feature on the crag is a pronounced silvery rib on the right of the crag and at its lowest point. Start on the edge immediately left of a recessed scoop.

1. 25m 5a. Climb the edge to trend back right above the scoop towards a small platform, old peg runner, vital Friend 1 below. Step back left round a rib and climb the unprotected crux slab to a patch of heather below a small tree.

2. 35m 4b. Step right on to the rib and climb up a crack to an easing on the edge before climbing the steep lichenous edge on good flat holds to a final clean slab and belays above by a flake.

3. 25m. Continue up the much easier rib above which avoids heather.

Absent Friends – 70m VS. J. R. Mackenzie, R. Brown (alt). 12th September, 1996.
Start a couple of metres right of the toe of the rib.

1. 45m 4c. Climb up to a short vertical crack. Continue on good rock keeping near the left edge of the rib to meet a heather mantle. Continue up on rock and lichen to gain the edge and clean slab of Friends Essential and belay beside the flake.

2. 25m. Finish as for Friends Essential.

To the right is an overhang-topped bay with a steep clean rib on the right with a beak-like overhang high up. The holds here are incut and the routes more strenuous and better protected, giving exhilarating climbing on rock which is easier than it looks.

Predator – 40m VS**. R. Brown, J. R. Mackenzie (alt.). 12th September, 1996.
An excellent climb that has a most fierce appearance. Start at the back of the grassy bay.

1. 20m 4c. Traverse right on a heather ledge and climb the fine white slab to the overhanging headwall. Step left to a block and surmount this to a curved crack. Traverse back right (crux) to the lip of the beak in a great position.

2. 20m 4a. Step right and climb the exposed arête on excellent holds.

Raptor – 55m E2*. J. R. Mackenzie, R. Brown (alt). 12th September, 1996.
Start at the foot of the grassy bay to the right of Predator below a short overhanging chimney.

1. 35m 5c. Climb the chimney on gigantic holds to gain the white slab. Climb the slab to the headwall. Step right to below a thin crack and climb the overhanging wall to its right to a difficult mantle on to the floor of the beak.

2. 20m 4a. Continue up the overhang above and finish as for Predator.

Scavenger – 60m E1**. R. Brown, J. R. Mackenzie (alt.). 17th September, 1996.
Another good climb taking in the best positions.

1. 35m 5b. Climb Raptor to the headwall but instead of climbing the wall, move up right into a scoop to the right of the beak (crux). Continue up the groove to belay on the floor of the beak.

2. 25m 5b. Step left and climb a wall to a loose ledge and traverse left (care with

loose blocks) to below the roof with a hanging corner above. Climb up to and over the roof on sound rock in a tremendous position.

CREAG AN FHITHICH (near Kinlochbervie; Map Ref. NC 258 538):

Gaff – 25m HVS 5a. N. Wilson, N. Stevenson. 27th June, 1996.
Climbs the prominent diagonal crack in the grey wall at the left end of the crag. Start at a steep groove right of the crack. Climb the groove, then the crack to finish left of the vegetated niche at the top.

Gropist's Boulevard – 30m E2 5c. Climbs the obvious right to left diagonal line across the steep central red wall. Start right of the obvious black swirl and follow the fault to its end. Belay on vegetated ground above. Low in its grade.

EILEAN NA H-AITEAG:

Swim Two Birds – 25m VS 4c. S. Campbell, N. Wilson. April, 1995.
Start as for Pebble Dash. Traverse left below the roof; continue up a corner to a ledge. Step left and finish by a short steep crack. For the full experience, observe that the tide has come in, abandon all climbing gear and swim ashore.

SHEIGRA, First Geo:

Turning left at the bottom of the descent is a small steep red buttress (containing Second Option – VS) and the following two routes.
Wind Frazzled – 10m E3 6a. I. Taylor, T. Fryer. 13th June, 1996.
Start just left of a large white boulder and climb a line through a number of roofs, finishing with an awkward pull out left.
Note: Here and Now (1996 SMCJ, p 82) has been reconsidered as E6 6b (not E5).
Short and Crappy – 10m E2 5c. T. Fryer, I. Taylor. 13th June, 1996.
Start just right of the white boulder and climb a groove, keeping to its left side.

Second Geo:

Dolphins and Whales – 30m E4 6a. G. Latter, P.T horburn. 16th June, 1996.
The pocket-infested wall above the slabby corner of Shark Crack. Belay higher up the slabby lower ramp of Shark Crack, beneath the centre of the wall. Follow a line of huge pockets diagonally leftwards to a break running across the centre of the wall. Continue up in the same line to a huge pocket just right of the arête. Move up to a good finger pocket, then head out rightwards to a good vertical slot. Directly above on better holds to a sloping finish. Many large friends useful. The final short crux wall could be avoided by escaping up the left side of the arête, giving a superb E2 5b.

Treasure Island Wall (From right to left):

Pieces I've Ate – 35m E3 5c. G. Latter, C. Murray. 13th June, 1996.
Start from near the left end of a tapering reddish ledge just above the high tide line, opposite the north end of the long rocky ridge that forms a narrow turbulent inlet along the base of the right side of the crag. (Spike belay, or nut belay 5m up and R if tide high). Climb a line of pockets just right of the prominent thin crack to some sharp pockets on the right. Move hard left to better holds, then direct to a small ledge. Continue much more easily in a fine position up the rib midway between two shallow grooves above.

Billy Bones – 55m VS 4b. G. Latter (solo). 13th June, 1996.
Continuing farther left is a large low ledge system which peters out.
1. 30m. Traverse diagonally left then up on huge pockets to a steepening near the

top. Step left and up to a ledge. Continue up the shorter right-most of two black corners to a large ledge above.

2. There is a choice of lines to finish, with the best looking a quartz crack in the slab.

Long John Silver – 45m E2. G. Latter, K. Martin. 16th June, 1996.

Start from the left end of a lower, narrower ledge, beneath a flake system just left of a thin crack system (often wet). A sparsely-protected pitch.

1. 25m 5b. Up the flakes and good pockets to good incut holds in the tiny left-slanting ramp. Move slightly right and up to large ledge.

2. 10m. Scramble up right to below a small wall.

3. 10m 4c. Climb on good holds near the right side of the wall, past a spike on the right near the top.

CREAG RIABHACH:

Jackercrack – 165m E1. N. Stevenson, N. Wilson. 19th August, 1995.

An entertaining route for the traditionalist involving chimneys and off-widths. Used on pitch 5 were a Camalot 4, a car jack (Halford's Big Jumbo) and large hexes (9,10,11). Start 20m left of the central bay at a dirty chimney with a parallel left-facing corner 5m to its left.

1. 25m 5b. Climb the left-facing corner. Exit left below an overlap and up a rib to belay in a grassy niche.

2. 20m 4b. Climb the corner behind the belay, then scramble across a terrace to belay below an open chimney.

3. 20m 4c. Climb the excellent chimney to a good stance.

4. 25m 5a. Climb the narrowing chimney above, through the roof to a good ledge.

5. 30m 5b. Climb the widening corner crack to grovel on to a grass ledge at its top. Escape out right. Climb up leftwards past a small roof to belay.

6. 45m 4a. Corners and slabs above lead to the top.

FOINAVEN, Creag Dubh:

Gully of the Dogs – III. S. Campbell, N. Stevenson, N. Wilson. 31st December, 1996.

The huge gully left of NE Buttress, splitting the crag. Numerous short pitches, including a cave pitch.

Creag Coire na Lice (Map Ref. 330 491):

Original Route – 80m VS 4c. N. Stevenson, N. Wilson. 24th June, 1996.

Climbs a chimney line towards the left end of the terrace, left of a huge wet dripping area. As seen from the lochan at Map Ref. 330 493.

1. 45m. Start below the prominent chimney-slot at the top of the crag. Aim for this via a rib, groove and short left traverse. Belay in the base of the chimney.

2. 35m. Climb the chimney to the upper terrace. Escape by scrambling up right.

CREAG NA FAOILINN:

God Slot – 170m H. Severe. N. Joss, J. Walker, N. Wilson. June, 1995.

To the left of Monkey Gull is an obvious deep slot in an area of multi-coloured rock. Climb loose rock, vegetation, bluebells etc. to this slot. Slither up the slot (crux). Continue upwards to easier ground.

CREAG SHOMHAIRLE:

The Flying Fensman – 100m E2. J. L. Bermudez, N. Wilson. June, 1995.

Start beneath an obvious cave 50m right of Harrier.

1. 35m. Climb the rib to the left of a grassy ramp to the foot of a small wall. Climb to belay 5m below and left of a large cave.
2. 30m 5c. Make hard moves leftwards over the wall and on up a slab to a small cave. Exit the right end of this cave to reach a spike. Stand on this and make thin moves on to and up the small slab above. Climb a short groove and move rightwards and climb another groove, awkward and sustained.
3. 35m 4c. Continue up slabs, climbing a steep crack, to a tree belay at the start of easy ground. Abseil, or climb the jungle above (150m).

The Black Crack – 75m E1. J. L. Bermudez, N. Wilson. June, 1995.
Well to the right of The Flying Fensman is an obvious slanting crack.
1. 25m 5a. Climb the crack to before it trends left.
2. 25m 5b. Continue up the crack/chimney to slabs.
3. 25m 4c. Traverse left over the slabs, then up into the forest. Abseil off.

BEN LOYAL, Sgor Chaonasaid, North Face:
The Great Game – 300m V,5. N. Stevenson, N. Wilson. 4th February, 1996.
A direct line. Start by following the line of a stream issuing from a large gully in the centre of the face. Follow this, then break out left to gain the base of the rocks. Start near the centre of these overlapping slabs at a large spike below right-trending turf ramps.
1. Climb a zigzag line through the slabs for 30m to a belay at an undercut groove.
2. Traverse up and right to the skyline, then follow easy mixed ground into the central depression below the headwall. Belay below and left of a prominent left-facing corner.
3. Climb into the corner, then back left to a parallel groove. Go up this to exit right and finish straight up.

BEINN CEANNABEINNE:
In the Land of Mince and Tatties – 30m E2 5c. I. Taylor, T. Fryer. 14th June, 1996.
At the right-hand side of the crag is a discontinuous crackline. Climb brittle pink rock to gain the crackline and follow it to the top with minor deviations.

CREAG ARNABOLL (Sheet 9, Map Ref. 461 596):
Thin Boy – 25m VS 4c. S. Myles, N. Wilson. June, 1995.
Climb the obvious open-book corner, traverse right across the wall below the roof and finish up the arête.

Lightning Crack – 20m VS 5a. J. L. Bermudez, N. Wilson. June, 1995.
About 8m right of Thin Boy is an obvious jagged crack. Not sustained.

SKERRAY SEA CLIFFS (Sheet 10, Map Ref. 669 632):
These crags lie to the east of Skerray. Park up a small side road, on the bend of the road, just beyond a gate. The climbing is in three main areas, all lying to the NE. Walking over the brow of the hill to the NE, the first area reached is a geo with a smooth slabby east-facing wall. The routes are as follows:
Unnamed – 30m H. Severe 4b. N. Wilson. June, 1987.
Starting from the high tide mark, climb the cleanest area of rock.

Unnamed – 30m H. Severe 4b. R. Wild, N. Wilson. 1985.
There is a broken scrappy corner halfway along the slab. Climb the slab to its left. Access by abseil.

Unnamed – 30m VS 4b. R. Wild, N. Wilson. 1985.
Climb the slab to the right of the corner over a steepening at one third height. Access by abseil.

The next area reached is a grassy prow with the remains of a wall visible at the neck of an isthmus. The prow contains a large east-facing red cliff, with a prominent grassy cone at the base. Access either by scrambling down a stream to the east, or abseiling off the in situ peg set in a boulder well back from the cliff edge (placed in 1992), or use the wooden stake.

Rumblefish – 45m VS 4c. A. Forsyth, N. Wilson. April, 1992.
Just to the left of the base of the grassy cone is an obvious slot. Climb this and continuation grooves, slanting left, before breaking out right at half height.

Asthedaygo Zawn – 30m E1 5a. S. Campbell, J. Walker, N. Wilson. April, 1992.
From the top of the grassy cone, pick a line trending slightly left to the top.

Walking farther east, one comes to a picturesque area bounded on the west by a narrow ridge with a small sea arch, and on the east by a larger promontory, also with a sea arch. Most of the routes are in this area (plan provided). Routes described NW to SE, from fin tip to inland. Access by abseil, except the first route.

Unnamed – 15m Diff. N. Joss, J. Walker. August, 1996.
Climb the east face of the obvious fin.

Wee Arête – 20m H. Severe. A. Forsyth, N. Wilson. April, 1992.
Climb the slabby arête at the start of the main section of the cliff.

Angens Corner – 20m HVS 5a. A. Forsyth, N. Wilson. April, 1992.
The corner to the left of the previous route.

Whale Arête – 20m VS 4c. A. Forsyth, N. Wilson. April, 1992.
Climb the arête to the left, delicate at first.

Monks in the Gym – 25m HVS 5a. S. Campbell, J. Walker, N. Wilson. September, 1992.
The pink wall immediately to the left of the previous line gives a tremendous route.

Wall of Attrition – 25m E2 5b. J. L. Bermudez, N. Wilson. April, 1995.
Start as for the following route, then swing across the roof to the right, utilising a small spike, and continue up the steep wall above.

Arch – 25m Diff. S. Campbell, J. Walker, N. Wilson. September, 1992.
Climb the obvious left-slanting grooves to finish above the arch.

Cradle Snatcher – 15m Severe. Same party as for Arch.
The corner to the south of the arch.

Native Tongue – 15m HVS 5a. As above.
The thin corner-crack to the left. Excellent.

Farther SE is an east-facing smooth cliff with a chimney towards its NW end. Again, access by abseil. Next four routes by S. Campbell, J. Walker, N. Wilson in September, 1992.

Unnamed – 25m HVS 5a.
Lies just to the right of the chimney.

Unnamed – 25m HVS 5a.
Just left of the chimney.

Unnamed – 25m Severe.
Climb the easier area of rock.

Unnamed – 25m E1 5b.
The smooth wall to the left of the previous route, crux at one third height.

Farther east, the rock is less friendly. There is a pink and black streaky wall facing west. The smooth corner at its left end gives the following route. the best here. The pink slab to the left of the east sea arch gives Pink Slab, 25m, V.Diff, by S.C., J.W., N.W., Sept 1992.

Ishmael – 35m E2 5c. N. Stevenson, N. Wilson. 27th August, 1995.
A superb sustained pitch up the huge corner in the prow of the buttress. Climb the corner to the capping overhangs. Move right and up a loose groove to finish. Large selection of micro wires essential.

ORKNEY Mainland, Castle of Yesnaby:
Yes Please – 25m E3 6a. M. Fowler, J. Freeman-Attwood, C. Jones. 19th July, 1996.
The route takes the flying finger crack in the seaward edge of the stack. Start from a sloping ledge at the seaward end. A very fine pitch. Start on the right-hand side. Move up and swing round to the left-hand side on a good hold (poor peg runner). Climb boldly up right to a resting place on the arête. Follow the strenuous finger crack on excellent rock through an overhang and up a final overhanging hand jamming crack.

HOY, St. John's Head:
M. Fowler and C. Jones note a free and one-day ascent of Original Route on 15th July, 1996. There was one pitch of 6a.

Rora Head:
Action Replay – 55m E3. C. Jones, M. Fowler. 16th July, 1996.
Takes the front face of the buttress just round the corner from Rosamund's Birthday. Approach as for Rosamund's Birthday and walk easily round the corner. Start just right of the arête.
1. 20m 4c. Climb sandy corners and breaks to the right of the arête, then make an awkward traverse right to the base of a groove which marks the right-hand side of a black bulge.
2. 20m 5c. Climb the groove and its capstone. Move up to flakes on the steep wall above (rest point) and then climb diagonally left to reach a ledge at the foot of another groove.
3. 15m 5b. Up the groove to the top.

Roarer – 40m E1. M. Fowler, C. Jones. 16th July, 1996.
Takes the right-hand prominent crackline in the east-facing wall of Gully 3. Approach by abseiling down the gully to a line of ledges leading out to the foot of the crack.
1. 10m. Traverse the ledge system leftwards to belay where it ends.
2. 30m 5b. Step up and hand traverse leftwards for 3m to gain the crack. Follow it to the top. A good pitch.

The Berry:
Beri beri – 220m XS. M. Fowler, C. Jones (alt.). 17th July, 1996.
The route lies up the huge red wall which forms the skyline edge of The Berry when viewed from the clifftop above The Needle. The approach given is that taken by the first ascentionists and is only possible for a couple of hours either side of low tide. Abseil directly into the sea from an stake (in situ) and swim across the narrow geo

to ledges on the far side (as for The Needle). Continue traversing at greasy 5b to reach exposed boulders. On the far side more greasy 5b leads to tunnels leading through the next buttress. Continue until an awkward diagonal abseil from a poor peg (in situ) is necessary to gain exposed boulders. Walk through the arch/tunnel to gain the next bay. The route is now clearly visible. On the far side of the bay a surprise geo cuts deeply back into the cliff and necessitates a 25m swim to gain ledges which lead easily to beneath the route. Scramble up to the start of a crackline just right of the left-bounding arête.

1. 25m. Climb up through an awkward overhang to a ledge beneath large projecting plates of crenellated rock.

2. 25m. Tackle the difficult overhangs above via the right-hand weakness. Move back left and continue up the main fault line to more overhangs. Traverse 5m right to belay.

3. 25m. Move up right from the belay, traverse right and break through a further band of overhangs to gain a grass ledge.

4. 25m. Make a rising traverse rightwards across slabs and climb a short awkward corner forming the left side of a prominent block. Belay on the block.

5. 25m. Steep pulls above the belay lead to ledges. Climb up and left to belay directly beneath a prominent overhanging corner capped by a bomb-bay chimney (this is about 15m right of an obvious crackline close to the arête).

6. 10m. Climb up to and aid (about 4 points) a short overhanging red bulge to gain the foot of the corner proper.

7. 25m. Climb the corner to the seriously overhanging upper section (leader used some aid to rest/clean – second free climbed). Use 3-4 points of aid, the last one being a very fortuitously-positioned natural chockstone, to gain the outer edge of the bomb-bay chimney which leads quickly to a stance.

8. 10m. Climb easily up right to the foot of a prominent grey corner.

9. 30m. Up the corner to the roof, then traverse left across the unprotected wall to a small ledge. Make a series of strenuous moves to reach a ledge.

10. 20m. Move back right into the grey groove and follow this to the top.

CAIRNGORMS

LOCHNAGAR, Central Buttress:
White Wizard – 120m V,6. S. Richardson, S. Venables. 29th November, 1996.
A worthwhile mixed climb to the right of Sciolist, finishing up the fine hanging V-groove on the left edge of the square-topped tower just below the pinnacles on Central Buttress. Start at the foot of Shallow Gully.

1. 45m. Move up for 10m, trend right along a narrow ramp and continue in the same line up turf and snow to a stance below the left of two steep fault lines, about 15m left of Shallow Gully.

2. 45m. Climb a short steep groove and continue over a steep bulge. Trend up and right over easier ground to the foot of the square-topped tower.

3. 30m. Climb the V-groove on the tower's left edge, and pull over the capping roof on the left. A sustained pitch in an excellent position. Continue up Central Buttress to the plateau.

Shadow Buttress A:
Doldrum – 75m VI,7. B. S. Findlay, G. S. Strange. 27th December, 1996.
The right-hand of the three groove lines on the lower buttress. Go up short steep walls to a ledge with good belay cracks on the right (20m). Climb awkwardly to gain

a large pointed flake in the left-facing corner. Continue up the corner and make a hard turfy exit out left to reach and climb a ramp to belay right of the shallow continuation groove (25m). Traverse right, climb the narrow chimney of Vortex, then go up left to another ramp and the Spiral Terrace (30m).

Note: An ascent of Shadow Buttress B by starting up Raeburn's Groove, then taking a diagonal line right to join Bell's Route at its crux moves, was thought to be the most aesthetic line at V,6 by J. Currie and G. Robertson, February 1997.

Black Spout Pinnacle:

The Extremist – 40m E5. W. Moir, P. Allen, J. Lines. 16th June, 1996.

Start just right of Nihilist Direct Start.

1. 18m 6b. Climb an awkward corner/ramp, then make hard moves up and right to gain the obvious niche. Continue up the steep crackline to belay above the overhanging wall.

2. 22m 5b. Continue in the same line up twin cracks veering leftwards to join, and finish up, the final corner of An Saobh-Chreideach.

Steep Frowning Glories – 155m E5/6. W. Moir, N. Morrison (alt. on sight). 21st July, 1996.

Start 5m up from Black Spout Wall.

1. 14m 5c. Climb a crackline up a pillar (just left of a shallow corner) to a ledge.

2. 18m 5c. Continue up the crackline to a roof. Go left under the roof and pull out to ledges leading left to the Black Spout Wall belay.

3. 18m 6b. Go back right along the ledge and climb cracks up rightwards, gaining the pedestal beneath the roof-crack from the right. Climb the roof-crack, belaying just above (full set of Friends up to 4 desirable).

4. 45m 5c. Climb the continuation crack and corner just left of the belay and continue up to join Black Spout Wall at the slabby shelves, moving right to gain the arête which is climbed to belay beneath the gable-end wall.

5 and 6. 25m 5c, 35m. As for Black Spout Wall to the Pinnacle crest.

Note: The Existentialist was repeated by N. Morrison, grade confirmed and thought outstanding despite a persistent wet streak in the initial groove.

The Stack:

The Undertaker – 115m VII,7. C. Cartwright, S. Richardson. 10th November, 1996.

A superb natural line, taking a left to right rising traverse across The Stack with a sensational finish up the right edge of the buttress. Start in Black Spout Left Branch, about 10m below the start of Crumbling Cranny, where a horizontal shelf cuts across the impending right wall of the gully.

1. 40m. Follow the shelf for 10m to a steep step. Climb this and continue traversing right to a stance on the edge of the buttress directly above the fork in the Black Spout.

2. 15m. Climb the line of cracks on the right to join The Stack at the 'alcove above the jammed boulders'.

3. 40m. Step down 3m and gain the lower of two traverse lines. Follow this for 15m to steep left-facing corner. Climb this to an exit on a slab, then move up and diagonally right to the cave belay of Torquing Corpse.

4. 20m. Move right up a curving shelf, transfer to an upper shelf to reach a small exposed niche on the right edge of the buttress. Move steeply up and left (crux – bold and wild) to reach a turfy groove which leads to the top.

Black Spout Buttress:

Queue Jump – 80m IV,5. G. S. Strange, B. S. Findlay. 10th November, 1996.
A variation start to Black Spout Buttress on the side wall opposite the Black Spout Pinnacle. Go up an obvious easy ramp alongside the Black Spout, then climb up and slightly left following short walls and narrow ramps to gain the crest about 25m below the level section of the normal route.

The Stuic:

New Boot Groove – 90m III,4. J. Ashbridge, S. Richardson. 19th January, 1997.
Start just right of The Stooee Chimney and follow the line of turfy grooves with several steep steps to easier ground and the top.

Bathtime Buttress – 70m II. J. Ashbridge, S. Richardson. 8th December, 1996.
The buttress just left of centre on the north-east face of The Stuic. Start up a short groove left of a prominent 30m pillar, then move right and up to reach the crest and the top.

Plug Groove – 70m III. C. Cartwright, S. Richardson. 12th January, 1997.
The icy depression in the centre of the north-east face. Climb a groove on the left side of the depression to a belay on the left (40m) and continue up easier ground on the right to the top.

CREAG AN DUBH LOCH, Central Gully Wall, Frontal Face, 'The Buff Slabs':

The following routes lie in the area of clean rock between Dragonfly and Caterpillar Crack. All give excellent, if bold climbing, finishing on The Caterpillar. All follow faint cracklines and are most easily described going right to left from the base of Caterpillar Crack. Another useful and interesting point of reference is the large arch or hole at the base of the cliff, formed by a huge exfoliating flake. Until an abseil point is established, Stark and Naked require an exit up and right into False Gully.

The Holiday Boys – 30m E3 5c *. N. Morrison, N. Ritchie. 15th July, 1996.
The faint rightmost crackline, reaching Caterpillar Crack just below the first rock section, is climbed in its entirety. Runners (RPs) appear just when you really need them. Descend Caterpillar Crack. Climbed on sight.

Naked – 50m E4 5c**. N. Morrison, N. Ritchie. 16th July,1996.
The next line left, starting right of the hole, passing the right side of a steeper red wall and finishing up a cracked red headwall. The crackline is followed with moves up a slab on the right to gain the base of a steepening (a traverse left and step down to a lower slab provides a good runner). Climb the steepening using a hollow hold and move boldly up left to cracks and a left-slanting ramp. A short corner (Friend 0 on left at the top) and crack in the headwall lead to The Caterpillar. Cleaned on abseil.

Stark – 100m E3*. N. Morrison, J. Wilson. 27th July, 1996.
This route is based on the twin crackline/seam starting at the left side of the hole and passing the left-hand side of the steeper red wall. Start 5m left of the hole at a small red corner.
1. 20m 5b. Climb the corner on to a bold rippled slab, then cracks on the right until a traverse right leads to a belay below the twin cracks.
2. 30m 5c. Climb the twin cracks, initially up a corner, to bolder moves on to the slab above. Belay below the upper wall; an awkward step up is required to place gear for his. A superb pitch.

3. 50m 5b. Step left from the belay, then move up to follow the junction of the slab and wall to a nose (as for The Prowl). Go up the nose and corner above to gain a belay on The Caterpillar.

Climbed on sight, the obvious direct start awaits a lightweight team while a true finish requires drier conditions and the attentions of a scrubber.

North-West Gully Buttress:
Baal – 50m E4. W. Moir, J. Lines (alt.). 15th July, 1996.
A direct line starting as for Jezebel.
1. 10m 5c. Climb jugs rightwards through the overhanging wall, as for Jezebel.
2. 20m 6a. Climb Jezebel cracks direct with a final move up and right from the top of the left-hand crack to reach a good break. Traverse left to belay in the big corner.
3. 20m 6a. Climb the thin crackline up the arête above and the continuation flake curving right on the the bare slab-arête which leads to a belay. Easy to the top.

Forte Declivite – 55m E5. W. Moir, N. Morrison, J. Wilson. 27th July, 1996.
A quick-drying direct line through the Sous Les Toits buttress. Scramble up the first pitch of The Caterpillar to belay by a dark seep patch.
1. 30m 6b. Go over the bulge and climb the right-slanting corner to join Sous Les Toits. Move left up twin cracks, then pull out right on to a shelf beneath the big A-shaped roof. Climb the roof, going up to its apex and pulling out left. Go across the slab rightwards to gain a layaway hold at the base of the groove. Make bold moves up into the groove and continue to belay at a good slot below some flakes.
2. 25m 4c. Go up the flakes to a heather ledge. Step left and climb twin slabby cracks to belay at the top right end of the buttress.
Note: From D. Wright. The original winter ascent of Pink Elephant (SMCJ 1994, p483) is to be renamed Chuchulain in honour of the late Norman Keir.
Note: From N. Morrison. Baal repeated and thought to be E5 due to the nasty ledge waiting below the crux on the second pitch. Jezebel is normally climbed in three pitches to avoid rope drag, the first being to the belay at the base of Late Night Final corner. The Crowd on the Diamond Slab should be 6b for pitch 1. Howff Dweller climbs a right-facing corner, not left as described in the Guide.

EAGLE'S ROCK:
Numbod – 80m III,5. G. Robertson (unsec). 2nd January, 1997.
A good, but highly escapable, route following the four-tiered icefall immediately right of Green Gully, approximating to the line of Nimrod. The second tier is the steepest, a short free-standing finger of ice.

DRIESH, Winter Corrie:
The Vice Squad – 150m V,6. P. Thorburn, A. D. Robertson. 5th December, 1996.
Climb an obvious 30m icefall on the buttress right of Easy Gully (probably done before), then 80m of easy ground to the foot of the steep cracked buttress between the two branches of Easy Gully. The wide left-trending diagonal crack leads to a recess which is passed with difficulty (crux). The off-width above is laybacked precariously to easier ground.

Sun Rock Blues – 165m IV,5. A. D. Robertson, J. Currie. 5th January, 1997.
Ascends the obvious cracked, stepped pillar to the left of Wiggle. Start below the line at a small rock pedestal.
1. 40m. Climb the crackline past three steep steps, the middle providing the crux, to a good ledge.

2. 45m. Climb directly behind the belay on turf to reach a steeper corner which leads to a small cave.

3. 35m. Traverse left 3m beneath a steep wall, then climb directly to easier ground.

4. 45m. Easy mixed ground leads to the top.

Note: A steep direct finish to Wiggle at IV,6 by G. Scott and A. T. Robertson in January, 1997.

CREAG OF GOWAL:

It's Good to Torque – 190m V,7. A. D. Robertson, P. Thorburn, G. Latter. 22nd December, 1996.

Ascends the diamond-shaped slabby buttress about 100m up and right of The Gowk. Good varied climbing, particularly on the crux pitch. Start roughly in the centre of the buttress.

1 and 2. 70m. Climb mixed ground to the base of an obvious pair of leftward trending cracks in a steep slab.

3. 40m. Climb the cracks (turfy in places, but technical) past two small ledges to a pull-out left into a small left-facing corner.

4. 50m. Continue up, then slightly right to a final steep icy headwall, easiest on the right.

5. 30m. Easy snow to the top.

GLEN CALLATER:

The Bastion – 200m II. S. Richardson. 23rd February, 1997.

A fine natural mountaineering line up the right side of the central bastion – exposed and open. Climb the left-to-right ramp in the lower half of the face, and exit by a short step on to snow slopes. Trend left up mixed ground and to gain a second snow field which curves up and right to reach the apex of the face.

BEINN A' BHUIRD, Coire an Dubh Lochain:

The Whip – 110m VII,7. A. Crofton, G. Robertson. 1st December, 1996.

The obvious groove system between The Scent and Bloodhound Buttress, becoming more defined higher up, gives an excellent and serious route following a good natural line. Start 20m down and left from Bloodhound Buttress and climb turfy grooves up and slightly leftwards past an awkward section at a prominent spike, then continue rightwards up easier ground to belay just below a large recess forming an impasse (40m). Step delicately out right, then continue up past flakes moving left above the level of the recess to regain the groove line and mantle on to a sloping ledge. Continue straight up until a bulge forces moves right to a steep off-width crack which leads strenuously to a short chimney and rest on a Hex 10. The chimney ends immediately above so move strenuously out right to mantel on to a ledge (30m, crux). Make a few moves across right to enter the final groove/gully of Bloodhound Buttress and follow this to the top (40m).

Fever Pitch – 30m E4 5c. J. Lines. 25th June, 1996.

Climbs the clean slab to the right of The Streak. Start directly below the left end of a tiny curving overlap at 8m. Climb up to it, cross its left end and smear delicately diagonally leftwards up a faint line to gain a hold. Stand on the hold, then move up and right to below a large overlap. Pull over this in the centre and finish by scrambling up and right.

Garbh Choire, Squareface Buttress, North Wall:

The face below the Crucible contained four parallel icefalls in perhaps exceptional conditions. The two regular icefalls directly below and thinner ones either side. Each route had a big 50m pitch requiring ice-screw runners (the rock has few cracks). Descent was easy via The Sneck or the big ramp diagonally down under Squareface.

Pot Luck – 190m IV,5. B. Davison, A. Nisbet. 10th March, 1997.
The thin far left fall running up a right-sloping ramp. Start up the gully as for Gold Coast, then briefly up the left side of its slabby ice pitch until possible to move up left over ribs to the well-defined section of the icefall. Climb the icefall and up to snow left of the Crucible. Traverse rightwards across this to the break in the cornice.

Gold Coast Direct – 180m V,5. B. Davison, A. Nisbet. 10th March, 1997.
The left icefall climbed direct.

Crucible Direct – 180m VI,5. B. Davison, A. Nisbet. 10th March, 1997.
Two consecutive iced grooves in the slabby ground right of the initial gully of Gold Coast led to the right-hand Crucible icefall, climbed direct. Steeper for longer than the Gold Coast icefall, but low in the grade.

Fool's Gold – 170m VI,5. B. Davison, A. Nisbet. 10th March, 1997.
The thin far right fall. Start up iced slabs right of Crucible Direct to gain the icefall. Climb this (on this occasion thin ice covered with crusty snow - serious and scary!) which leads into a left curving groove which enters the Crucible at its extreme right edge (and therefore catches drainage from it).

Mitre Ridge:
West Side Story – 180m VII,8. S. Richardson, C. Cartwright. 22nd December, 1996.
A sustained expedition taking a natural left-to-right rising line across the West Wall of Mitre Ridge. Start as for Mitre Ridge, Original Route.
1. 35m. Climb Mitre Ridge, Original Route to the top of the initial chimney.
2. 20m. At the top of the chimney take the slanting chimney-slot on the right to gain the top of the first chimney of the Cumming-Crofton Route. Continue across the shallow groove of the Cumming-Crofton Route to a small stance below a corner leading up right on the edge of the West Wall.
3. 20m. Climb the corner to a large ledge (The Chancel pitch 3).
4. 10m. Climb the blank vertical wall just left of centre starting from a short rock spike to reach a stepped series of flat edges leading left to a good narrow ledge (The Chancel pitch 4).
5. 50m. Traverse right for 5m to reach the slanting fault line. Follow this to where it joins the gully of Commando Route. Cross this and continue in the same line up a diagonal fault to beneath the headwall on the west side of the Second Tower.
6. 15m. Climb the wall above to enter a right-facing chimney-corner. Follow this to its top and step left to reach the top of the Second Tower. (Bell's Variation finishes here).
7. 40m. Continue along the crest to the top.

BRAERIACH, Garbh Coire Mor:
Coronet Arête – 120m IV,5. C. Cartwright, S. Richardson. 15th December, 1996.
An enjoyable mixed climb up the well defined arête to the left of the upper groove of Crown Buttress. Easier than it looks from below. Start 10m left of the buttress edge.

1 and 2. 70m. Climb easy grooves to where the buttress steepens.

3. 20m. Continue up the corner system above, and belay on a small platform below the steep headwall.

4. 30m. Move up to a ledge, step left and climb a short wall to reach a steep groove on the left side of the headwall. Follow the groove and its continuation to the top.

Cherokee Chimney - 90m V,6. C. Cartwright, S. Richardson. 17th November, 1996.

An excellent technical climb up the overhanging chimney-slot to the right of Little Big Chimney. High in the grade, but easier and better protected than its more imposing twin to the left. Start 5m right of Little Big Chimney.

1. 25m. Climb the chimney over a bulge with a chockstone, to a niche.

2. 25m. Continue up the overhanging slot and short continuation corner to a ledge.

3. 40m. Move up the slabby wall above, and climb the right-hand of two corners to reach easy ground and the top.

Custer Corner – 50m IV,4. S. Richardson, C. Cartwright. 15th December, 1996.

The square-cut corner 20m right of Cherokee Chimney completes the triptych of lines on the steep left wall of Great Gully. Good sustained mixed climbing up the corner leads to an exposed step right at the top to finish.

Great Gully, Right-Hand Finish – 50m III. C. Cartwright, S. Richardson. 15th December, 1996.

The narrow groove which cuts into She-Devil's Buttress starting opposite the foot of Custer Corner. Climb the groove to a steep exit and pass the cornice on the right. Late in the season the route will bank out, but in these conditions the cornice is likely to be impassable.

Femme Fatale – 120m VI,6. S. Richardson, C. Cartwright. 1st February, 1997.

A superb mixed route following the line of grooves on the right edge of She-Devil's Buttress overlooking the prominent corner taken by the original winter route.

1. 50m. Follow easy grooves 20m right of She-Devil's Buttress to below the right edge of the steep upper buttress.

2. 20m. Climb the stepped groove system left of She-Devil's Buttress, Corner Line to a good stance on the left.

3. 20m. Continue up the steep corner on the right and gain a groove on the right arête. Follow this to a ledge, then move up and left to a slabby stance.

4. 30m. Climb short groove for 3m to top of a block, then traverse right to the edge overlooking the corner of She-Devil's Buttress, Corner Line. Climb the narrow groove for 10m to reach a sharp spike. Swing left on to easier ground and finish up a short snow arête to the cornice. An excellent pitch.

Coire Bhrochain:

The Compleatist – 90m IV,6. N. Wilson, N. Stevenson. 10th November, 1996.

Approximately follows the summer line of Braeriach Direct: its relationship with Midwinter is unsure. Climbed in early-season conditions. Start at the lowest point of the crest above Bhrochain Slabs. Climb the slabs to belay on a large ledge. Climb a left-rising ramp above to the crest, then traverse horizontally right to belay left of a prominent slab in a niche. Cross the slab rightwards, climb the left-hand groove above to the crest, then swing right into an overhung niche. Climb the groove above and another on the right to the Terrace.

COIRE SPUTAN DEARG:

Spectre – 90m E1. W. Church, G. S. Strange. 14th July, 1996.
On the rocks right of Pilgrim's Groove (Grey Man's Crag). Start just right of Pilgrim's grassy entry.
1. 45m. Climb an easy slab ramp for about 8m, then go up right to gain a higher ramp. Follow this to an optional belay in a slight bay. Continue up the ramp, break out right and climb slabby rock through a bulge to belay on a large platform at the apex of the lower buttress.
2. 45m 5b. Follow Lucifer Route to the traverse of Grey Slab, then continue up right and climb a rising slab ramp round the headwall to finish at the top of Ferlas Mor.

Grey Man's Crack – 30m E1 5c G. S. Strange, W. Church. 14th July, 1996.
The prominent crack in a left-facing groove just left of Hanging Dyke. Climb the crack to either join the second pitch of Ferlas Mor or, as on this ascent, move out right at a small square overhang to belay on Hanging Dyke.

Rootin' Tootin' Sputin' – 120m III. A. Nisbet. 13th December, 1996.
Climbs a ramp with shallow chimneys tucked in to the left side of the Janus buttress. Follow the ramp and chimneys until it steepens towards the top. Bend right via two awkward short chimneys to reach the crest of the buttress at the plateau.
Note: A. and G. Nisbet made a free ascent of Janus at III,5 on 13th December, 1996.

CREAGAN A' CHOIRE ETCHACHAN:

Talismaniac – 40m E4 6a. J. Lines, S. Harper. 4th August, 1996.
Essentially an extended start to Talismanic, which gives a superb bold pitch. Start right of Talisman Direct Start. Climb up the centre of the scooped wall to a bulge. Pull through the bulge to gain an obvious quartz blotch, move delicately right, then up the arête to better holds to join the normal route.

Green-House Effect – 110m VII,7. G. Lennox, D. Alexander. 25th January, 1997.
Climbs a version of The Dagger without ice. Climb the first pitch of Stiletto using bulging turf-filled cracks, then traverse right to belay on The Dagger (25m). The Dagger corner to the spike belay (35m, crux). Pull out right and climb a turfy corner (initially same as Scabbard winter) passing two overlaps on their left. Where the corner peters out, step left into the turfy groove of The Dagger. Continue to the top of The Terrace (50m).

CARN ETCHACHAN, Upper Tier:

Nathrach Dubh – 100m VI,6. G. Ettle, J. Lyall, J. Preston. 16th December, 1996.
A good direct crackline running straight up the amphitheatre between Boa and The Guillotine. From the terrace the finish can be seen as a W-shaped notch on the skyline. Start just left of The Guillotine and follow a ramp left until possible to break out right and climb the cracks up into the central right-facing corners (35m). Follow the three-tiered corners, the last being the hardest, to below the headwall (30m). Follow the groove, crack and chimney to finish just left of big roofs at the W-shaped notch (35m). Sustained and well protected.
Summer: H. Severe. E. Kane, J. Lyall. 14th September, 1996.
A good top pitch but better in winter.

Snake Charmer – 90m VI,6. J. Lyall, A. Nisbet, E. Pirie 23rd December, 1996.
The back left corner of the above bay, just right of Boa. Start as for Guillotine, then trend left crossing Nathrach Dubh at its middle corner to belay below the final crack of Boa (this is the summer line of Boa, taking the easiest choice) – 55m. Climb a

turfy crack just right of the corner right of Boa for about 10m, then make a short traverse left into the corner and follow it to the top, finishing by a flake and chockstone (35m).

Red Garter – 80m VI,6. G. Ettle, J. Lyall. 20th January, 1997.
A faint parallel fault up the wall right of Pagan Slit. A ledge leads right from the base of Pagan Slit ending at a large block. Start 4m left of the block and climb twin cracks to a turf ledge. Move right and up cracks to a big ledge (20m). Climb straight up a shallow slabby chimney and continue up the fault to belay in a gully (25m). Follow the gully and gain Hairpin Loop at the short crack. Finish up this.

SHELTER STONE CRAG:
Consolation Groove – 160m VII,7. B. Davison, A. Nisbet. 21st January, 1997.
The original winter ascent climbed all bar 50m of Raeburn's Buttress, where it abseiled into Consolation Groove to climb a pitch. This seems a much better winter version. Start as for Threadbare, at the same place as Rib Tickler, immediately beside the rock column.
1. 40m. Climb the left-hand and turfier of two corners and move left to a ledge (this is the first pitch of Threadbare). Work up and leftwards, keeping immediately under short steep walls until about 6m below the pitch 3 groove of Consolation Groove summer.
2. 30m. Move left and up the right corner of a slab to below a well-cracked overlap. Pull over this to a block and step right to a turfy groove with an overhanging start. Climb this and at its top traverse right to a big flake just left of the Consolation groove. Climb this flake to a second flake, the summer belay and to where the previous winter ascent abseiled. Though a less direct pitch than the summer line (which should be feasible), it contains some good climbing and we were lost.
3. 40m. Continue up the grooves of the summer route.
4. 50m. Move left to finish up the deep narrow chimney of Raeburn's Buttress (as did the original ascent) to the platform.

Central Slabs:
Immortal Start (to Thor and other routes) – 35m E4 6a. J. Lines, R. Campbell. 20th July, 1996.
Start at the left end of the lower slabs at a right-facing corner leading into an arching roof. Climb the corner easily to the roof, pull over and follow a crackline upwards to its termination (RP1 at top). Move right to gain better holds, step up above a small overlap and delicately traverse right to gain a huge loose flake/block on the original route.

Notes: N. Morrison notes an ascent of Run of the Arrow and considers it E6. Also that the E6 opinion outnumbers E5 *(agreed-Ed)*. The hammered wire has now disappeared and there is no alternative at this point. A Friend 0 is an important runner for the crux, not mentioned in the Guide.

A free winter ascent of Citadel by A. Cave and Slovak partner in February, 1997. Citadel Winter Variations. The new Guide does not say that R. Anderson and G. Nicoll freed what they considered to be a complete route from Citadel lower crux through to their independent finish.

Western Union – 210m IV,6. A. Cave, G. Ettle, J. Jeglic, A. Stremfelj. 14th February, 1997.
An easy, yet direct, line between Clach Dhian Chimney and Western Grooves.

Follow an easy gully system for 100m to a point where one can move right into a shallow groove. Climb this direct into and up the large chimney which joins Clach Dhian and Western Grooves. Climb directly to a steep cracked groove just right of the deep V-groove of Clach Dhian Direct Finish. Climb this cracked groove, crux.

HELL'S LUM CRAG, Low Slab (SMCJ 1996):
Hell's Gate – 50m HVS 4c. P. Allen, N. Morrison. 14th August, 1996.
Climb the cracks left of Cerberus to easier ground, trend left to finish directly into a right-facing corner.
Notes: From N. Morrison. Pluto was repeated and thought to be 50m, E1 5a.
Cerberus was thought 50m, E3 5c, but perhaps not the same line, as it is possible to move off right after 25m and this ascent continued up and left for a fine finish.

STAG ROCKS:
Bambi – 70m IV,5. G. Ettle, J. Finlay. 18th December, 1995.
The large groove immediately right of Final Selection. Start 5m right of the main groove.
1. 30m. Ascend a few metres to traverse right across a slab to gain the base of the groove. Climb this till it steepens, then climb a thin crack on the slab to the right. A few insecure moves on the rib gain a good ledge.
2. 40m. Climb the corner-crack on the right, moving right to easier ground.

Bambi Variation – 70m IV,5. A. Fyffe, G. MacEwan. December, 1996.
Links the start of Bambi with the finish of Final Selection. Climb Bambi to the foot of the big corner. Climb the corner a short way and gain the steep flake-crack on the left wall. This leads to a ledge and Final Selection which is climbed to the top.
Note: Final Selection is probably IV,5, or even harder.

STAC AN FHARAIDH:
Broad Buttress – 140m III. G. Ettle, J. Lyall. 28th December, 1996.
Follows a long shallow fault line up the left side of the broad broken buttress to the left of Narrow Gully.

COIRE AN T-SNEACHDA, The Mess of Pottage:
Crystal Gale – 45m V,6. D. Jarvis, D. Sanderson, B. Fyffe. April, 1996.
Climbs the slab to the left of No Blue Skies by the large right-facing corner. Start 3m right of Wachacha Direct Start beneath the right-hand end of the roof. Climb a short wall and sloping ledge leading rightwards into the corner. Follow the corner passing a small cave (roof) on good ice. Follow cracks above and move left into the easy ground of Wachacha. From the small cave, a short traverse right would lead to No Blue Skies.

Aladdin's Buttress:
Original Summer Route, True Finish – 60m IV,6. G. Ettle, B. Goodlad, A. Huntington. 4th November, 1995.
Previously, the summer route extended to the plateau via the steep rib just right of Aladdin's Couloir, rather indirectly. This winter ascent climbed the rib direct with one excursion on the right wall via a doubtful flake.

Fiacaill Buttress:
Straight to Jail – 55m V,6. D. Jarvis, B. Ottewell. April, 1996.
Takes a steep groove above the start of Escapologist. As for Escapologist past the

obvious ledge, then move right to gain the steep groove, followed to the terrace. Sustained but on good ice.

White Dwarf – 45m VS 5a. J. Lyall, S. Roberts. 7th September, 1997.
Followed the winter line, except for one short deviation on the left. Much better in winter.

Northern Whites – 35m V,7. G. Ettle, P. Munford. 23rd November, 1996.
Ascends the tapering wall to the right of The Hurting via an obvious roof. From the right-hand end of the wall east ground leads up to a big flake under the roof. Gain the roof and good protection, then traverse left underneath to pull up on to a ledge on the left. Move left 3m to ascend a crack rightwards and a further large flake to finish.

COIRE AN LOCHAIN:
Ventricle – VII,9. B. Davison, A. Nisbet. 8th March, 1997.
A free ascent of the original winter line, providing a series of desperate technical, but well protected, problems separated by ledges. The first overhanging groove was climbed by using a thin crack on the right (summer line), then stepping left into it. Ideal conditions; ice in the grooves and ledges was helpful, as was the lack of snow on the smooth walls.

Adventure – 50m V,5. G. Ettle, R. Mansfield. 19th November, 1996.
This route ascends cracks and grooves on the rib to the right of Inventive.
1. 35m. Ascend a short chimney to a step left to gain good cracks. Follow these to steep corners with precarious blocks and climb to ledges.
2. 15m. A continuation groove to finish.

Lateral Thinking – 100m IV,6. B. Davison, A. Nisbet. 23rd January, 1997.
A girdle traverse of No.1 Buttress. Start in The Vent immediately above its difficulties. Go diagonally out left on to the buttress and up to the base of the final corner of Inventive. Descend left until under the wide crack of Ventricle. Climb a blocky crack starting from the lip of the Ventricle corner below to gain a ledge on the crest. The ledge has a flake traversed until under the thin crack of Ventriloquist, climbed for one step (crux) to allow a further traverse left into Auricle. A short awkward chimney allowed a continuing traverse, finishing by a short descent into the easy finishing gully of Iron Butterfly.

Minute Man – 100m VI,7. B. Davison, A. Nisbet. 25th January, 1997.
Climbs a crackline in the tower left of Appetite for Destruction. Start up Milky Way and belay below the line. Climb an overhanging inverted V-groove and continue up the crack in two stages. A short crest and wall leads to the top.

Rear Entry – 60m IV,6. G. Ettle, A. Hyslop. 7th December, 1995.
Ascends the groove on the right wall of The Couloir, below the narrows. A good early season route, as it will shorten later.
1. 30m. Ascend a steep orange groove to join the crest of Ewen Buttress.
2. 30m. Climb the crest direct over two interesting pinnacles and a short wall to finish.

Migrant Direct – VII,7. W. Garrett, A. Coull. 13th December, 1996.
The huge corner-groove which Migrant avoids. Sustained. Gear adequate but hard to place.

Nocando Crack – VII,8. B. Davison, A. Nisbet. 20th January, 1997.
Finally climbed free. The second pitch (previously free) was the crux. The third

pitch was started up a crack in the wall just right of the big flake to gain a back and foot rest, then continuing up the flake to its top and traverse left as for summer.

Siberia – 60m E3. I. Taylor, C. Forrest. August, 1996.

Climbs the stunning arête between The Vicar and The Demon. Start as for The Demon.

1. 30m 5c. Go up for 3m, then step left into a groove and follow it to the roof. Pull leftwards over the roof, follow cracks in the arête and pass the next roof round on the left.

2. 30m 5c. Follow twin cracks until a move left gains the edge. Climb the roof using a flake on its left side and continue more easily to the top.

Never Mind, Mindless Finish – 25m E3 5c. A. Nisbet, A. T. Robertson. 25th June, 1996.

A corner, right of the crest and well seen from the other side of Y-Gully Right Branch, provides an alternative and free finish to the original line. The start of Never Mind is best reached by one abseil from the plateau at the tip of the pillar down the Left Branch side. Below the final pitch, belay just to the right beside a detached pillar. Traverse right round the pillar into a right-facing corner. Climb the corner for about 10m (well protected) past an overhanging section and an unexpected rest until a sloping hold can be gained on the slab out left. Traverse left past a bulge and go up to a scary mantelshelf finish (on the original route).

Transformer – 90m VII,8. G. Ettle, A. Huntington. 16th December, 1995.

Based on the summer route, this audacious line gives an outstanding experience to rank with any.

1. 25m. Gain the groove of Bulgy direct, which is followed to belay at the same level as twin cracks going right.

2. 25m Move right on the arête and follow twin cracks into Savage Slit. Cross a ledge line out right to a step down into Prore. Ascend a wall rightwards to a ledge round the arête.

3. 10m. Traverse right to a large block and descend into Fallout Corner. Descend the right arête to a ledge.

4. 30m. Move right, starting low to traverse a mossy break which eases on to blocky ledges rightwards, crossing War and Peace to gain the roof on Procrastination. Turn this on the right to traverse right to a block belay on Third Man. Abseiled off from here (failed headtorch). Finishing up Sidewinder or continuing right would be easy.

Note: R.Anderson notes that the winter ascent of Inquisition did not involve a rest point. G. Ettle says that he fell off and was lowered to a good ledge. Not knowing whether yo-yoing counted as a rest point, one was declared. Since falling off has not often in the past been declared, it would seem fair if the rest point was ignored. But it is a difficult issue, since rest points could often be missed out by yo-yoing. So can either be left to conscience or a policy can be decided (opinions welcome) but it should be noted that many of the Grade VIIIs have involved a fall (e.g. Guerdon Grooves, Rat-Trap, Needle etc.). R. Anderson's free ascent of Citadel's lower crux (a previous note) also involved a fall and yo-yo, although the rope was pulled through. The free ascent this winter is also rumoured to have involved a fall. R. Anderson also notes that The Executioner was climbed in winter conditions, not snowy but heavily verglassed.

Gaffers Groove: The winter ascent of the summer route was by R. Anderson, P. Long on 6th December, 1987.

Grade opinions (G. Lennox): Prore – VII,8. No Blue Skies – VI,8. Nightline – VI,7.

NORTH EAST OUTCROPS
With page reference to the guide.

North Doonies Yawn, North Face (p.30):
Rufus – 8m E3 5c. W. Moir. 9th May, 1994.
A slanting roofed corner from the only real platform below the wall.

Fettie Freaks – 10m E3 6a. W. Moir. 7th May, 1994.
The overhanging crackline.

Shady Proposition – 10m E1 5a. W. Moir. 9th May, 1994.
Move right from below Fettie Feaks on to a slab and climb up to a notch via a quartzy layback flange.

Red Rocks, Long Slough (p.37):
Polka Dot – 12m E3 6a. W. Moir, P. Allen. June, 1995.
Start up Blue Dot, then bridge up over the overhang and up a thin crack to reach left and rejoin Blue Dot.

Rednecks – 12m E5 6a. W. Moir. June, 1995.
The arête left of Blue Dot. Start on the right side and climb boldly to a break. Use the thin crack above to gain a little groove and finish more easily.

Liquid Dancing Firelight – 13m E5 6a. W. Moir, G. Elrick. June, 1995.
The undercut knife-edge at the seaward end of the crag. Climb easily up the left side, then traverse right on the lip of the overhang. Swing round and climb the right side of the edge to the top.

Seal's Hole (p.42):
Ello's Desert Island – 20m E3 5b. W. Moir. 26th June, 1996.
Abseil to the flake island to belay at the narrowest gap between the island and the main cliff. Step across the gap and find a way up into the corner above (loose). Pull out right around the prow. Short wall to the top.

Cove, The Priest (p.58):
Invertebrates Wall – 15m E5 6a. W. Moir, P. Allen. 27th June, 1996.
The wall between The Mitre and Spinechiller. Belay at the foot of The Mitre. Start up the initial moves of the corner, then go right along a shelf to its end. Pull up to enter a tiny corner leading to an undercut horizontal crack. Gain jugs above, then go left and climb a groove. A quartzy edge leads to the top.

South Cove (p.64):
Procreation – 33m E6. W. Moir, P. Allen. 11th June, 1994.
1. 18m 6b. Start up Procrastination. Where this route goes left under the small roof, continue up the crackline to gain the perch on Space Rats. Continue up Space Rats over its crux roof to belay.
2. 15m 5c. As for pitch 3 Space Rats.

Existentialism – 25m E2 5c. W. Moir, P. Allen (on sight). June, 1995 (p.65).
Belay as for The Hedonist. Climb a crackline up the slab-pillar to a ledge. Move up the stepped right-slanting corner, then pull left round a rib to finish up an open corner.

Beyond The Fringe – 11m E5 6b. W. Moir, N. Ritchie. 10th September, 1994 (p.68).
The wall below Lunatic Fringe. Belay on barnacled ledges below the right arête.

Start briefly up The Waterfront, take the hand traverse break right to the arête and move up to another break. Pull right round the arête on a little flake (crucial RP 3 on right). Layback up to a horizontal break and continue up the quartzy wall to belay below Lunatic Fringe.

Sickle Row (p78):
Obvious Risk – 15m E4 5c. M. Reed. 9th February, 1997.
Start just left of Mao and climb directly up the wall between Mao and Trunk aiming for a short vertical crack. From this, reach up to a break (crux), then easy to the top. Top-roped then soloed.

The following route was missed out of the guide by the type-setters.
Demokratisatsiya – 25m E4 6a. W. Moir, C. Stewart. June, 1989.
The left-facing corner right of Perestroika is climbed to reach a sloping ledge on the right. Make a couple of moves up, then climb the left-slanting ramp to the ledge of Glasnost/Perestroika. Finish as for these routes.

Findon, Rock Band Cliff (p98):
A steep slab adjoining the Red Band Cliff (to its south) gives the following routes. From left to right. All August, 1994.
Extreme – 12m V. Diff. W. Moir. The obvious crack via a quartz block.
Nirvana – 13m E2 5c. P. Allen, W. Moir. The vague central crackline.
Soundgarden – 13m E3 5c. P. Allen, W. Moir. Overlap and left-facing, left-slanting grey corner.
Stone-Temple Pilots – 15m HVS 5b. W. Moir. Undercut black corner, beak, slab and V-notch.

Orchestra Cave (p.103):
Unchained Melody – 20m E5 6a. W. Moir, N. Ritchie (on sight). 8th October, 1994.
At the right-hand side of the crag at the junction between the pink and black rock is a crack. Climb this to a rest on the slab, then the left-slanting corner above.

Findon contd. (p.104):
Armistice – 25m E2 5b. W. Moir, N. Morrison. 5th August, 1994.
Just left of Armed Conflict is a crack. Climb this, then the thin right-hand crack in the gold wall to ledges. Finish up the slabby arête above.

Pow Kebbuck (New Crag, see map, p.77):
Pow-Wow – 18m E3 6a. W. Moir, P. Allen. September, 1996.
The obvious right-slanting line of the crag. The first 3m are loose. Thereafter excellent climbing up the diedre and roof-crack.

Berrymuir Head (p112):
Visiting Jo – 20m HVS 5a. D. Borthwick, O. Clem. 23rd February, 1997.
Start as for The Notch and climb steeply up to the large recess/cave. Step left under the roof until possible to follow a corner-crack through the roof on delightful holds to the upper steep wall.

Craig Stirling (p.126):
Hell and High Water – 40m E5. W. Moir, P. Allen, N. Morrison. 20th August, 1994.
1. 15m 5c. Pitch 1 of Between the Devil, or Jack Sprat if the tide is in.
2. 25m 6c. Go up from the belay to a horizontal crack. Climb the twin converging cracks and slap for a break above. Pull over and climb the right-facing corner, then veer right over bulges to gain ledges. Move right and finish as for Between the Devil.

The Terminator – 16m E5 6b. W. Moir, N. Ritchie. 28th August, 1994.
The wildly overhanging arête right of When the North Wind Blows.

Jeux Sans Frontiers – 20m E3 5c. W. Moir. 19th June, 1994 (p.127).
The twin roof cracks 5m left of Petite Diedre. Continue up twin cracks above and climb the right side of the arête to the top.

John's Heugh (p.136):
Veinspotting – 25m E4 6b. W. Moir, P. Allen. 5th October, 1996.
Start 4m right of Jaded Ledge Lizard. Climb up to a huge hold at the base of the brown scooped corners. Use a layaway here to reach for a good hold up on the left (crux). Continue up the corner and exit left. Follow the obvious line leftwards and up to the top.

Clochindare Crags (p138):
CID Wall – 12m HVS 5a. W. Moir. November, 1996.
The line of intermittent cracks right of The Secret Policeman's Other Ball.

Vespa Vulgaris – 14m E4 6a. W. Moir, G. Elrick. November, 1996.
The overhanging corner and crackline left of Wasp Slab.

The Secret Policeman's Ball (Direct) – 14m E1 5b. W. Moir. November, 1996.
The overhanging groove in the arête. Continue up the edge (original route) to the top.

Solar Eclipse – 14m E1 5a. P. Allen, A. Robertson, W. Moir. November, 1996.
The thin crack up the steep slab (the original Secret Policeman's Ball started up this).

Willie Truthful – 20m E1 5a. P. Allen, J. Reid, W. Moir. November, 1996.
The line just left of Billy Liar, joining that route at mid height.

Veracious Vera – 20m E2 5c. W. Moir, P. Allen, J. Reid. November, 1996.
The hanging black corners just left of Willie Truthful.

Hellgate Cliff (p.187-188):
A massive chunk of this cliff has fallen into the sea. The following routes no longer exist. The Left Hand of Darkness, Right of Way, Green Void. Also, The Beast/ Pretty Vacant finish looks decidedly inadvisable at present.
Akimbo – 20m HVS 4c. G. Latter, J. Reid, P. Allen. 9th October, 1996 .
Bridge up the centre of the deep Hellgate Chimney, utilising the newly-formed crack-line splitting the pillar for protection. At the top, step onto the pillar and finish carefully up this.

Red Wall (p194):
Hundred Acre Wood – 15m E5 6b. G. Latter, J. Reid (both led), P. Allen. 9th October, 1996 .
A powerful technical problem breaching the roof left Pooh Corner. Start directly beneath the tiny groove. Up to a good break under the roof (Fs #0 and #2), then place a clutch of small nuts in the groove. Make hard moves to gain good diagonal breaks over the lip. Finish more easily rightwards up the wall.

Crimson Tide (p.196) – 20m E2 5c. W. Moir, P. Allen. 5th October, 1996.
The crackline between Pink Fink and Pinkosubversive.

Red Tower (p.210):
Wasted Years (aka. The Bare Necessities) – 20m E6 6c. M. Ingham. 29th November, 1994.

The wall right of Bagheera. Climb right-trending cracks and move left to the horizontal break (Bagheera peg available on left). A tricky step up reaches a good hold. Make a hard move to stand on this and reach a triangular hold in the grey rock out right. Move up to jugs and finish easily.

Meackie Point (p224):
Route One – 10m VS 4c. M. Reed, T. Rankin. 20th March, 1997.
Takes steep cracks just around the corner left of Thieves Like Us.

HIGHLAND OUTCROPS

Most routes have been passed on to the author, Kev Howett. Apologies, but a large number of routes have not been published over recent years and, despite the new policy of publishing all the year's routes, whether or not they are about to appear in a guidebook, it seems pointless to do so for this area.

CREAG DUBH, Bedtime Buttress:
Cup of Tea – 25m VI,8. M. Garthwaite (unsec). 30th December, 1995.
The very wet steep wall on the extreme left-hand side of the crag forms a thin icicle in very cold years. Hard mixed moves with marginal gear to gain the ice, which is followed to where it runs out, then up the thin crack on the left.

BINNEIN SHUAS, West Sector, The Fortress:
The Rubaiyat – 70m E2. G. Latter, J. Hartley. 30th August, 1996.
A direct line up the right edge of the dome-shaped buttress containing Kubla Khan. Start down and right of that route, beneath twin parallel cracks.
1. 20m 4c. Climb direct, passing a tiny rowan sapling near the top to pull onto a heather terrace.
2. 50m 5a. Climb an easy niche which leads to a flared-crack in the slab. Follow this past a thin section low down (poorly protected – crux) and continue in the same line to a prominent right-slanting break. Shuffle right along this and continue in the same line, to finish up a wider crack. Move out left to belay as for Kubla Khan. Either continue up this, or abseil off. Not easy to protect.

The Keep, Alternative Start – 25m E1 5b. G. Latter, R. Kerr. 21st June, 1996.
Start at the toe of the buttress, on the front face, to the left of the long grassy ramp that leads up to the normal start. Follow twin parallel cracks up the front face, to finish on good holds on the arête. Scramble up heather to the block belay at the base of the main pitch.

BEN NEVIS, AONACHS, CREAG MEAGHAIDH

BEN NEVIS, The Comb:
Tower Face of the Comb, Direct Start – 80m VI,6. A. Clarke, J. Main. 28th February, 1993.
A logical but harder alternative to the original route.
1. 30m. Start as for Don't Die of Ignorance along the obvious ramp at the bottom of the buttress, and climb a left-slanting crack (delicate) to a ledge below a short wall.
2. 50m. Climb the short wall to join the groove of the original winter line. Belay at the collection of broken blocks.

Tower Face of the Comb, Central Wall Variation – 45m V,5. A. Clarke, J. Main. 28th February, 1993.
A winter ascent approximating to Kellett's 1943 variation. From the top of the steep

wall which is turned on the left (pitch 3 in Ben Nevis Guide), traverse right to enter a chimney. Climb this to join the original route at the flake window.

Secondary Tower Ridge:
Stringfellow, Direct Finish – 50m V,5. J. Currie, A. Crofton. 2nd April, 1996.
The logical finish up the final headwall avoided by pitch 5 of the original route (due to unconsolidated snow). Start from the large platform at the top of pitch 4.
1. 15m. Climb up to the steep headwall, and move left to a notch. Swing up and left, then traverse left along an awkward narrow ledge to gain a prominent wide gap formed by a pinnacle.
2. 35m. Pass through the gap to gain a groove which leads up and right to the top of the buttress. Follow the level broken crest to reach the Western Traverse.

Creag Coire na Ciste:
Cornucopia – 100m VII,9. C. Cartwright, S. Richardson. 14th April, 1996.
The smooth, steep corner on the right wall of Number Three Gully. Very sustained and technical, especially pitch 2. Start at the foot of Number Three Gully, opposite Winter Chimney, below the left edge of Creag Coire na Ciste.
1. 20m. Climb up and left of some large blocks to reach an awkward slabby corner which leads to a small stance below the main corner-line.
2. 25m. Follow the crack-line in the right wall of the corner for 5m, then step left into the corner (thread runner used for rest on first ascent). Climb the impending corner with increasing difficulty (crux) to a welcome alcove. Traverse right along a narrow ledge, and move up to a good, but small and exposed stance on the edge of the buttress.
3. 20m. Climb the booming flake above the stance to its top (3m), then step down and left into the corner which is now a narrow chimney. Climb this, past two chockstones, to gain the large platform above. Another difficult pitch.
4. 35m. Move up over blocks and snow to the top right corner of the platform. Pull up an overhanging wall just left of an arête with a large spike, and continue up easier ground to the top.

Darth Vader – 100m VII,8. S. Richardson, C. Cartwright. 30th March, 1997.
This outstanding mixed climb takes the striking-chimney crack which slices through the blank vertical wall at the left end of Creag Coire na Ciste. Start at the left end of the crag, directly below the chimney and just right of Number Three Gully.
1. 25m. Climb an open icy groove to a ledge running beneath the vertical wall. Move right to belay on blocks just right of the chimney-crack.
2. 20m. Entry to the chimney is barred by a 3m wall. Climb this (awkward) and continue up the chimney to a magnificent hidden cave stance.
3. 25m. Pull over the roof of the cave and enter a bottomless groove (crux). Continue up the chimney above to belay on a large platform (as for Cornucopia).
4. 30m. Continue in the same line by taking the chimney at the back of the platform, and move up and right to finish.

South Sea Bubble – 110m VII,7. S. Richardson, C. Cartwright. 8th March 1997.
A very steep and intimidating icy mixed route up the previously unclimbed wall to the left of South Gully. It links two prominent right-to-left ice ramps with a free-hanging icicle that leads through the overhanging headwall.
1. 30m. Climb the initial ramp of South Gully and belay directly below the hanging icicle (old peg).

2. 40m. Traverse up and left across mixed ground to reach a groove line leading to the first ice ramp. Climb the ramp for 5m then climb the vertical wall above (bold and strenuous) to gain the foot of the second ramp. Climb this to its top, then traverse right to belay on the right side of the hanging icicle. (Hanging stance – large nuts useful).

3. 40m. Climb the icicle and continue up the snow basin to the top.

Tinkerbell – 100m IV,5. C. Cartwright, S. Richardson. 2nd March 1997.
A counter-diagonal to Wendigo. Start 10m right of Wendigo directly below the final tower of Central Rib.

1. 40m. Climb mixed ground then a narrow left-facing icy corner to a snowy depression. Junction with Wendigo.

2. 45m. Continue in the same line up the steep icefall directly above to reach an icy groove. Follow this to where it ends below the final tower of Central Rib.

3. 15m. Climb easy snow left of the tower and avoid the cornice on the right.

Carn Dearg:
The Blind – 100m VS*. D. Brooks, C. Moody. 7th September, 1996.
1. 45m 4b. Climb the corner of The Curtain for 35m, traverse left 4m, then move up on damp rock (bold). Step left to reach a belay.

2. 25m 4b. Move up left to climb a groove, then easily up right to pegs (in situ).

3. 30m 4b. Go right to the watercourse, follow it for 4m, then move right and climb a wall to the top.

Note: Mourning Slab (not described in the 'comprehensive' guide) starts up the same corner, then traverses well left after 20m on to the rib. The groove on pitch 2 of The Blind is shared with part of pitch 3 of Mourning Slab.

AONACH MOR, Coire an Lochain:
Spider Rib – 90m II. S. Richardson, C. Cartwright. 16th November, 1996.
The buttress between Easy Gully and the icy chimney of The Web. In common with other routes on this part of the cliff, most of the climb will bank out under heavy snow. Start just left of Easy Gully.

1. 45m. Climb an easy snow gully to where the buttress steepens. Move up and left to the foot of a short wide crack. Climb this and exit left at the top.

2. 45m. Finish up easy mixed ground, then snow, to the cornice.

Hammerhead Pillar – 100m VI,6. C. Cartwright, S. Richardson. 9th February 1997.
A good direct line up the buttress taken by Gondola with the Wind. The steep headwall provides an exciting finish. Start as for Maneater.

1. 40m. Move up into the base of the amphitheatre, then follow Gondola with the Wind for 10m up the ramp to the right. Climb a short open groove on the left edge of the buttress to a stance below a steep headwall.

2. 30m. Climb the wall and continue up the groove above to a stance below the headwall.

3. 30m. Climb the steep groove in the centre of the wall (difficult to start), then step left at the top to gain a hanging V-groove. Climb this and finish up a short snow slope to the cornice.

Alien Abduction – 120m VII,8. A. Powell, A. Benson. 22nd December, 1996.
Takes the grooves and stepped corner right of Hurricane Arête. Start 5m up Left Twin at a platform on the left.

1. 35m. Climb the groove and crack line up the right edge of Central Buttress. Belay

on the right (level with the belay on Hurricane Arête) below a right facing corner containing several overhangs.

2. 25m. Step left to enter the corner system. The second roof is large and very smooth above (1 axe rest and 1 PA - in situ). Above the third roof step up and left to a block belay. A very taxing pitch.

3. 40m. Continue 5m up left and pull onto a slab which leads to easier ground.

4. Climb increasingly snowy ground to the cornice.

Note: The second roof is 6a/6b terrain. The best chance to free it could be with monopoints for the cracks as there are no handholds for 12ft.

West Face:
The Red Eye Routine – III. O. Metherell, J. Marsham. 13th December, 1996.
Start 30m right of Solitaire at a small snow bay just right of a large pink block. Climb up the snow bay and move left up the short gull – serious (30m). For the next seven pitches continue up by the line of least resistance (mainly on turf). There is a short chimney on the sixth pitch. Easy ground leads to the plateau.

AONACH BEAG, West Face, Raw Egg Buttress:
Stalking Horse – 70m HVS. J. L. Bermudez, N. Wilson. June, 1995.
At the toe of the buttress, left of the existing summer routes, is an obvious chimney-corner, the route.

1. 35m 5a. Climb the initial wall, then thrash up the chimney.
2. 35m 4c. Climb the right-angle corner above to easier ground.

MAMORES, STOB BAN, North Buttress:
Foxtrot – 150m III. M. Cooper, C. Bailey. 5th December, 1996.
The broad north-facing ridge that descends from the upper section of the East Ridge. An obvious gully (grade I) can be seen immediately to the left of the route. Start just right of the foot of the ridge below a narrow chimney. Climb to the base of the chimney then make moves out left and up to the crest of the ridge, block belays (20m). Follow the crest of the ridge for two pitches to easier ground which leads to the upper slope of the East Ridge.

South Buttress:
North Groove – 160m III,4. S. Kennedy, A. Paul. 30th December, 1996.
Starts about 30m up from the foot of South Gully at a prominent rocky recess on the right. Traverse out rightwards below a steep wall, then move up and back left into a deep groove which runs up to the top of the buttress (45m). Continue directly up the groove over a steep step to more broken ground (45m). Climb to the ridge (North Ridge) which is followed easily to the summit (70m).

SGOR AN IUBHAIR, North Face:
Solo Gully – II. P. Azzi, M. Kann. 19th December, 1996.
Follows the obvious long and narrow gully on the right-hand side of the face.

AM BODACH, North-East Face:
Solstice Gully – III. P. Azzi, M. Kann, A. Snell. 21st December, 1996.
Climbs a gully hidden behind a buttress when seen from Glen Nevis direction but becomes apparent from below the face. It joins the more visible gully to the left shortly beneath the upper snowfields. Once here, the central option was taken to the summit ridge, climbing up the left side of a rocky outcrop, then left to a break in the cornice.

MONADHLIATH, Carn Dearg, Loch Dubh Crag:
Note: A. Keith notes that he and P. Brownsort climbed Tunnel Vision (SMCJ 1995) on 24th January, 1988 and called it The Wee Walk, Grade II ('aiming for an obvious keyhole on the skyline which turns out to be a chimney'). The location of The Great Trek (Nevis Guide, p284) is a mystery to him, but presumably, must be similar to this route, although overgraded.

He also soloed The Broken Link (SMCJ 1996) on the same day. It was named Loch Dubh Waterslide and the poor impression of its quality was improved by a recent ascent in icier conditions 'quite good, although extremely escapable'.

BEN ALDER, Maiden Crag:
Melting Maiden – 250m III. N. Anderson, A. Bratt. 2nd March, 1996.
A mixed route which takes the far left branch of the snow bay at the foot of the icefall of Ice Maiden. Start as for Ice Maiden.
1. 40m. Climb a snowy gully to the back of the snow bay at the foot of Ice Maiden icefall.
2. 25m. Exit the bay by the far left branch, a slanting ramp. Belay below an icefall.
3. 50m. Climb the first icefall to an easy snow gully, then up a second icefall.
4, 5. 100m. The large upper snowfield leads to the rock headwall.
6. 35m Exit to the plateau by a narrow iced gully in the left-hand side of the headwall.

AONACH BEAG, North-East Face, Loch Cheap Crag (Sheet 42, GR 480 752):
The crag is not named on the map and lies above Loch Coire Cheap. It is up to 200m high and is dominated by a large ice sheet cascading down its centre. Stairway to Heaven takes the obvious direct line. Descent is by the wide gully on the right side of the crag (The Ocean). Protection is generally poor.
Stairway to Heaven – 130m IV,4. N. Anderson, A. Bratt. 16th March, 1996.
1. 45m. Climb the left-hand side of the icefall direct. Belay at an outcrop on the left.
2. 50m. An easy snow slope leads to a second icefall. Climb this into a large snow bay. Belay at the base of the final rock headwall.
3. 35m. Exit the snow bay on its left side by a gully with a third ice pitch.
Gallows Pole – 130m III,4. A. Bratt, N. Anderson. 16th March, 1996.
Start 7m to the right of Stairway to Heaven and to the left of the prominent rock arête.
1. 50m. Climb the ice sheet direct to an overhang in the rock outcrop at 25m. Avoid this on the right by an iced ramp.
2. 50m. Climb easy snow slopes to the headwall at the top of the bay.
3. 30m. Exit to the plateau directly through mixed ground.
Misty Mountain Hop – 125m III. N. Anderson, A. Bratt, A. West. 17th March, 1996.
Start 10m right of Gallows Pole on the right-hand side of the central arête.
1. 50m. Climb an icefall to the right wall of the arête. Continue up a groove to an iced chimney and climb this.
2. 50m. Ascend the easy snow slope on the far right side of the snow bay to the headwall.
3. 30m. Mixed climbing through the right side of the headwall.
Ramble On – 120m II. N. Anderson, A. Bratt. 3rd March, 1996.
A large snowy recess lies 20m right of Gallows Pole. This takes the iced gully at the top of the recess.
The Ocean – 70m I. N. Anderson, A. Bratt (descent). 16th March, 1996.
The far right-hand side of the crag is split by a wide snow gully which provides a rapid descent back to Loch Coire Cheap and the base of the crag.

GLEN COE

BUACHAILLE ETIVE MOR, Great Gully Upper Buttress:
Curried Yak – 40m HVS 5a. D. Gardner, G. Robertson. Summer, 1993.
The broken crackline to the right of May Crack.

Coire na Tulaich:
A fairly compact group of crags exist high on the eastern slopes of the corrie, the first of which are about 100m up and right of the obvious slab containing The Dial. The crags comprise small individual buttresses and are grouped roughly in the shape of an arc. The area gets the benefit of any afternoon or evening sun. The first route described is on a small clean buttress just below the main crags and is the first reached.
Pinball Wizard – 30m HVS 5a. C. Grindley, S. Kennedy, A. Nelson. 5th September, 1996.
Start at the lowest point of the buttress and climb a short steep wall by some flakes to a horizontal break. Step right and climb directly to a prominent right-facing corner. Climb the right wall of the corner to the top.

The following routes are located on the rightmost (southmost) buttress which is pale-coloured and has a large 'blotch' (recess) on its left side. A small pinnacle sits at the foot of the buttress. The crag has become known as Blotch Buttress.
The Shield – 35m HVS 5a. C. Grindley, S. Kennedy. 31st August, 1996.
Follows an obvious flakeline starting just right of the pinnacle. Climb the flake, then traverse rightwards along the top of the flake before climbing the wall directly above. Step right just below the top wall to finish up the crest.

Crack Cocaine – 30m E1 5b. C. Grindley, S. Kennedy. 7th September, 1996.
Climb the obvious crackline immediately behind the pinnacle. Finish by a small ramp on the right, below the final wall. Alternatively, finish out left.

Slack Alan – 25m E2 5b. A. Findlay, A. Nelson. 7th September, 1996.
Start just left of the pinnacle. Climb a thin flake, then cracks through a bulge at mid height to a peg belay on a grass ledge. Peg left in place for abseil descent.

The Sentinel – 30m E1 5b. A Findlay, A. Nelson. 29th August, 1996.
Start at a juniper bush at the bottom left side of the buttress (left side of recess). Go up a thin flake into the recess (the Blotch). Exit the recess on the right by a crack which is followed to the top.

Stob Coire Altruim:
Cerberus – 80m V,7. M. Bass, J. Clamp, S. Yearsley (alt.). 6th December, 1996.
This route climbs the steep buttress to the right of Dalmatian Couloir by the corner and chimney system on its right hand edge. Start at the foot of the first corner to the right of Dalmatian Couloir.
1. 10m. Climb mixed ground to the foot of the rightwards curving corner. Climb the corner and then the bulging right wall by thin moves to a poor stance and good belay at the foot of the obvious narrow chimney.
2. 20m. Thrutch up the chimney and make strenuous moves to gain the groove above. Climb this (on this ascent up unconsolidated snow and good turf) over several short steep steps to a snow terrace. Follow the right hand edge of the terrace to belay under a chockstone.
3. 50m. Go under the chockstone, then up onto it, and follow the groove above

passing two chockstones and a col overlooking Dalmatian Couloir to finish up easier ground below the summit.

Note: Good ice and consolidated snow will probably be found above the narrow chimney later in the season. However, as the hardest part of the route lies below the narrow chimney the overall grade will not be affected.

BIDEAN NAM BIAN, Beinn Fhada, North Face:
Most of the routes on Beinn Fhada come into condition quite often, can easily be identified from the road and are very accessible. Descent from most routes can be made by abseil. Routes described right to left.

Time for Tiffin – 150m IV. P. Moores, A. Paul. 27th January, 1996.
Climbs the rightmost icefall.

Time for Tree – 150m III/IV. P. Moores, A. Paul. 28th January, 1996.
Climbs the central ice smears.

Solicitors Slot – 150m IV. P. Moores, A. Paul. 29th January, 1996.
Starts up St Valentine's Climb for one pitch and branches off rightwards into an obvious rocky chimney.

St. Valentine's Climb – III. The next line left.

Andy's Folly – 140m IV. P. Moores, A. Paul. 31st January, 1996.
Climbs the uppermost ice smear at the top of the rocky parallel (to St. Valentine's?) gash. The first pitch was a rocky mixed pitch.

Kriter – 120m IV. P. Moores, A. Paul. 1st February, 1996.
Climbs the lower ice smears in the middle section of the parallel gash as seen from the road.

Lost Valley Buttress:
Cold Feetus – 80m V,6. M. Garthwaite, N. Gresham. 24th February, 1996.
1. 20m. Start up right from Tyrannosaur at the base of a deep cleft. Climb the left wall via a slim groove to the base of a prominent vertical corner.
2. 10m. Climb the corner to the buttress crest.
3. 50m. Finish up Directosaur.

Klu Klux Cleft – 100m V,7. M. Garthwaite, N. Gresham. 28th November, 1996.
1. 30m. Climbs the obvious deep chimney on the left of the rib left of Pterodactyl. Climb the steep wall at the back of the gully past a peg into the deeper part of the chimney. Back and foot to a pull out right on to a balcony on the rib.
2. 10m. Climb the groove line of Pterodactyl to belay below an overhanging chimney-groove.
3. 10m. Climb the chimney-groove to the buttress crest.
4. 50m. Snow grooves to the top.

Barbarian – 80m V,6. M. Gray, R. McAllister. 29th December 1995.
Start 8m right from the ramp of Barracuda/Savage.
1. 30m. Go up a groove for 10m (start of Trilobite?) until it is possible to pull left round an overhanging bulge on to a block. This gains the base of a chimney crack parallel and right of Barracuda and which leads to a turfy ledge and belay.
2. 50m. The chimney leads rightwards to easy snow slopes and the top.

AONACH DUBH, Far Eastern Buttress:
Hu-a-Choy – 85m IV. B.Ottewell, D. McCarthy, S. McCarthy. February, 1996.
Starts just left of Orient Express.

1. 50m. Climb an iced chimney and short steps to a ledge on the left.
2. 35m. Take the wide corner-crack leading up and right to belay to the large boulder as for Orient Express.
Variation: 1a. 35m III. Start from a ledge round and left up a rightward-slanting groove to the belay. Photodiagram and photos supplied.

STOB COIRE NAN LOCHAIN:
E. Brunskill notes that on an ascent of Spectre, it was thought to be V,6 and a lot harder than it's neighbour, Scabbard. A more logical direct start was also climbed at V,6 taking a shallow corner crack directly into the main line. (Conditions were lean? Significant? – Ed)

STOB COIRE NAM BEITH, West Buttress (see SMCJ 1996, p104):
Arthur's Corner – 95m IV,5. A. Paul, G. Reilly. 31st March, 1996.
Climbs the open right-facing corner bounding the right side of the buttress, to the right of The Gathering. Steep moves at the bottom and a tricky finish. Probably the hardest of the routes here.

AONACH EAGACH, South Side:
Findlay's Tail – 130m IV. P. Moores, A. Paul. 27th January, 1996.
The icefall to the right of Blue Riband.

SRON NA CREISE, North Face (Map Ref. 242 525):
Two icefalls form low down to the left of the North Ridge.
King's Tear – 170m III/IV. P. Moores, W. Samuels. 4th January, 1997.
The right-hand icefall, taking the steepest line.

The Weep – 250m II/III. P. Harrop, S. Kennedy, D. Sinclair. 5th January, 1997.
The left icefall. Continuous easy-angled ice.

STOB COIR' AN ALBANNAICH, North Coire:
Plumbline – 70m IV,4. S. Kennedy, A. Nelson, S. Thirgood. 22nd December, 1996.
Takes the line of the prominent corner which is situated roughly in the centre of the buttress below the summit. Climb mixed ground directly to the base of the corner (25m). Climb the corner directly to a large block belay (30m). Finish up easier ground (15m). Probably a grade easier with a large build-up later in the season.
Note: The route described in SMCJ 1995, p682 lies to the left of the above route and is called Plumeline.??????

GARBH BHEINN, ARDGOUR:
Banangle – 90m M. Severe. K. M. Edgar, K. Schwartz. 27th May, 1996.
On the obvious curved narrow slab near the bealach. Go steeply up to and along the left edge of the slab for 50m. Then zigzag up between bits of vegetation (40m).

South Wall of the Great Ridge:
The Epeeist – 50m E5 6b. P. Thorburn, G. Latter. 23rd June, 1996.
Excellent varied climbing up the central blocky crack in the leaning wall, directly above the very prominent black seep. From the top of the initial chimney of Sgian Dubh, first hand then foot traverse the shelf out right with increasing difficulty to the base of the crack. Pull the ropes and move the belayer to below (or drop a third rope). Up the crack with a hard move low down to follow excellent holds which lead out left near the top. Finish up the easier wall above on excellent rock to spike belay. Scramble off.

Lower Tier:
The Gay Blade – 40m E3 6a. G. Latter, P. Thorburn. 24th June, 1996.
The prominent thin crack-line up the wall left of Scimitar. Start 3m left the broken
rising ledge system of Scimitar. Climb the initial cracked wall with difficulty (crux)
to move right at the prominent horizontal break to join Gralloch. Continue up the
crack, moving right on sidepulls into the steep finger-crack which soon relents.
Continue more easily in the same line, past a short steep wall near the top

BEINN NA SEILG (Ardnamurchan), Hebrides Wall:
Rhumb Line – 35m H. Severe. D. Kirk, L. Snowdon. 6th April, 1996.
Climbs an obvious crackline in the steep wall between Trident Climb and Faradh
Dubh. Start at the foot of an obvious slanting ramp leading diagonally right to the
main crack. Move boldly up the ramp to gain the crack. Follow the crack up the
steep wall until the angle eases (this point is just to the right of Trident Climb 2nd
pitch traverse). Continue directly up slabby rock, passing a large flange, to the end
of difficulties (25m). Easy to the top (10m).

SOUTHERN HIGHLANDS

BRIDGE OF ORCHY, Beinn an Dothaidh, North-East Coire:
Jobseekers Allowance – 125m IV,6. E. W. Brunskill, D. Crawford, S. Burns. 23rd
November, 1996.
A varied line threading the large overhangs on the leftside of the North Buttress.
Start just left of the large square snow bay, at the bottom of a shallow right-facing
groove.
1. 15m. Climb the groove to a recess below a bulge.
2. 30m. Climb the bulge (crux) and continue up the groove exiting out left just
below the start of the overhangs, to reach a small terrace. Traverse left along the
terrace for about 10m to reach a deep and narrow chimney.
3. 40m. Climb the chimney and steep continuation groove above exiting out right
to reach easier ground.
4. 35m. Trend leftwards to reach easy ground.
A choice of finishes is possible, either continue up the broken buttress to join Taxus
near the summit or if conditions and visibility allow, traverse leftwards to reach one
of the easier gullies and descend.

Emel Ridge – 200m II. J. Mount, K. Schwartz. 9th February, 1978.
The ridge between East and Central Gullies, climbed directly to the summit.

The Beechgrove Garden – K. Schwartz, 24th January, 1978.

Pedant's Corner – 110m V,7. A. Powell, R. Cross, S. Elworthy. November, 1996
Climbs the prominent edge left of Haar.
1. 40m. Climb the edge of the buttress left of Haar to the foot of a prominent steep
corner.
2. 20m. The corner is very strenuous. Easier turf walls follow above.
3. 50m. Steady climbing leads to easier ground near the summit.

Haar – The right-hand corner climbed at IV,4 by K. Schwartz, T. Groves, 13th
January, 1984. (See new Guide).

West Buttress:
Stormbringer, Direct Start – 50m V,6. C. Cartwright, S. Richardson. 24th November, 1996.

Good steep climbing following the true line of the Stormbringer fault. Start midway between Haar and the fault-line of West Buttress Direct Start, below a vertical right-facing corner.

1. 25m. Climb the corner, and pull over a bulge to a good ledge.

2. 25m. Continue over an impending wedged block to enter the lower section of the main Stormbringer corner. Follow this for 20m to where the original line comes in from the left.

Can't, Won't, Shan't – 65m VII,6. M. Garthwaite, N. Gresham. 30th December, 1996.

Climbs a very thin streak up the right edge of the slab right of Cirrus and right of Carte Blanche. Scramble up Far West Buttress for 20m to a small flat belay ledge below the slab.

1. 25m. Climb precariously straight up the slab linking small blobs of turf heading for the 'frogs eyes' above. Belay up and left. Tied off warthogs and a Bulldog hook for gear.

2. 40m. Finish up the obvious steep chimney-groove system taken by Carte Blanche.

Missplaced – 135m III,4. M. Boyle, E. Kane. 23rd December, 1995.

Starts right of Quickstep, then crosses it to finish. Climb broken stepped rock bounding the right side of Far West Buttress to belay below a steep wall (35m). Traverse right to a steep corner/chimney breaching the wall and climb it (15m, crux). A rising traverse left leads back into the corner, crossing Quickstep and belay above Clonus (45m). Continue up a corner/gully to the top.

Coire an Dothaidh:

Highway to Hell, Right Branch – 200m II-III. K. Schwartz. 3rd February, 1996. The escapable right branch is climbed throughout.

BEINN UDLAIDH:

Hot Keks – 95m IV,5. K. Schwartz, K. M. Edgar. 3rd April, 1996.

Between White Caterpillar and West Gully. Climb steep ice on the left to a diagonal traverse up and right to a vague rib (50m). A long traverse right and up a two-step icefall (45m).

THE COBBLER, South Peak:

Viva Glasvegas – 50m VIII,7. M. Garthwaite, A. Coish. 13th January, 1996.

1. 25m. Start at the very base of Gibber Crack after the initial scramble. Follow the diagonal crack on the left wall over a small overlap to a turfy ledge (warthog for protection). Climb straight up, then rock over right (hard) to gain the base of a hanging groove. Follow this to belay. Serious pitch.

2. 25m. Climb up and move left round a small roof, then straight up to belay on North Wall traverse. Easy escape right.

Centre Peak Buttress:

Drugs are for Mugs – 90m V,6. R. McAllister, D. McGimpsey. December, 1996. A line just left of Cave Route with good climbing on pitch 1. Full description in new guide.

THE BRACK:

Resolution – 145m VI,7. R. McAllister, D. McGimpsey, A.Fraser. 1st January, 1997.

A superb mixed line up the great slab right of Great Central Groove, followed by a technical corner through the headwall immediately above. Start at the bottom toe of the slab.

1. 40m. Climb to, then up an easy right-trending turf ramp and move up to a higher turf ledge. Follow this left to its end. Difficult moves lead left, then directly to a ledge.

2. 45m. Move right above the ledge, then traverse hard left above the ledge. Continue more directly by the line of most turf and least resistance to belay on a good ledge at the top of the slab. An excellent pitch.

3. 35m. Traverse right for 3m until possible to gain, with difficulty, the left end of a narrow ledge. From this ledge move directly up turfy ground above, heading for a right-trending corner capped by an overhang (there are three corners in the headwall, the left being the right-hand finish of Great Central Groove, this being the central one and the right one being the tapering corner of Mainline). Difficult moves lead across the slab under the overhang to gain a turfy groove; belay at its top.

4. 25m. Move right and surmount a rock step to gain a good ledge. To the right is a blocky rightward-trending and surprisingly easy crack splitting the final headwall.

Plunge, Variants – R. McAllister, A. Fraser, S. Mearns. 9th January, 1997.
Direct start: The lower section of the gully was climbed directly (25m IV,5), avoiding the initial two turf pitches to the right.
Alternative finish: The icicle was not present and the steep turfed wall 7m to the right was climbed (V,5).

Small Fry – 100m III. K. Schwartz. 21st December, 1995.
Climb the gully right of Big Game to a chockstone, passed with difficulty to a 5m slab and easier gully above. Chockstone would be easier with a bigger build-up but can be avoided by an easier branch to the right.

BEINN AN LOCHAIN:
K. Schwartz notes that Twin Caves Gully deserves Grade III in lean conditions.

GLEN CROE:
K. Schwartz notes that Cosmic Corner deserves VS 4b.

KNAPDALE, Creag nam Fitheach:
The Changeling – 25m E5 6a. D. Griffiths, I. Griffiths. 16th September, 1995.
Climbs the left arete of Metamorphosis. Start at the crack just right of the rowan tree to gain the top of a detached block. Climb directly up the arete to a semi-rest on a large foothold. Continue up the slabby wall before moving right to gain a hanging crack. Just before it meets Metamorphosis move left to a ledge and up a ramp to finish. Bolt belay.

BEN CRUACHAN, Stob Dearg, North-East Face:
Angel Face – 200m IV,4. S. Kennedy, A. Nelson. March, 1995.
The route climbs the open slabby face between Original Route and Central Grooves. Start just right of the icefall which forms the direct start to Original Route. Climb diagonally up rightwards to belay below a groove line almost in the middle of the face (50m). Climb directly up the groove (45m). Traverse out left to a snow bay below a steep wall which is passed on the left (45m). Finish up broken ground (60m). Climbed in very icy conditions.

Meall nan Each, North-East Face:

The main cliff (100m in height) is dominated by a band of overlaps at two-thirds height. Right of this, the crag falls back into easier-angled gullies and ribs before ending at a deeply recessed left-slanting gully (possible descent, Grade I).

Epona Gully – 90m II. A. Matthewson, J. Andrew. 24th February, 1996.
The open gully just to the right of the main cliff. At the final impasse, exits are possible left or right.

White Horse Grooves – 120m III. J. Andrew, A. Matthewson. 24th February, 1996.
Mixed climbing following a right-slanting line up the lower section of the main cliff to the edge overlooking Epona Gully. Start at the lowest rocks.
1. 45m. Zigzag up and right via a turf-tuft slab to belay in the fault line.
2. 35m. Pass a thin spike by a groove on the left, then traverse right under corners to a notch on the buttress edge; belay above.
3. 40m. Move up, then step right into Epona Gully, finishing directly.

ARRAN

BEINN TARSUINN, Meadow Face:
Blunderbuss Finish to Blundecral (SMCJ 1996) – 150m HVS 5a. A. Fraser, R. McAllister. 31st August, 1995.
This long finish gives a spectacularly positioned mystery tour. The Blundecral/Blunderbuss combination is 215m, E2 5c** and perhaps the best route on the crag.
4a. 25m 5a. Climb the fine diagonal rock ramp of pitch 4 of the original route, step left on to the continuation ramp and follow this for 6m to a spectacular position on the ramp.
5a. 25m 4b. Continue up the ramp for 3m, then move up to a higher ramp. Follow this left until it leads to a wide grassy fault (Brobdignag). Go up this for 7m to a cave belay under a rock arch.
6a. 25m 5a. Depart the herbiage of Brobdignag by jumping on to the grass ledge to the right of the belay. Follow this right and down to its end. Above is a crack which leads to a chimney, then another chimney where the left chimney is followed to a good ledge.
7a. 50m 4c. Climb the slab at the extreme left end of the face to its apex, move right with difficulty, then continue to and up leftward-trending flake cracks above.
8a. 25m 4a. Pleasant climbing up walls and cracks to the top.

Blundecral, True Finish – 25m E5 6a/b**. R. McAllister, D. McGimpsey. July, 1996.
The best and most direct finish. From the poorish flake belay after pitch 4 of Blundecral, climb directly up the middle of the steep slab to a rounded break. Traverse this leftwards with increasing difficulty to a hard step up and foot traverse round the blunt arete. Climb up to an obvious short chimney (good runner) and spike belay at its top – bold. Now in the cracks (which lead to the chimneys) on pitch 6a of the Blunderbuss Finish.

Gulliver's Travels – 300m E2**. A.Fraser, R. McAllister. 20th September, 1995.
A natural rising traverse, using the leftward trend and ledged nature of the cliff. A fine adventure with good climbing and spectacular positions making up for the relative shortage of new ground.
1-5. 140m 4b 4b 5a 5b 5c. Start as for The Rake Alternative Start and follow this for five pitches to belay in Boggle.

6. 30m 5a. Move up to a ledge on the left and follow this left to a crack (Brachistochrone). Descend this for 3m past a chockstone, then follow a ramp up left past an awkward break to belay as for Blunderbuss Finish pitch 4a.

7. 30m 4b. Pitch 5a of Blunderbuss, then traverse left to a block belay overlooking The Blinder.

8. 40m 5c. A sensational and intimidating traverse leads into The Blinder (a rope looped over the top of the arch lowers the fall potential). Continue to a chimney which is climbed via a chockstone to exit on to the floor of a great square recess (Hanging Gully).

9. 30m 4c. Finish as for the last pitch of The Blinder.

Note: The 35m crux pitch of The Rake was thought worthy of E2 5c without the original protection pegs, which have long gone. The initial slabs, minus the scrambling at the bottom, were 90m rather than the quoted 65m.

LOWLAND OUTCROPS

THE GALLOWAY HILLS, MULLWHARCHAR:
Brigadoon – 70m E1 5b. A. Fraser, R. McAllister. 4th May, 1995.
The huge corner on the left side of the crag, 7m left of Yucatan (SMCJ 1996), climbed in two pitches (25m, 5b: 45m, 4b). A somewhat gothic classic.

Unnamed – 20m E1 5b. P. Brown. May, 1995.
The corner to the right of the initial corner of Dungeonmaster. Thin.

CAIRNSMORE OF FLEET (Guide p152; Map Ref. 501 671; Sheet 83): Clints of the Spout (Map Ref. 509 667):
Very remote with a wonderful atmosphere. The easiest approach is to turn off the A75, just south of Palnure, to Muirfad. At the old viaduct, fork right up the private road towards Cairnsmore House and then fork right again, circumnavigate the old coach house and take the second left to a car park (Map Ref. 471 641). From here follow the tourist path to the summit of Cairnsmore and descend north-east to a col between Cairnsmore of Fleet and Meikle Mulltaggart (Nick of the Saddle) and then southward to the cliffs (2hr.). A much harder but very spectacular approach is from the car park near Dunkitterick Cottage (MR 502 720). Follow the footpath to the ruined cottage and a break in the forest to open land. Strike up the hillside diagonally rightwards to the summit of Craignelder and descend to the plateau beyond. Contour the north-west slope of Meikle Mulltaggart to a col and descend into the east-facing corrie (3hr.).

The Clints of the Spout is too broken to offer good rock climbing but it provides a classic gully and one other excellent winter route. The crag is east facing and catches the sun all morning. A prolonged freeze of a fortnight would seem to be essential for good conditions.

Spout of the Clints – 160m VS. S. Reid, A. Moore, J. Campbell. 19th May, 1992.
The obvious watercourse in the centre of the crag may become easier in a drought.

1. 50m 4b. Scramble up the gully bed with a hard move to overcome a chockstone.

2. 60m 4c. Can be split. Climb the waterchute first on the left, then on the right.

3. 50m 4c. Climb the left wall of the gully, well back from the fall to gain a right-slanting ramp. Follow this back into the gully and the top.

Note: The route was originally named Lost Pilots Gully after the debris from a crashed aircraft that litters the climb and the corrie floor – Spout of the Clints is the correct name.

Winter: V,4. C. Bonington, S. Reid (alt.). 5th January, 1997.
A superb sustained climb. The final pitch is the crux and not well protected.

Smear Test – 120m IV,4. S. Reid, D. Scott (alt.). 7th January, 1997.
The spectacular ice smear on the right of the crag gives an excellent climb with the final pitch the crux.
1. 40m. Climb easy ice, steepening to a heather ledge.
2. 50m. A steep start eases to a ledge (possible belay). Climb steepening ice above to a groove which leads to a stance.
3. 30m. Climb the thin smear up the slab to the top.

DUMFRIES OUTCROPS, CLIFTON CRAG, Dirl Chimney Area:
Gramercy – 13m Severe 4a. S. Reid, J. Reid. 9th May, 1996.
A pleasant route with a fine finish up the buttress left of Dirl Chimney. Start below Dirl Chimney. Climb the short crack on the left of Dirl Chimney's start and follow an easy ramp up leftwards to a huge block. Climb the crack on the left side of the block to a ledge. Follow the crack on the right on to the front of the buttress and a bold direct finish. Taking the crack on the left from the ledge reduces the grade to V. Diff.

SOUTH-WEST SEA CLIFFS, MEIKLE ROSS, Main Cliff:
Spectacular Bid – 40m E5 6b. R. McAllister, S. Mearns, E. Brunskill. 1995?
A last great problem taking the blank wall between Crack Track and Sidetrack. Serious in its lower half. Start midway between Crack Track and Sidetrack. Step off a boulder into a horizontal break, then move up to a good hold (skyhook, not tied). Make a committing thin traverse left for 3m, then climb up until a traverse left leads to a break (Friends 1, 1.5). Step off a rib on the right and move leftward up the wall to an intimidating rock up into a small niche (wallnut 3 in slot on left). Climb out of the niche on small edges (crux) to mantle on to a ledge, then ascend a fine thin rightward-slanting crack on fingerlocks to finish.

ROADSIDE CRAG, Yellow Lichen Wall:
At the end of this wall there is a pillar buttress.
Ranti-Crack – 8m E2 5c. T. Rankin. 28th May, 1995.
Climb the obvious thin corner on the right side of the buttress.
Variation: E1 5b. Climb the crack to the sloping ledge at 5m, then step right to the holds on the arete. Finish leftwards.

Catapult Suzie – 10m E3 5c. T. Rankin. 28th May, 1995.
Bold and committing with groundfall potential. Climb the shale-filled crack on the left to a handrail on the main face above a small roof (runners in the thin corner-crack on the left). Make hard moves up using both arêtes to stand on a handrail, then straight up to finish.

Trainspotters Traverse – 12m VS 4c. T. Rankin. 14th October, 1995.
Right of Wee Pig are four parallel cracks. This climbs the third crack until underneath the overhang, then traverses left on good holds to finish at the top of Wee Pig.

Pause for Thought – 10m E2 6a. T. Rankin. 14th October, 1995.
This climbs the third crack direct to the top through the overhang and open groove.

FINNARTS POINT (Sheet 76, Map Ref. 044 742):
A series of cliffs situated on that isolated section of coast south of Ballantrae. The *piece de resistance* is the main cliff, a ferociously steep wall of perfect rock. This is definitely a cliff in the modern idiom, ranking with the best outcrops in Galloway, if not elsewhere. The other cliffs, while less stunning, provide good routes in interesting situations. Outlook is pleasant on to the north end of Loch Ryan (a must for ferry

spotters). The cliffs dry quickly after showers but after prolonged rain there will be seepage and two-three days of dry weather is advised. There are seabirds and the crags are worth avoiding during the nesting season (end April to start August).

Access: From Ballantrae follow the A77 (Glasgow to Stranraer road) south. South of Ballantrae the road winds uphill through some bad corners. About three miles south of Ballantrae, 0.5 mile after the road straightens out, there is a right turn signposted to a pottery/craft shop. Follow this for 200m to a junction at the pottery. Take the left turn and follow this for four miles along a gradually deteriorating road, then a track, through a number of gates (at three miles the road forks and the left fork is again taken). The track swings southwards and eventually Loch Ryan and the top end of the Mull of Galloway/Stranraer peninsula becomes visible. Shortly thereafter and situated between two gates, there is an area of gorse bordering the road, immediately before the track swings sharply uphill to the left. Park here and walk SW towards the Mull/Stranraer peninsula, towards a small rocky cleft on the edge of the moor. From this cleft descend the fern gully directly to the sea. Walk south (left) above the main cliff until possible to gain access from its southern end –15 minutes. It will come as no surprise that the cliff was discovered from the sea.

Main Cliff:
Access to the main cliff is from its southern end, down an easy rib on the seaward side of the cliff. This provides a grandstand view of the cliff. The main features from the left are:
1. The overhanging arête at the left end (Edge of the Abyss).
2. A central area of slightly easier angle, with a corner running nearly the length of the cliff.
3. A final undercut area with an obvious hand crack at its top left end (Lloyd Quinan). Routes can all be accessed from the end of the rib except for a short period at high tide when access is by abseil or by a traverse from the north at Severe. Routes are described left to right.

Edge of the Abyss – 25m E4 6a***. R. McAllister, A. Fraser. 22nd August, 1996.
An outstanding route, macho fantastico, both strenuous and sustained. Protection is good if you are strong enough to place it. The route takes the overhanging grooved arête at the left end of the face. Climb the arête to a spike and step left off the spike into a hanging groove. Difficult moves up this lead to a ledge. The final wall is climbed on the arete to the left.

Red Hot and Blue – 25m E3 6a*. R. McAllister, D. McGimpsey, S. Mearns. 28th August, 1996.
To the right is an uncompromisingly steep area of rock, with a ledge leading rightwards across the middle of the face to join the top of a crack. This crack runs nearly the length of the cliff and is this route, a fine climb up an obvious feature. The crack is reached by boldish climbing. The crack itself is sustained but excellently protected. At the top of the crack a swing left leads to an easier finish.

I Should Coco – 25m E2 5c. R. McAllister, D. McGimpsey, S. Mearns. 18th September, 1995.
To the right is an apparently easier-angled area with a large corner. The route climbs the corner, reached directly from below by a wall. While not as sustained as some of the other routes, the top steepening of the corner is technical.

Rhythm Nation – 25m E2 5b*. R. McAllister, S. Christie. September, 1995.
An interesting and varied route. Start as for I Should Coco and climb its initial wall to the foot of the corner. Traverse right round a rib and climb up and right to gain a

corner. Follow this for a few moves until possible to traverse out left on to the arête. This is followed to the top.

Lloyd Quinan is a Weatherman – 22m E3 5c**. D. McGimpsey, R. McAllister, S. Mearns. 28th August, 1996.

Another fine line of contrasting styles. To the right of the previous area the crag steepens and is undercut. At its top left side is a fine and prominent fist crack. Start 3m to the right of the fist crack. Step off a flake and climb a short but very intimidating undercut wall on underclings to a flake. Traverse left along the flake to the fist crack and finish up this.

Baywatch Babes – 20m E1 5b. S. Mearns, R. McAllister, D. McGimpsey. 18th September, 1995.

A good introduction to the wall. Start at the extreme right of the crag and traverse left (the traverse line would eventually lead to the crack of Lloyd Quinan) to below a short corner. Climb this, then continue above to the top.

Surfin' Seal Bay:
This is the next large bay south of the main cliff. There is only one short route to date, situated on the south face of a block at the north end of the bay (i.e. nearest the main cliff). The block presently has a stake on its top. Access is from the top of the rib to the main cliff, then turn left and down short cliffs with difficulty. Alternatively, and probably preferably, abseil from the block down the route.

Bustin' Surfboards – 8m E2 5b. R. McAllister, A. Fraser. 29th March, 1995.

On the southern (left) side of the bay is a small block of good rock. This route climbs the centre of the face and, while short, has some excellent moves. Start at the left of the face and climb up to clip a peg above an overlap. Move up and right to a precarious mantelshelf on to a small ledge. Continue directly to the top.

Smugglers Zawn:
This is the next bay to the south, difficult of access from either land or sea and with a large unfrequented cave at its head. The best access is by abseiling from blocks at the top of the following route.

Electric Brae – 45m HVS 5a**. A. Fraser, R. McAllister. 22nd August, 1996.

A good route in a remote setting. A further curio is the changing geology on the route. At the back of the zawn, about 50m left of the cave, is the biggest sweep of clean rock on the crag. At mid height on the right side is an obvious capped corner. This route climbs the face below the corner, then the corner. At the top of the corner swing out left and continue more easily up the friendly rock above.

Smugglers Ridge – 40m V. Diff. A. Fraser. 15th August, 1996.

This is the ridge to the right of the large cave at the back of the zawn. While useful as an escape out of the zawn and is not a bad route, the top moves are on turf and definitely not recommended as a descent route.

PORTOBELLO, Slab Cove:
The following two routes lie on the wall on the north side of the cove, on the opposite side from The Man from Del Monte cliff.

Brain Dead Fred – 10m E3 5c. R. McAllister, S. Christie, D. McGimpsey. April, 1995.

This is the intermittent crackline in the centre of the wall. Bold moves up the grey shield of rock gain twin pegs. Continue up on small edges to exit with difficulty.

Grim Reefer – 10m E1/2 5b. R. McAllister, S. Christie. April, 1995.

Climbs the wall to the left via long reaches on pockets. Poorly protected.

Cracked Block Cove:

A Close Shave – 13m E1 5b. A. Fraser, C. French, D. McGimpsey, T. Prentice, R. McAllister. 10th March, 1996.

At the right end of the loose and stratified wall at the back of the cove. To the right of the cracked block are twin cracks. These give steep and unusual climbing, better than appearances might suggest.

Carrycots of Fire – 12m E1 5a. A. Fraser, R. McAllister, R. Rankin. 16th March, 1997.

Climbs the left side of the block's seaward wall, moving slightly left at the top to cross the bulge at its widest point. Worthwhile, with adequate if tricky protection.

St. Elmo's Fire, Right-Hand Start – E2 5b. R. McAllister, D. McGimpsey, A. Fraser. 10th March, 1996.

An easier though unsatisfying start. Climb the wall immediately left of the gully until it is possible to rejoin the parent route at the good holds above its crux.

KILN O' THE FUFFOCK, The Orange Wall:

Fifty metres north of Main Cliff is a north-facing steep and compact wall. The rock is very good quality.

Stonehead – 10m E3 5c*. R. McAllister, M. Reed (both solo). September, 1996.

Climbs the central line to a rounded finish.

Ocean Colour Scene – 10m E4 6a**. R. McAllister, D. McGimpsey, S. Mearns. September, 1996.

Climbs the left arête of the main face. Poorly protected.

Spinning Wheel – 10m E2 5c. R. McAllister, D. McGimpsey, S. Mearns. September, 1996.

The crack to the left. Climb the crack until possible to step right 2m below the top and finish up Ocean Colour Scene.

Hate Thy Neighbour – 10m E1 5b. M. Reed, R. McAllister, J. Hagan. September, 1996.

The crack left of the previous route.

LAGGANTULLACH HEAD, Small Bay:

Stolen Moments – 25m E1 5c. M. Reed, R. McAllister. 17th September, 1995.

A fine well-protected and sustained route. At the back (landward) end of the bay is a prominent corner which gives the route.

CRAMMAG HEAD, Kittiwake Zawn:

Beers, Smears and Queers – 25m E4 6b. R. McAllister, D. McGimpsey. 1st May, 1995.

A magnificent route. Though prone to seepage, direct sun will temporarily dry it. Well protected. This is the main open corner line in the back of the zawn. Access from the south by traverse or by free abseil. Climb a fine overhanging flake crack for 3m, then step rightwards into a niche. Make a committing high step up on to a good foothold. Using undercuts, climb up the wall to some sidepulls. Hard moves gain a pocket and good flange, then pull up on to a hanging ramp. Go up this to sloping ledges, then move out right on to a rib. Climb this to its top, then undercut up and right until below a roof. Exit via an awkward and precarious slab, then leave this on big sloping holds to ascend the much easier finishing corner.

CENTRAL OUTCROPS, CAMBUSBARRON QUARRY:

The line described as Rats up a Drainpipe (SMCJ 1996) had previously been climbed by M. Worsley and C. Pettigrew in May, 1994 and named Pig Route but had accidentally been missed from the guide.

Blockbuster – 15m MVS 4c. C. Adam, S. Baker. June, 1994.
In the large corner to the left of Power of Endurance, scramble over large boulders to the obvious wide crack at half height and climb it.

Bo's Groove – 12m MVS 4c. C. Adam, C. Lennox. 14th May, 1996.
About 10m left of Power of Endurance a blunt arete protrudes. Climb the groove with a thin crack on the right to a tree belay.

Bo's Arête – 12m HVS 5a. C. Adam, C. Lennox. 14th May, 1996.
From the bottom of the groove make an interesting move out right to takle the blunt arete face on. Gear out on the right, then left.

Bo's Arête Direct – 12m E1 5c. C. Adam. 14th May, 1996.
The face returning to the right of the arête provides an interesting variation. Climb to the hold above the V-shaped pocket, then swing left to join Bo's Arête.

Contortionism – 20m E6 6c. G. Lennox, D. Parr. 30th August, 1996.
Climbs straight up the corner right of Economy Drive. The route is well protected but very sustained with a vicious crux section.

Anabolic Steroids – 20m E7 6c. G. Lennox, C. Adam. 14th May, 1996.
Climbs the overhanging crackline above the friction boulder problems at the back of the quarry. Bold dynamic climbing leads to a break at 4m. Hard and sustained but well protected climbing follows.

CAMBUSBARRON WEST QUARRY:
High on the west wall is a prominent squat pillar with two short but striking cracklines on its right flank. It is level with the north end of a fenced-off planted area on the quarry floor, and above the north end of the biggest of the piles of rubble below the west wall of the quarry.

The Rock of Crack – E3 5c. M. Worsley, T. Wood. August, 1996.
The left-hand crack.

Confessions of a Speed Freak – E2 5b. M. Worsley, T. Wood. August, 1996.
The right-hand crack.

Gear Freak – 15m E6 6c. G. Lennox. April, 1997.
An ascent of Production Line without pegs, which seem to have been removed in revenge for the bolt chopping. Climb the crack on the right placing a high side runner. Climb down and across to horizontal crack. Move up to small roof and make very hard move to triangular hold. Pull up to crack and carefully scale loose ground above.

Bird Nest's Crack – E1 5b. M. Worsley, T. Wood. July, 1996.
On the east wall and 14m right of Production Line, just left of Assassin, is a pillar split by a vertical off-hand crack. Requires care at the top.

FASTCASTLE SEACLIFFS, The Soutar Area:
Tubigripper – 12m E1 5a. C. Pasteur, A. Matthewson, J. Andrew. 20th May, 1996.
Sustained climbing between Sentry Box and Daytrippers (SMCJ, 1996). Start 4m right of Sentry Box, and directly up the centre of the huge protruding block above.

BENARTY HILL (Fife):
The cliff remains an esoteric backwater, probably justifiably.

Pamela Anderson – 15m E4 6b. J. Andrew. 13th June, 1996.
The curvaceous off-width crack right of Dolly Parton is harder than it looks, even more so in the nesting season (fulmar). A car-jack runner was employed.

Wizard – VS 5a. A. Matthewson, A. Hume, C. Pasteur. 13th June, 1996.
A short clean prow near the left end of the cliff.

MISCELLANEOUS NOTES

The W. H. Murray Literary Prize.

As a tribute to the late Bill Murray, whose mountain and environment writings have been an inspiration to many a budding mountaineer, the SMC have started a modest writing prize, to be run through the pages of the Journal. The basic rules are set out below, and will be re-printed each year. The first year open to contributions will be 1998, with a deadline, as is normal, of the end of January that same year. So assuming you are reading this in early July, you have, for the first year of the competition, six months in which to set the pencil, pen or word processor on fire.

The Rules:

1. There shall be a competition for the best entry on Scottish Mountaineering published in the *Scottish Mountaineering Club Journal*. The competition shall be called the 'W. H. Murray Literary Prize', hereafter called the 'Prize.'

2. The judging panel shall consist of, in the first instance, the following: The current Editor of the *SMC Journal;* The current President of the SMC; and two or three lay members, who will be drawn from the membership of the SMC. The lay members of the panel will sit for three years after which they will be replaced.

3. If, in the view of the panel, there is in any year no entries suitable for the Prize, then there shall be no award that year.

4. Entries shall be writing on the general theme of 'Scottish Mountaineering', and may be prose articles of up to approximately 5000 words in length, or shorter verse. Entries may be fictional.

5. Panel members may not enter for the competition during the period of their membership.

6. Entries must be of original, previously unpublished material. Entries should be submitted to the Editor of the *SMC Journal* before the end of January for consideration that year. Lengthy contributions are preferably word-processed and submitted either on 3.5" PC disk or sent via e-mail. (See Office Bearers page at end of this Journal for address etc.) Any contributor to the SMC Journal is entitled to exclude their material from consideration of the Prize and should so notify the Editor of this wish in advance.

7. The prize will be a cheque for the amount £250.

8. Contributors may make different submissions in different years.

9. The decision of the panel is final.

10. Any winning entry will be announced in the *SMC Journal* and will be published in the *SMC Journal* and on the SMC Web site. Thereafter, authors retain copyright.

First recorded Scottish Avalanche?

BOB AITKEN reports: The following item appears in a new book by John Kerr, who writes a lot of slightly eccentric history about Atholl, called *The Living Wilderness: Atholl Deer Forests* (Perth: Jamieson & Munro, 1996). It's a terrible curate's egg of a book, full of fascinating detail about the historical minutiae of deer forest life and management (much of it out of Atholl estate papers previously almost untouched by researchers), but entirely devoid of any wider political or critical context. However the point of interest is Chapter 8, Tilt and Beinn a' Ghlo Forest, pp 79-80:

'Commonplace events in the glen are well covered in reports submitted by the factor and keepers, providing an insight into life there nearly two hundred years ago:

March 10, 1799. Thomas Palliser, factor.

There is no scarcity of either harts or hinds in the forest. John Crerar has been here since Wednesday. I went up to Forest Lodge with him, after which we looked into Glen Criny and Glen Mark, where we saw a great number of deer. The snow in many places there will not be off in the course of next summer, some of the wreaths are as high as this house.'

One of Robertson's sons in Dalnagelsich (925 734) had a very narrow escape when out looking after the sheep near to the side of the Tilt: 'He heard a great noise; on looking up he saw a considerable quantity of snow comeing *[sic]* from the top of the hill, he got in below a rock and called his dog to come to him, but it refused, and was carried away by the snow into the river, and was lost. The snow rushed down with such violence into the river that it threw out to the opposite side several birch trees, a great deal of ice, and some trout, about fifty yards into the field behind the stables.'

The source is given as the Blair Castle Charter Room. The bit about the flying fish has a slight whiff of the shaggy dog about it (if that's not over-mixing the metaphor), but perhaps it's the kind of unlikely detail that confirms the truth of the tale . . .

Apart from its intrinsic interest this may be the first written record of an avalanche in the Highlands, since it predates by one year the Loss of Gaick. Perhaps they had a run of good winters at the turn of the century.

IAN THOMSON writes:– Jean's Hut, for many years a haven from wind, rain and snow in Coire Cas on the northern side of Cairn Gorm, and, from 1965, in Coire an Lochain, was demolished in 1986 owing largely to the depredations of weather and vandalism. The origins, construction and subsequent history of the Hut provide an interesting story, worth recounting.

At Easter 1948, the Scottish Section of the Central Council of Physical Recreation (CCPR) organised two one-week mountaincraft courses in the Northern Cairngorms, based at the Aviemore Hotel. They were well-attended, but marred by the fatal accident which led to the building of Jean's Hut. A 21-year-old physiotherapist, Jean McIntyre Smith, the daughter of a Scottish doctor, was full of enthusiasm for the outdoors. The war was over, and the nation making a return to a peace-time economy. The 40 students were transported from the hotel to Glenmore Lodge where the forestry track terminated, and those who were skiing had to walk with their heavy hickory ex-army skis the five uphill kilometres to

Coire Cas. On March 17, Jean's party was descending the Fiacaill ridge of Cairn Gorm after a langlauf excursion on the plateau on the final day of the first course when Jean lost her balance, accelerated into the corrie and had the misfortune to strike a rock with her head, and was killed. She loved the hills, and a year after the accident, her ashes were scattered beside Clach Bharraig, the prominent erratic on the western flank of An t-Aonach overlooking Loch Morlich and Glen More.

By the beginning of 1950, Glenmore Lodge, which had opened as the Scottish Centre of Outdoor Training four months after the accident, was offering courses almost throughout the year. These were courses for the public at the popular holiday times, for final-year students in colleges of physical education, for military personnel and for schoolchildren. Dr. Smith wanted to erect a memorial appropriate to his daughter, and in 1949 he suggested that a hut should be built in Coire Cas, with custody given to Glenmore Lodge. The idea was warmly welcomed by the CCPR and the Lodge staff: most of the skiing was in the corrie which was also frequently visited by hillwalking parties from the Lodge, and boulders were the only protection against the elements there. Permission was sought and received from Inverness County Council and the Forestry Commissioners.

Cowieson of Glasgow were approached to provide plans for a prefabricated hut designed for the hostile area in which it would stand, and, when these were approved, they manufactured the sections. It was to have wooden walls and a corrugated aluminium roof, with benches fixed to the walls, and a cupboard. The firm specialised in making bodies for railway wagons, so the walls were stoutly made. They were to have concrete foundations, and a concrete block, set into the earthen floor, was to be provided for cooking stoves. To protect the door from the elements, particularly wind and snow, there was a porch along that side also with a door, and a wooden bench along its inside wall.

From early 1950, a great deal of work was done by the Glenmore staff and students, especially the schoolchildren, carrying the materials to the site. Of those required, only two lay within reasonable distance: boulders, which were rolled down the hillside to form the foundations, and gravel, which was gathered from near the Clach Bharraig Bothy, a kilometre away. Over many months, every party heading for the Cairngorm plateau went by way of the Bothy, filled a little bag with gravel and took it to the site. The rest of the material had to be carried from the Lodge. Fortunately, they had the assistance of a garron for carrying the cement and Loch Morlich sand. Many a journey she made up the path alongside the Allt Mor, with her human companions chasing behind. All the prefabricated sections and other timber work, together with the roof sections, had to be manhandled all the way from the Lodge, although, when conditions allowed, the Lodge's old Nansen sledge was pressed into service. It took 18 months to assemble all the materials on site. In an article about the Hut entitled, *A Cairngorm Shelter,* published, a week after its erection, in *The Glasgow Herald* of September 13, 1951, Alastair Hetherington said: 'Most of the hauling was not done by adults but by schoolchildren from Glasgow and Lanarkshire attending special courses at Glenmore Lodge. It was part of their training in outdoor life and in meeting the challenge of the hills. And a fierce challenge it must have been in the early spring. Parties of boys and girls aged 15 and 16 camped out for a week at a time to help in moving the sections. With snow and wind it was hard camping, so hard that one night the tents were blown down by a gale. But they seem to have enjoyed it – certainly it was a change from city schools.'

However, the Hut was quickly erected. Once the concrete base was laid, the walls and roof were bolted into place in one day. Initially, the interior remained bare, but over the summer of 1952, Andy McGinn, a teacher of technical education and a voluntary instructor at the Lodge, completed the Hut by fixing the benches to the walls, and providing it with the cupboard. In October 1952, an inscribed plaque was set in place. It read: 'In memory of Jean McIntyre Smith, who trod this way joyfully. *Cha till i tuilidh.* [She will not return.]'

The porch was always left unlocked so that anyone could use it, and it contained a Duff stretcher, while some additional First-Aid equipment was kept in the main part. In this way the Hut became the outpost of mountain rescue in the area. The inner door was initially kept locked to prevent misuse and vandalism, but the key was placed in a glass-fronted box for emergency use, and one was kept at the Lodge. Parties were allowed to use the Hut with consent from the Lodge, but too often the key was taken from its box in non-emergency situations, and it was eventually hidden on a hook behind the downpipe. Unfortunately, this led to the Hut being forcibly entered on occasions, and from time to time it was decided to leave it open.

Jean's Hut offered a marvellous sanctuary in Coire Cas, particularly when the wind blew and the rain fell. It had a stove on which water could be boiled for tea or cocoa – endless amounts of which were consumed over the years. Metal mugs, some with strips of sticking plaster along the rim to protect lips from hot metal, were kept there. They were seldom washed, and the plasters became dirty, but what did that matter when they revitalised the cold and weary. In 1955, Karl Fuchs opened his ski school at Carrbridge, and taught his students in Coire Cas where they, too, availed themselves of the Hut. When the weather was particularly foul, it could be filled to overflowing, 50 or so, the entire skiing population in the corrie in the days before the opening of the new ski road in 1960 – crammed inside. Dougie Stewart, a member of the Glenmore permanent staff from 1958 to 1960, remembers one such day:

'One bleak winter's day, with a wet sleet blizzard developing, I baled out with my climbers from Coire an t-Sneachda, and headed for the hut. It was already jammed full of wet, miserable skiers and climbers, and the only heating was the gas cooker. The place was thick with steaming bodies, and Jack Thomson (a member of the Glenmore staff for 30 years until his retirement in 1982) said: "We'll need to try something to get these folk warmed up." So the Jean's Hut Olympics were inaugurated. In the rafters there were dozens of garden canes, used for slalom practice. Jack got everyone organised with a cane each, and divided the occupants into the west team and the east team. He screwed up a newspaper into a ball and threw it up in the middle-for the most compressed game of hockey in history as everyone flailed about, trying to force the "ball" to the other end of the hut. After some time of this mayhem, with everyone now in a frisky mood, Jack announced the next event – the relay race. The door was opened and one runner from each team tore round the hut, slithering and falling over snow and rock foundations, came back in, shouted "East" or "West", and the next runner shot off. Non-running team members had to jump up and down in the hut, cheering on their team. In no time everyone was sweating and cheery. One guy said to me it was the best day he'd ever had in Coire Cas!'

Jean's Hut was used as a base for three-day expeditions undertaken by the schoolchildren. As it was not too distant from the Lodge, it was suitable for some of the less fit, and from it day-long tramps could be made. It was also used as overnight accommodation for those who were continuing to the Shelter Stone or the Etchachan Hut. Using benches and floor, it could take up to 18, although the normal complement was 10 children and one instructor. A good thick layer of heather on the floor helped make sleeping easier, but many still found themselves stiff in the morning. The benches may have been warmer, but their ribbing was uncomfortable. On fine nights in summer, there was always the option of sleeping alfresco on a bed of heather.

The advent of the road to Coire Cas in 1960 and the development of skiing brought to an end the golden days of Jean's Hut. There was a continuous increase in human activity in the area-skiing, walking, climbing – and the Hut suffered from the start. In the absence of any accommodation for skiers – the Shieling was not opened until 1963 – the Hut was broken into on a number of occasions and in the end it was decided to leave it unlocked. In the absence of adequate toilet and litter-disposal facilities, it was used as a lavatory and a litter bin. In truth, it was now in quite the wrong place. In this country, a mountain hut should not be sited where large numbers of people congregate, especially if it is unwardened and alternative facilities are available. Moreover, it no longer had the same value as overnight accommodation for Lodge expeditions. The road made it too accessible, and the area was too busy. It was clear that, if it remained in Coire Cas, it would soon degenerate to the point where it would have to be demolished.

After discussion, in the summer of 1962 it was decided to move the Hut three kilometres to the south-west into Coire an Lochain where it would serve as a useful base for climbers in one of the most popular winter-climbing corries, and allow the Cairngorm Mountain Rescue Team, who kept a stretcher in a box there, to store more equipment. A good start was made by a party of soldiers camping in the area. They dismantled the Hut and transported all the smaller parts to the corrie, leaving the rest stacked on the original site. Moving the main sections proved a much harder task. Four Glenmore Lodge staff or six Glasgow schoolboys, accompanied by a relief team, were required for each section, and in practice it was not possible to move more than one section a day to the new site. Bill Blackwood, who operated a ski-tow in the area, offered the hire of himself and his caterpillar tractor to assist in the task but, despite the efforts of tractor, schoolboy and staff, over a three-week period only two-thirds of the sections were moved. Finally, when the tractor suffered its third major breakdown, this method of transportation had to be abandoned. The sections in Coire an Lochain were tied down and heavily cairned for the winter, while those remaining in Coire Cas were taken down to the Lodge and stored in a garage.

The Army was approached for assistance under its Military Aid to the Civil Community (OPMACC) scheme. The response was positive, and it was hoped that the remainder of the Hut would be taken into Coire an Lochain by a military vehicle the following June and re-erected. However, when the time came the vehicle was not available, and it was not until 1964 that the job was done. In early November of that year, men from 300 Para Squadron (TA), under the command of Capt. Stanley Peake, arrived with Capt. Graham Owens, the mastermind of the project. At their disposal was an RNAS Lossiemouth helicopter which flew the remaining sections and all required materials in an underslung net to the new site. The opportunity was taken to replace the bench on one wall with upper and lower bunks, and the completed structure, which was given a concrete floor, was strengthened with steel roof-stay cables anchored to the ground. The whole operation took about a fortnight.

Jean's Hut survived there for 22 years. However, although the Scottish Sports Council (SSC), through the Lodge, maintained its special responsibility for the Hut, the Hut lost its old connection with the Lodge. At different times – with the support and encouragement of the Mountain Bothies Association and Glenmore Lodge – the Strathspey Mountain Club, the Cairngorm Ranger Service, the Jacobites Mountaineering Club and the Ellon Hillwalking Club looked after the Hut. But it was a constant battle. As the years passed, it suffered the ravages of weather and vandalism, and again litter became a problem. From time to time, it was mended and cleaned up, but soon reverted to its former condition – and the structure deteriorated progressively. Its proximity to the top of the ski-road and the Shieling continued to make its existence questionable, and increasing numbers walked into Coire an Lochain. Moreover, in the 1970s, prompted by the tragic loss of five Edinburgh schoolchildren and an instructor on the Cairn Gorm-Ben Macdui plateau in November 1971, an influential body of opinion emerged, opposing all bothies and mountain huts on the grounds that they could be difficult or impossible to find in darkness and poor visibility, and in winter they might be covered by snow or so frozen that they could not be opened. In this way the inexperienced might be lured into danger. (In January 1984, three men in a party of four died when they became lost in a blizzard as they made their way from the Coire Cas car park to the Hut.) Others argued that huts were out of character with wilderness areas and aesthetically displeasing, although Jean's Hut, being wooden, was not as inappropriate to its surroundings as some.

By early 1979, the SSC was anxious to have the Hut demolished, and secured the consent of Jean Smith's family, but it lingered on. By 1986, it was in very poor condition and the majority opinion was that it should go. The Cairngorm Mountain Rescue Team accepted this, but argued that it should be replaced to continue to provide a store for equipment, a forward base for rescue operations, and a shelter for rescuers and rescued in bad weather. They approached the Army for assistance, but the weight of opinion was against them, and in the end they had to concede defeat. The Hut was demolished in June 1986.

Today, all that remains of Jean's Hut are its original 1952 plaque and another commemorating its removal to Coire an Lochain – both now attached to a memorial pillar to Ben Beattie in the grounds of Glenmore Lodge – and two stout nesting-boxes, still in use and both called, 'Jean's Hut', made from timber rescued at the time of its demolition.

SMC Above

The following aerial view of Scotland is sent in by Iain Smart with apologies for getting a bit above himself.

There are many kinds of artificial aids for arriving over the top of a mountain. One no more disreputable than any other is by light aircraft. True, unless things go badly wrong your feet do not actually touch the summit but then what is the difference between a few hundred feet of air and the high-tech boot-sole of the conventional climber? This analogy is not entirely convincing and so the following accounts of airborne Munro-bagging are given with a feeling of guilt. Ringing the quiet hills with so many decibels wrung out of the blue belfry of a peaceful sky is, I suppose, the auditory equivalent of orange peel.

The flights described here were made in a Cessna 152 out of Riverside Airfield, Dundee. This aircraft is a highwing monoplane with two seats and a cruising speed of about 90 knots. Real airmen consider it a very boring aircraft and refer to it as a 'spam can' but to an inexperienced pilot like myself it feels like being at the controls of a Sopwith Camel heading into peril. This feeling, however, sharpens up the senses; the familiar hills beneath gain a new magic as the vertical dimension is suddenly enlarged, made mobile and put under your own personal control. The accounts below are not given in the spirit of Biggles, nor with the gravid introspection of St. Exupery; they are responses to the high aesthetics of soaring above the fair land of Scotland in its different moods, to the privilege of travel in four dimensions with all senses heavily engaged in responding to the total ambience, yet with the practical need to keep one's hands on the control systems connecting the appreciative brain with the uncompromising reality of aerodynamics.

Spring Song: This flight was made on a fine day in May. I flew north over fertile Strathmore, parquet-floored with fields of winter brown and the fresh green of brairding crops. Then up to 8000ft above the scattering of fair-weather cumulus clouds of the type that angels recline upon with their harps. You occasionally see them in the distance; many are clearly recognisable as former members of the Club. Far below were the sun-dappled moorlands of Strathardle and bonnie Glenshee and there by the silver river was my house. Over the Ben Iutharns the clouds ended and the captured Feshie could be seen right-angling into the Spey instead of the Dee. Above the Garbh Coire Mor I throttled back, put down half-flap and commenced a lazy, circling descent in a clockwise direction over the snow-wreathed hills.

The old familiar landmarks appeared on the horizon one after the other: the Monadhliath, the great forests of Rothiemurchus and Nethy, Ben Avon and Bennachie and the plains of Aberdeenshire beyond, then Lochnagar, Glen Clunie with its rolling green slopes, Beinn a' Ghlo and the Drumochter hills and back to the Monadhliath. The Lairig Ghru meanwhile spiralled up from below growing in texture and detail with each circle. At five grand I levelled out and made a turn round Braeriach, wing tip pointed at the cairn and eyes checking the dials for slip, bank, height and speed – you can't be too careful. Nevertheless, there was enough cerebral capacity left over to appreciate the total situation. You could see into sunlit Coire Bhrochain where we had camped in deep snow on Hogmanay 1948 when the hills were empty. There was the little lochan below Cairn Toul and now the textured floor of the Garbh Coire Mor itself sparking the memory of that winter day when the great quilt of cloud cascaded off the edge of the plateau into the gloom of the coire, then the Wells of Dee of the memorable June bivouac in perfect weather and now Rothiemurchus once wild and lonely with only a rutted track to Glenmore Lodge which lay on the edge of the then known world.

I am telling you all this to illustrate how much parallel processing the creatively-stressed brain can accomplish as it wheels about in time and space above a landscape heavily associated with the brain's own formative experiences. Then on over the trackless Macdhui plateau, now well and truly tracked, a look into Loch Avon where Broon kept a lonely Hogmanay long ago when there actually were deep mid-winters, over barnacled Ben Mheadhoin where I once drowsed fawnlike one youthful summer *apres midi,* past Beinn a' Bhuird of the frost-bitten toe and the Mitre Ridge of high ecstasy, then back south by dark Lochnagar and many-branched Glen Clova, an eastward curve over the Howe of the Mearns to the silvery

Tay and a near-perfect landing at Dundee. I walked away from the plane six inches above the ground having lived a full three weeks in an hour-and-a-quarter of elapsed real time.

High Summer: This was a windless day, slightly overcast with a thin layer of high cloud and enough sunshine to give a hint of shadow. Below the cloud the air was clear to the sharp horizon as it often is after rain. The first leg to Inverness lay over the detailed landscape of the rolling eastern Grampians. Loch Builg, Tomintoul, Loch Garten, the Spey and the Findhorn all appeared below uncannily in the order predicted by the map. After a coffee in the International Lounge and an altercation with the security guards who wanted to see documents we didn't have, we were escorted back to the plane by an embarrassed local who apologised for the extra-terrestrials who seemed to be running the place. Then the flight to the rough bounds of Wester Ross and Sutherland. First direct to Loch Maree at four grand. Between us and the far horizon lay the fabled lands of the West from the Skerries to the Lewes.

To the left the textured lands of Torridon and to our right the wilderness of Sutherland whither we were bound. It is good to be lucky but magnitudes better to actually know you are lucky; this privilege was being bestowed on a receptive mind. I thought I would mention this because the few readers who actually reach this remote corner of the Journal will be people of discrimination and may think I was being just thoughtlessly exuberant, behaving like a sort of airborne trendy. The whole brain was, in fact, dedicated to appreciating the total situation – no mean task.

We made a descending circle over the shaggy islands of the reflecting loch with Slioch as a backdrop, then over by Airidh Charr to the Fionn Loch with herons circling the only wooded island. Over Strath na Seallag you could make out Sheneval and Larachantivore before passing by mighty An Teallach and crossing the Loch Brooms to Coigach.

From this vantage you could see that the North West was the ragged fringe of Scotland, the edge of Europe, the end of the road for folk migrations from the Eurasian hinterland. Below us the present-day Gaels were being displaced in their turn by poor souls driven out of their homes in the south by the collapse of their own community. This time the sack of the homeland was being carried out by the most recent wave of barbarians, wielding the naked sword of market forces untram-melled by educational, cultural or moral constraints. At the end of the Achiltibuie road I could see the croft of Cul na Creag where in the late Forties I had stayed in a Gaelic-speaking household, still rich in song and story; probably they speak some form of broad Yorkshire there now. In another 200 years maybe the Gaelo-Yorkshire tongue will be replaced by Urdu and Wee Shias may reign with all the tolerance of the Wee Frees. From up here you gain a certain perspective on these transient human population movements. Nevertheless, the loss of a creative culture and its songs should be taken at least as seriously as the loss of some squawking bird.

The flight continued with a low circle round Stac Pollaidh then round mighty, gloomy Suilven with its head moodily in a cloud.

Back in Inverness, we refuelled, flew down the Great Glen, turned left up Glen Coe flying below the summits – that was exciting – then we hung a louis over Kingshouse to take us along Loch Laidon where the super camping island is, then by Rannoch and Tummel to Pitlochry, grabbed a roger here and so back to Dundee. The four hours in the air now required months to unravel. The soul, as is well known, travels at walking pace, requires frequent rests and is left far behind as the present relentlessly pursues the future.

Autumn over Schiehallion: This was as fine an autumn day as you could wish for. There was a bit of a temperature inversion. A big glacier of cloud filled the upper Tay from Pitlochry to fair Strathmore. Elsewhere the glens were clear, the sun was brightly shining and the Highland summits stretched away to the horizon dusted with early snow. The autumn colours were aglow – russet bracken, yellow-gold birch and yellow-ochre larch. The great Schiehallion from which Fujiyama was copied lay ahead and to its left the long view over Loch Tummel and Loch Rannoch to Lochaber and the clichés of the Isles. A wide, climbing turn over the sacred mountain took us to ten grand, the ceiling of the aircraft. Scotland lay below from the Sgurr of Eigg to the Bass Rock looking like a brighter version of a Bartholomew's map.

There are times when it might be possible to exclaim: 'Oh, joy, oh, rapture!' and get away with it. I wish I had had the nerve to try on this occasion; it would be nice to be a tearaway and let yourself go, just once in your life. Alas, I flew stolidly homeward, frightened of committing a solecism. An hour later I was sitting at my desk wondering if it had all happened.

Above the Clouds: This flight to the west was made part of the way above the clouds. This is perfectly legal provided you remain within sight of the ground and a certain distance from the cloud. Within these constraints you can explore the great hills and glens of the upper air, the great one-off landscapes that will never be repeated, the transient country of beauty and mystery you traverse on the way to a conventional destination. I have never seen anyone else up there on these rolling snowfields, although doubtless there are marauding military jets, setting an objective danger like avalanches or collapsing seracs. This high territory is one of the last great wilderness areas. It's like the mountains below used to be before the industrial age, before our bizarre activity became just another sector of the market economy. It's like sailing still is once you get to the western coasts of the outer isles and keep away from the St. Kilda run.

We were on our way to Mull. There were glimpses of Ben Lui and Ben Cruachan at the bottom of crevasses in the high snows below. At Taynuilt the cloud ended and in calm, sunny weather we landed at Glenforsa on the meadow that serves as the airport. The skylarks were singing; lunch was out of doors. An hour later we flew over Ardnamurchan, the beaches at Arisaig and Morar (but at a discreet height and distance) halfway up Loch Morar a turn south over the rough bounds of Moidart to the Ben, a circle here for admiration and homage, then back over Luibelt, Loch Ossian and Loch Ericht before leaving the rugged terrain and entering the contrasting lands of far eastern Scotland.

Envoi: This flight will never take place. Nevertheless, I am going to tell you about it. It would be made on a clear, windless winter night with a full moon. The lochs will be frozen and there will have been a heavy snowfall. I have made a training flight under these conditions and it was indeed an exhilarating experience with Strathmore and its surrounding mountains all a-glimmer below and town, village and even individual farmhouse lights twinkling and identifiable. Circling the aircraft in level flight from pole star back to pole star while the well-known constellations pass in procession before the windscreen is an exacting test, particularly when you are asked to continue for a second round to make sure the first time wasn't a fluke.

On this final flight I'll fly north over Braemar, then low between Cairngorm of Derry and Ben Macdhui. By Carn Etchachan I'll put down full-flap and descend into the head of Loch Avon with a glance from the corner of the eye at the Shelter Stone and its crag, then fly over the twinkling snow on the loch and through the bealach to the Nethy, then climb high over Strath Spey and continue north again. Maybe keep on going over the Monadhliath and the Great Glen to Stac Pollaidh and Suilven, ghostly in the moonlight. Maybe even keep on going over the sea until summer.

But to do something irresponsible like that would provoke an air-sea rescue, generate disagreeable headlines and would almost certainly invalidate your insurance, and if they never found you it would be legally inconvenient for your heirs. It would also mean the destruction of a perfectly good aeroplane. To be a serious romantic you have to be ruthless and to be both ruthless and romantic you have to lack insight and if you lack insight you can't really be fully aware of what you are doing and if you do have insight enterprises of great pith and moment like this become sicklied over with the pale cast of thought and lose the name of action; thus conscience doth make Hamlets of us all. And Hamlet was a wally. I think maybe I'd keep pointing towards the pole star and just keep on going after all and increase the entropy of the universe with a modest bang rather than a whimper.

The Scottish Mountaineering Trust – 1996/97

DURING the year the Trust has continued successfully with its publication programme and managed to provide some financial assistance to all of the applications which have come before it and which Trustees have adjudged to be within their remit.

As the publications operation has developed, it has become clear that meetings of Trustees, which take place normally two or three times annually, are insufficient to manage what is now, in effect, a small company. Many decisions involving the day-to-day management are commercial by nature requiring perhaps particular skills or a more immediate response. The role of the Publications Company has therefore been enhanced and management of the publications operation is now wholly the Company's responsibility leaving the Trustees free to respond to the successes or failures of the directors and to handle the distribution of grants. All editorial responsibility including selection of titles, authors and design and specification will, of course, remain with the Publications Sub-Committee of the Club. The new arrangement gives every indication of working well.

The 1996 publication programme saw the production of the climbing guides *Selected Scottish Winter Climbs* and *Skye and The Hebrides* together with reprints of *Glen Coe Rock & Ice Climbs* and *The Corbetts*. This year includes climbing guides to *Arran and Arrochar, Highland Outcrops* and *The Munroists Companion*. Members might be surprised to know that the number of titles covered by the Trust is now more than 30.

Over the last 10 years, during which mountaineering books generally have begun to produce profits, the Trust has had no doubt over its obligation to return this income to the mountaineering community through the distribution of grants and details of these are listed below. The Club is, of course, a major recipient of Trust assistance and in the past year this has supported Journal costs, royalty payments, Lagangarbh and the Club library. Individuals also receive honoraria and authorship royalties.

The work carried out by the Trust grows annually and this falls on the backs of both Trustees and officials who give voluntarily of their time and to whom we should all record our thanks. The present Trustees are R. N. Campbell (chair), D. C. Anderson, C. D. Grant, A. Kassyk, W. A. McNicol, S. Murdoch, D. C. Page, R. T. Richardson, D. Sommerville and N. M. Suess.

J. R. R. Fowler.

General Grant Fund

Grants paid		
	Dundee Mountain Film Festival	£400
	Grampian MC – Inbhirfhaolain	£2015
	Gupta Peak Expedition	£500
	Jonathan Colville Trust	£665
	LSCC – Milehouse renovation	£5000
	MC of S – Conference booklet	£1300
	MC of S – core funding	£11,215
	MC of S – conference expenses	£100
	NTS – bridge over Allt Gniomhaidh	£750
	NTS – Tarmachan appeal	£1000
	NTS – Ben Lawers	£800
	Ochils MC – hut renovation	£1500
	Scottish Film Archive	£1740
	SMC Greenland Expedition 1996	£800
	SMC – Lagangarbh roof repair	£2870
	SMC – Lagangarbh tree planting	£918
	SMC – Library	£840
	Stirling University photographic exhibition	£100
Total		£32,513
Grants committed		£25,043

Footpath Fund

Grants paid		
	Balmoral Estates – Lochnagar	£3868
	NTS – Torridon and Glen Coe	£13,000
	Ross and Cromarty Footpath Trust	
	Annat and Carnmor	£8519
	Annat and Carnmor	£3819
Total		£29,206
Grants committed		£24,900

Journal Bequest

SEVERAL years ago, the *SMC Journal* received a cheque for £500, no strings attached, from the Walton family. The father, Robert, had been a member of the Club, and had, apparently, a soft spot for the Journal. His son, Ian, as will be seen elsewhere in this issue, remains active outdoors. This generous gift was put to good use recently, and has enabled the New Climbs Editor both to modernise his computer and be connected to the Internet, enabling switched on young climbers to communicate with him more rapidly.

Of Beer and Boats.

Some more notes on Harold Raeburn, from researches by K. V. Crocket and J. R. R. Fowler.

K. V. Crocket begins: Lacking the time and skills of a full-time researcher into such matters, it can be quite a lengthy process to unearth even basic facts on a person's life. Unknown to both of us, each of us had, in our small ways, been slowly gnawing away at Raeburn's details. Our inestimable Secretary for example, had been tramping round the burial grounds of Edinburgh, in search of the Raeburn headstone. In this he was ultimately successful, as he details below. As for my own researches, they led to me being photographed in an Edinburgh street, sitting on someone's shoulders with me dressed as a modern rock climber and my living step-ladder dressed in tweeds and false handle-bar moustache. It also led to Harold Raeburn's photograph being used for a brewer's promotional poster. And I have the T-shirt to prove it. If this intrigues you read on.

Our personal interest in Raeburn, as with many climbers, stems from a knowledge of many of his ascents in Scotland, as well as his own writings. Little need to expand on these here. I even wrote a short story purporting to be an account of the schoolboy Raeburn's first steps on rock. It may well have been fictional, but the footnotes included genuine details of his Birth and Death Certificates. To repeat the first of these: Entry No. 729 for the District of Newington, in the City of Edinburgh records the birth of Harold Andrew Raeburn on July 21, 1865 at 12 Grange Loan, Edinburgh. His father was William Raeburn, Brewer, his mother, Jessie Raeburn, maiden name Ramsay. The Certificate also records that William and Jessie married on October 5, 1849. As my short story accurately describes, Harold had two sisters, Ruth and Ethel, with Ruth quite often mentioned in later years as a climbing and walking activist.

This basic data, along with Raeburn's Death Certificate, sufficed for some time, until I received a communication from a large, International advertising company. They were, it seemed, involved with the launch of a new beer, and were toying with the name Raeburn. Could I help? As few climbers could spurn the scent of a free pint I was easily intrigued. It seemed that the company's researchers had thrown up three Raeburns. There was Raeburn the brewer, Raeburn the artist, and a Raeburn who apparently lived as a hermit in Ayrshire. Obviously, the latter did not much appeal as a name on which to launch a new ale!

Some of my other findings of more than a decade ago helped confirm that not only was Raeburn the brewer a relative of Harold, but that Harold himself worked as a brewer. Referring to the Edinburgh Post Office Directory Log for 1893-1894, for example, there was a listing for 'W. & J. Raeburn, brewers, 12 Merchant St.' Another entry was from 1905-1906, 'W. & J., brewers & maltsters, Craigmillar', and finally 'Raeburn, John (W. & J. R.), 49 Manor Place'. All of these addresses were in Edinburgh, though intriguingly, I found that Raeburn had actually lived for a short spell in Partick, Glasgow, while involved in the war effort. I have so far been unable to discover the street physically however, and it very likely has been pulled down and rebuilt, in good old Glasgow manner.

In 1905, a Julian Baker wrote:

'A brewer has to be a man of many parts. A knowledge of engineering, chemistry and biology is essential to one who takes an intelligent interest in his work and who wishes to be well provided for in the keen competitive style of the present times . . . and most important of all, he must be a judge and manager of men, for untold damage may be done by discontented and malicious workmen.'

A brewer also had to expect a rapid staff turnover. The annual fatality rate in the

Raeburn brewery, for example, was more than 8%, a grim reminder of past working conditions in an admittedly dangerous business, given the presence of so much CO_2. William Raeburn was, of course, the father of the climber, with John his uncle. In 1861 the two brothers acquired the former Usher's Brewery, Merchant Street. This brewery probably dated back to the early 18th century. Under the Raeburns, it became known as the Merchant Street Brewery, becoming extensively reconstructed in 1876. By the 1890s problems were being experienced with the water supply, and in 1897 the property was offered to the governors of Heriot-Watt College. William Raeburn had been connected with the College since 1872; as a director, treasurer and Life Member of the College Committee. This, no doubt, eased the sale of the property going ahead in 1898, for £14,500. William died that same year. By then Harold Raeburn would have been 33, and we must suppose that he would have been working in the brewery for some time with his father and uncle.

The sale of the property, however, allowed John Raeburn to build a new brewery at the then-developing brewery community of Craigmillar, just east of Edinburgh, where there were good water supplies and rail connections. Five other breweries were already in existence, including a Drybrough's. In 1913, the nearly-new brewery was sold to Robert Younger Ltd., of the St. Ann's Brewery, Edinburgh. The 1914-18 War stopped brewing at Craigmillar, which recommenced in 1919, with all output heading south by rail to the North-east of England. Brewing ceased in 1931 due to falling demand.

The trademark of W. & J. Raeburn Ltd. was a Lion Rampant, similar to a Scottish flag.

This is a brief summary of the brewing side of the Raeburn family, but what of the sailing part? I was led into this line of research by a few enigmatic lines in *SMC Journal* articles, both by Raeburn himself, and by William Inglis Clark, another well-known Edinburgh climber. The articles are in the 1903 issue of the Journal, and follow one another. In Raeburn's article, *From Sea to Summit,* 'SMCJ 7, pp.194-198, 1903, Raeburn describes a date to meet up with the Clarks on Ben Nevis. The route they were in hot pursuit of was Observatory Buttress, but Raeburn was also in pursuit of other yachts, for he was racing in the Firth of Forth that weekend. Lack of wind meant a day's delay before he could catch the train to Fort William, the Clarks in the interim continuing their explorations of the Ben. (See the Introduction to the sailing articles, this issue.)

Raeburn had, in fact, become becalmed in the Firth, only picking up the buoy at 1am. After an hour's sleep he caught the 4am train to Fort William. The long, idle hours that day may well have led Raeburn to a philosophic frame of mind. His article begins by attempting to define mountaineering, then moves on to compare it with other sports. On the way to describing yachting in a favourable light, he roundly condemns golf, 'that insidious epidemic'. My first moves in looking into Raeburn's yachting exploits were to find the most suitable local yachting club. A suggestion to try the Royal Forth Yachting Club met with immediate success. In October 1995 the Archivist of the Club confirmed that Harold and John Raeburn were admitted as members of the club in 1900, and both ceased to be members in 1911. At first the archivist could find no more, but in November I received more details that the Archivist had succeeded in finding.

The Club House belonging to the RFYC that the Raeburns would have used was Eildon Lodge, at 1 Boswell Road (1881-1983). This was a fine building above the present harbour at Granton, but a bit back from the water. The present club house, at Middle Pier, Granton, was built new. The RFYC has a similar membership size to the SMC, at around 400.

Harold and John, already members of the RFYC for three years, bought the nine-ton cutter *Teal* in 1903. The Commodore of the club then was Sir Donald Curry, the multi-millionaire of the Curry Line. His boat was a bit bigger, at 999 tons, being the luxury steam yacht *Iolaire*. When I say luxury, we are talking of gold banisters. The wine cellar probably took the boat over the 1000-ton mark.

In 1904, the Raeburns won the RFYC Corinthian Match Challenge Cup, racing in the *Teal*. From 1905 to 1907 John Raeburn presented a prize for a series of three annual races. He was a member of the Sailing Committee of the club from 1905 to 1908. This committee organised all club sailing and racing.

In 1906, John bought the 30-linear rater *Armyne*, owning it until 1908. Sailing in the *Armyne*, John and Harold again won the Corinthian Cup, in 1906 and again in 1907. As they had now won it three times, they were presented with the cup (a practice which has since ceased). They in turn presented the cup back to the RFYC who re-named it the Raeburn Trophy. This is the name under which it is still raced for.

Round about 1988, at an SMC Committee Meeting, I suggested that the new Club Hut between Dalwhinnie and Newtonmore be named the Raeburn Hut. The earliest record of climbing exploration at nearby Creag Dubh was by Harold Raeburn, while the SMC already had Ling and CIC (Charles Inglis Clark) Huts, both named after prominent club members of the past. The Committee happily endorsed the suggestion.

As for the beer, I am happy to confirm that the new ales, developed by Scottish Brewers, and named after Raeburn, were up to standard. Through the company, I arranged for free beer at a Club dinner in Fort William. Unfortunately, and to the deep embarrassment of the brewery, a hitch in their internal communications meant that the Raeburn ale never reached the discerning palates of club members – the hotel provided free beer with what they had instead. On the same afternoon, the Hon. Editor and Hon. President were photographed quaffing beer at the foot of the Ben, to the considerable bewilderment of a descending walker (who ended up with a serendipitous pint of beer). Raeburn himself appears on the print of the assembled meet on the steam yacht *Erne*. He's the laid-back one on the left, holding onto a stay.

John Fowler continues: Raeburn had been noted as a man of outstanding vigour and energy which no doubt was why he was chosen to go to Everest with Howard-Bury in 1921. His health however, already chronically weakened by overwork during the Great War, failed during the expedition, and Raeburn was to spend the last years of his life in Craig House in Morningside – a sanatorium for the mentally ill (recently restored for similar purposes as part of Napier University). His last years must have been miserable

The Raeburn Trophy.

ones as institutional care had progressed only a little since Victorian times. The death certificate detailed below mentions melancholia.

So where does the man lie? Many of Edinburgh's graveyards are in an appalling condition – a perfect example of the wrong sort of property being in private hands. Ever since the closure of the city's main public graveyard (Greyfriars) in 1863 by the Medical Officer, Henry Duncan Littlejohn (the father of the forensic scientist who helped investigate the Arran murder), Edinburgh left interment to private companies. As graveyards became full and the popularity of cremation increased, profits dwindled and graveyards were abandoned to their fate. Inevitably, vandalism has since become rife. However, a few inquiries and an expedition with a machête revealed that Raeburn lies in Warriston Cemetery in a hellishly-desecrated corner. Fortunately, his monument is a mural one and this is well preserved. The inscriptions read:

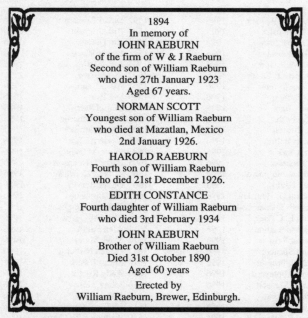

1894
In memory of
JOHN RAEBURN
of the firm of W & J Raeburn
Second son of William Raeburn
who died 27th January 1923
Aged 67 years.

NORMAN SCOTT
Youngest son of William Raeburn
who died at Mazatlan, Mexico
2nd January 1926.

HAROLD RAEBURN
Fourth son of William Raeburn
who died 21st December 1926.

EDITH CONSTANCE
Fourth daughter of William Raeburn
who died 3rd February 1934

JOHN RAEBURN
Brother of William Raeburn
Died 31st October 1890
Aged 60 years

Erected by
William Raeburn, Brewer, Edinburgh.

And here the story closes but for one thing. The descendants of Raeburn and Munro may have forgotten the mountaineering heritage created by their ancestors and allowed the grave sites to become visual wrecks. Perhaps some person or Club should not.

Footnotes: We are grateful to the following sources for information on the Raeburn family, both as brewers and sailors! Gerald Glancy, Archivist, Royal Forth Yachting Club. Charles McMaster, Scottish Brewing Archive. Ian Hamilton, McCann-Erickson Advertising.

Raeburn's Death Certificate. Entry No. 683 in the register of Deaths for the District of Morningside, Edinburgh, records the death of Harold Andrew Raeburn, Brewer (retired), at 6 am on the morning of December 21, 1926, at Craig House, Edinburgh. The usual place of residence was given as 14 Abercromby Place, where he lived with his sister, Ethel. The reason for death was given as 'Exhaustion from Melancholia 4 yrs 10 months 13 days. Endocrine Insufficiency 4 yrs. 10 mos. 13 days'.

MUNRO MATTERS

By C. M. Huntley (Clerk of the List)

This year the Clerk of the List has been kept busy with a record number of new Munroists to be added to the List. The 170 new names are listed below with the Munroist number and year of compleation of the Munros, Tops and Furths. Of the additions 10 have included the Tops and seven the Furths. * SMC member.

1536 Craig Allardice	1996		
1537 Danny Rafferty	1995		
1538 D. Hillman	1996		
1539 Andrew M. James*	1996		
1540 Willie Black	1996		
1541 Mary Macrae	1995		
1542 Alex Macrae	1995	1995	
1543 W. Angus Wallace	1996		
1544 Pat McIntosh	1995		
1545 Calum McIntosh	1995		
1546 Tod Bainbridge	1996		
1547 John McPartlin	1996		
1548 Elizabeth B Smith	1996		
1549 Eleanor Symon	1996		
1550 Scot Symon	1996		
1551 Danny Barr	1996		
1552 Colin Firth	1996		
1553 Bill Buriton	1996		
1554 Adrian Belton	1996		
1555 John Clark	1996		
1556 Ian Dickson	1996		
1557 Andrew Moignard	1996		
1558 Andy Heald	1996		
1559 Graham G. Hemsley	1996		
1560 Kenneth J. Campbell	1996		
1561 Robin L. Calder	1996		
1562 Jock Mackinnon	1996		
1563 Murray Reid	1996		
1564 David Spencer	1996	1994	
1565 Ruaridh Pringle	1996		
1566 David Appleyard	1996	1996	
1567 Peter J. Mansell	1996	1996	
1568 Richard Bryan	1996		
1569 Janice Butcher	1996		
1570 David Butcher	1996		
1571 Robert D. Veitch	1996		
1572 David Eccles	1996		
1573 James Garvie	1996		
1574 John Samuel	1996		
1575 Thomas Mason	1996		
1576 Ken Ross	1996		
1577 Alan Gibson	1996		
1578 Harry Morton	1996		
1579 Richard Wheeler	1996		
1580 Ron W. Elder	1996		
1581 David Broadmeadow	1996		
1582 William Lawrence	1996		
1583 Fred C. Alexander	1996		
1584 Edward H. Noble	1996		
1585 Hamish Stewart	1996		
1586 Iain F. D. Gilmour	1996		
1587 John M. Moore	1996		
1588 Iain S. Dickinson	1996		
1589 Ethel S. Thomson	1996		
1590 David L. MacGregor	1996		
1591 Michael B. Howard	1996		
1592 David Graham	1996		
1593 Bill Grierson	1996		
1594 Jim Dixon	1996		
1595 Lynda Woods	1996		
1596 Jonathan Woods	1996		
1597 Sue Jardine	1996		
1598 Allan Bantick	1996		
1599 Del Evans	1996		
1600 Muriel Parry	1996		
1601 Doris Matheson	1995		
1602 Alex Matheson	1995		
1603 Kevin A. Tait	1996		
1604 Susan M. White	1996		
1605 Barry J. Hodgson	1996		
1606 A. Neil K. Brown	1996		
1607 David Harvey	1996	1996	
1608 Eric Simpson	1996		
1609 Robert J. Ferguson	1996	1996	
1610 Elizabeth Harwood	1996		
1611 Alex Smith	1996		
1612 Steve Mann	1996		
1613 Gillian Nisbet	1996		
1614 Susan J. Park	1996	1996	
1615 Andy Ritchie	1996		
1616 John Calder	1996		
1617 Ron Neville	1996		
1618 Molly E. Grant	1996		
1619 Andrew J. H. Grant	1996		
1620 Euan Pyper	1996		
1621 Mhairi Ross	1996		
1622 Jim Ross	1996		
1623 Mike Dales	1996		
1624 Chris Bull	1996		
1625 Thomas Paton	1996		
1626 Cameron J. Johnston	1996	1996	
1627 Alastair Bruce	1996		
1628 Roy Bell	1996		
1629 Steve Frearson	1996		
1630 J. M. Thomson	1996		
1631 Robert J. Barton	1996		
1632 Andrew R. Dickson	1996		
1633 Shona Malcolm	1996		

1634	Bruce Malcolm	1996	
1635	Eric Young	1996	
1636	James A. Bennett	1996	
1637	Nancy McCombie	1996	
1638	John Stevenson	1995	
1639	Graham Sage	1996	
1640	Geoff Scott	1994	
1641	W. Michael Gollan	1994	
1642	Matthew Runciman	1996	
1643	Ian MacPherson	1996	
1644	Gerald McPartlin	1996	1996
1645	David Gemmell	1996	
1646	Anne Stokes	1996	
1647	Euan Nicol	1996	
1648	Andrew Wright	1996	1996
1649	Gordon Maclachlan	1996	
1650	John J. Fleming	1996	
1651	Ron Lyall	1996	
1652	Barry K. Smith	1996	
1653	Peter Standing	1996	
1654	Ken Coote	1996	
1655	Roger Cumming	1996	
1656	Ian Rowe	1996	
1657	Des Slavin	1996	
1658	John M. Dougherty	1996	
1659	David Ritchie	1996	
1660	John Kirkham	1996	
1661	Mary Duncan	1995	
1662	Jeanette Fenner	1996	1996
1663	W. Weiglhofer	1995	
1664	Ian H. Hill	1996	
1665	Kenneth Robertson	1996	
1666	David Ollerton	1996	
1667	Andrew Ollerton	1996	
1668	Leslie Barrie	1996	
1669	Jim Lawson	1996	

1670	Richard D. Humble	1996		
1671	Graham Daniels	1992	1992	
1672	Flora Hunt	1996		
1673	Tim Hall	1996		
1674	Sam Johnston	1996		
1675	Paul Caban	1996		
1676	Edward J. Haggarty	1996	1996	
1677	John Patterson	1996		
1678	Tom Gailey	1996	1996	1996
1679	Elliot S. Sloan	1996		
1680	Elizabeth Carnduff	1996		
1681	Peter Hastie	1996		
1682	David F. Beaumont	1996		
1683	John G. Robin	1996		
1684	Jonathan Bellarby	1996		
1685	James Bellarby	1996		
1686	Graham Clark	1996		
1687	Rob Black	1997		
1688	Jennifer M. Thomson	1996		
1689	Keith Taylor	1995		
1690	Gordon A. Winton	1996		
1691	George W. Graham	1996		
1692	Stuart H. Clarke	1996		
1693	Graeme Findlay	1996		
1694	Graeme Reid	1996	1996	1996
1695	G. W. Roy Goodwin	1996		
1696	Brenda Lawson	1996		
1697	S. L. Grice	1997		
1698	Alison Curle	1996		
1699	Keith R. Stratton	1996		
1700	Nick J. Wild	1997		
1701	Simon C. Jefferies	1996		
1702	John Ferguson	1995		
1703	Gill Lyons	1995		
1704	Brian Tomlinson	1996		
1705	Dave Delaet	1997		

AMENDMENTS

Only number of rounds and the year of the latest round are given. The columns given are Munros, Tops and Furths.

		Munros	Tops	Furths
107	Andy Nisbet*	1993 x3		
153	A. N. Darbyshire	1977		1990
248	Lindsay Wyllie	1996 x2		
251	Chris Townsend	1996 x2	1996 x1	
254	Jim Renny	1996 x2	1994 x1	
256	Hugh F. Barron	1981	1988	1997
327	Stewart Logan	1996 x8	1996 x8	
336	Stephen T. Ramsden	1996 x3		1989
486	Peter Bellarby	1987	1987	1987
636	John Allen	1988	1996	
707	Robert F. Gibson	1989	1996	
780	Eddie Sutherland	1996 x2	1996	
781	Norma Sutherland	1996 x2		
876	Elsa Yates	1996 x2		
877	R. Yates	1996 x2		
910	Eric Drew	1991	1992	1993
1066	John Peel	1992	1996	
1087	Tim Pickles	1992		1996
1113	Kenneth Oliver	1996 x2	1991	
1119	Ronald H. MacGregor	1992		1996
1135	James Ashby	1992		1996
1192	David Unsworth	1996 x2	1995	1994
1284	John D. Taylor	1994	1994	1996
1336	David Smith	1994		1996
1422	Stephen A. Glasper	1995	1995	1995
1432	Karl Nelson	1995	1995	1996
1441	Jim Bryce	1995	1995	

When I started issuing the Munroist Certificate in August 1996, I wondered if this was likely to increase the number of claimants to a position on the List, and I suspect it may have encouraged a few to put pen to paper. However, I am sure that the chance of a certificate is the last thing on a potential Munroist's mind as he or she tries to decide whether to leave the security of the car, tent or bothy in a downpour, and it is probably not going to be the spur to keep you going on an exposed windswept ridge during a white-out.

Is this a new record? continues to be a common question in my correspondence. Gerald McPartlin (1644) was hoping that his party of five Munroists would set a record for *Munrosis multi* when he, David Gemmell (1645), Anne Stokes (1646), Euan Nicol (1647), and Andrew Wright (1648) compleated on Sgurr Mor (Loch Quoich) supported by 28 friends and a dog (176 Munros). Gerald had written prior to the event to inquire about the record and all I can say is 'probably'.

I have often said that on each Saturday in June, July and August there is a high chance of a walker finding a Last Munro party taking place on the top of Beinn na Lap, but I have not heard of many party clashes. Equally, Kevin Tait (1603) and Steve Mann (1612) were surprised to find themselves sharing parties, each group having ascended from different directions and met at the summit. Of course, many couples and friends share compleations and this year these have included Susan White (1604) and Barry Hodgson (1605), Elizabeth Carnduff (1680) and Peter Hastie (1681), Matthew Runciman (1642) and Ian MacPherson (1643), and finally Doris and Alex Matheson (1601, 1602).

Family connections seemed to abound this year. Susan Park(1614) joins her father G. Martin (304), brother Andrew (249) and husband David (1041) on the List. Similarly, Mary Duncan (1661) was preceded by her father G. Binnie (974), her husband Stuart(1383) and a brother-in-law Leonard Thomson (747). There are three more father-and-son teams. David Ollerton (1666) and son David (1667) compleating together; Euan Pyper (1620) son of Ian (1087), and Jonathan and James Bellarby (1684,1685) sons of Peter (484).

When Willie Black (1540) signed up for a course in Skye he only had the 11 Munros left to compleat and all in Skye. However, he had not planned that with a bit of manoeuvring he would actually be able to do the full traverse, with bivi's as necessary, on the course. Hence quite unplanned he found himself with Andy Nisbet (106), as instructor, on Sgurr nan Eag having traversed the whole ridge but with no alcohol to celebrate his compleation. Slightly later in the year, I expect Andy ensured the right supplies were on hand to celebrate his wife Gillian's (1613) compleation.

Not surprisingly, many Munroists comment on their use of the bothies maintained by the MBA, and how grateful they are to the MBA for their existence. This year there are more leading members of the association now joining the List of Munroists, showing that Maintenance Organisers must allow some time off during bothy work parties. Mhairi and Jim Ross (1621,1622) and Linda and Jonathan Woods (1595, 1596) all compleated this year, while still managing to hold down positions of responsibility in the MBA. In Mhairi's letter she describes two non-MBA 'highlights'; one missing the true top of Stuic a' Chroin and not realising their mistake until they had descended and the second getting caught by a lightning storm in Glen Affric. Bothy stories were left to the comment 'but that's another story'.

John Dougherty's (1658) disappointment at not reaching the top of Sgurr nan Gillean was similar, although he knew he was only 20 yards away, it was just that he didn't have the confidence to continue. This, however, encouraged him into guided help and a short while later he had ticked all the harder Skye hills.

Adventures on Loch Mullardoch continue to be reported. Eleanor and Scot Syman (1549, 50) regretted the time they took advantage of a boat to the head of the loch, planning to walk back over the hills. Unfortunately, the plans did not take into account the severe change in weather, and by the time it hit, they were on the ridge and the boat had departed, leaving them committed to the walk back.

Other experiences included Nick Wilds's (1701) companion being lifted by the wind and accelerated past him on Beinn Narnain, and Cameron Johnston (1626) being sucked into a peat pool up to his waist. Escaping from the peat is probably a skill Tom Gailey (1678) was not taught on his Glenmore Lodge Course. Early in his hill walking days, he realised while descending Bidean nan Bian that he was severely lacking in snow and ice expertise and after surviving the experience, with only a few cuts and bruises signed up for a Lodge course. On a better note Keith Taylor (1689) recounted his day on the hills above Culra Bothy when his group set off in strong winds and low cloud to find themselves appearing almost instantly out of the mist into bright sunshine, as they walked between the second and third summit of the day.

Munro longus belongs to Flora Hunt (1672) and Kenneth Robertson (1665) with rounds of 50 and 62 years respectively. Molly and Andrew Grant (1618, 1619) might have reported a fairly lengthy round but decided that on reaching the age of 50 they would wipe the slate clean, start all over again and do the Munros together. In years to come Edward Haggarty's (1676) sons may feel aggrieved that they had been within 100 yards of the top of Ben Nevis, when their father decided to stop, have lunch at that spot and then descend. This was in order that their first Munro was saved to be his last one. Adrian Belton (1554) had a very variable pace as he ticked off the hills. From start to compleation has taken 21 years but on one occasion he traversed 28 Lochaber hills in 24 hours.

If I often comment on the sedentary pace of some Munro rounds, I have to mention Brenda Lawson (1696) who accelerated her round when she found she was expecting a baby and had 33 summits to go. By the time she wrote to me the Munros and the birth had been accomplished and her baby had been up his first hill.

Striking up a conversation with a stranger while on the hill can be one of the pleasures of a day out. Elliot Sloan (1679) spoke to one such person on Conival and asked: 'Where are you going?' His reply came from Hugh Symonds (777) and was: 'Actually, I'm attempting all the Munros non-stop without transport.' It transpired this was Hugh's third day out and he indeed did go on to compleat in 67 days. I wonder what a stranger would have made of sharing Peter Standing's (1653) last Munro. He compleated on his own in Strathfarrar and to celebrate he found himself uttering a 'primal scream' more commonly heard in remote American canyons!

While Hugh Symonds compleated without the use of a car, Sam Johnston (1674) and Leslie Barrie (1668) have both prided themselves on compleating without actually owning a car. However, they must have had a number of sympathetic friends.

The amendments almost deserve a section of their own but I limit my comments to Chris Townsend's (251) self-propelled traverse of all the Munros and Tops, covering 1700 miles and 575,000ft. to do so. A bike was used on some long road sections and used to return from Skye via the bridge. Perhaps we should be expecting a book?

Methods of publicising the opportunity to record your compleation have been widened this year to include the Internet. The Scottish Mountaineering Club now has a WEB site, which Rob Black (1687) came across, and which prompted him to write in (http://www.smc.org.uk/smc/). Other sources continue to be the magazines such as *High, Climber, Great Outdoors, Trail* and, of course, the *SMC Journal*.

Finally, I received an inquiry concerning a copy of *Munro's Tables* bought in a second-hand bookshop. Derek Bradley was intrigued to find that all the Munros and Tops had been ticked and would be happy to return the copy to the original owner. There is no name of owner, but he or she seems to have compleated on August 31, 1971 on An Riabhachan or An Socach and a frequent companion was D. L. Browning. Any ideas should be sent to me and I will pass them on.

For those who wish to be registered on the List of Compleat Munroist they should write to the Clerk at the address below. I am always pleased to hear of your experiences, time take on the round, age, etc. and I always prefer to hear direct from the Munroist.

If an A4 stamped-addressed envelope is enclosed I will return a colour A4 certificate to mark their Compleation. Also, if those already on the List would like a certificate they should write to me with a reference to their Munroist number (and enclose suitable SAE please). All Notification should be sent to Dr. C. M. Huntley, Old Medwyn, Spittal, Carnwath, Lanarkshire. ML11 8LY. Once registered, Munroists can rightfully purchase a tie and/or Brooch.

Coire an t-Sneachda from Loch Morlich   john mitchell 1997.

MOUNTAIN RESCUE COMMITTEE OF SCOTLAND
Accident Reports 1996
Compiled by John Hinde

N.B. Due to an error, 1995 narratives for Central Highlands were not included last year, although this error did not affect the statistics. Both 1995 and 1996 narratives for Central Highlands are published this year. Police have not been mentioned in each incident as they are involved in all.

NORTHERN HIGHLANDS

JANUARY 6 – Two missing girls found by Coastguard ground teams near Durness. HMCG helicopter.

FEBRUARY 24-25 – Compound incident. Cramponing unroped up a gully on W Face 10m below the summit of Beinn Eighe (Ruadh-stac Mor 1010m) a women (26) slipped on hard névé. Sliding, she knocked off one of her six companions, another woman (27). Both fell 50m and both had clavicle fractures, one with pelvic injuries and the other with minor head injuries. Difficult night stretcher carry by Kinloss and Torridon MRTs. HMCG and RAF helicopters had to withdraw. Later Dundonnell helped carry to HMCG airlift at head of Coire Dubh Mor. 485.

MARCH 9 – Male caver suffered severe arm injury and significant blood loss caused by rockfall in Claonaite Cave, Allt nan Uamh, Inchnadamh. Casualty walked to ambulance. Rescue from site would have been difficult. Assynt Team helped Scottish Cave Rescue Org. 6.

MARCH 16 – Walker (23) slipped on ice on track 1km NW of Choiremor Bothy, Strath Mulzie, breaking her ankle. Rescued by Assynt MRT using ambulance. 33

APRIL 6 – Leader (36) on a new ice route in No. 2 Gully, Sail Mhor, Beinn Eighe, dislodged a rock when on 4th pitch 100m from top. The rock caused more to fall, one of which knocked him off. His top runner failed so he fell 25m with chest and arm injuries. He was held below his second's belay, who got him off the crag in a series of lowers. Torridon MRT, HMCG helicopter. 52.

APRIL 11 – Scrambling down one of the pinnacles of Am Fasarinen, Liathach, a student (20) wrenched his arm, dislocating the shoulder. Torridon MRT, RAF Sea King. 28.

MAY 5 – Descending Horns of Alligin path a walker (50) tripped, injuring her ankle by a fall into a burn. Torridon MRT, RN Sea King. 55.

MAY 16 – Lost in mist on top of Sgurr Fiona, An Teallach, an experienced walker (52) was overdue but he got down to Ardessie unaided. Dundonnell MRT. 22.

MAY 26 – A member of Assynt MRT was not far away when a woman (31) slipped descending wet rock, sustaining serious multiple injuries. She fell 10m from a scrambly bit of the otherwise easy path south from Sail Gorm, Quinag. Winched by RAF Sea King. 10.

JUNE 11-12 – Fishing a complicated system of hill lochs south of A894 between Scourie and Laxford Bridge an angler (56) was lost overnight. He walked out to Geisgeil next day. Searches by Assynt and Kinloss MRTs, SARDA, RAF and HMCG helicopters. 269.

JUNE 15 – Walker (64) broke her ankle on Handa Island. HMCG helicopter.

JULY 9 – A retired man (60) was overdue from the Fisherfield Forest Munros, but walked out unaided. Search of bothies and track by Dundonnell MRT. 9.

JULY 11. HMCG helicopter helped police in search for man (75) missing near Golspie.

JULY 14 – Rescuer on exercise (24), leading or soloing fell off Jetty Buttress, Gruinard Bay. He fell 6m injuring head, back and legs. Evacuation by HMCG helicopter. 13.

JULY 20-21 – Two people walked 18km from Shenaval to Letterewe believing there was a ferry across Loch Maree. Attempting a further 14km to A832 one of them collapsed (f33) from exhaustion at Kinlochewe River about 2km from a farm. Stretchered by Torridon MRT. 16.

JULY 25 – One of five German students (18) slipped near Fionn Loch Causeway injuring her ankle. Rescued by estate boat. Dundonnell MRT. 8.

AUGUST 5-11 – Search by Assynt and Kinloss MRTs, SARDA and RAF Sea King after an American's rucksack was found at the SW Bealach of Ben Klibreck. He turned up in Thurso some days later. 202

AUGUST 6-7 – Assynt MRT searched moorland overnight for a woman after a car was abandoned at Balnakiel, Durness. Found uninjured by Police at 08.00 on roadside at Loch Eriboll. SARDA, HMCG helicopter. 212.

AUGUST 6-7 - A group on An Teallach reported an accident but the subject was found safe at Corrie Hallie. They had seen him climbing a gully above Loch Toll an Lochain. As cloud descended they heard a large rockfall. When cloud cleared they could not find him. Dundonnell MRT. 125.

AUGUST 8-9 – Going well ahead of his three companions traversing An Teallach from N. to S. man (25) was out of sight of them when he was killed by a fall from the Bad Step of Corrag Buidhe. Two followed him over the pinnacles, and one went round by the path, but he was not missed till the three returned to the car park. Victim recovered by winching by RAF Sea King from 250m below Bad Step. Dundonnell MRT and SARDA. 63

AUGUST 9-10 – Two women climbing Pigott's Route on Central Buttress of Beinn Eighe went off route in deteriorating light and weather and decided to stay the night. They were found abseiling off by RAF Sea King next morning. Torridon MRT. 24.

Note: Pigott is incorrectly spelt in new guide books.

AUGUST 13-19 – Dundonnell, Kinloss, SARDA, Torridon and volunteers searched Loch Garve shoreline, forests, road and rail verges for a missing woman (83) who was known to often walk along the railway. Body recovered from the loch on 19th by her nephew. 629.

SEPTEMBER 4 – Man (34) went bouldering when his seven companions stopped for a break at Coire Dubh Beag, Liathach. The rock he was on broke away and fell on top of him. He fell 55m and was killed. Torridon MRT, RAF Sea King. 57.

SEPTEMBER 10 – Injured walker lifted from Sandwood Bay (9.2km S of Cape Wrath) by HMCG helicopter. 5.

SEPTEMBER 21 – Climber (20s) fell 12m with serious skull and arm injuries. His abseil point failed when roping off Diabeg Pillar. His helmet was shattered at rear. That, his fitness, oxygen and speedy evacuation by Torridon MRT and RAF Sea King probably saved his life. 18.

SEPTEMBER 22 – Aged 17, one of five girls walking rough coast path Diabeg to Alligin Shuas, complained of stomach cramps and weary legs. Torridon MRT evacuated her by boat. 46.

OCTOBER 8-9 – Assynt and Kinloss MRTs, SARDA and RAF Sea King searched for six wives (36-49) missing from a stalking party. They had a map but no compass. Intending to walk round Beinn Uidhe, Inchnadamph, they retreated from the pathless section and got benighted. Found by air search suffering mild hypothermia which could have been much more serious. 96.

OCTOBER 15 – Woman (34) slipped on Garvie Beach (Enard Bay coast of Coigach Peninsula) twisting her ankle. Stretchered by Dundonnell MRT, then by local boat to ambulance access point. 25.

NOVEMBER 23 – Lost man (27) tired in deep snow night winched uninjured by HMCG helicopter from 650m on W. Ridge Eididh nan Clach Geala (6km E of head of Loch Broom and 3km from position he reported on mobile phone. During search phone batteries went flat). Strong wind, freezing. Dundonnell and Kinloss MRTs. 68.

DECEMBER 9-10 – Man (66) separated from companions shooting in woods at Tore, Black Isle. Dundonnell and Kinloss MRTs and SARDA. Found by line search dead from heart attack. 34.

DECEMBER 18-21 – Assynt MRT, SARDA, RAF and HMCG helicopters searched moorland and rugged coast around Drumbeg, Sutherland for a woman (51) who turned up suffering overdoses. 263.

WESTERN HIGHLANDS

MARCH 28 – Forcan Ridge of The Saddle. Army sergeant (25) on a course, fell 60m from a pinnacle two-thirds up the ridge. She lost her ice-axe on the way down. She stopped on a snow slope only 15m above another severe drop, sustaining very nasty facial and jaw injuries. Crampons carried but not worn. Helmet not carried. Kintail MRT, RAF Sea King. 37.

APRIL 21-23 – Kintail MRT mobilised for a pair (m42,f39) overdue from South Cluanie Ridge. After a camping epic on the ridge at Maol Chinn Dearg in a gale and rain they had been delayed by the woman getting an inflamed knee from descending with a heavy rucksack. From Glen Quoich they got back to Cluanie Hotel at 02.00 on third day. Found at 07.00 sleeping in a car. RAF Sea King. 9.

MAY 1-2 – Search by RAF Sea King with Kintail MRT aboard after white flares were reported seen on Beinn Fhada from Affric Youth Hostel. False alarm probably caused by meteorites. 27.

MAY 12 – After 12 days walking on a challenge expedition, a woman diabetic (42) camping with her husband at Affric YH became ill from blood sugar problems. She responded to hospital treatment after airlift by RAF Sea King. 8.

MAY 10-14 – Kintail and Lochaber MRTs and RAF Sea King searched Glen Dessary to Shielbridge routes for a man reported overdue. It was a false alarm because he was in Canada. 104.

MAY 25 – Accompanied by a friend walking between bothies (Corryhully to A'Chuil), a student (f27) slipped and fell 5m into a gorge in Gleann a'Chaorainn. Airlift with leg injuries by RAF Sea King. Lochaber MRT. 22.

MAY 26 – Student (20) airlifted by RN Sea King from Essan Bothy, Loch Eilt. With three companions, he slipped on grass, breaking a leg and was carried to the bothy. Lochaber MRT. 19.

JUNE 5 – Crossing a river at Kinlochbeoraid, man (25) slipped, injuring his knee. Airlift by RN Sea King. Lochaber MRT. 18.

Note: A natural bridge spans a spectacular gorge at NM 863850 but the boulder is not easy to cross.

JUNE 24 – Man (46) stayed an extra day walking Loch Arkaig to Knoydart area without informing anyone. Lochaber MRT, RAF Sea King. 49.

JULY 20 – When 10m up South Wall of Great Ridge, Garbh Bheinn of Ardgour, man (32), who was leading, fell on to his back when his right handhold came away.

Winched off by RAF Sea King on exercise, which uplifted four members of Lochaber MRT. Treated for spine fracture (not permanently damaged). 9.

AUGUST 23-24 – Two women (47, 36) benighted on Meallan Odhar, The Saddle, turned up as search began. Glenelg and Kintail MRTs. 26.

SEPTEMBER 11-12 – Failing to meet a friend on Carn Eighe summit, a man (38) went down because he was cold and wet. He stayed in a bothy at Loch Mullardoch and was found walking east along the loch next day by Dundonnell MRT and SARDA in a keeper's boat. 43

OCTOBER 2-3 – Student (36) descending Sgurr na Moraich (NW Peak Five Sisters) got benighted. His torch failed so he stayed put till morning then walked out OK. Kintail MRT. 8.

OCTOBER 11 – Man (68) stalking in Knoydart (on Druim na Cluain-airighe) was descending a slight heathery slope when he slipped, knocked his head on ground and cracked two ribs falling on his binoculars. With help he managed to walk off hill. Mallaig lifeboat to Mallaig, then airlift by RAF Sea King to Broadford. 40.

NOVEMBER 3 – With a companion on steep, broken ground on the Loch Morar side of Carn Mor (829m) and about 60m from the summit, man (23) dived out of the way of a rock rolling towards him. The rock hit him on the right hand causing bad fractures and cuts. They walked to Glendessarry and were taken by the stalker to ambulance at Achnacarry.

BEN NEVIS

FEBRUARY 3 – With two companions walking from Halfway Lochan to CIC Hut, man (50) tripped and fell on his shoulder, dislocating it. Lochaber MRT and R.137 RAF Sea King.19.

FEBRUARY 11 – In crampons, leading a group of 16 up Nevis via Carn Mor Dearg, man (31) put his weight on his ice-axe, dislocating a shoulder. Self evacuation escorted by Lochaber MRT. 4.

FEBRUARY 17-18 – Climbing near the top of No. 2 Gully when it was snowing, a leader (30) and his second (31) were swept down by an avalanche (possible cornice collapse). Their belay held but the leader was hit on the head by an ice-axe making him incoherent. The second blew his whistle to get help.

FEBRUARY 17-18 – Three nearby men climbed up to rescue the above pair, hoping to take a rope up over the plateau edge not far above them. All five were avalanched 250m stopping on the debris fan at the bottom. The leader (first incident) got more bruising and a clavicle fracture. His second got a back injury and one of the rescuing trio got back and leg injuries. Due to bad weather RAF Sea King could not get in till later. Carries by Lochaber and Turkish MRTs. 313.

FEBRUARY 22-23 – Three men (50, 43, 38) benighted on NE Buttress used mobile phone at 11.45 hours next day to allay fears. RAF Sea King cancelled and Lochaber MRT stood down. 20.

MARCH 22 – Ice climber (36) was killed by a fall from Boomer's Requiem, Carn Dearg Buttress. Independent from a companion, he fell before they had roped up for the harder part of the climb. Lochaber MRT and RAF Sea King. 54.

MARCH 28 – Tower Face of the Comb. At about 18m into the climb an axe came out of a crack and the climber (22) fell 3m spraining his ankle before the rope took hold. Able to walk out to Lochaber MRT vehicle at the Dam. 2.

APRIL 2 – A Dutch tour guide (28) walking alone on the plateau section of the Ben Path in mist fell through Gardyloo Gully Cornice into Observatory Gully. He was seen falling (probably from below?). Fatal. Winched by RAF Sea King. Lochaber MRT. 17.

MAY 9-10 – A shepherd (m49) and two students (m21, m19) started climbing Tower Ridge at 11.30. At 21.30 they met difficulties going along a traverse so they back-tracked and bivvied for the night. At 10.30 next day they saw a party walking towards CIC Hut so they fired flares and blew whistles. Winched by RAF Sea King. The youngest needed hospital treatment for cold feet. Lochaber MRT. 27.

MAY 11 – Suffering from severe abdominal pains descending the Ben Path a man (56) twice tried to continue down. Eventually, a passer-by called for rescuers on a mobile phone. Lochaber MRT, RAF Sea King. 33.

MAY 25 – Already dealing with an incident in Glenfinnan, RAF Sea King then flew to Nevis to lift an exhausted man (80). Passers by had helped him descend snowfields and he had been stretchered down the Ben Path to Halfway Lochan. Lochaber MRT. 18.

MAY 26 – Man (43) got knee pain descending Ben Path snowfield. At aluminium bridges his knee locked. Lochaber MRT walked/carried him down. 44.

MAY 26 – Man (30) stumbled and sprained a knee descending the Ben Path. Lochaber MRT. Airlift by helicopter. 24.

JUNE 24-25 – Starting to climb Tower Ridge at 17.00 and underestimating the time they needed, four male students (18, 18, 18, 17) spent the night below the Great Tower when it got dark and were reported overdue. Airlifted by RAF Sea King from summit plateau at 09.30 after they finished climb. Lochaber MRT. 24.

JULY 9 – Woman (34) with husband attempted Nevis Path. At West Flank Zigzags they descended due to her collapsing with abdominal pain. She collapsed several times before they met passers by. Winched by RAF Sea King. Lochaber MRT. 39.

JULY 13 – Student (26) walking Nevis Gorge Path stumbled and sprained her ankle. Stretchered out by Lochaber MRT. 80.

JULY 14 – Accompanied by her husband descending Ben Path at Red Burn, woman (48) slipped and injured her ankle. RAF Sea King, Lochaber MRT. 22.

JULY 14 – At 15.41, one minute after the above incident, a Dutch student nurse (21), in a party of nine, slipped at the same location while descending. She also suffered an ankle injury. Both women were winched into the same RAF Sea King. Lochaber MRT. 22.

JULY 20 – Schoolboy (9) fell 5m down rockface at Lower Falls Bridge, Glen Nevis. Both wrists broken and head gash. Airlift by RAF Sea King on exercise locally. Lochaber MRT on site. 3.

JULY 21 – Man (53) competing in Half Nevis Run slipped near aluminium bridges with slight leg injury. Stretchered by Lochaber MRT. 19.

JULY 21 – Crossing the wire bridge at Steall, man (33) slipped and dislocated a shoulder. Helped out by Lochaber MRT. 16.

AUGUST 1 – Because of a poor belay, when a student (17) slipped climbing Roadside Crag, Polldubh, he suffered cervical spine and head injuries. Lochaber MRT and Ambulance (paramedics). 22.

AUGUST 4 – Woman (26) slipped off the path 300m below CIC Hut heading for Halfway Lochan, sustaining minor injuries.

AUGUST 4 – Going to help the woman in the above incident, her male companion (32) also slipped with minor injuries. He used a mobile phone to alert Lochaber MRT and RAF Sea King. 80.

AUGUST 30 – Seconding Tower Ridge, woman (31) slipped on wet rock descending into Tower Gap in mist. She fell 6m down Glover's Chimney, fracturing a patella, and was stopped by the rope. Nearby climbers alerted Lochaber MRT by mobile phone. Airlift by RAF Sea King. 74.

SEPTEMBER 2 – Descending Coire Eoghainn Waterslide to Glen Nevis top car park with three companions, a student (25) slipped on wet slabs, breaking tibia and fibula. He was stretchered down by Lochaber MRT from about 200m up the Waterslide. 24.

SEPTEMBER 13 – Losing the route up Tower Ridge two men (26, 21) retreated from a sheer chimney but got cragfast and used mobile phone to call Lochaber MRT. Airlift by RAF Sea King. 22.

SEPTEMBER 15 – Woman (33) slipped on a damp, loose boulder descending Ben Path causing a triple fracture/dislocation of an ankle. RN Sea King and Lochaber MRT. 23.

SEPTEMBER 19 – Leading Tutor's Rib at Polldubh Crags, a man (59) placed a nut runner at 5m then pulled on it to test it. The nut pulled out and he fell 5m on to his back. Stretchered down by Lochaber MRT and paramedics. 23.

SEPTEMBER 29 – Four people walking Ben Path separated into three parties. A pair mis-navigating went down Eoghainn Waterslide, being reported overdue, but all got down OK. Lochaber. 2.

OCTOBER 5 – Descending Ben Path, a woman (35) tripped near the top aluminium bridge, falling 15m into the gorge, fracturing ribs and cutting her head. Winched by RAF Sea King. Lochaber MRT. 26.

OCTOBER 25 – A Dutch marine (24) ascending Ben Nevis via Carn Mor Dearg Arête suffered severe abdominal pain when 300m from the summit. Carried by 10 of his 40 companions to Coire Leis Refuge then airlifted by RAF Sea King. 33.

DECEMBER 25 – Man (53) from Bristol was last reported as being seen at top car park, Glen Nevis, by a companion who arranged to meet him at 16.00. He had the car keys if he wanted to sit in the car. He had no crampons and because there was ice on higher ground he intended just to walk up and down Glen Nevis. Searches by Glencoe, Kinloss, Lochaber, RAF St. Athan MRTs and RAF Sea King on 26th found no trace. Subsequent searches by the above, Leuchars and SARDA on 27th and searches by Lochaber on 28. 12. 96 and 18.1.97 were negative. Region of incident may prove to be 'Other Central Highlands'. 882.

DECEMBER 28 – Descending Tower Gully wearing crampons and unroped, man (34) lost control and rolled down. He managed to ice-axe self-arrest, but not at the first attempt and he fractured an ankle. Companion used radio at CIC Hut. Winched by RAF Sea King, Lochaber MRT. 17.

GLEN COE 1996
(Including Buachaille Etive Mor)

JANUARY 23-24 – Four overdue students (f23, 19, m20, 20) lost above Lost Valley eventually walked out to Glen Etive. Glen Coe MRT and SARDA. 34.

FEBRUARY 2 – Unroped climber (34) fractured both ankles in a fall when the toe clip of one of his crampons loosened or snapped. With a companion he was near the top of the final ice pitch of Great Gully (II). Winched by RAF Sea King. Glen Coe MRT. 44.

FEBRUARY 7-8 – Delayed by difficult snow and ice conditions traversing Aonach Eagach W to E, two men (38, 31) got cragfast in the dark E of Am Bodach. Escorted off by Glen Coe MRT. 95.

FEBRUARY 12-13 – North Face Aonach Dubh. Party of three had been near summit when avalanched by windslab. Mountain guide (42) was killed by a fall of 180m. Two women had been shallowly buried and extricated themselves. Next day the victim was found at GR 148 561, half buried in debris and winched off by RAF

Sea King. Use was made of photographs taken by the women of the actual position of the dead man's disappearance. Glen Coe and Kinloss MRTs. 408.

FEBRUARY 17 – Glen Coe and Leuchars MRTs stretchered a walker (23) from Stob Coire nan Lochan after dark. Descending with three others, a crampon jammed in snow breaking his leg. RAF Wessex from N. Ireland unable to help due to location. 105.

FEBRUARY 17-18 – Two snow climbers (39, 27) were overdue from Sgor na h-Ulaidh. Glen Coe and Leuchars MRTs assembled at Gleann-leac-na-muidhe (Glen Coe side) next morning, but the two men walked out on the Etive side due to poor navigation. 46.

FEBRUARY 22-23 – Having completed E to W traverse of Aonach Eagach two men got cragfast and benighted descending the higher slopes of the Loch Achtriochtan side of Sgorr nam Fiannaidh. Glen Coe MRT assisted them down. 35.

FEBRUARY 24-25 – Two walkers (52, 49) decided to bivouac on Buachaille Etive Mor due to wind and snow. Both men were spotted by Glen Coe MRT making their own way down Coire na Tulaich next morning. 28.

FEBRUARY 29-30 – A man (32) and woman (29) intended to climb B Buttress of Aonach Dubh, but got cragfast in No. 2 Gully due to poor navigation. Escorted down by Glen Coe MRT in darkness. 72.

MARCH 4-5 – Two men (28, 26) alerted Glen Coe MRT by torch flashes. After a Great Gully ascent to Buachaille Etive Mor they attempted to find Coire na Tulaich descent route but got stuck on areas of sheet ice in Staircase Gully. Airlift by RAF Sea King. 85.

MARCH 10 – After a climb on Stob Coire nam Beith man (30) arsaded down a snowfield wearing crampons. A crampon caught in the snow fracturing his ankle. Stretchered by Glen Coe MRT to an airlift by RN Sea King. 85.

MARCH 17 – A student (27) descending south from Bidean nam Bian into Gleann Fhaolain lost her footing, falling about 100m over snow, ice and boulders. First aid for scalp cuts and collar bone fracture by Glen Coe MRT and winch by RAF Sea King. 107.

MARCH 17-18 – Glen Coe team searched for two youths (19), lost and benighted after climbing No. 2 Gully, Aonach Dubh. They bivouacked, used a mobile phone to call help, then walked off unaided. 76.

MARCH 23 – Solo descending An t-Sron Corrie of Stob Coire nam Beith, which he had just climbed up, a man (41) stopped to clear snow from his crampons, slipped and fell 30m, fracturing an ankle. Winched by RAF Sea King after alert by a mountain guide who saw the fall. Glen Coe MRT. 52.

MARCH 23 – Having completed No. 6 Gully, West Face of Aonach Dubh, a man (34) wearing crampons slipped and fell 45m fracturing a tibia and fibula. Winched by RAF Sea King. Glen Coe MRT. 48.

APRIL 7 – Three Spanish men crossed The Gorge from A82 in daylight onto hillside where they fell asleep. Waking in darkness they could not return to A82 though but 30m from it. Guided by GMRT. 2.

APRIL 9-10 – Dutch couple (m28, f27) got cragfast descending Clachaig Gully path, losing path in dark and strong winds after Aonach Eagach traverse. Torch signals alerted GMRT for escort down. 54.

MAY 14 – Woman (61) in a pair descending path out of Lost Valley stumbled on scree causing ankle injury. Glen Coe MRT. 43.

MAY 14 – Lost Valley Face of Stob Coire nan Lochan. Man (43) slipped on scree spraining an ankle. Glen Coe MRT, R137 RAF Sea King. 67.

MAY 23 – Man (31) was walking at foot of Curved Ridge, Buachaille Etive Mor when his knee locked. Glen Coe MRT, RAF Sea King. 44.

MAY 27 – Glen Coe MRT stretchered man (41) down from upper reaches of Coire na Tulaich, Buachaille Etive Mor. Accompanied, he suffered a heart attack, tried to walk down, but failed to get any farther. 24.

JUNE 9 – Retired man (63) had almost reached summit Buachaille Etive Beag with two companions when he died from a heart attack. Glen Coe MRT, RAF R137 Sea King. 69.

JUNE 16 – South side of Buachaille Etive Mor. Man (25) was soloing the lower waterfall in Coire Cloiche Finne. He fell back 20m into the bottom of the gully, causing serious pelvic injuries, when loose rock fell away from the face. One of two friends went for help. Glen Coe MRT, R137 RAF Sea King. 46.

JUNE 23 – Schoolgirl (15) sustained serious head injuries. Descending the path from Bidean nam Bian she slipped on rock, falling 10m into the gully bed at the lower waterfall in Coire nam Beithe. Glen Coe MRT put her in a stretcher for winching by RN Sea King. 62.

JULY 7 – Glen Coe Team and RN helicopter carried out a negative search of the head of Lost Valley following reported calls for help. 54.

JULY 16 – A twist caused his shoulder to dislocate when man (28) was traversing Aonach Eagach (Meall Dearg section) with a friend. Mobile phone used. GMRT reduced dislocation. All winched off by RAF Sea King. 35.

SEPTEMBER 11 – Suffering abdominal pains when on summit of Stob Coire Sgreamach (Bidean) with four companions, a student (18) was lifted by RAF Sea King. She was released from hospital after treatment. Glen Coe MRT. 54.

SEPTEMBER 27-28 – Because he thought he was slowing down his three companions on an E to W traverse of Aonach Eagach, man (28) tried to escape south halfway along the ridge. After a short distance he fell sustaining a deep cut to the top of his head. Glen Coe MRT found him when he flashed a torch and a flash gun. He was very cold. He was stretchered down to safer ground for airlift by RAF Sea King. 70.

OCTOBER 5 – Traversing Aonach Eagach E to W with a companion, man (26) slipped while climbing (dry rock) over a large boulder between Meall Dearg and Stob Coire Leith. He fell backwards over the N side for about 100m. Found at 20.00 with fatal injuries by Glen Coe MRT and stretchered down. RAF Sea King unable to help with evacuation due to weather. 148.

OCTOBER 9 – After E to W traverse of Aonach Eagach two men (26,19) got cragfast descending to Loch Achtriochtan and made torch distress signals. Escorted down by Glen Coe MRT. 32.

OCTOBER 20-21 – Stob na Doire of Buachaille Etive Mor. RN Sea King recovered solo walker (m32) by stretcher transfer. Glen Coe MRT had reached him earlier. Head, pelvic and leg injuries, cuts, bruises and cold trauma from a fall at 15.00 when a scree ledge gave way under him. Unconscious for some time he had climbed back up to a gully and blew a whistle for nine hours till found by two walkers at 14.15 next day, as he had not left a route plan. 83.

OCTOBER 23 – Glen Coe MRT and RAF Sea King checked a smoke flare on Beinn Fhada. Nothing found. 38.

OCTOBER 28 – Pair split up at foot of Curved Ridge, Buachaille Etive Mor. One descended due to poor weather. Her companion (m31) continued with the route. He was found by Glen Coe MRT at the foot of Crowberry Gully with fatal injuries. Stretcher lower. 145.

NOVEMBER 29-30 - Descending from Bidean nam Bian via Stob Coire nan Lochan three men (37, 36, 33) took a wrong route and bivvied overnight. They got down OK at 11.30, Glen Coe MRT having delayed a full callout. 8.

DECEMBER 10 - Pair started W to E Aonach Eagach traverse at 10.00. Man (50) found terrain difficult and was worried they would not complete before dark. They descended at the pinnacles. Casualty fell and cut his arm. After first aid he fell again and cut the other arm. Companion went to alert Glen Coe MRT. Winched out by RAF Sea King.

DECEMBER 22 – Starting W to E Traverse, Aonach Eagach at 10.00 a pair decided to take most direct route down from Meall Dearg when light faded. One got down leaving companion (21) cragfast. He made torch signals. Assisted down uninjured by Glen Coe MRT. 41.

DECEMBER 30-31 – A couple (f31, m29) attempted Curved Ridge, Buachaille Etive Mor. Due to a navigation error they got cragfast in Crowberry Gully. Winched out by RAF Sea King. Glen Coe MRT. 120.

OTHER CENTRAL HIGHLANDS (1995)

JANUARY 2 –The leader of a walking holidays group (47) slipped crossing a dyke at Grey Mare's Waterfall, Kinlochmore, Loch Leven. Her foot slipped on an icy stone and jammed in the wall breaking an ankle. Glencoe MRT. 10.

FEBRUARY 10-14 – Solo walker (25) arranged to meet companions at White Corries Ski Tow. He set off alone but there had been sightings of him high on Meall a'Bhuiridh. On 13th a witness said the missing man had asked him the way off the summit of Creise on 10th. His body was found on the Glen Etive side of the North Ridge of Sron na Creise. Massive searches in poor weather and avalanche conditions over the Black Mount Range had involved Arrochar, Glencoe, Kinloss, Leuchars, Lochaber, Ochils, Strathclyde MRTs, SARDA, RAF and RN Sea Kings. 3162.

FEBRUARY 11 – Walker (42) fell on Beinn a'Chlachair. With head injuries he got to Gallovie, Kinlochlaggan. Conveyed to hospital with hypothermia.

FEBRUARY 18 – Cairngorm MRT helped Lochaber MRT carry two casualties (30, 28) off The Wand, Creag Meagaidh as helicopter could not fly (airlift later). RN and RAF Sea Kings involved. The leader (30) had slipped, the belay failed and both men fell to the bottom. Both had very serious injuries and the leader later died in hospital. 280.

FEBRUARY 18-19 – Crossing one of the cols between Ben Starav and Glas Bheinn Mhor, one of a pair (47) fell through a cornice. Both men conversed by shouting to 'meet at the road' but only one got down that night. He met Leuchars MRT next day after snowcaving. Searches in dangerous avalanche conditions by Glencoe, Strathclyde and Arrochar MRTs, SARDA. 718.

FEBRUARY 18 – A party of three was descending Sgurr Eilde Mor, Mamores when a man (53) slipped in snow. Bruised, he was able to walk then got tired. Rescued by gamekeeper in 4WD vehicle. Glencoe MRT. 3.

FEBRUARY 23-24 – Poor navigation in mist caused a walker (36) on the Ring of Steall to get his descent blocked at the top of Steall Waterfall. He bivouacked at 23.00. Descending by the proper glen next morning he was lifted by RAF Sea King. 8.

FEBRUARY 24 – Man (28) skied over a cornice just south of the Centre Top of Beinn a'Chaorainn in poor visibility and fell 50m sustaining a cut head. His companion went for help. RAF Sea King met bad weather and wiper failed, but Lochaber MRT met the teacher walking off the hill with a passer-by. 61.

Note: Not many years seem to go by without someone going through this particular cornice. It seems almost as attractive as Steall Waterfall.

FEBRUARY 25-26 – Walker (39) on Sgor Gaibhre fell through a snow hole. Stuck overnight he walked out to Corrour, Loch Ossian. Lochaber MRT.

MARCH 1 – Mamores in bad visibility. Walking ahead of a companion on a bearing, with a compass in his hand, NE of Am Bodach, man (32) went through a cornice. He fell 240m with fatal injuries. He was stretchered off by Glencoe MRT because RAF Sea King was unable to help due to heavy snowfall. 80.

MARCH 1-2 – Man and woman missing overnight in Glen Strae, Dalmally were found safe.

MARCH 8 – Cries for help from Coire Ardair, Creag Meagaidh, turned out to be climbers shouting to each other. Lochaber team, RN Sea King, SARDA. 68.

MARCH 17 – Man in front (32) leading a party of three on a bearing on Stob a'Choire Mheadhoin fell through a cornice. Others went for help. Lochaber MRT and RAF Sea King started but were called off when he walked down, suffering a cut eye from his ice-axe. 9.

MARCH 19 – Deciding the visibility was too bad to ski 'over the back' and down into Coire Dubh off Aonach Mor, a woman (25) skied down the edge of the cornice towards the top of Warrens Run. The cornice gave way. She fell 50m uninjured. Rescued by Nevis Range (also Lochaber MRT). 7.

MARCH 25 – Climbing Cinderella, Creag Meagaidh unroped, five students and friends were avalanched (wet snow) and fell 70m. Female (27) and male (25) had broken legs needing stretchering; male (25) had cuts. Lochaber MRT, RAF Sea King. Cairngorm MRT called but returned when helicopter was able to get in. 80.

MARCH 25-27 – Overdue from two days' Munro bagging two men (30, 27) were delayed by soft snow and spent second night out. Airlifted from head of Glen Nevis (Tom an Eite) by RN Sea King. Lochaber MRT. 30.

APRIL 1 – 'Un-ewe-sual' (but genuine) rescue of a heavily-pregnant sheep from a 15m crag at Crubenbeg, Laggan by Cairngorm MRT. 32.

APRIL 14-15 – Party of four was going up the north ridge (Sgor a'Chaolais) which abuts on the main ridge of Sgor Dhonuill, Ballachulish, 400m east of the summit. They could not climb steep rocks of the ridge so dropped on to its east flank to traverse below them. While descending, victim (very experienced climber 28) slipped on scree, rock and snow with tumbling fall into a gully then on to a large snowfield. He then fell on to boulders with severe head and chest injuries. Glencoe MRT used ventilated breathing, oxygen, cannula, collar. Winched by RAF Sea King. 42.

MAY 13-14 – A woman (25) sitting on a rock face with a sprained ankle at Steall Waterfall attracted attention of others by shouts at 18.00. They had seen her through binoculars and reported her predicament at 23.00. Winched by RAF Sea King. Lochaber MRT. 42.

MAY 14 – Hillwalker (63) above Steall Ruin in Coire Giubhsachan slipped and broke her ankle. Lochaber MRT, RAF Sea King. 28.

MAY 28 – A compound incident: just below The Window, Creag Meagaidh, three walkers were descending into Coire Ardair; a woman (54) slipped on ice, falling 65m and sustaining severe bruising around the pelvis; her husband (55) deliberately sat on the ice trying to make his way down, tumbling on to rocks below causing broken ribs and arm, with abdominal injuries. The third took a safer route. None had any winter climbing gear. Casualties winched by RAF Sea King. 10.

JUNE 4 – Beyond Steall Bothy a walker (23) slipped on muddy ground injuring his knee. Stretchered down Nevis Gorge. Lochaber MRT. 35.

JUNE 18 – RAF Sea King retasked to Sgairneach Mhor, Drumochter, for hillwalker with suspected heart attack – not required.

JUNE 22-23 – One man (37) and his dog walked the Grey Corries without allowing enough time, so they spent the night in a bothy (probably Lairig Leacach). Met at the level crossing by Lochaber MRT. RAF Sea King involved. 20.

JUNE 27 – Witness said he found a rucksack and gas cooker on the Grey Corries. He had earlier seen an old man carrying the same easily recognisable grey Bergen and he was worried about him. Searches of Coire na Gaibhre by Lochaber MRT and SARDA found nothing. 67.

JUNE 28 – Man (39) descending from Ring of Steall got cragfast on Steall Waterfall but extricated himself before Lochaber team arrived. 8.

JULY 14 – Boy (15) on Devil's Staircase was victim of an unknown condition which had occured before; prone to collapse on steep slopes. Conscious but confused when Glencoe team arrived he later became deeply unconscious, though breathing, pulse etc. were OK. He was stretchered to an ambulance. 34.

JULY 21 – Woman (36) fell off the wire bridge at Steall Cottage banging her head and injuring a knee. Stretchered by Lochaber MRT. 24.

AUGUST 5-9 – A remarkable survival epic on Stob Dubh, Glen Etive, an intimidating peak with its South Face deeply scored by a diagonal gorge rising W to E. A man (56) was reported overdue late on August 6 having left a four-day route card of Glen Etive and Black Mount peaks from Thurs. 3. to Sun. 6th. After eight peaks on Friday (no note left of completion) he chose Stob Dubh on Sat. 5th. as an easy day. Descending from the summit he fell into the gorge and was unconscious till he heard RN helicopter on Mon 7. He knew he had damaged both arms, skull, hip and ankle. Tuesday was a blank. On Wednesday he climbed almost to the top of the gorge, perhaps 100m, then fell again almost to the same place fracturing his top lumbar vertebra. After noon he removed his green jacket to show a bright T-shirt. A massive three-day search by Arrochar, Kinloss, Leuchars, Glencoe and Strathclyde MRTs and SARDA was being abandoned when he was spotted by RN Sea King. He was on the very edge of a 35m vertical drop on the true right of the gorge and could not be winched for fear of downdraught dislodging him, so the helicopter went to refuel. Members of three MRTs reached him and rescued him by helicopter stretcher winch using hi-line technique to prevent swinging and rotation of casualty. After an artificial joint and vertebra bone grafts he will walk again, but always wearing bright clothing. 3824 .

AUGUST 13 – Woman (53) slipped on scree at Craigellachie Nature Trail, Aviemore fracturing her ankle. Airlift by RAF Sea King. 15.

AUGUST 15 – A Belgian woman (25) member of a survival club slipped crossing Abhainn Rath at Luibeilt, injuring a knee. Friends carried her down river to Creaguanach Lodge, Loch Treig. Stretchered to Corrour Station by Lochaber MRT. 70.

AUGUST 19 – Man (52) got leg cramp on steep west slopes of Carn Beag Dearg (Nevis group) but walked off as Lochaber team mustered. Two RAF Sea King recalled – not required.

AUGUST 21 - The menace of the mobile phone! Rider (40) of All Terrain Vehicle (motor quadcycle) on Corrieyairack Hill (896m) overturned it dislocating his shoulder. Companion with mobile phone reported head and back injuries. No aircraft available. Further messages said there were no back injuries and casualty was 'fed up' waiting for rescue and would ride out. Met by doctor at Drummin and injected. Cairngorm MRT. 31.

AUGUST 26 – Ascending Aonach Mor on scree and damp grass a man (47) slipped and fell 100m on to scree near the bealach between Aonach Mor and Carn Mor Dearg. His injuries were to: ribs, head, thorax and scapula. Lochaber MRT, RAF Sea King. 65.

SEPTEMBER 25-26 – Benighted after losing equipment when crossing the river immediately below Blackwater Dam, two men (both 22) walked out after a morning search by Glencoe MRT and SARDA had started. 14.

OCTOBER 7-8 – Two men (43, 42) got separated from their party of eight ascending Sgurr a'Mhaim, trying to finish Ring of Steall. The two men descended in cloud on a wrong bearing and got on to steep, rocky ground. It was getting dark with wind and rain so they used bivouac bags and settled down for the night. Lochaber MRT found them descending early next day. 21.

OCTOBER 8-9 - Woman (17) became ill at Culra Bothy (Ben Alder) and was lifted by RAF Sea King. Discharged from hospital next day. 8.

OCTOBER 10-11 - Couple left Garva Bridge at 18.00 to cross Corrieyairack Pass on hired trail motorbikes. Woman (47) crashed on a wooden bridge at altitude 550m severely injuring her knee. Alerted by mobile phone at 21.00 rescuers went in from Laggan and from Fort Augustus in 4WD vehicles. Patient was hypothermic when found at 23.30 and rescued. Cairngorm MRT. 30.

OCTOBER 14 - After deerstalking was finished in the area for the day, two women (39, 38) decided to walk to the summit of Sgurr a'Choise (663m. 3km. S. of Ballachulish). They got lost and benighted. Found by Glencoe MRT and SARDA. 38.

OCTOBER 19 – RAF Sea King evacuated seven cold and wet military personnel from Coire Gabhalach, Mamores. Three of them had mild hypothermia.

OCTOBER 31-November – Descending An Gearanach from the Ring of Steall, a solo walker (34) got benighted. Losing the path he bivouacked below crags. He was found uninjured in Glen Nevis by Lochaber MRT. Kinloss MRT and RAF Sea King involved. 65.

NOVEMBER 22 – On a steep hillside NW of Garbh Bheinn, Kinlochleven, one of 10 soldiers (age 20) on exercise lost consciousness from exhaustion. He was winched by RAF Sea King and flown to hospital. 8.

DECEMBER 9-12 – After lodging a route card with Police for a walk on Dec. 8 from Corrour Station to Glen Nevis, a man (19) did not report as planned. A vain search of the route was carried out by three Police plus one. The man appeared at Corrour Station on Dec. 12. He had been camping nearby and he had not done the route. 30.

DECEMBER 20-21 – Member of a party walking from Ballachulish to Duror got lost on forestry roads but turned up unharmed. Glencoe MRT. 6.

OTHER CENTRAL HIGHLANDS 1996

JANUARY 7 – Two men (both 27) tried to ascend Creag Meagaidh from Carn Liath via The Window. They failed to find summit and could not navigate off plateau because their unprotected map was a soggy mess. They snowholed for the night and got down unaided at 11.20. Searches by Kinloss and Lochaber MRTs, SARDA, RAF Sea King. 362.

JANUARY 20 – Walker (32) slipped and fell into River Kinglass, breaking his leg when crossing the bridge at Innseag-na-h-Luraiche. Airlifted by RN Sea King. Strathclyde Police MRT. 22.

JANUARY 20-21 – Cairngorm and Kinloss MRTs, SARDA and RAF Sea King vainly searched a large area of Monadhliath Range for an overdue hotel guest, male about 29, who had left a vague route plan and no luggage. 360.

FEBRUARY 3 – Man (21) went out of control on steep ground skiing Summit Run, Aonach Mor, landing on rocks and tearing ligaments in his back. Lochaber MRT and RAF Sea King on scene. 7.

FEBRUARY 17 – Two companions thought a student (21) had a broken ankle when he slipped on ice (no crampons) from summit of Na Gruagaichean, Mamores, sliding 150m. Lochaber and Glencoe MRTs, RAF Sea King. 20.

FEBRUARY 17 – Three people climbing Icicle Gully, E. Face Aonach Mor, stopped to rope up. Man (46) slid down when his snow steps collapsed. He knocked off another climber (41). Both men wore crampons. Both fell 22m. The older broke an ankle; the other had cuts and bruises to face and head. Lochaber and Turkish MRTs stretchered them to a tracked vehicle and Ski Gondola. 46.

FEBRUARY 18-19 – Two men (45, 37) got on to a crag in error, descending in the dark and getting cragfast above an ice pitch 150m above foot of Staghorn Gully. Both men in good heart were lowered off by Lochaber MRT, and then walked out. RAF Sea King. 250.

FEBRUARY 18-19 – Attempting four Munros west of Drumochter in foul weather five members of a climbing club went down the wrong side of Geal Charn (917m) and had a long walk out up the SE Shore of Loch Ericht. Cairngorm MRT, RAF Sea King. 26.

MARCH 6 – Four Kinloss MRT flown by RAF Sea King to Coire Ardair, Creag Meagaidh. A mountain guide (m29) had fallen from Centre Post Direct with chest and back injuries. His foothold had collapsed and he fell 30m and had been lowered to a safe place by a companion. Stretchered to helicopter. Lochaber MRT. 81.

MARCH 28 – Experienced ice-climber (35) leading 1st pitch Smith's Gully, Creag Meagaidh when his axes pulled out of soft ice. He fell 10m breaking a lower leg. Lowered by his second. Further lower by Lochaber MRT to airlift by RN Sea King. 63.

MARCH 30-31 – Eighteen University OTC students (seven female, 11 male aged 21-18) with two male members of HM Forces (both 36) lost path on Am Bodach, Mamores. A student (21) slipped injuring her leg. Two male casualties (20, 19) had bruising. They had difficulty in descending 800m to Glen Nevis in snow because there was only one ice-axe, one rope and one pair of crampons in the group. An instructor went for help. All airlifted by RAF Sea King. Lochaber MRT. 63.

APRIL 4 – Having climbed above the difficulties of The Pumpkin, Creag Meagaidh two men (41, 32) stopped for lunch and unroped. The older man had put his helmet in his rucksack and carried the rope. The younger man ahead, just metres from the top, disturbed a small snow slab which carried both down. The older man was killed by a fall of 300m. The younger man's crampons lodged in stones causing an ankle injury, but he completed the climb and was helped down by other climbers. RAF Sea King unable to help due to wind conditions. Both casualties evacuated on stretchers. Kinloss and Lochaber MRTs. 297.

APRIL 23-24 – Man (71) left Achintee to go via Carn Mor Dearg and CMD Arête to Ben Nevis. When he was overdue a search started next morning. His body was found by RAF Sea King at G.R. 41NN 168 724 which is on WSW slopes Carn Dearg Mheadhonach, about 300m NE of CIC Hut. Carrying ice-axe and crampons he is presumed to have slipped on scree/snow and died of chest injuries. Lochaber MRT. 102.

MAY 25 – Woman (36) fell off mountain bike on West Highland Way 5km west of Kinlochleven suffering a minor leg injury. She was evacuated by Glencoe MRT Land-Rover. 11.

JUNE 14-15 – Man (56) got separated from three companions on NW slopes of Carn Beag Dearg, Fort William in good weather. He was partially sighted. Despite a search his party could not find him. Located by Lochaber MRT sweep searching in the small hours. 23.

JUNE 20 – Sixteen-year-old on an award hike collapsed from exhaustion in Lairig Leacach, Grey Corries. He was airlifted by RAF. Lochaber MRT. 17.

JULY 1996 – Body of man (c50) who shot himself, found on summit plateau of Ben Alder.

JULY 17 - Two paragliders launched off Aonach Mor. When his canopy collapsed, French Air Force navigator (32) fell 45m into Allt Daim, fracturing a femur and opposite wrist. RAF airlift, Lochaber MRT. 29.

JULY 17 – One of five Germans walking West Highland Way near Tigh-na-Sleubhaich collapsed with heat exhaustion. Passer-by used mobile phone. RAF Sea King in area for paraglider rescue attended, but walker had recovered and he declined help. 2.

JULY 20 – Angler (76) banged his head. He tripped on a rock returning to A82 from Loch Ba, Rannoch Muir, with three companions. Lifted by RAF Sea King (as location was 4km from road) and detained overnight for observation. Glencoe MRT. 33.

AUGUST 4-6 – Search by Lochaber and Kinloss MRTs (Leuchars later) for man (32) overdue from walking Ring of Steall, Mamores. On the morning of third day he was found dead by RAF Sea King on steep, wooded slopes 200m west of Steall Waterfall. 749.

AUGUST 5 - Above col Aonach Mor/Carn Mor Dearg. Man (28) slipped on rock, falling 6m with scalp laceration (eight stitches needed). Lochaber MRT already on hill for above search. RAF airlift. 5.

AUGUST 5-6 – Dutch male student on outdoor course expedition was lunching at Prince Charlie's Cave above Ben Alder Cottage. Messing about throwing food at each other he stepped back, fell 5m and banged his head. He suffered memory loss. Instructor walked 16km to phone at Ben Alder Lodge. Flown out by RN Sea King and treated for minor head injury. 14.

AUGUST 11 – Near North Top, Beinn a'Chaorainn, Loch Laggan, one of eighteen suffered a heart attack. A male (70) he was treated with oxygen and airlifted by RN Sea King. Lochaber MRT. 43.

SEPTEMBER 9 – A party of three adults with three children was overdue walking from Corrour Station to Glen Nevis top car park. All turned up safe as search by Lochaber MRT and RAF Sea King started. 11.

SEPTEMBER 14-15 – Two men got benighted at Steall Waterfall descending from anti-clockwise circuit of Ring of Steall. Escorted down overnight by Lochaber MRT but failed to report details to Police. 56.

SEPTEMBER 20-21 – Retreating from a walk to Ben Alder from Loch Ossian Youth Hostel because of high winds, a man (27) did not inform anyone of his return. Next day he returned by train after drinking at Rannoch while Lochaber MRT and RAF Sea King searched for him. 74.

OCTOBER 21 - Party of four walking Rannoch Moor from Rannoch Station to Kingshouse Hotel were overdue well after dark. Lifted in Glencoe MRT Landrover. One woman (69) had fallen and sprained a wrist. All had overestimated distance and their ability. 17.

OCTOBER 25 – Search by Lochaber MRT and RAF Sea King for a schoolboy (14) who was missing after a disagreement. He walked round Loch Oich. OK. 28.

NOVEMBER 9 - Walking north on the Rannoch Moor section of West Highland Way, a man (49) collapsed in a fit and then complained of chest pains (heart attack) at Ba Cottage. Airlifted to Belford Hospital by RAF Sea King. Glencoe MRT. 24.

NOVEMBER 24 - A pair attempted to get from Fort William to Bridge of Orchy on West Highland Way complete with mountain bikes. In worsening weather and heavy snow one (m27) became exhausted at Lairigmor, about 14km from the start. Evacuated by Land-Rover. Lochaber MRT. 16.

DECEMBER 13 - Aviemore Police rescued a female German tourist trapped by darkness on Craigellachie, west of Aviemore. Cairngorm MRT. 6.

DECEMBER 15-16 - A man (24) and a female student (20) were climbing Upper Couloir, Stob Gabhar when the snow they were on collapsed. Student received abrasions from fall into deep gully. Man went to help then both got cragfast. Escorted to open ground for airlift by RAF Sea King. Strathclyde Police and Glencoe MRTs. 306.

DECEMBER 27 – Despite wearing crampons, two women walkers (36, 30) got cragfast due to ice on summit of Stob Coire na h-Eirghe (a peak just south of main ridge of Mamores near Sgurr an Iubhair). One from another party used mobile phone. Other climbers also helped them. Airlift by RAF Sea King with Lochaber MRT aboard diverted from another job. 8.

DECEMBER 28 – One of a party of three RAF Leuchars MRT (38) fell descending Am Bodach (Mamores). He tried to ice-axe self arrest but failed due to ice. Crampons then caught resulting in a long, tumbling fall down N. slopes. Serious head injuries. Leuchars and Lochaber teams. Winched by RAF Sea King already on search in the area. 30.

DECEMBER 30 – Ascending Right Twin on East Face of Aonach Dubh (near ski complex, not Glencoe) a roped climber (32) put his axe into a soft snow cornice believing it to be ice. He fell 30m spraining an ankle and bruising nose and chest. He managed to get to gondola without Lochaber callout. 2.

CAIRNGORMS

JANUARY 21-22 – Couple (f52, m50) overdue on Monega Hill above Glen Isla walked out to Glenshee Ski Centre after night in a snow cave. Overnight snow searches by Tayside teams and RAF Sea King. No route plan left. No map and compass. 240.

JANUARY 27 – Two students reported overdue on Lochnagar were found at Scott's Bothy, Derry Lodge, having changed plans without telling anyone. Aberdeen MRT.

JANUARY 27-28 – Having completed Sidewinder, Coire an Lochan at 17.10 hours, a pair (m23, f19) went too far south on the plateau avoiding the crags. Lost in a white-out and gale they bivvied in a snow scoop. Rescuers on the plateau were beaten back by weather and those in the corrie found conditions very hard. Pair found next day by SARDA dog and handler, cold but well, coming off the plateau on correct bearings. Cairngorm and Leuchars MRTs, RAF Sea King. 500.

JANUARY 28 – Pair reported overdue from White Magic, Coire an t-Sneachda. Report was too early for rescuers to be very concerned for climbers on such a hard route. As expected they turned up OK. Cairngorm MRT.

FEBRUARY 3 – Roped pair were climbing Salamander, Hell's Lum Crag, in very thin ice conditions. Leader (25) fell above crux pitch when ice gave way. Belay held but he sustained head and arm injuries. Winched by Rescue 137 (RAF Sea King). Cairngorm MRT. 96.

FEBRUARY 7 – Ski instructor (f23) lifted from Cairngorm Top Station by RAF Sea King. Hospital release followed treatment for mild hypothermia.

FEBRUARY 18 – A party of four split into two singles and a pair when attempting three Munros around Glas Maol. In strong winds and white-out the only map blew away. The two singles got down, one reporting the pair overdue, but they escaped unharmed. Braemar MRT. 21.

FEBRUARY 18 – Son (11) got separated from mother by her falling off Cairnwell T Bar Tow. He got lost in a white-out and the Ski Centre closed because of gales.

Braemar MRT and Chairlift staff found him not far from top of tow, because he had sheltered and not wandered. Aberdeen MRT stand-by. 80.

FEBRUARY 22 – Leader's axes pulled out and he (27) fell 18m, sustaining a compound lower leg fracture, on one of the Cascade routes, Stag Rocks. Winched by R.137 RAF Sea King. Winchman was on ground for 45 minutes. 12.

FEBRUARY 24 – A pair left carpark at 09.00 and think they climbed Invernookie, Coire an t-Sneachda, gaining plateau at 18.30, but had no explanation why they did not get back to carpark till 23.00. Cairngorm MRT. 3.

FEBRUARY 24-25 – Leading the second pitch of SE Buttress, Creag an Dubh Loch, man (27) placed a runner 15m above his second. Some 15m above the runner one of his axes pulled out, the runner failed and he fell 50m over snow and rock with serious open fractures to a lower leg. Braemar MRT members were twice struck by avalanches during his evacuation. 202.

MARCH 2 - Climber (23) on Fingers Ridge, Coire an t-Sneachda, slipped, fell 5m unhurt, lost both his axes and got cragfast. He was rope lowered by another climber because his companion (29) could not help. Descending in bad weather they met Cairngorm MRT. 68.

MARCH 3-4 – The pair involved in the above incident went to look for lost gear. They got lost soon after leaving Ptarmigan Chairlift, possibly because map and compass were among lost items. Sheltering overnight near Stag Rocks the 29-year-old got cold, so the 23-year-old went for help. The hypothermic one was found by walkers who raised alarm and he was rescued by RAF Sea King. 150.

MARCH 3-4 – See above two incidents. The man (23) who went for help was overdue. Braemar, Cairngorm, Kinloss MRTs and RAF Sea King searched. He wandered about all day. By good luck when somewhere east of Cairngorm there was a cloud window and he saw the Ciste carpark. Found uninjured by a passer-by in Coire na Ciste. 150.

MARCH 4 – Woman (42) slipped on Shank of Drumfallow, Glen Doll, injuring her leg. Carried by eight passers-by on a Pigott (improvised rope) stretcher and a farmer's quad ATV. 20.

MARCH 16 – On foot, but carrying skis after a ski traverse of three Munros, three Kinloss MRT members followed a cornice line north to find the NW Ridge of Glas Maol for a safe descent line in falling snow and high wind. Summits were scoured of snow but west facing slopes were loaded. They were at 1000m on a convex slope immediately above a steeper part of the W Face of Glas Maol. Finding soft slab they started to retrace south to find a way down off Craig Leacach but one man collapsed the cornice and was carried down, stopping unhurt on top of the debris. Not knowing where the other two men were he used a mobile phone to contact Rescue Control and carried out an avalanche transceiver search. The avalanche had swept 240m height by 100m wide with a crown wall height of 2m. Radios contacted the two still above the avalanche danger who were extracted by Glenshee Piste Machine from Glas Maol summit. Braemar, Kinloss MRTs. 28.

MARCH 23 – Two climbers overdue from Shelter Stone Crag turned up safe. Cairngorm MRT callout. 5.

MARCH 30 – Boy (3) got separated from older friends who thought he was going home. He got lost in woods north of Bennachie, near Insch. Aberdeen and Braemar MRTs and RAF Sea King searched by night in forest. His jacket was found then he was located unhurt, but cold, by Police dog, having travelled 1500m through thick undergrowth. 120.

MARCH 30 – Poorly clad walker (43) 'just stopped' in Glen Dee when half-way round a 24km circuit of Carn a' Mhaim, with a companion. Rescued by

Grampian Police Land-Rover he was very cold and complained of sore legs but refused medical assistance. 4.

MARCH 31- April 1 – Three schoolboys (15, 14, 14) mountain biking from Rothiemurchus Lodge got lost. Found before midnight by Police dog handler. Cairngorm MRT, SARDA. 66.

APRIL 1 – Leading Spiral Gully, Coire an t-Sneachda, a candidate (26) for Mountain Instructor's Certificate had a problem with a running belay below him. Climbing down to rectify it, he lost footing, sliding 30m down the gully breaking a lower leg. He failed to ice-axe brake but the rope stopped him. With legs bound together he was lowered by his assessor and stretchered by Glenmore Lodge MRT. Airlift by RAF Sea King. 40.

APRIL 2 – Skier (16) off piste on the remote plateau 1.7km south of the head of Loch Einich stumbled causing a slight leg injury. Flown out by RAF Sea King. 13.

APRIL 5 – Man (48) climbed partially fallen tree when walking near Derry Lodge. Descending he fell and broke tibia and fibula. RAF airlift. 9.

APRIL 5-6 – Two males (17, 15) wearing trainers and jeans undertook a 48km, two-day walk in moors west of Knockando, Strathspey, as training for an award hike. Fortunately, the weather was good because they soon got lost, wandering off route. They pitched a tent in a gully among thick whins, and stayed there, not far from habitation, till they were out of food. Found by RAF Sea King. Grampian Police MRT. 40.

APRIL 7 – Walker (70) suffered a minor stroke walking on NE Shoulder, Morrone, Braemar. Air Ambulance evacuation as he was not close to 4WD Track. Grampian Police MRT. 5.

APRIL 8 – Man (51) walking path west of Baddoch Burn, Braemar fell sustaining compound fracture of wrist. Walked out by companion to a waiting Police vehicle. 2.

APRIL 11-12 – Jock's Road. Two men (both 31) got lost above Glen Doll and used mobile phone. Stayed put in worsening conditions and walked off at first light. Searches overnight by Tayside MRTs. 154.

MAY 5 – Climber (m29) roped on Beech Tree Wall, Craig a' Barns fell to base of crag because of poor belay. Leg injury. Tayside MRTs. 6.

MAY 7-8 – Six men starting at Cairngorm Car Park at 11.30 got lost in white-out returning from Derry Cairngorm at Garbh Uisge Beag. Going west then east they stayed overnight at Fords of Avon, reaching Glenmore 07.45. Cairngorm, Kinloss MRTs, RAF Sea King. 132.

MAY 17-18 – Solo walker (39) slipped on rough path at head of Loch Avon and heard ankle snap. Crawled to sandy beach and stayed in tent overnight. No response to shouts and whistles in overcast weather with frequent snow/sleet showers. Painfully hobbled 6km to Dubh Lochan (Lairig an Laoigh) where he met passer-by. Airlift by RAF Sea King. Braemar MRT. 22.

MAY 26 – Couple (m42, f40) got broken arms when ex-Army tracked vehicle toppled over on steep ground on north side Bogha-cloiche (897m), Gaick, Glen Trommie. Two of party of 22 went to phone but rang off before giving full details. Search and airlift by Air Ambulance and RAF Sea King helicopters. 29.

MAY 30 – Solo walker (70s) caused concern to passers-by. Attempting Macdui from Linn of Dee he had several adventures attempting river crossing and got part way up Sron Riach in mist, rain and sleet. Braemar MRT doctor found him hypoglaecaemic and hypothermic. Walked to Land-Rover track with help after chocolate feed. Recovered after treatment. 6.

JUNE 6 – Schoolgirl (14) slipped on dry scree on Craig Maud, Gen Doll and struck head on a rock. Tayside MRTs, RAF Sea King.

JUNE 6 – Man (35) slipped on small snowfield on Stob Coire an t-Sneachda, Cairngorm, breaking his ankle. Passers-by used mobile phone. RAF Sea King and Police. 14.

JUNE 29 – Man (50) climbed a crag east of Loch Loch. Rockfall caused abdominal and chest injuries. Stretchered by Tayside MRTs.

JUNE 30 – Loaded with food and gear for a 7 day expedition a Danish scout (19) slipped on rocks crossing R. Gairn breaking her ankle. She was stretchered to a vehicle by Braemar MRT. 15.

JULY 3 – Man (59) tripped on path two miles north of Derry Lodge twisting an ankle. He and his son abandoned plan to return to Aviemore and phoned from Derry Lodge. Grampian Police vehicle. 1.

JULY 14 – Mountain biker skidded on loose surface of Derry Lodge track causing 10-stitch cut to his knee. Police and Ambulance. 3.

JULY 17 – On third day of an award exploration, an overweight teenager (17) bent down to pick up an object when sitting on a wall in Glen Luibeg. Due to his weight (159kg.) he strained back muscles so that he could not continue. Braemar MRT Land-Rover. 1.

JULY 27 – A 26km leg (Tarf Bothy to Baddoch/Clunie) of a sponsored solo coast-to-coast run took the exhausted runner nine hours to walk. None of his back-up team had mobile phones. Due to poor timing a helicopter searched the route. The runner (29) reached Glen Clunie, Braemar but abandoned the undertaking. 17.

JULY 27 – Solo bouldering at foot of Craig a' Barns, Dunkeld, a man slipped on dry rock, causing head and arm injuries. Tayside MRTs. 5.

JULY 29 – Heading up track to Lochnagar, a student (18) had abdominal pains after recent appendix op. Grampian Police, RAF Sea King. 10.

JULY 31 – Man (34) twisted his knee aggravating an old injury descending Allt Clais an t-Sabhail from Cairn Toul. Grampian Police vehicle to above Derry Lodge. 2.

AUGUST 1 – RAF Sea King lifted walker (59) from Chalamain Gap. She slipped twice, injuring ankle, then knee. 11.

AUGUST 5 – A large foothold fell out, causing a man (36) leading Savage Slit, Coire an Lochain, to fall 10m on to ledges before the rope stopped him. Stretchered down by Glenmore Lodge MRT and airlift by RAF Sea King. 28.

AUGUST 16 – Female student (c18) slipped on path above Bachnagairn, Glen Clova with bad ankle sprain. Stretcher carry by Tayside MRTs. 35.

AUGUST 17 – One of 11 walkers (m56) collapsed from a heart attack at Balluderon Hill, Sidlaws. Rescue by Ambulance Service and local 4WD vehicle.

SEPTEMBER 1 – One of a party of 28 hillwalkers (m57) died of a heart attack at the summit cairn of Devil's Point. Braemar MRT, RAF Sea King. 54.

SEPTEMBER 4-5 – Starting to climb at 13.00 it got dark when three men (22, 21, 20) had completed Eagle Ridge, Lochnagar. They bivvied not knowing they were at the very lip of the corrie. Found descending path, unaware of search, by Braemar MRT. 25.

SEPTEMBER 27 to date – Man (34) missing from home. His unlocked car with keys in ignition found at Spittal of Genmuick. Usual walk with his dog was to waterfall on Glas-Allt. Large-scale searches of a broad area carried out by Aberdeen, Braemar, Grampian Police MRTs, RAF Sea King. Not traced. 627.

OCTOBER 20 – Woman (40) separated from three other walkers in mist between Mayar and Dreish, reaching Glen Prosen four hours later. Search by Tayside MRTs and SARDA. 28.

NOVEMBER 8-10 – Three London men (36, 35, 32) were overdue according to their lodged route card. Reaching Devil's point from Cairngorm they walked to Linn o' Dee because of deep snow. Cairngorm MRT, RAF Sea King. 17.

NOVEMBER 18 – Group of eight overdue at Crow Craigies (where they had arranged to meet informant) completed Jock's Road walk to Glen Clova OK. Tayside MRTs and SARDA called out. 3.

NOVEMBER 24 – During snowfall a pair were swept 200m by slab avalanche when descending Fiacaill a' Choire Chais. Poor visibility caused them to go east under corrie headwall. Student (22) got back injury. His fellow student (19) dug him out despite injury to his own leg, then went for help and found others with mobile phone. Stretchered by Cairngorm MRT. 180.

NOVEMBER 24-25 – Note in Cas car park found at 11.30 Monday said two climbers were due back from Braeriach Sunday pm. Turned up 14.50 Monday. Cairngorm MRT. 14.

NOVEMBER 28-29 – Two from Cas car park intended to do round of Northern Corries and Lurchers to Chalamain Gap. Man (59) exhausted in poor weather and waist deep snow. Lost, they went down into Lairig Ghru and casualty was put in bivvy bag. Companion found way down Allt Druidh and used mobile phone. Search by Cairngorm MRT. RAF airlift. 164

DECEMBER 24 – RAF Sea King airlifted a hillwalker, one of a party of four, (m35) with neck and breastbone injuries from Loch Avon area. Using crampons and ice-axe he had slipped in corrie west of Coire Domhain. Cairngorm MRT. 17.

DECEMBER 25 – Woman (41) slipped on icy rock in good weather on Meall a'Buachaille, above Ryvoan Bothy injuring an ankle. On the path, she wore plastic boots without crampons. Airlift by RAF Sea King. 11.

DECEMBER 27 – With a companion, and carrying a large rucksack containing a parachute and gear, a man (32) was ascending Craigendarroch, Ballater. His intention was to paraglide from the summit (405m) but he slipped on ice on the way up, injuring an ankle. He managed to walk down using a broom as a crutch. Braemar MRT. 7.

DECEMBER 29-30 – Leaving rucksacks and food at Day Lodge, Cairngorm car park, two snowboarders (17, 16) lost near Ptarmigan Restaurant in mist. The two boys went down to Loch Avon, followed fresh tracks in snow to a tent and waited there till two men returned. The men took them to Fords of Avon Bothy, giving them a bivvy bag. They shared cramped accommodation and food with three others. Next day rescuers made contact with one of the tent men. Airlift by RAF Sea King. Cairngorm, Kinloss and Leuchars MRTs, SARDA. 338.

SOUTHERN HIGHLANDS

JUNE 4, 1995 (Three late reports) – One of six scrambling up part of Spearhead Ridge, Beinn Narnain dislodged a boulder which lacerated another's leg. Arrochar MRT, RN Sea King.

SEPTEMBER 16, 1995 – Man descending beside Buttermilk Burn, above Narnain Boulders, felt 'crack' in ankle/foot and could not continue. Stretchered by Arrochar and Dumbarton Police MRTs.

SEPTEMBER 30, 1995 – Lost solo walker with mobile phone on Beinn Ime met a lost group of four with another phone. They had a map but no compass. They reported they were on a scree slope and frightened. Located and escorted by Arrochar MRT who spotted torch light.

JANUARY 5, 1996 – Descending dry grass with her daughter on Sron a' Chlachain,

Glen Lochay, a woman (75) stumbled, injuring a lower leg. Stretcher carry by Killin MRT. 8.

JANUARY 21-22 – A man (43) descending Beinn Ime with a companion sustained fatal injuries in a fall. Not far below the summit they went off route in poor conditions, finding themselves on very steep ground on the south side. Deceased tried to climb down rock face but slipped on ice, falling 15m on to rocks. Companion retraced steps and went for help. Arrochar, Leuchars and Strathclyde teams, SARDA, RN Sea King and Police helicopter. 727.

JANUARY 29 – Ochils MRT called out to Commonedge Hill, Dollar for a scantily-clad male walker (36) trying to avoid re-admission to hospital. 82.

FEBRUARY 2 – Steep East Face of SE Ridge, Ben Ledi. Scrambling unroped on snow/ice man (49) slipped and fell 60m with fatal head injuries. He was not using helmet, ice-axe or crampons. Stretchered by Killin MRT to airlift by RN Sea King. 36.

FEBRUARY 13 – Flares reported on The Law, Tillicoultry. Two members of Ochils MRT checked. It transpired that a meteorite had crossed Central Scotland at that time. 6.

FEBRUARY 18 – Black Linn Reservoir NE of Dumbarton. Walker (41) in a party of three slipped on a muddy hill path on Lang Craigs breaking her lower leg. Stretchered by Strathclyde Police MRT. 7.

FEBRUARY 22-23 – Crianlarich man (36) was walking in hills around his home and was overdue. His body was found by SARDA dog at 01.15 hours in Bogle Glen. Wearing army boots he probably slipped on an icy path or wet grass. Stretchered by Killin MRT. 88.

MARCH 29 – Report of lights near Dumyat summit. False alarm.

MARCH 31 – Woman (36) walking on Ben Ledi began to suffer abnormal eyesight and speech. Her daughter went for help but the woman slithered down through trees till found with hypothermia on a forest road by Killin MRT. 15.

APRIL 2 – Report of lights and shouts east of Dumyat. False alarm.

APRIL 9 – Man (37) descending a snow slope on Beinn nan Eachan (Tarmachan Ridge) twisted a knee when his foot went through a hole. A member of the party of six contacted help with a mobile phone. RN Sea King airlift and Killin MRT. 13.

APRIL 13 – Man (47) slipped on a snow slope, falling over a ledge on to rocks on the ENE Ridge, Ben Vane. Suffering chest and arm injuries he was winched by RN Sea King. Strathclyde Police and Arrochar MRTs. 74.

APRIL 11-13 – A student (m26) set out for An Caisteall and Beinn a'Chroin (by *The Munros* route) on 11th, got stuck on a ledge of Beinn a' Chroin, went up and down the hill on 12th and walked out to Balquhidder on 13th suffering mild hypothermia, abrasions and possibly cracked ribs. Meantime three SARDA dogs, RN Sea King, Killin, Leuchars, Lomond and Ochils MRTs searched for him. 15 search dogs on call. 1264.

MAY 8 – RN Sea King winched walker (58) from east side of Ben More. Descending grass, she stumbled, breaking a tibia and fibula. Killin MRT. 48.

MAY 12 – Walker (45) descending from Ben Venue summit to Achray Hotel. His foot stuck in boggy ground and he fell forward breaking an ankle. Winched by RN Sea King. Killin MRT. 26.

Jamie Andrew on 'Alopecia' E4 6a, Ratho Quarry. Photo: Alastair Matthewson.

MAY 15 – Descending The Law from Ben Cleuch a schoolboy (13) slipped on a path cutting his leg. Ochils MRT. 15.

MAY 19-20 – Soldier carrying very heavy rucksack on ridges west of Cnoc Coinnich (Lochgoilhead) slipped, twisting his back. Arrochar MRT and RN Sea King.

JUNE 2 – Killin and Leuchars MRTs, SARDA and RN Sea King searched for a dementia sufferer (84). She was found in Brig o' Turk, having walked 13km from Ballimore, Balquhidder. 126.

JUNE 17 – Woman (74) slipped on a wet, grassy path on lower slopes of Craigleith, Alva. Rescued with leg injuries by Ambulance Service.

JUNE 18-19 – Central Scotland Police Underwater Unit recovered the body of a man (64) from 6m of water. He had slipped when photographing Falls of Dochart unseen by other tourist walkers. Killin and Leuchars MRTs, RN Sea King. 457.

JUNE 21-22 – Camping with five others in the Campsies, a girl (14) fell 24m into ravine. With extensive injuries she was winched at night by RN Sea King. Winchman and stretcher had to be lowered 54m through tree canopy into bottom of ravine. Balfron Ambulance. 20.

JUNE 23 – Casualty (21) was camping with three friends near the top of Dumgoyach, Strathblane (Duntreath Castle). Obeying a call of nature at 04.45 he slipped down a 20m crag and collided with a tree. Stretchered by Lomond MRT to airlift by RN Sea King. 40.

JULY 12 – A party of two in mist descended east-facing crags of SE Ridge of Ben Lui. One of them (57) slipped on grass and rock at about 700m. He died from skull and other fractures from a fall of 30m. Killin and Lomond MRTs, RAF and RN Sea Kings. 17.

JULY 12-13 – Ill-equipped and using a photo-copied page of a Trossachs walkers' guide, pair (f49, m 46) got lost descending Ben Venue in mist. They reached the roadless south shore of Loch Katrine. Evacuated from a remote farm by ambulance (woman hypothermic), Police and Strathclyde Water Board. Lomond MRT stood down. 34.

JULY 17 – Solo walker (67) parked car on A82 1.6km north of Tyndrum. At 12.30 two walkers found him dead from a heart attack on Beinn Odhar 150m from West Highland Way. Killin MRT 4.

JULY 27 – On a family outing to climb Ben A'n, a woman (67) died from a heart attack 100m up the path. Central Police. 5.

AUGUST 3 (could be 95?) – Arrochar MRT splinted a French woman walker's arm at Narnain Boulders.

AUGUST 6 – His wife went for help when a poorly-equipped man (49) got stranded in a steep gully descending Ben Venue off the Achray path. The incident is not classified as 'cragfast' because he got himself out. Killin MRT. 10.

AUGUST 22 – 50m from Ben Lomond summit, man (57) died from a heart attack. Lomond MRT, RN Sea King. 15.

AUGUST 25 – Ochils MRT stretchered a young walker (10). A makeshift rope swing on a tree broke when he was playing on it in Alva Glen. Leg lacerations. 15.

AUGUST 25 – Hillwalker (58) descending Alva Glen fell 30m into the gorge when a path gave way, sustaining skull and spine injuries. Rescued from a pool by his wife and sustained by her, a passing nurse and two teenagers till four ambulance men arrived. 12. (Site of a fatal recovery by Ochils MRT on 3. 2. 94).

AUGUST 29 – Dehydrated and with kidney problems a walker (33) on Ben Lomond

Duncan Chessell climbing the south summit of Mount Cook. Photo: David Ritchie.

was escorted down by other walkers. He declined medical assistance. Lomond MRT. 10.

AUGUST 31 – Male with arm injuries from a slip in Dollar Glen, Ochils.

SEPTEMBER 8 – Trying to get down from Ben Lui, a woman (32) collapsed from heat exhaustion. Killin MRT, RN Sea King. 18.

SEPTEMBER 22 – Party got stuck on a 6m cliff descending Ben Venue. Father got down but daughter (22) with dog stayed put. Roped down by Killin MRT. 5.

SEPTEMBER 27 – Student (21) walking on forest road 3.5km NW of Callander tripped spraining his ankle. Killin MRT. 14.

SEPTEMBER 29 – SARDA standby for three boys overdue on West Highland Way, Inversnaid, Loch Lomond.

OCTOBER 2 – Walker (m57) collapsed and died on Ben Chonzie above Loch Turret. RAF Sea King.

OCTOBER 6 – Man (59) walking south on Glen Ogle Nature Trail, nearing Lochearnhead, slipped on wet grass fracturing a tibia and fibula. Stretchered by Killin MRT. 3.

OCTOBER 19 – Three members RAF Leuchars MRT on exercise saw a woman blown over by strong winds near Ben Lawers summit. Carried/supported to Visitor Centre with ankle injury. 13.

OCTOBER 19 – An untraced woman reported to a farmer that a female hillwalker had fallen and injured a leg on Meall Ghaordie. Searches by Killin MRT and RAF Sea King revealed nothing. 84.

OCTOBER 24 – Family party were separated in mist near Dumyat summit. Boy (14) found during search by Ochils MRT and RN Sea King. 35.

NOVEMBER 9 – Two members RAF Leuchars MRT, told by an eye witness, transported a male walker with injured lower leg on West Highland Way near Tyndrum to Oban Hospital. 7.

NOVEMBER 20 – Slip on icy path to Cobbler above Succoth (SE slopes Beinn Narnain) by a woman (54) caused leg injury. Camera flash used by casualty and friend speeded location by RN Sea King for winching. Arrochar and Strathclyde Police MRTs. 34.

NOVEMBER 24-25 – Two males (36, 28) tried to cross Stobinian and Ben More from Balquhidder to Crianlarich. Caught in blizzard and unstable snow so stayed overnight in an igloo at Bealach-eadar-dha Beinn. Killin, Leuchars and Lomond MRTs and SARDA searched. Spotted and winched by RN Sea King due west of Ben More at half-height. 124.

DECEMBER 9-10 – Starting late, walker (52) spent night out on Ben Vorlich (route from Ardvorlich, Loch Earn) after dropping his rucksack down a cliff. Turned up as Killin and Tayside teams assembled next morning. Thaw conditions. 84.

SKYE

MARCH 12-13 – Deceased (23) with three companions left Sligachan at 11.00 to climb Pinnacle Ridge, Sgurr nan Gillean. Descending in snowfall and wind he left companions at foot of climb to navigate down Coire a' Bhasteir by torchlight at 23.00. After 100m he slipped on verglas and ice on boiler slabs falling 250m. His ice-axe was attached to his rucksack and crampons in it. Skye MRT, R137 RAF Sea King. 144.

MARCH 21-22 – Responding to a mobile phone call to Sligachan that 'his friend had been hurt, and to be transferred to the Police on 999', RAF Sea King, Kinloss and Skye MRTs searched North Cuillin ridges and corries, paths and parked vehicles. Nothing found. 210.

APRIL 1 – Climber (17) continued ascending after his father stopped on the Tourist Route, Sgurr nan Gillean. When his son was descending from the summit the father heard falling rock; on looking over the edge of the ridge he saw the deceased lying 250m below in a boulder field clear of snow. Crampons were found in his rucksack. Correct way was walkable as snow had melted off south side of East Ridge. He went too far down the top slabs, failing to turn right to get the best line, turned left and slipped on hard neve over two cliff edges, then sliding down snow into the boulders. RAF Sea King. Skye MRT. 55.

MAY 19 – Seven people were descending from the summit of Sgurr Mhic Coinnich during snowfall. A man (50) slipped on wet rock and fell just over one metre breaking a tibia and fibula. Skye MRT and RAF Sea King. 112.

MAY 20 – Four walkers were crossing an area of loose rock on West Ridge near summit of Sgurr nan Gillean. A man (41) lost his footing, tried to regain balance by grasping a large rock but it gave way. He was killed when he fell more than 300m into Coire a' Bhasteir. Skye MRT, HMCG helicopter. 194.

MAY 26 – Five climbers finished a route but took a wrong turn descending Coire a' Ghrunnda. Retracing steps one (28) slipped and fell 12m down a slab causing hairline hip fracture and leg ligament damage. Skye MRT, RAF Sea King. 84.

Date?????HMCG helicopter evacuated female with broken ankle from beach at outlet of Kilmarie River, Strathaird. 8.

JUNE 8 – A man (48) separated from his four companions in poor weather on South Top, Sgurr na Banachdich. His body was found 90m below his last known position. Skye MRT, RAF Sea King. 93.

JUNE 20 – Three climbers in a chimney on the ridge between Sgurr Dubh Mor and Sgurr Dubh Beag. Leader was sack hauling. The rucksack dislodged a rock which struck a companion (42) fracturing his skull. No helmet carried. Skye MRT, RAF Sea King. 28.

JULY13 – HMCG helicopter evacuated hillwalker (f73) with broken ankle from hills 1.3km north of Armadale Bay. Ambulance Service. 16.

JULY 14 – Man (18) could not continue walking due to sudden fatigue, attributed to medication change. Assisted from East Ridge, Beinn Dearg Beag (Red Cuillin) by Skye MRT. 6.

AUGUST 22-23 – Descending Coire na Banachdich near Window Buttress, three walkers (f28, m27, f25) benighted, made several wrong turns, then sheltered, shouting for help every 15 minutes. At 0100 they were heard by another walker who informed Skye MRT. Team had already been alerted and found party at 11.35. Airlift by RAF Sea King. 60.

AUGUST 29 – Descending Coire Scamadal near Bealach a' Chuirn, The Storr, woman (33) slipped on rock breaking her ankle. Skye MRT, RAF Sea King. 36.

SEPTEMBER 5-6 – Solo walker (41) cragfast 300m to north of Blaven path in Coire Uagneich. Helped down from top of a stack by Skye MRT. 36.

SEPTEMBER 6 – Walking with her husband in Storr Sanctuary, Trotternish, a woman (65) broke her ankle on a scree slope. Skye MRT, HMCG helicopter. 14.

SEPTEMBER 9-10 – After finishing a climb in Coire Lagan two men (42, 29) bivouacked when it got dark. They were reported overdue but walked off unaided at first light.

SEPTEMBER 9-10 – Rope of 3 (m22, m21, f20) got cragfast on Integrity, Sron na Ciche as climb took longer than anticipated. They spent night on a ledge having whistled for help. Whistles were heard by friends of the pair benighted in concurrent incident (above). Trio winched off by 202 Sqdn RAF Sea King. 12.

SEPTEMBER 12 – A stone rolled under the foot of a walker (21) on South Ridge, Sgurr na Banachdich. He injured leg muscles. Skye MRT, RAF Sea King. 23.

SEPTEMBER 23-25 – Man (41) got lost with his wife near Sgurr Thearlaich. They stayed in bivvy bags. It was rainy and misty again next day so after wandering a bit they got back into bivvy bags. Descending at 11.00 man slid over ledge, falling 20m breaking an ankle. Wife climbed to ridge and blew whistle at 12.00 to get help. Alerted at 17.00, Skye MRT were lifted by RAF Sea King to below cloud at 300m. Found bivvy site but casualty could not hear them. Team bivvied at 900m in rain, strong wind and hail. Found on third day at 09.30 and lowered into a gully, stretchered into Coire an Lochain to airlift by R137. Only injury was ankle. 381.

OCTOBER 4-7 – Leaving Camasunary on October 4, three males (56, 27, 15) got to Loch Coruisk on 6th. Report on 7th that they were exhausted and trapped by spate rivers. Airlifted by RAF Sea King, Skye MRT. Released from Broadford Hospital after examination. 18.

OCTOBER 23-24 – Party of two men (both 42) and a woman (31) attempted Bruach na Frithe from Coire a' Mhadaidh. Lost in atrocious weather they bivouacked in a cave and were found descending next morning by RAF Sea King. Team told they went up NW Ridge. Kinloss and Skye MRTs. 122.

NOVEMBER 18-22 – Searches by Kinloss and Skye MRTs, SARDA, HMCG and RAF helicopters followed report of a car at Fiskavaig road end. Alcohol was found, then the body of a Swiss student (m23) at the foot of a 100m sea cliff, near waterfall. 583.

NOVEMBER 23-24 – Returning across the Main Ridge from Coruisk when it was snowing, and off route on Bidein Druim na Ramh, a pair roped, lowering themselves down small rock shelves. Man (32) slipped, causing knee injury. Companion left him next day in a tent. During winching by RAF Sea King, Mayday was called when an engine failed, possibly due to ice ingress. Aircraft landed at Glenbrittle on one engine. Skye MRT. 139.

ISLANDS OTHER THAN SKYE

MAY 4 – Rescue of one of five members of Deaf and Dumb Mountaineering Club caused some communication problems for Arran MRT and RN Sea King. Man (36) slipped on dry path on Caisteal Abhail with leg injuries, cuts and bruises. 20.

MAY 12 – Fatal fall on Askival, Rum, by man (67) in a party of seven. He fell 100m down scree. Lochaber MRT, RAF R137 Sea King. 29.

MAY 18 – Group member used mobile phone to say casualty (23) on Caisteal Abhail was very cold and in shock. Examined in hospital after airlift by RN Sea King. He was discharged with only obvious injury torn ligaments. 58.

JUNE 12 – Wearing golf shoes, a woman (49) slipped at White Water, Corrie, injuring a leg. Stretchered by Arran MRT. 50.

JULY 19 – Youth (16) finished an abseil on Dun Caan, Raasay. Walking down east side, just below summit he tripped on grassy scree and fell 18m stopping against a rock. Airlift by HMCG. No significant injury. 28.

JULY 21-22 – Taking wrong path and meeting river crossing problems , four males (34, 11, 11, 9) with no compass on Beinn Nuis benighted. Arran MRT, RN Sea King. 152.

AUGUST 6 – HMCG helicopter found missing girl (17) unhurt. Arnol area of Lewis. 20.

AUGUST 11-12 – Three males (48, 15, 15) overdue at 22.00 in Glean Easan Borach, Lochranza. Arran MRT. 4.

AUGUST 21-22 – Attempting to cross 20 km of uninhabited moor from Loch Meavaig, North Harris to Morsgail Lodge, Lewis, walker (50) got stopped by Abhainn a' Loin, a river flowing into Loch Morsgail less than 1 km from the Lodge. Airlift by HMCG helicopter. 54.

SEPTEMBER 5 – At Dun Fion (Castle 3.2km SE of Brodick Pier) a woman (72) slipped on a grass path injuring a leg. She wore fabric boots. Arran MRT. 27.

OCTOBER 27 – A gunner (25) collapsed with hypothermia when on exercise in remote loch/hill country in east of Benbecula (Druim na Lice). Airlifted to Skye by RAF Sea King. 23.

NOVEMBER 13 – HMCG helicopter helped police search for missing hill walker in South Uist. Found by HMCG ground team. 9.

SOUTHERN UPLANDS

JANUARY 15-16 – Walking near his home, a retired man (67) with Parkinson's disease fell when a spar of a gate broke. He got hypothermic because he lay for 11 hours, unable to get up and frightened in case he fell into a nearby burn. Found by Moffat MRT sweep search. Stretchered to hospital and detained for two days. 201.

FEBRUARY 8 – Tweed Valley MRT and SARDA searched for a forest worker who had driven into forest in deep snow. He was found in a caravan 10km from the abandoned vehicle. Rescue by Land-Rover. 50.

FEBRUARY 18 – Borders SARU, Tweed Valley MRT and SARDA searched Lammermuirs (Twin Law Cairns) in a blizzard for three overdue women walkers (over 40) as it was getting dark. Found safe by Police. Really a separation incident because those reported overdue had been searching for a woman (80) who had turned back, gone adrift and reported them missing. 26.

APRIL 6 – Galloway MRT called out to search for a schoolboy (8) who got separated from his parents walking a forest trail ahead of them in Glen Trool. Police found him safe when he wandered on to the Southern Upland Way. 20.

APRIL 11-12 – HWWR, Galloway MRT, SARDA and RN Sea King called out for 4 males (17-14) on scout expedition. They had been refused admission to Backhill of Bush Bothy, having to camp outside in wind and snow. Suffered hypothermia crossing Rhinns of Kells to Black Craig next day. They walked out to Garryhorn Farm. 34.

MAY 2 – Three walkers overdue on S.Upland Way, west of Moffat, delayed by male (40+) with very bad blisters and bruised foot, turned up safe. Tweed Valley MRT. 5.

MAY 14 – Southern Upland Way 2km NE of Dalry. Galloway MRT called out for man (38) ill with fever, vomiting and diarrhoea. 3.

MAY 15– Staff outing plan went wrong: to do reciprocal walks on Southern Upland Way from Loch Trool to Auchinleck, with westbound party changing car keys with eastbound at White Laggan Bothy. Some went ahead so that three older women were left behind missing the turn off to the bothy south of Loch Dee. From 'non-turn off' they had to walk 13km to A712. Galloway MRT. 3.

MAY 15-16– Family of four bikers totally lost in Kielder Forest on a very cold night used mobile phone, being found by air search. Tweed Valley MRT called to search from Scottish side after dark. Northumbrian Services, Police helicopter, light aircraft. 30.

MAY 24 – Borders SARU searched Hirsel Estate, Coldstream. Evacuated drowned body of missing man (76) from loch in estate. 39.

MAY 26 – Galloway MRT standby for schoolboy (14) separated from 24 others in a sponsored walk of Cairnsmore of Fleet in mist. Alarm by mobile phone from leader, but boy turned up uninjured. 7.

JUNE 3-4 – Tweed Valley MRT, Borders SARU, SARDA and Police searched Galashiels and countryside for missing man (54) very sick with a life-threatening condition. He had wandered from home on to the hill. Found in time. 452.

JUNE 8-9 – His wife anxious when a Dane (71) walking Southern Upland Way in New Luce area could not get her on his mobile phone. He camped and phoned her next morning just as Galloway MRT were setting out. 2.

JUNE 22-23 – Borders and Tweed Valley teams searched woodland policies and immediate areas of a nursing home for a disoriented patient (77) missing from ward wearing only indoor clothing. Bruised from a slip, a wall obstructed re-entry to grounds. He was rescued by providing a ladder. 62.

JUNE 29 – Moffat MRT helped fell runner on Saddle Yoke. His ankle had been injured by a slip on scree. 6.

JUNE 29 – Moffat MRT searched Hart Fell for a runner who had missed two check points in mist. She was found in the glen. 24.

JULY 7 – Tweed Valley MRT searched for adult male who seriously injured himself and took to the hill naked. 5.

JULY 27 – Land-Rover used to recover walker with injured leg who had slipped on grass. One of a party of three near Winterhopeburn (5 km NNE of White Coomb). Tweed Valley MRT. 9.

AUGUST 6 – Borders SARU call out cancelled when three overdue mountain bikers turned up at Heatherhope, Hownam, Cheviot Hills. 6.

AUGUST 26 – Woman (53) collapsed exhausted on Craig Ronald (3km NE of Cairnsmore of Fleet) in strong wind and rain. Airlift by RAF Sea King. Released from hospital same day. Galloway MRT. 11.

SEPTEMBER 1-2 – Four girls and two boys (all 14) undergoing an award expedition in wind, rain and mist on Hartsgarth Fell (8.5km NE of Langholm) lost map on high level route and got lost. Camping, they found some bits of their tents deficient. Overnight search by Borders, Moffat and Tweed Valley teams and SARDA. Found sheltering under fly-sheets. 667.

SEPTEMBER 8-10 – Pair (f53, m47) ascended Benyellary and Merrick from Bruce's Stone, Loch Trool intending to descend same route. They got lost in mist near

843m summit, spending night on the hill. Next day they went down West Ridge, not SW as intended, almost reaching derelict house at Kirriemore and only 2km from a road. A local saw them wave at Rescue 177 RN helicopter, then they went uphill. After second night out with very poor gear they continued uphill to under the crags of Black Gairy, where they were found by rescuers, suffering cold and mild shock. Galloway, Leuchars and Moffat teams, SARDA. 880.

OCTOBER 17 – Male patient needing medical attention ran from casualty department with threat of going into surrounding hills. Found as Tweed Valley MRT arrived. 20.

OCTOBER 26 – Runner (m67) in mountain marathon slipped crossing a burn east of Tarfessock suffering pelvic and leg injuries (cold trauma later). Galloway MRT and SARDA dropped by RN Sea King west of Tarfessock due to low cloud. Later winched with casualty. Worsening weather caused large number of entrants to be called off. 200.

OCTOBER 26 – Runner (37) winched by RN Sea King with leg injuries after he slipped at Loch Valley. Galloway MRT. 37.

OCTOBER 27 – Runner (m20+) winched by RN Sea King from Larg Hill suffering hypothermia during mountain marathon. Galloway MRT and SARDA helped with various (other) First Aid jobs. 142.

NOVEMBER 1 – Tweed Valley MRT called out for missing boy (10) who turned up before team mobilised.

NOVEMBER 28-29 – Moffat MRT night searched for a walker (56) who used his bivvy bag when lost in a whiteout on Hartfell/Swatte Fell. Weather cleared at 01.00 and he found his own way down about 02.30 as Borders and Galloway MRTs and SARDA prepared. No compass, torch broken. 130.

NON-MOUNTAINEERING

JANUARY 1-2 – Kinloss MRT searched sand dunes and forest east of Lossiemouth for a woman (51) with sleeping tablets. Not found. 42.

FEBRUARY 5-6 – Moffat MRT delivered food to snowbound motorists and coach passengers, evacuating many people to emergency centres. Some were suffering illnesses or conditions including heart ailments, diabetes and epilepsy. Several were treated for cold trauma. 320.

FEBRUARY 8 – SARDA (South Scotland and Lakes) and police dogs on standby to locate people in cars buried in snowdrifts.

FEBRUARY 9 – Cairngorm MRT used 4WD vehicles to help Police and snow plough crews ferry 117 people to safety when buses, cars and lorries were trapped in snowdrifts and white-outs between Ralia and Dalwhinnie. 45.

MARCH 7 – SARDA searched Carbeth, Milngavie and West Highland Way for a male missing from home at Carbeth since February 22. Body found a few days later on West Highland Way just outside Milngavie. 5.

MARCH 31 – At the request of Central Scotland Police, Lomond MRT evacuated the body of a man (37) from a ledge on the face of disused Muirton Quarry, Blanefield. Spotted by a passer-by earlier that day he had been missing from Glasgow since December 29, 1995. 40.

JUNE 2-4 – SARDA handlers and dogs from three regions searched Galashiels for a man (54) missing from home. Found suffering hypothermia by a passer-by. 7.

JUNE 21 – In the early morning at Poca Buidhe Bothy (10km from main road near Gairloch) man (18) fell down stairs fracturing his lumbar spine. Evacuation RAF Sea King. 12.

JULY 2 – RAF Sea King evacuated man (32) from Alltbeithe Youth Hostel, Glen Affric. A medical condition caused a trapped nerve near his spine. The injury was sustained at the hostel, not on the hill. Kintail MRT. 20.

JULY 8 – Tweed Valley MRT called out for a missing woman (over 70) who was safe at a friend's home. 5.

JULY 11-30 – Searches by Assynt and Kinloss MRTs, SARDA, RAF and HMCG helicopters for man (75) possibly missing in Ben Bhragaidh area. Later found dead on Peterhead foreshore. 176.

AUGUST 10 – Moffat MRT on standby for boy (11) who ran off from home but turned up safe. 3.

AUGUST 11 – Tweed Valley MRT mobilised. Child turned up safe at Dinlabyre, Newcastleton. He went missing as family picked mushrooms. 2.

OCTOBER 16 – Two people were killed when a light aircaft flying from Edinburgh to Perth crashed on Meall nam Fuaran (805m) 15km NNW of Crieff. Boulmer and Lossiemouth RAF helicopters, Leuchars and Tayside MRTs involved in search and recovery. Cloudbase 750m. 88.

OCTOBER 20 – Requiring regular insulin, a teenager was missing from home for 14 hours. Searches by Tayside MRTs and SARDA. She was safe at a friend's house despite missing several shots. 26.

NOVEMBER 4 – Tweed Valley MRT leader flew in helicopter searching forest roads for car belonging to missing person. Nothing found.

NOVEMBER 5 – Follow on from previous incident. Tweed Valley MRT searched forest round an abandoned car – no connection. However, Police found missing person dead in another car in another forest 16km distant.

NOVEMBER 9 – Boy (9) missing from home in Drymen found in village square before SARDA dog (South Scotland) was deployed.

NOVEMBER 12-13 – HMCG helicopter helped Police search near Stornoway Castle for missing woman. Nothing found. Later found dead in water. 6.

NOVEMBER 16-17 – Man (48) left car in woods north of Bridge of Allan. Search by Kinloss, Lomond (SARDA), and Ochils MRTs, Strathclyde Police helicopter. Some medication belonging to the missing man was found, then he was found dead hanging from a tree. 281.

NOVEMBER 18-19 – Police dogs and underwater unit, SARDA and RN Sea King searched River Forth near Stirling for man (40) suspected drowned after evading capture over a wall and down river bank. 26.

NOVEMBER 25 – Motor vehicle found in wooded picnic area at Dubh Chnoc, Loch Venachar, Trossachs. Driver was missing. Killin MRT member and SARDA dog handler found man (44) dead hanging from a tree. 58.

DECEMBER 19 – Before SARDA dog team was deployed a man (86) missing from home near Falkirk was found 3km away on a building site.

DECEMBER 25 – SARDA alerted for a woman (25) who ran off, lightly dressed in cold weather. She was found safe by Police at a wood edge near Killearn.

IN MEMORIAM

DOUGLAS B. BARCLAY j. 1961

"I met someone last week who, I think, would be an excellent climbing companion for you," said the girl – and so I first heard of Douglas.

The year was 1954, and I had recently joined the JMCS of which club Douglas was already a member. As it was late spring, Friday evening club meetings in Rowan's Smoking Room had ceased for the summer, and it was some weeks before we met on the then well-known Sunday morning excursion train on the West Highland line, which allowed a reasonably-priced day at Arrochar or Crianlarich.

Thereafter we climbed and hillwalked regularly for the next 15 to 16 years until Douglas's heavy involvement with the nascent Strathspey Railway made regular outings increasingly difficult to fit into a busy timetable.

Douglas was a splendid companion on the hills and a very strong walker and quite tireless. We had many trips to most parts of the Highlands and many long, hard, enjoyable days. He was always willing and invariably good tempered. We did a little rock climbing and were comfortable up to V-Diff standard. In winter we did some of the easier snow climbs.

On one occasion, in Glen Sligachan, camped in a favourite nook, wet and blowing as only it can with a Sou-Wester in that glen, the back pole of the 'Guinea' tent broke during a furious gust. Immediately, we were enveloped in wet cotton, so I seized the upper part of the pole and pushed it up. 'Pack up Douglas,' I shouted, he replied: 'Just let me finish my chapter.'

We had two trips to Norway, one to Sunnmore and and one to Lyngen. In Sunnmore we were having a second crack at Smorskretind. It was a lovely autumn day and we were nearing the summit up a snowy chimney. On taking a high step, Douglas, in the lead, split the inside seam of one trouser leg. My future wife, who was with us, searched her pockets and rucksack and produced seven safety pins. These were used to effect a repair. Thus patched, and the requirements of modesty satisfied, we made the summit in triumph minutes later.

The following year in Lyngen, the highlight of the holiday, was to climb Jaekkevarri, a most enjoyable day.

In 1961, we both joined the SMC and both completed our Munros in 1966.

From 1972 onwards, Douglas and his wife, Catherine, became heavily involved with the Strathspey Railway, but fortunately his wife also loved the hills, and they continued to climb together for many happy years. Recently, he had led hillwalks with his church's hillwalking group. Douglas completed his Munros for the second time in 1992.

Douglas was an enthusiastic skier, and for years he and his wife went to Switzerland in February or March for a skiing holiday.

For many years, Douglas was auditor to the club, The Scottish Mountaineering Trust, and the John Muir Trust.

Last July, he started up Beinn Odhar, near Tyndrum, on his own on a warm morning and was seen to collapse. Thus passed a good companion and a keen lover of the hills.

G. King.

IAN GRANT CUMMING j. 1957

He died in a Kent Hospice, but Ian Cumming's heart was in the Highlands. Exiled through necessity, he and his family made annual pilgrimages north. They were regulars at the Glenisla Games, in his wife Mary's home glen.

Ian graduated with first-class honours in Maths and Physics from Glasgow University in 1946 and joined ICI in Ardeer. His early climbing was in Arran and Glen Coe and then farther afield in Scotland, frequently with members of the Club.

He collaborated in the 1950s with Malcolm Slesser in research on climbing ropes. The results *Evaluation of a Risk* were published in the 1957 and 1958 editions of the Journal.

In addition to being a life member of the SMC, Ian had the distinction of having been president of three widely-scattered mountaineering clubs. While with ICI, and based in Dumfries, he formed the Galloway MC, was first meet secretary and second president.

When work took him to Dounreay he helped found, and was first president of, Caithness MC. Then he moved to head the Physics Department at the British Jute Trade Research Association in Dundee, joined the Grampian Club and was president 1967-70.

Ian was an all-rounder who enjoyed rock, snow, ice, skiing – and dooking in river and lochan. Over about 10 years I enjoyed his company on the hill all over the Highlands and Skye. An abiding memory among many is of his quite incredible speed in descent, regardless of conditions. In any party Ian was always first off the hill.

Apart from mountains, his interests were wide-ranging. Music, literature, the Gaelic language, gardening and cooking all had a part in his life. He enjoyed wine and was a connoisseur of malt whisky long before malt was fashionable.

A devoted husband and father with a busy professional life, he was treasurer of the local Duke of Edinburgh Award Scheme in Kent. Both his son and daughter gained the Gold Award.

Ian made friends easily. This was borne out by the company of more than 100 who attended his funeral in Kent. One of the speakers on that occasion declared in truth that he was 'in the very finest sense, a nationalistic Scot, loving the hills and glens and his native land'.

D. Green.

DOUGLAS JAMIESON FRASER j. 1936.

Douglas Jamieson Fraser, who died on December 13, 1996 aged 86 was an Edinburgh man. Educated at George Heriot's School he spent his entire working life with the Standard Life Assurance Co. His heart, however, was always in the hills and wild places.

After a number of years with the Edinburgh JMCS he was elected to the Club in 1936 and attended a considerable number of Easter and other Meets over the next 50 years. In 1940 he offered his services as a Army climbing instructor but was called up to serve in the National Fire Service. Also in 1940, he married Eva who, with their three children, survive him.

Douglas climbed many classic routes in Glen Coe, Ben Nevis and elsewhere with his friend, Alan Home, and paid several visits to climb in Norway and the Pyrenees with his brother, Barclay. He was one of a handful of members who attended both the Golden Jubilee Dinner of the Club and the Centenary Dinner.

Quiet and modest by nature with a pawky sense of humour, he was a man of considerable culture. He painted well in oils and was a superb photographer contributing regularly to the annual exhibition of the Edinburgh photographic Society.

It was as a poet that he became best known, contributing to the Club Journal, *The Scots Magazine* and other periodicals. His poetry covered many aspects of life and was always perceptive and often humorous. He published four books of verse, the first *Landscape of Delight,* at the age of 57. His best known publication *Rhymes o' Auld Reekie,* first published in 1973, went to a second edition in 1988, something rarely achieved by a modern Scottish poet.

Two verses from his *Freedom of the Hills* sum up Douglas's feelings for the hills:

When winter grips the mountains in a vice,
Silently stifling with its pall of snow,
Checking the streams, draping the rocks in ice,
Still to their mantled summits I would go.

Sun-drenched, I sense the message they impart;
Storm-lashed, I hear it sing through every vein;
Among the snows it whispers to my heart
'Here is your freedom. Taste-and come again.'

W. M. S. Myles.

MALCOLM R. D. DUFF j. 1985

I FIRST met Mal when he invited Brian Sprunt and I to join himself and Adrian Clifford for an attempt on the West Ridge of Nuptse in 1981. I already knew him by reputation as a keen rock climber with new routes around Dunkeld and Creag Dubh, but when he was persuading me (with ease) to go to Nuptse, I soon discovered his enthusiasm for exploring mountains world-wide. In fact, he was never intimidated by the reputation of person, route or mountain, as we soon found out seeing the awesome West Ridge. He even went back the following year for a second attempt, this time with his client turned partner, Sandy Allan. He and Sandy later tried an even more audacious, positively outrageous, line up the south face of Lhotse Shar.

To finance an annual Himalayan expedition, usually trying a hard new line, (and he succeeded on one in particular on Mera Peak), he would run winter courses in Scotland, based in Glen Coe/Ben Nevis. This gave him the chance to explore extensively and find new lines to climb at the weekend, or even sometimes with the courses. The opportunity was there but few would have had the energy or enthusiasm to work on the hills and still go climbing at the weekend. It's a measure of this enthusiasm that few folk are aware that he climbed more First Winter Ascents on the Ben over a 10-year period, including the early and mid-eighties, than anyone else.

Perhaps his favourite and finest achievement was Point Blank, second hardest in the Nevis Guide graded list and which survived several attempts with different partners until he guided it with his most regular client, Rick Nowak. Not just the Ben but hard new routes in Glen Coe and Creag Meaghaidh made him one of the most important pioneers in recent years.

Mal's Scottish courses were running for some 15 years, a quiet operation but one which introduced so many to winter climbing. Certainly important for me, as I did my first instructional work in the hills for Mal and his encouragement pushed through my change in career. It always used to surprise me how many climbers I met who had started on one of Mal's courses and had been inspired by his low-key approach.

Like all climbing professionals he received plenty of stick from the amateurs who always seem to resent one being paid to go to the hills. If only they knew it wasn't as easy as that, but the stick never came from his clients. In recent times his business expanded greatly into guided expeditions, including a successful ascent of Cho Oyo in 1994, and he spent much time away from Scotland, but always returning for the winter.

After a successful trip to the Mustagh Tower in 1984, making the second ascent of the Brown/Patey route, Mal was back in Rawalpindi when he was offered the permit for the North-East Ridge of Everest the following spring. Always the opportunist and such things weren't to be turned down.

The organisational element expanded way beyond his expectation as he raised a large amount of sponsorship and at the same time recruited many of Britain's best young climbers (the boy racers) and a supposed sensible element (the old farts). To control such a keen and independent group, but with little Himalayan experience, was an impossible task, yet the expedition reached a high altitude and we all came back in good health. It shows the difficulty of the route that it was only climbed last year by a big Japanese expedition with imported sherpas.

Mal always had a deep love of the mountains; for him the profit side came secondary, if there ever was a profit side. The mountain guide has always at least to pretend to be efficient and serious, perhaps keeping his true feelings to himself. But the giveaway picture which is a hint of Mal's true attitude to the mountains is Rick Nowak's first naked ascent of Elliot's Downfall, encouraged and led up by Mal, but who was never so ostentatious as to do it himself.

Andy Nisbet.

IAN F. ROBERTS j. 1951

IAN'S ASHES were scattered on Lochnagar last summer. His passing recalls that happy dawn of post-war climbing in Aberdeen. This movement started in the Thirties tradition of Ewen and Bell, continued through Mac Smith and company, the Brooker-Patey group, the Kincorth Club and lasted a decade. Their uniform was Army windproofs, woollen balaclavas, tricounis and ice-axes (at fifteen shillings and ninepence – 84p) from Campbells.

Early on their experience, and sometimes their attitude, was confined to homely weekend Deeside – Mount Keen, Lochnagar and Derry Lodge. Their way furth to other Scottish ranges was barred by the vastness of Ben Macdhui, the shortness of recreational time and the cost of distant travel. But what a good time they had – and what deeds were done (remember, too, the long march-ins and exhausting march-outs).

While in his teens at Aberdeen Grammar School, Ian started to explore Aberdeen's hinterland of adventure. He trained as an accountant until called up for war service. He spent five years in the Royal Air Force. In Kenya, away from duty, he enjoyed the high country, including a small expedition to climb Mount Elgon.

Returning to Aberdeen he completed his CA training. It was during this time, often in the company of his brother, George, and other Cairngorm Club worthies, that he developed his climbing skills. From 1948 to 1950 he worked in London where he was very active in the JMCS section. He frequented Harrison's and had weekends in North Wales, often with another exiled accountant, Ken Armstrong.

He moved to Inverness in 1950. His activities, often with John Frew, in the Northern Cairngorms, Nevis and Skye, led to his election to the Club in 1951.

He set up practice in Peterhead in 1952 and married shortly afterwards. He immersed himself in family life, in exemplary business practice and in valuable community work. In that remote seafaring place he set a standard and was wholly respected for it. For Ian, I think, that became more important than the wilderness of mountains. But the gleam of memory, the warmth of past comradeship, the laughter of old folly were always there. All his days, with his black hair, erect gait, sparkling eye and ready laugh he retained the appearance of youth.

His interest in the Club remained strong. He was Honorary Auditor from 1964-77.

In his later years, and after his retirement in 1991 to Aberdeen, he resumed his old acquaintance with the lower hills and glens of Deeside as far as he was able.

He died, aged 75, having failed to recover from surgery.

J. M. Taylor.

DAN PIGGOTT j. 1978

IT WAS only when preparing this notice that I realised Dan must have been at Cambridge about the same time as Gino Watkins, Spencer Chapman, Jack Longland and similar personalities of the venturesome world. As he climbed with the CUMC, used skis in the Alps, canoed and sailed, I cannot imagine why he too did not become one of the 'Young Men in the Arctic'. But rather than the ice it was to the heat of tropical Africa he went, as a District Officer in the then Colonial Service in Tanganyika and Uganda. At that time such a job would no doubt have given him plenty of adventure, especially during the War when he was sometimes rather isolated.

After the War ended he went on an Alpine Club Training Meet to Zermatt, climbing the standard peaks, but including the Zmutt Ridge (with a Guide for whose presence I gather he was rather grateful!) In 1949 he came back on leave to the UK where he met and married Marjory Kennedy Fraser a move which, apart from the usual family results, had a major effect on his subsequent activities. However, he did find time to climb Kilimanjaro (before the crowds came) and several peaks of the Rowenzori massif, including Alexandra, at that time a major exploit. On retiral from the Service he was still relatively young (as was usual) and active (which was probably less so) and settled with his family in Scotland, Marjory being of the direct line. They came to Edinburgh in 1957, where as a result of devious LSCC connections I was deputised to introduce him to Scottish rock.

We went to Skye for a week or so and did a number of the usual routes. As Dan had not then been introduced to Vibram soles he climbed in a pair of boots nailed (more or less) with Tricounis which gave me a respect for his abilities when he led severe rock. Thereafter we became constant partners.

Although his initial application to join the Club was unsuccessful on the grounds that he had not climbed enough in Scotland, he went to the hills with me and other SMC parties, with whom he was a popular, if rather unusual, companion, whom some folk regarded as a 'throw back' to the days when climbing was the pastime of a more gentlemanly generation. They were wrong, of course. Dan was no throw back – he was an original article who had brought the aura with him – and was none the worse for that. He had wide interests and was well-informed about many of them and so was an entertaining man to have about on the hill, but he also had the unassuming self-confidence which seems to have been possessed by so many of his 'Oxbridge' contemporaries. I doubt if he ever thought twice about the fact that he had canoed across the Baltic and down the Rhone, and cycled to Istanbul. If you wanted to do it – why not?

He was lightly-built and strong with it and like his near-contemporary at Cambridge, Ivan Waller, was outstandingly active for his age, so he certainly stood out among his companions on the hill, some of whom found his 'ready for anything' attitude slightly eccentric, but he made many friends.

In the days before Winters died, the hills seemed to have snow cover for weeks and gave us all the sport we needed without having to get stuck in cold, icy clefts. Not that Dan was averse to a bit of ice – with Myles Hutchinson he did Glover's Chimney before the vogue for pegs, screws and front points, while we did get involved in several snow-covered rock routes, including Tower Ridge (under modest cover, but tricouni-shod).

We went regularly with the JMCS bus out of Edinburgh or Glasgow but later went for longer periods, including one glorious week when we got snowed up in the Ling Hut. The car was stuck, but the mountains were in prime condition. Dan acquired a camper van and ranged widely throughout Scotland transporting me and usually one or two others for winter weeks. That was adventure enough for the time and the company was good.

In summer, however, Dan turned to his other love – sailing. Marjory and her sister acquired a cottage on the Ross of Mull in a location of which I am sure their grandmother would have approved. There, with his equally web-footed brother-in-law, he carried out some adventurous sailing in small open boats rigged for the conditions. He regularly put the wind up me, but I admit that if you have not approached Staffa in wild weather, exposed as the Vikings were, then you have missed a lot of its true atmosphere.

Not that climbing was ignored, as we worked out numerous routes up (and along) the granite sea cliffs and even on larger (but still unrecorded) minor crags of gabbro where you may find the odd cairn in unexpected places.

Dan went to the Jotunheim and the Dauphine with me and in the former area had some good summer rock climbing without the benefit of much in the way of guide books – a circumstance much suited to his attitude to mountains. In the latter area the prize was, of course, the Ecrins, but the adventure came a few days later when we were caught in a bad storm high up on the Pic Sans Nom with an epic blizzard descent. This presaged a period of bad weather and we retired north via numerous cathedrals about whose stained glass Dan was knowledgeable and wanted to tick off on his list, He was one of these folk who seemed to be able to rise to any occasion.

As commitments (and age) took their toll and ski trips with a Europe-based grandfamily took up my winter time I was on the hill less with Dan (although spending a lot of time with him in Mull) but in 1978 he joined the Club and went out regularly with the older (and some younger) members of the Eastern District.

We met at Meets where his performance on the hill was astonishing – he could still run downhill in his 70s. He made several solo cross-country trips in the North West, using minimal gear and carefully – estimated minimum food. With Marjory he made several randonees in France and Italy.

We were last on the hills together at the Easter Meet of 1993 at Elphin. It was a good one for us to finish on, although despite advancing problems connected with a terminal illness Dan still went walking with Marjory as circumstances allowed.

Scott Johnstone.

JAMES McK. STEWART j. 1938

I WRITE this appreciation largely from the archive and personal knowledge from a few brief meetings as perhaps few members will remember Jimmy Stewart who died in Edinburgh on March 5, 1996.

A small, dapper man, he seemed always eager to talk about the hills at Eastern District lunches even although family circumstances and advancing years had prevented serious hill-going for some time. During his most active years, however, he was clearly no slouch, being active with the Edinburgh Section of the JMCS (becoming Honorary President) in the company of Annand, Gorrie, Peat and Ogilvie all of whom aspired to the senior Club.

In the 1930s, when merely the ownership of a rope elevated one's mountaineering status, Jimmy recorded winter ascents of the North East Buttress (a bit icy on the last 1000ft!) and Crowberry Ridge. He climbed the Chasm with Ogilvie. The same period records much rock climbing in North Wales (including some winter ascents) and a visit to Ireland. He had three good Alpine seasons before Europe was closed to sensible pastimes in 1939.

He was a Life Member of the Club and served as Meets Secretary from 1945-47, and an attractive photograph by him taken on a Club meet appears in Volume 23. I wish that I could write more but it has been most pleasant looking back over the career of a very active member from a period when the hills were quieter.

J. R. R. Fowler.

CHARLES GORRIE j. 1937

CHARLES GORRIE was educated at Dunfermline High School and studied Engineering at Edinburgh University. He was in the army during the war but left after sustaining a fractured femur. He went back to work again as an engineer in exile in the South. During this time he climbed in North Wales and Harrison's Rocks with another well-known exile, Iain Ogilvie. He also climbed on the 'somewhat fragile' cliffs of Beachy Head where he used primitive pitons home-made from angle iron and 3ft long! He introduced J. H. B. Bell to Beachy Head climbing – in which, as Gorrie wryly observed, 'the rock being somewhat insecure, he revelled'.

Iain and Charlie made many trips to the Alps together and he also visited Corsica. One of Charlie's best mountains was the Bietschorn which he did with George Dwyer, an expatriate Dundonian.

Tiring of his job in the South, he returned home and entered Teacher Training. At one time he was a colleague of Hamish Brown at the famous Braehead School in Fife. His transport at that time was initially an Aston Martin but later he reverted to the more practical, if less prestigious, Transit van.

One time, he and Oliver made a marathon circuit of Ben Alder at the end of which they drank a bottle of whisky for supper. It is necessary here to read in between the lines.

His distinctions include dropping a rock on the head of George Waterston, a well-known ornithologist and being charged with vandalising a railway compartment after using the luggage rack as a climbing frame.

In his latter years he attended many Club Meets where his humour and experience made him a pleasant companion for younger members. Anyone who did not know Charlie in real life can still meet him by reading his reflective article *An Educational Experience* in SMCJ, xxxiv, 182, 573-577, 1991.

A. H. Hendry.

IVAN WALLER j. 1981

'WHY DON'T you take up climbing?' This was the advice given to the young Ivan Waller by his housemaster as he was going up to Cambridge in 1924 to read engineering. He needed some form of exercise, being hopeless at the traditional ball games of the Public Schools. Seldom can a schoolmaster's advice been followed with such enthusiasm and relentless determination; apart from his work in the motor industry and motor racing, at which he excelled, mountaineering became his dominant interest. His early rock climbing included King's College Chapel and the tower of St. John's College, Cambridgeshire, but he was soon going out with the leading men of his day including Jack Longland, Charles Warren and Colin Kirkus. His first ascent of Belle Vue Bastion on Tryfan, to the accompaniment of ragtime played on a portable gramophone, placed on the ledge above, is part of climbing folklore. Fifty-eight years later he repeated the route, still graded VS. He seconded Colin Kirkus on the first ascent of Mickledore Grooves, a fine Lakeland classic on Scafell, and around this time he climbed up, and down, Beachy Head in crampons.

After Cambridge, Ivan Waller held various jobs in the motor industry which made it easier for him to compete in motor racing: the Monte Carlo Rally from Budapest, hill climbing racing at Brooklands and at Phoenix Park, Dublin where he won. He eventually joined Rolls-Royce where he was soon put in charge of experimental endurance testing in the car division. This was the perfect job, test-driving fast, glamorous cars along the open roads of central France, covering huge distances at high speed, sometimes to the Pyrenees to snatch a quick climb, or to the Nurburgring for the German Grand Prix in 1938 where he later saw Hitler's troops march into Czechoslovakia.

On the outbreak of war he was transferred to the Aero Division where he worked in the experimental flight test department. In 1940 he was involved in an exciting adventure which nearly cost him his life. While on a test flight over the Firth of Clyde in a flying-boat the engines failed and the order was given to bale out. When Ivan's parachute became entangled with the tail plane he edged his way along the outside of the fuselage, using wire cables for handholds with his feet against the shell of the plane in a sort of hand-traverse. He managed to untangle his parachute and landed in the sea from where he was eventually rescued. He always claimed, and we can believe him, that without his rock climbing experience he would never have made it. For his work in the industry he was awarded the George Stephenson Research Prize by the Institute of Mechanical Engineers.

MAL DUFF. *Photo: Bob Ross.*

DAN PIGGOTT. *Photo: G. Scott Johnstone.*

GEORGE RITCHIE. *Photo: J. R. Marshall.*

IVAN WALLER. *Photo: Oliver Turnbull.*

Family commitments after the War somewhat restricted his activities, but he found time for several trips to the Alps, on one occasion narrowly failing to reach the summit of Mt. Blanc, on skis, with Gaston Rebuffat. He also took part in the 1951 Le Mans 24-hour race with Robert Laurie. They finished 11th, the leading privately-entered team and Ivan's wife, Helen, was embraced by President Auriol.

On retirement in 1969 Ivan moved to the Lake District, to a house which he himself designed. Here he was free from the tedious necessity of earning his living and he made the most of it. This was a period of intensive rock climbing activity, much of it in the Lake District with Jim Ingham, a Kendal dentist. But he did not ignore Scotland, indeed the achievement which perhaps gave him the greatest satisfaction of all occurred in June 1977 when he completed two traverses of the Cuillin Ridge. The first, with Jim, was by way of being a reconnaissance for the more serious attempt two weeks' later with his old friend, Charles Warren. In perfect weather the two septuagenarians, following an afternoon start from Glenbrittle, enjoyed a prearranged bivouac on the ridge high above Coire a' Ghrunnda after completing the southern end of the ridge. When they reached Sgurr nan Gillean the next day an incredulous lone climber was the first to congratulate the triumphant pair and insisted on their accepting prepayment for the first round of drinks on their arrival at Sligachan.

During all this time Ivan had steadily added to his list of Munros, but by 1978 he was only half-way there. Then in an astonishing burst of energy for one of his age he climbed the remaining 140 Munros inside two years. He was now ready to join the SMC. He continued regular visits to Scotland for Easter meets and more extended trips in summer with Helen. My last serious day out with him was at Easter 1984. Starting from Cannich in the early morning we were at the CIC Hut by 11am, then climbed Tower ridge in superb winter conditions. During this wonderful day we never had a moment of hesitation nor anxiety, pausing only to admire the view.

Sturdily built with a muscular frame and with great powers of endurance, Ivan was physically equipped for mountaineering well into old age. His engineering training had given him the habit of neatness and order, with a high regard for safety. An early proponent of the double axe technique his vast sack was always filled with equipment for any emergency, sometimes to the consternation of his companions who were less used to carrying such loads. His inquiring mind, remarkable memory for mountain detail, his sense of humour and ever-roving eye produced a ceaseless flow of anecdote and instruction, and above all his stories many of which were hilariously unprintable. He was the best of companions. How he would have enjoyed the Yacht Meet, advising the crew on rope management, arguing points of navigation with the skipper or tinkering with the engine, he would have been in his element!

No account of Ivan's life can be complete without mentioning his devoted wife, Helen, and his long-suffering support of his numerous activities. Wedged aboard the motor bike, with a tent at her back, surrounded by loads of equipment all carefully strapped into place for a continental holiday, she must sometimes have had a bumpy ride. Later the purchase of a Dormobile gave her more material comfort, even though she endured many anxious moments patiently awaiting the return of her man from the hill. (For an account of a typical Ivan adventure see his article in *SMC Journal* 180 pp 215-18).

Ivan died at Kendal on October 3, aged 89. To Helen and the family we extend our sympathy.

Oliver Turnbull.

GEORGE J. RITCHIE j. 1947

WITHOUT doubt, George defied categorisation, the much-used eulogy when God made him, he broke the mould moves us, his friends, to ponder whether God would do so out of frustration or delight, the normal paradoxical outcome of spending time on the hill with George.

At the height of his career, he held a dignified post as one of Midlothian Council's Depute County Clerks and in the city, dressed in his lawyer's suit, he looked rather dapper, strongly reminiscent of film stars of the black-and-white era.

He was forever rushing about sorting things out or helping some cause or other, seemingly without respite other than the occasional escape to the hills, where the other self emerged, somewhat evocative of the ancient mariner, specially after a hard day on the hills, a small figure, quick of movement, bright-eyed with a mop of wild hair, dressed in several layers of out-at-elbow Shetland jerseys and the most voluminous tweed plus-fours.

He carried little food and ate sparingly yet was capable of great endurance and seemed indifferent to hardship during wilder times on the hills, today we would call him hyper-active, seeming only to cat nap to recover, for any time I awoke through the night, George was bright-eyed and ready to chat till I dropped off again.

Surprisingly, or maybe not so; given his forte for saying the wrong thing at the right time, he never really had a steady climbing partner, though Archie and George did come to form a memorable duo in later years.

George enjoyed associating with the *avant garde* and sought to attach himself to the 'top' climbers of the day, little appreciating they were doing the same, higher up the chain.

He was totally ingenuous in these manoeuvres but the outcome could be quite awkward as he found himself out in the Alps without, or abandoned by his higher associates with recourse only to us, to save his holiday.

I always enjoyed his company, perhaps for the entertainment of his impact on some unsuspecting colleague, indeed I well remember descending from the Réquin where the trying heat of the glacier finally melted the forbearance of one of the party who had been talked down to all morning by George and as he was about to start in on him again, the victim grabbed George by the collar, waved his axe before his nose, snarling, 'say another word, I'll stick this right between your eyes', devastatingly George said: 'It's all right son, I often have this effect on people' at which point I had to dive between them and ensure safe distance for the rest of the day.

'Higglety pigglety, hear that clutch' or some such words, were Smith's reference to George's driving. I remember one evening he said he knew a short cut round Perth, this went by diminishing road standards, eventually to tracks with grass in the middle. As usual, Ronnie and I were rolling about in the back creased in mirth and alcohol, offering to get out and turn the car round, but typically, George persevered until the tracks once again became roads and we found ourselves on the way to Stirling instead of the Cairngorms.

Mind you, he once told me he had ridden one of the early Minis, solo to Moscow, an amazing feat for the roads in these days, we of course, found endless entertainment in our journeys with George.

Typhoo was the undoubted king of the road, so when we were stuck behind a queue of traffic, which was quite horrendous in these days, we would all chorus:

'Typhoo would just nip out and burn this lot off.' George always rose to the bait, leaving us in abject fear and wonderment.

Another testament to his driving was that Archie, a model motorist would always travel with George, holding onto the passenger door handle, ready to abandon ship should things go adrift.

He was one of several notable climbers who founded the EUMC and in association with Haworth, a fellow member and outstanding rock climber of the 1940s made the first ascent of Surgeon's Gully, a typical outing where George rose to the occasion to achieve great results by virtue of tenacity.

Another time with Haworth, riding pillion on the way home from the Gorms in the darkening light, anxious to catch the ferry, Haworth misjudged a bend somewhere in Glenshee and went through a hedge into someone's garden, the lights were switching on as they manhandled the bike back through the hedge and roared off down the road, George had to keep wiping stuff off his head but didn't give it much thought, until they were on the last ferry over the Forth when Haworth expressed concern at George's blood-covered face, only to discover the blood was his, he had torn his scalp back on breaching the hedge and the slipstream delivered the gore across George.

On another occasion, three of us had done the Mer de Glace face of the Grépon and decided to return to the Envers des Aiguilles in the face of an imminent storm.

As expected, it broke just as we embarked on the belt of huge easy slabs and with the fading light and torrential rain we lost the track, floundering around, trying to keep contact in the thunderous noise of the storm, dodging huge boulders bouncing across the slabs, traced only by the impact sparks or seen in the blinding lightning flashes as we made mad rushes up the slabs hoping to find the path.

It was all very dramatic. I pounded up one particular section, which steepened more than expected, losing momentum till I teetered in desperation, aware of the hellish roll to come, when George's long piolet appeared out of the gloom above to provide all I needed to reach to reach the safety of the path – an occasion never to be forgotten.

I never had any problems tying on with George, mostly we climbed things beyond his mental barriers but within his real capabilities, if he found it hard, I would embark on a flow of invective and heave on the rope, which always worked, though sometimes it did seem it may not.

On a couple of these particular occasions, on the disparate flanks of Ben Nevis and the Plan he expended energy in the effort to surmount critical overhangs, only on succeeding, to stand on his famous plus-fours and bomb off, leaving it all to be done again.

These few memories of our mercurial George (there are many more) are not written in mockery for I salute his memory, he was a lovely, sincerely humble man who rarely mentioned his long list of exciting exploits on and off the hill; a man bold enough to father two families with wholesome love and compassion, yet able to rollick about with us in our mountain madness.

We don't need tears for his passing, I last saw him, in his late Seventies, rolling a huge boulder around to improve some obscure aspect of his beloved garden, still showing the inner strengths which impressed us in the fullness of life, a strength which in his final years kept him alive long after the medics had given him up for good.

J. R. Marshall

PROCEEDINGS OF THE CLUB

New members

The following were admitted or re-admitted to the Club in 1996-97.
We welcome –

Edward R. Allen, (55), Civil Engineer, Cumbria.

Paul Allen (31), Data Communications Analyst, Aberdeen.

Jameson R. Andrew (27), Rope Access Instructor, Edinburgh.

Jason Currie (27), Teacher, Aberdeen.

David Cuthbertson, Mountain Guide, Ballachulish.

Robin McAllister (30), Farmer, Ballintrae, Ayrshire.

David McGimpsey (27), Mudlogger, Holmston, Ayr.

Donald W. Macleod (30), Teacher, Hamilton.

Wilson Moir (34), Teacher, Stonehaven, Kincardineshire.

Christopher C. Pasteur (32), Civil Engineer, Edinburgh.

Christopher R. Ravey (27), Engineering Geologist, Bridge of Allan, Stirling.

Alastair D. Robertson (27), Research Scientist, Broughty Ferry, Dundee.

Mark S. Ryle (26), Teacher, Edinburgh.

James Thomson (30), Licensed Aircraft Engineer, Dundonald, Ayrshire.

David W. M. Whalley (43), Royal Air Force, Forres, Morayshire.

EASTER MEET – LOCH DUICH HOTEL

Although Easter was early this year there was no snow on the ridges, in marked contrast to the wonderful winter conditions last year. Nor was the weather so kind, although it must be said it was a lot better than most of our recent meets. High winds were the order of the day with broken cloud and sporadic showers, Those favouring the long ridges were well advised to keep the wind in their backs, even though this meant the unrelenting grind up from Kintail on to the Five Sisters.

Turn-out was much the same as last year; a few old friends dropped out but they were replaced by new or, as the case may be, much older ones. Eighteen members and guests eventually sat down to dinner on Saturday night. Special mention should be made of Douglas Scott, who with Audrey, got within sight of the Falls of Glomach from below, while more junior members of the Club took the easier option of the high route. Also worth recording was the arrival, on Saturday evening of John Hay by boat and then a long walk from his Loch Mullardoch retreat. We trust he made it back the next day.

Hills ascended include: The Saddle, Ben Attow, the Five Sisters, Sguman Coinntich, Aonach Buidhe, Sgurr Mhic Bharraich, Sgurr a' Bhac Caolais plus the falls of Glomach and other low-level outings.

Those present included the President Bob Richardson, Robin Campbell, Iain Smart, Bill Wallace, Malcolm Slessor, Rick Allen, Bryan Fleming, John Fowler, John Hay, Douglas Scott, Audrey Scott (guest), Nigel Suess, Oliver Turnbull, Colwyn Jones, Anne Macpherson (guest), Ian Cumming (guest), Noel Williams and Paul Brian.

Oliver Turnbull.

The One-Hundreth-and-Seventh AGM, Reception and Dinner

It was all Bill Brooker's fault – the lone voice at the 1995 AGM who suggested Strathpeffer. The Committee took the idea to heart and so it was that the annual carnival headed north to the Victorian spa village near Dingwall. But we were in safe hands. The local laird has much influence in these parts and happens to be our Vice-President and from his modest cott arrangements were well directed.

The Ben Wyvis Hotel had seen better days but the Club settled in with its accustomed ease and the President seemed particularly happy with the lofty pink-walled dining room, if not with the disgraceful piano which seemed to cope with a few snatches of his jazz repertoire but was to labour under the accompaniment to the Club song.

The show kicked off with a well-attended lecture by our only paid-up Everester, Charlie Hornsby (Haston having been a victim of Rule 11). Fine slides and a modest delivery belied a fine achievement and members left feeling confident that with this level of mountaineering performance the Club was in good heart.

We re-convened for the formal bit in a long slot of a room where those sitting at the rear were conveniently inaudible to the Chair. This meeting was more wide-ranging than those of recent years and members got to grips with property deals in the North West, mobile phone pylons, car parking in Glen Coe and seemed much more enthusiastic on the idea of national parks. Agreement to an increased subscription for 1998 did no favours to the proposal to extract a levy from hut users to support the reconstruction costs of footpaths.

Pre-dinner drinking was a trial – there was only one beer tap in the bar but we eventually shuffled through to entertain Ann Murray of the LSCC, Ken Wilson of the Climbers' Club and representatives of the Fell & Rock, JMCS and Yorkshire Ramblers to a very good meal. The speeches followed – oh dear! Hamish Irvine toasted the guests in good style but extended this to a standard teaching period, the President investigated the high incidence of Willies in the membership history of the Club (although strangely omitting Mr Ling) and Ken Wilson, between adverts, could only recite a list of Scottish climbers whom he had met, before filling in his expenses claim.

The evening closed with the handing over of Presidential office to Bob Richardson who told us that history has its place but the Club must move on. We wait to see where, but in the meantime, I can tell you that this December we are going back to Fort William.

J. R. R. Fowler.

JMCS REPORTS

Perth Mountaineering Club (JMCS, Perth Section): Activities for 1996 returned to the normal Scottish-based programme after the most successful five-day excursion to Northern Ireland in August 1995 which neatly fitted in with the brilliant summer. That made it a hard act to follow – so attempts to do so were avoided.

Meets throughout the year were generally well attended – except the one or two where forseeable bad weather had a calamitous effect. It seems that the shift in the weather pattern is markedly affecting what used to be the reliable third weekend of May camping weekend at Glenbrittle, and both 1995 and 1996 have broken a good run of eight to 10 years.

The climbing scene has been particularly active – regular Wednesdays through the winter at the Dumfermline Climbing Wall followed by spring and summer activities based on Craig a' Barns, Dunkeld, but going farther afield in Tayside and Fife Coastal areas at times. Thanks particularly to the efforts of Mel and Grahame Nicoll – there have been nearly 20 attendances on some evenings.

Club membership is on the controlled way upwards, and there are currently 24 people seeking active participation on a trial basis. We are slightly formalising our methods on dealing with potential new members in line with the 'Duty of Care' scenario.

At last November's AGM it was unanimously agreed to give our long-standing and long-suffering Treasurer, Tom Rix the title of Honorary Member, which should at least fix him with the job for a good while yet.

After the recent poor winter for snow and ice climbing we look forward to a good spring season and a possible repeat of the summer 1995 conditions. This will no doubt prove too much to expect.

C. J. Bond.

London Section:– Members continue to get lost in some fine surroundings, with Senior and Dalgarno descending to Borrowdale instead of Langdale, Fryer and Dalgarno's best left unmentioned northern Coires confusion, and Walker and Jordan muddling up two better-known gullies on the Ben, albeit in poor emotional and climatic conditions (I thought that second pitch was steep . . .). The fine tradition of terrorising the gullible and less-experienced continued – this time the equation involved Centre Post Direct and the gentle AI Stockold (with walking axes and bendies). Predictably Fryer and Dalagrno were involved.

Big Steve did an excellent meets programme, arranging the usual wide-ranging locations, bad behaviour, some fine weather and occasionally some climbing. Scotland featured highly, as always, in our formal and informal gatherings: meets at the CIC, Milehouse, and Blackrock being supplemented with too numerous trips to Meagaidh, Lochnagar, Lochinver, The Northern Coires etc. The CIC was a great event enlivened by the camping contingent's sound system carried up by Krazy Kev. Other notable happenings included Borrowdale, the ever-beautiful Low Hall Garth and the never-beautiful Glanafon.

A dazzling array of exotic overseas trips reflected improved employment prospects rather than any paradigmatic shift in climbing ability. These included trips to Ama Dablam, Malaysia, and Yosemite. Nepal was further eroded by the likes of Dave and Dawn Edmunds, Hugh Jordan, Tony Buj and Hilary Ross. The poorer went to Lundy, Cornwall and Devon; the less socially-integrated sailed small boats to Iceland and around Anglesey. Members also went up new routes in Wales, Lundy and Pembroke, and fell down old routes in the Alps.

As usual, helicopters and ambulances were a common form of post meet transport, with ironically one of the few medically qualified being the first to bite the quartzite when Cheesmond interfaced with Gogarth. Subsequent bodies shovelled in to helicopters included the predictable figures of Fryer (Wales) and Walker (Half Dome and Ducati). Hibbert also sought attention by laboriously inserting bits of trials bike through his post-Burns body in a too hasty attempt to regain the pub . . . er . . . sorry, Dow Crag. The ever-sympathetic Senior being fortunately present to withdraw metal from flesh. The mature influence of club elders was also felt (mainly by roadside crash barriers) as Stokes and Perkins hurled their new sports bikes down the road.

Somehow the older members stuck around to show their tolerance and share their guiding wisdom, notably Dave Hughes, Hugh Jordan and Dave Edmunds. An innovative self-catered (all right, we've been banned everywhere) club dinner was superbly catered for by Steve and Jill at Tranearth, Coniston, but unfortunately, the newly-eligible females unreasonably refused to do the washing up.

The cognitively challenged Nigel the Mad was thrown off the committee but not before he'd confused us all with four circulars and mis-managed the work (-less) meet. Steve Gladstone set new standards of club communication by bringing out timely, regular and understandable missives. Gordon and Dave fiddled the books, while the committee absconded to the pub to avoid Gladstone's impeccably (over) organised meetings. We welcomed youngsters, Blake and Fryer, to the committe, to complete its total loss of credibility and cater for the special needs of the under 60s.

The Club survived the hideous spectre of mass-matrimony for the uglier, desperate and more insecure, with Clavey, Perkins, Blake, and Milner biting the dust, among other things.

The coming year looks horribly tiring with trips planned to Nepal, the US, Isle of Mann and Greenland by boat (hopefully with much Tilmanesque hardship), the usual alpine nonsense, and return visits to the ClC, etc. We also look forward to hosting the whole club dinner in the Coe, which we hope both the Glasgow Section can attend. Here's to the crack.

President: Andrew Walker, 1 Hancock Court, Main Road, Bamford, Derbyshire, S30 2AY Tel: 01433 651707. *Hut bookings:* Glanafon, Snowdonia: Rod Kleckham, 129 Weydon Hill Road, Farnham, Surrey GU9 8NZ. *Secretary:* Steve Gladstone, 36 Meadow Close, Hockley Heath, Solihull, B94 6PG.

Andrew Walker.

Edinburgh Section:– The Section hosted the Whole Club AGM at the Highlander Hotel, Newtonmore, in April 1996. On this historic occasion the club voted with a decisive majority for the motion that women should be admitted as full members of the club – we have finally caught up with the SMC in this respect! It will be of considerable interest to see how enthusiastically this new policy is pursued by the various sections.

Membership of the Club started the year with about 70 members (finally a number of gifted female climbers were allowed to emerge from their legal loopholes) and has been fortified during the year with about 10 keen new members.

Despite the Club's stringent selection procedures, the committee has failed to prevent the election of some new members who turn out to regularly lead E-grade routes.

Both the Wednesday evening meets and the weekend meets continued to be well-attended throughout the year. The summer-evening meets covered the Lowland outcrops and, on the longer nights, ranged farther afield from Bowden Doors to Dunkeld. During the weekend meets – held approximately every second weekend – the club's own *pieds-a-terre* in Newtonmore and Dundonnell were frequently visited and many other trips to (wild) campsites and huts were also organised. In addition, members went off on any unofficial gatherings whenever the weather was benevolent (and often when it was not). Members explored and enjoyed themselves on the Scottish ice and rock faces in areas such as Glen Nevis, Glen Coe, the Cairngorms, Torridon, Arran, Ardgour, Skye, as well as the Outer Hebrides (where new routes were boldly explored by Fraser Fotheringham and even documented in full frightening colours in High).

The Lake District and the Peak District provided a welcome respite from the midges. On many of these occasions, members' palates were stimulated by strange and spicy foods, washed down with a variety of alcoholic beverages – as some of the members culinary skills kept pace with their improving climbing standards. (Although some diehards insisted on sticking to their menu of iron rations and powdered milk).

On the international front, a number of excursions were undertaken to the Continent and farther afield: The Alps, France, Spain, Frankenjura, Arctic Norway, British Columbia, Shawangunks, Nepal and Pakistan were all visited.

Both huts were regularly used by members, as well as by other parties. Thanks to the dedication of the hut custodians and the enthusiasm of the work parties, the huts continue to be a valuable asset.

Officials elected: *President,* Brian Finlayson; *Vice-president,* Nick Cruden, *Treasurer,* Charles Stupart, *Secretary,* Frederike van Wijck, *Newletter/Website Editor,* Chris Eilbeck; *Meets Secretary,* Kate Holden; *Smiddy Custodian,* Fraser Fotheringham, Tigh Na Sith, Braes, Ullapool, 01854-612 354; *Jock's Spot Custodian,* Alistair Borthwick, 2 Aytoun Grove, Dunfermline, Fife, 01383-732 232. *Committee:* Euan Scott, Robin Sinclair; *Honorary Committee Members:* John Fowler, Nigel Suess.

Information about the Club may be obtained from the Secretary: 21 Spottis-woode Road, Edinburgh EH9 1BJ. Tel: 0131-447 8162, also on email: F.vanWijck@shore.qmced.ac.uk, via the Web: http://www.ma.hw.ac.uk/jmcs/

F. Van Wijck and J. C. Eilbeck.

Lochaber Section:– Last year held a special importance for the Lochaber Section in that it celebrated its 50th year since formation. To mark the occasion the club organised an anniversary dinner held in the Alexandra Hotel, Fort William. The evening was a great success, attended by more than 70 members past and present and joined by guests from kindred clubs. Club President Ian Donaldson presided over the formalities, Robin Campbell, SMC President, was the guest speaker and he delivered a fine speech including some history of the Lochaber Section. Ian Sutherland and Paul Brian spoke on behalf of the club.

Membership of the Lochaber Section has risen slightly and now has the most paid-up members for several years. The Section continues to meet socially every Thursday evening in the Nevis Bank Hotel. Several meets were held throughout the year, the most popular being to Torridon, Braemar and the Lakes.

In August, the club was saddened by the death of Bill Robertson, once a very active and influential member of the Club. Again, in March this year, the Club grieved the death of Angus 'Wee Gus' MacLean – Gus was a long-time member of both the Club and the Lochaber Rescue Team dating back to the early Fifties and was still active on the hills up to his untimely death.

The Section continues to maintain and improve the Club's hut at Steall, Glen Nevis. This year will, hopefully, see a new roof and windows in place.

Office Bearers: *Hon. President,* Billy Munro; *Hon. Members,* B. Bissell, D. Scott; *President,* Ian Donaldson, *Vice-President,* Ian Walker; *Treasurer,* George Bruce; *Secretary,* Kenny Foggo, 4 Parkan Dubh, Inverlochy, Fort William. Tel: 01397 706299. *Hut Custodian,* John Mathieson, 43 Drumfada Terrace, Corpach, Fort William. Tel: 01397 772599. *General Committee,* Brian McDermott, Jim Paterson, Paul Brian.

Ken Foggo.

Glasgow Section:– Last year will go down as the year in which the JMCS finally changed 71 years of tradition by altering the constitution to allow women members. After many years of debate and failed attempts to change the constitution the change was adopted by 19 votes to 5 at the Whole Club AGM in Newtonmore in April.

Five new members joined the Section last year bringing the total to 87, of whom 19 are life members. We were saddened during the year by the loss of Bill Murray who had been our Honorary Member for longer than any of us can remember.

A total of 22 meets were held in Scotland and informal meets abroad. Activity abroad included trips to Jordan and New Zealand (David Ritchie), Greenland and Kenya (Colwyn Jones), Spain (many members), Ireland (Donald Ballance, Neil Craig and Ian Thomson) and, as usual, the Alps.

Early winter was extremely cold with a number of waterfalls receiving ascents. Unfortunately, the expected winter snows did not materialise and it was not until late March that good conditions appeared.

The summer once again started with rock climbing in the North West at the beginning of May but it was not until later in the year that there was significant rock activity. Notable rock climbing meets were held in Ardgour and Ardnamurchan, Reiff, Logie Head, Skye, Torridon and Ben Nevis.

Three members (Douglas McKeith, Colwyn Jones and Ken Koote) completed their Munros.

At the AGM in November the Section Constitution was changed to reflect the change to the Whole Club constitution and the following officials were elected: Hon. Member, Alan Thrippleton; Hon. President, Benny Swan; Hon. Vice-President, Neil Craig; President, Andrew Sommerville; Vice-President, Alasdair Reid; Secretary, Donald Ballance, 1/R 11 Airlie Street, Hyndland, Glasgow, G12 8QQ, (Tel: 0141 357 3073, Email: D.Ballance@mech.gla.ac.uk) URL="http://www.mech.gla.ac.uk/JMCS/"; Treasurer, Andrew Sommerville; Coruisk Hut Custodian, Sandy Donald, 15 Smeaton Avenue, Torrance, Stirlingshire, G64 4BG, (Tel: 01360 622541); Committee: Iain Cumming, Dave Eaton, Stevie Hazlett, David Lawson, David MacDonald, Neil Marshall, Ian Thomson.

Donald Ballance.

SMC AND JMCS ABROAD

Himalaya

HUGH JORDAN reports: I've never experienced death on the mountains. Yes, over nearly 50 years' of climbing several of my climbing friends have been chopped, but fortunately, I've never been around when the grim reaper has come knocking. Even when climbing at one's limit I was fearful of injury and pain, but never death. It was unreal, a joke. I well recall climbing on Wasted with the Steele brothers in the Sixties doing Rackstone Crib when a block detached itself from the rib and took a climber with it. I remember two sounds; the cannonball roar of the boulder thundering down the scree, and a squelching noise as something like a rag doll bounced down behind it. One of us said: 'God! I bet he drinks Carling Black Label.' He was injured, but he lived. Of course, he did! People don't die around me in the mountains.

Annapurna and Dhaulagiri are the two 8000m massifs that lie south of the main chain of the Nepalese Himalayas. Being that bit farther south there is no political complication with the Tibetan frontier, and it is possible to circumnavigate each mountain group without concern for the border. Annapurna is the more impressive, Dhaulagiri is the less frequented. Having left Pokhara, then Kusma, we eventually found ourselves climbing through the rain-forested valleys that led up to the deserted high grasslands of the Myagar plateau. At the upper limits of the forest we reached the last teahouse and while drinking tea found in a corner a porter standing over a shivering bundle. This was another hillman and John, who was a doctor, quickly diagnosed Acute Mountain Sickness, or Pulmonary Oedema if you're a medic. John literally shook some life into him, gave him an injection to keep him active. We made him eat a Mars Bar plus a couple of Diamox, which as a short-term measure was probably useless, and telling his mate to keep him walking sent them on down. He had a superficial wound on his leg which oozed blood so thick it resembled red treacle. His chances were not good since he had a good five miles to go before any appreciable loss of altitude. We went on, wondering which trekkers had sent them back virtually without any support.

Out of the forest the weather was fine, superb peaks, snow covered at 7000m on either side. Just above the Dhaulagiri base camp we met the first people we had seen since the hapless two. This was a group of four Irish who had just managed to extricate themselves from a severe storm on the other side of French Pass, 10 miles farther on and 2000ft higher. We were amazed that we had experienced nothing. Two days later we were camping on the other side of French Pass and the night was fine and cold at -8°C inside the tents. But next morning was different – warmer with total cloud cover and a distinct drop in pressure. We pressed on up to the Tharpa pass at 5500m and then started the traverse east This would go on contouring round the mountain for some seven miles before losing altitude. The sky was looking worse with that monochrome image so like a Scottish winter. The cloud was getting lower but not rapidly so.

It was mid-afternoon that we came across the first porter. A heap of wind-blown snow out of which stuck a bare hand and a foot wearing a cheap trainer. John wanted to examine the corpse but Anou, our sirdar, was most insistent that it was left strictly alone. Whether it be by law, custom, or practice, if one touches an abandoned body it becomes your responsibility. After 20 minutes we found two more. No hands or feet sticking out, just odd tatters of clothing and a heap of snow. At last we reached the end of the high traverse with what looked like a felt of thick cotton wool a few hundred feet above us. We started to lose height towards the valley. We camped at Yak Karka at 4800m and had a rushed luke-warm supper and went to bed before the snow started.

It was the most placid night's camping I have had. Warm, quiet, cosy, and my plastic piss bottle meant one didn't need to face the elements despite the Diamox. Dawn came with a sallow light and still the eerie silence. In particular, no friendly roar of the sherpas' primuses as they brewed tea. I started to unzip the tent flap, then quickly shut it, having been faced with a complete wall of snow. I was still contemplating the least messy way of getting out when a metal dinner plate serving as a shovel scraped down the fly sheet, the zip was undone and a brown hand, backed up by a grinning face, proffered the usual mug of steaming hot tea. Once up and outside one could see that the tents were almost completely covered – only purple canvas discs like small umbrellas showing. It speaks wonders for Phoenix geodesic tents that all three of them had taken the weight of snow without collapsing. Higher up the bodies would now be totally covered and remain there till next spring.

And still it snowed. With further loss of height it became wet snow, and eventually, stair-rod rain. We had to navigate round several large landslips without realising the tragedies they were causing all along the valley.

I was depressed about my personal comfort as we waded through the deep wet snow. Somewhere ahead in a porter's basket was a stuff sac containing my sleeping bag and down jacket. The sac was supposed to be proofed but not against this deluge. By mid-afternoon we bottomed-out into the Kali Kandarki at the village of Marpha, where we were told that there were eight dead porters on the traverse. They had been paid off at the Jonsom airstrip by a trekking group and had tried to take the short way home over the high passes to near Kusma when the first storm struck. They would eventually be removed by their own villagers who would come looking in the spring.

At the campsite I found Dowa the porter who had carried my gear. He was soaked to the skin. The piece of rip-stop plastic sheeting he used as a cape in bad weather had been carefully wrapped round my stuff sac which was bone dry. The extra 200-rupee tip I gave him at the end seemed very inadequate. To have a warm dry sleeping bag that night had to be worth at least £50.

Scottish Himalayan Kullu Eiger Expedition 1996

GRAHAM E. LITTLE reports:– Two days before departing for India, I received a Fax from the Indian Mountaineering Foundation indicating that the Government of India had not granted clearance for our expedition to Kishtwar. After the numbness had worn off, we set about achieving the impossible in identifying and obtaining permission for an alternative objective and maintaining the impetus of the expedition.

I had ample opportunity to view the impressive peak of Kullu Eiger on an expedition to the Parbati Valley, Himachel Pradesh, in 1985 and we quickly firmed-up on this as our alternative objective. At this stage we were uncertain as to whether it had already been climbed (subsequent research did not reveal any previous attempts on the peak). Sadly, as a result of this change, we no longer had the allocation of a Liaison Officer by the name of Miss Trupti Upadhya!

A wet but picturesque walk-in took us to a delightful campsite at 3740m directly under the peak. By Himalayan standards, Kullu Eiger at 5646m is of modest height, yet its North Face, towering a vertical 1900m above us, looked a serious enough challenge.

Our first attempt, after fixing 300m of rope on the First Band the day before, faltered, in the face of deteriorating weather, at 4690m. Our second attempt, a few days later, during a period of superb weather, proved successful. On September 21, 1996, Scott Muir, Graham Little and Jim Lowther stood on the summit in windless conditions, under a near cloudless sky. The round trip from Base Camp, which was largely climbed Alpine Style, involved three bivouacs. The overall grade of the route on the North Face/North-East Face was Alpine ED (El, AI and Scottish V) with nine pitches above the Central Icefield giving excellent Scottish character winter climbing. We named our line, The Mask, after a small distinctive icefield high on the face.

The summit team owe a debt of gratitude for the Base Camp support provided by John Finlay, Pasang Bodh and Prakash Bodh on what was a most harmonious and successful expedition.

Asia

PHIL GRIBBON reports:– The Bogda Ola range lies in the heart of the Central Asia plateau, soaring above the formidable void of the Takla Makan desert and visible from the age-old caravanserais of the Silk Road. This range is the most easterly outlying tail of the Tian Shan Mountains, translated as the Celestial Mountains, and lying 80 miles from Urumchi, the capital city of the Chinese desert province of Xinjiang. They are known to English-speaking mountaineers chiefly through the writings of those redoubtable exploratory mountaineers, Tilman and Shipton. With their typically slender resources they made a spirited reconnaissance of the range in 1947, identifying the climbing potential of the massif and climbing a couple of peaks over 4000m. In 1980 Mike Banks, exploiting the first relenting chink in the Maoist 'bamboo curtain', assessed the trekking potential of this remote pristine region and reached a couple of high points on the mountains. He was at once struck by the very attractive possibilities of the range for alpine-style climbing.

Once the range 'was opened to foreigners there have been many expeditions coming to climb in an endless stream', a quote with a touch of hyperbole from the XMA (Xinjiang Mountaineering Association) brochure presented to us on arrival at Urumchi. Yes, the short-stay trekking parties came and went, but the mountaineering parties laying siege to the highest summit of Bogda Feng (5445m) were few on the face. This spectacular peak was finally climbed after several previous attempts by a Sino-Japanese expedition in 1985, and a couple of years later our Sandy Allan, acting as a guide with a trekking party, went with a competent companion and stormed up and down its steep mixed ground in a fast three-day sortie. How could I resist an invitation to climb in this exotic area on a Saga Magazine-sponsored 'golden oldies' trip? This was to be the fourth in a series of biennial mountaineering expeditions under their sponsorship. The first two had been to attempt Jaonli, in the Garkwal Himalayas, and the third to climb 11 peaks on Sermersoq Island in SW Greenland.

Three of the team were veterans of previous Saga and other expeditions, the two septuagenarians, Mike Banks from Bath and Joss Lynam from Dublin, and the sexagenarian baby of the party, Paddy O'Leary from Co. Wicklow. Banks, of course, had made the first ascent of Rakaposhi (7742m) with Tom Patey in 1958. The other members were Barrie Page from Nottingham, Hugh Banner, who had to withdraw at the last moment, from North Wales, and myself.

All arrangements were made direct with a Chinese governmental body, XMA. In practice, this meant that they fitted in with our plans and for a considerable lump sum in dollars they provided hotel accommodation, road transport, the ferries on the loch, the pack horses and drivers to and from the camps, the base food and a mess tent, and our Chinese staff. A huge administrative burden was lifted by just one cheque!

The XMA, at 1 Renmin Road, P.O. Box 83002, Urumqi, China, currently have an ambitious mountaineering programme, not only to five places in the Tian Shan mountains, but to the Kunlun mountains, including Kongur and Muztagh Ata, the Altun and the Altay mountains. There also are Karakoram trips to K2, Broad Peak and the Gasherbrums with two months allowed to tackle these well-known summits from a common base camp on the Chinese side of the range. XMA also runs Tian Shan and Karakoram trekking, horse riding in our Bogda Ola range, exploration by camel in the Takla Makan desert, bike tours and river rafting. There is nothing like a bit of rampant commercialism to get you into the farthest flung corners of the world.

Our 1995 Tian Shan Saga-Mag expedition flew 6000 miles from Heathrow via Vienna to Beijing on July 30 in the comfort of an Austrian Airlines flight. It was then necessary to back track for 1500 miles flying over the Gobi Desert to Urumchi. There we were on the same latitude as the Pyrenees, with the coastline of the Arctic Ocean 2000 miles N, and Mount Everest directly due S across the deserts and the Tibetan plateau. We were met by an XMA staff member and from there to base camp all arrangements were in their capable hands. They delivered an excellent service and ensured our intricate programme went without a hitch – no mean achievement.

We left the ugly industrial city of Urumchi through a dark-Satanic-mill waste-land and crossed the dry landscape before our minibus followed a modern tarmac road up into the hills. We reached the road end at a tourist-ridden and litter-strewn loch endearingly called the Heavenly Pond at about 2000m. A motorised pleasure boat, designed to serve the hordes come to view the snowy heights, carried us along the loch to the overnight stop in a cosy nomad's yurt tent and the 'delicacies' of the South of Heaven restaurant. Here we met the local Kazak hillmen who would provide the pack animals needed to transport our month's supply of fresh food and equipment. These Kazaks are born horsemen, one of the several major ethnic groups that inhabit the Central Asian region known as Turkestan which spans the border between China and the former Soviet Union. They were dressed in Russian-style working men's caps and incongruous suits, they listened to Walkmans and had fallen into venal and time-wasting ways. Next day we were off, the wiry and sure-footed Kazak horses splashing through mountain torrents and stepping daintily across rough boulder scree. They toiled up the Zlayanzhan valley for about 1000m through fragrant conifer forests and then more open grasslands. Three members hired riding horses. One member who did not add extra padding to his saddle ended up with two huge raw blisters on his stern. Thereafter he walked.

A pleasant meadow was found for the first base camp at 3100m. Our Chinese staff consisted of a happy young Chinese cook, He Fen Gian, who worked wonders in the cramped mess tent with a hatchet, a chopping board, a wok and a gas ring; our friendly and charming interpreter, Leung Hua Sing, who was an English teacher and who rapidly became our friend; and our official 'minder' or liaison officer, Mai Ti, whose job allegedly was to make sure all the arrangements worked – they did, even if he did not. None had ever had any expedition or even mountain experience: 'No problem, we are very adaptable.'

We were not immediately taken with our surroundings. Our camp was sunk in a valley, the peaks were unimpressive, the weather was poor. However, our prospects became better after we had a fittening 700m slog up an easy scree mountainside and were able to scan the distinct summits astride the steep snowy glaciated northern flanks of the range. We then experienced a morale setback when it appeared that our team might not be up to the difficulties we seemed likely to encounter. Four of us attempted a gleaming white mountain christened Snow Dome (4203m) to receive a nasty surprise when we found the snow was wafer-thin with hard ice underneath. Unusually-warm temperatures for this altitude and latitude had stripped much of the snow away, and this meant front-pointing, pitched climbing and banging in lots of ice pitons, all very time consuming. We were struggling, unacclimatised, with a face from which melting and slithering snow induced a lack of resolve. We also had other problems. Page, who had somehow knocked himself out on a boulder at base camp, had to turn back with a crippling headache, and I accompanied him down. O'Leary and Banks pressed on, but Banks, although climbing well, was (at last!) at 72 showing his age, and at 4p.m. with lots more to climb they gingerly backed down the way they had come.

It was decided to try on the sunny southern side of the mountain. After enduring a rainy night in a bivouac, Banks and O'Leary found a long, and somewhat, tedious rock gully that led to a snow ridge high on the peak. As O'Leary hacked through a snow cornice he was able to see the summit of Snow Dome a few yards away. 'We're there.' The expedition had claimed its first summit. Under fairer conditions Page, Lynam and I repeated the route some days later.

Thwarted rock climbers had to look for more exciting options. O'Leary, Page and I reconnoitred the NE face of another mountain, Dinosaur Peak, and opted for the uncertainty of a rocky rib blocked by a leaning tower in its upper section that led on towards the main summit. We were avoiding an easy but less interesting line, and on the day of our attempt Banks was irritated. 'We're not here to climb up grotty rock. If you want to do that you can go to Glen Coe or Glendalough. I'm an expedition mountaineer to the greater ranges. I don't want to waste time on a futile attempt on loose rock.'

The route began too easily and ended up too hard. At the tower, rock forays to the left and straight up could not be pushed so a difficult snow exit was made but this only led to a subsidiary summit. Banks was right; it was too late and too far to the main top. Our reward for a gratifying day was an enjoyable 700m scree run and home to the base camp.

Driven by the demons, high on adrenaline, Banks and O'Leary quickly tried to make amends for our lack of success. After a glacier camp they followed an Aonach Eagach-like ridge in a near-blizzard with dense rushing cloud. There were plenty of rising traverses on hard ice and many changes in direction to keep them on their mettle. They reached this unclimbed summit, Isolde Peak (4520m), unsure that they had climbed the highest point until they had a clear view later from below. We now shifted to another base camp in a snowstorm crossing a pass to a lochan at the edge of the Daweigu glacier, formerly known as the Grachimailo Glacier, at 3500m and found ourselves in a more exciting, beautiful arena. The striking peaks of the range – Bogda Feng and its several subsidiaries, 'in shape just like a writing (sic!) brush rack' – dominated our view, and above us Schokalsky Peak (4813m) soared invitingly. Elegant, complicated lines to 5000m summits waited defiantly for young alpinists.

Here we were more at home in the wilderness. Some yaks snuffled and grazed on the hillsides. Eagles wafted on the thermal air currents. I found mouse tracks by my tent after an overnight snowfall and came across a rare snow leopard's pug marks imprinted on a snowbank as I traversed a high ridge above camp. Gentians, edelweiss and the strange carnivorous-looking snow lotus speckled the slopes. But here the age of the team, and the unsuitability of our logistic arrangements, combined to fuel further frustration. We had hoped to pass through a remarkable gorge called the Slot to gain the southern side of the range, to explore and attempt some worthwhile first ascents. But we were tied to a base camp that required a number of horses to shift it, horses that could not cope with the terrain we hoped to explore, and we were also umbilically attached to supplies which were unsuitable for back-packing.

So we turned to the challenge before our eyes, the main peak of Bogda Feng some 2000m above our base camp. A large Japanese team had arrived just before us and had been working on the mountain for some days. We began carrying loads up the glacier and established a camp sandwiched between a moraine and the boulder slopes of a ridge. O'Leary climbed most of the way to a col at 4700m and found that the young strong team had fixed 1600m of rope, mainly on the upper wall of the peak.

On our first carrying up to the proposed camp site Banks and I had an uncanny and unwished-for experience. I saw an ice axe coming through the melting snow surface, and then other lost bits and pieces of gear appeared at random around us. With a growing sense of unease I looked around and there 20m away was the mutilated and half-dressed body of a once-beautiful Japanese girl. No matter how hard we tried we could get no satisfactory explanation for the presence of a body that had disappeared some 15 years previously in a deep crevasse. It looked like a case for a Sherlock Holmes investigation in the Journal.

We made a tentative sortie along the flanks of the heavily-crevassed glacier that led to the col. It became apparent that ancient bones were not up to carrying loads up the steep icy route. It was decided we should try elsewhere, but the following morning and having mulled over our lack of moral fibre O'Leary and I agreed we should try after all. Even greybeards ought to manage with fixed ropes and we were both probably fit enough by now to manage the harder upper section of the mountain.

First, we temporarily put the whole plan out of our minds and had a less daunting day out. Banks and I were able to climb a pleasant peak N of the main massif. We called it Eric's Peak (4348m) because it was above a col first visited by Shipton. Our route involved an entertaining succession of rock steps with connecting snow passages, all most satisfying, while the view to the north wall of Bogda Feng was the Ben's Orion Face five times over, all quite overwhelming. On the same day O'Leary climbed to the col to get a closer look at the route to the summit. On his way up he met, much to his disappointment, the Japanese coming down and in the best environmental practice they were removing the final sections of their fixed rope gangway that they had used successfully to climb Bogda Feng in their fortnight's siege. His descent was somewhat fraught as he enjoyed (well, for most of the time) the hardest climbing of the expedition. Load carrying on such terrain would have been most telling on even the most technically proficient of older climbers so the removal of the fixed ropes put paid to our hopes on Bogda Feng. We had marched, like the Grand Old Duke of York's men, a wee bit up the hill and then down again.

O'Leary and I had one last major fling when we attempted a formidable rock peak of some 5000m on the western extremity of the massif. It gave us some good rock climbing, complicated route finding and an airy bivouac, but our attempt was defeated by the baffling nature of the rock architecture and by some unexpectedly hard ice. We had left our crampons and heavy plastic boots behind and had been treating the cracks and ledges of the north face of a 600m rock tower too cavalierly. We were rejected summarily for our temerity.

Our final outing took Page, Banks and Lynam up Jianshier Feng (4304m) with an ascent that involved climbing steep and massive scree on to a rambling ridge. The descent was down seemingly interminable fine-grained scree that gave splendid runs on a virgin slope not yet ruined by the feet of countless climbers. On the last day when I was wandering a high horseshoe ridge above base camp O'Leary shot out alone to climb both Jianshier Feng and Eric's Peak in a final flamboyant gesture.

Seven peaks over 4000m had been climbed, members attaining summits on 17 occasions in total – our leaders on their last major mountaineering expeditions (so they said!) claimed this to be a fair score for OAPs. It goes without saying that considerable scope remains for some challenging first ascents.

We made our way home by flying over the Takla Makan desert from Urumchi to Kashgar. We then drove 800 miles along the ancient Silk Road through the Pamir mountains following the recently completed, very spectacular and over-hyped Karakoram Highway. We crossed into Pakistan via the Khunjerab Pass, at 4730m the highest point we reached in the whole expedition. We flew back from Islamabad on September 12. Where to, next time?

JOHN STEELE reports – John Steele and Barbara Gibbons visited the Kulu area in the Indian Himalayas during October last year, principally to recce the approach routes to several well known peaks there. Early winter snows made access to the higher mountains (Deo Tibba, White Sail) problematic, however journeys were made into the Parbati, Malana and Tos valley systems and several important passes crossed. The Kulu Dussehra festival made for a colourful finale.

South East Asia

John Steele and Barbara Gibbons continued exploration (SMCJ 1995 p. 775). Ascents in Java included Gunung Arjuno (3300m) and its smoky neighbour Welirang (3100); the latter known for its sulphur mines. Better still were the island ascents of Agung (3100m) on Bali and Rinjani (3,700m) on ajoining Lombok. These last two peaks were followed by several days diving in the deep ocean trenches that are a feature of the Indonesian archipelego.

Antipodes
Aspiring to Summits in New Zealand

DEREK FABIAN reports: Few mountain expeditions begin with a cheese and wine party! I had been across to Edinburgh, helping Robin help Eddie to set up his exhibition of Rodel pots. We were late back and had to miss the Western District Thursday evening lecture. It was November, and Robin decided to give a miss, also, to the cheese and wine that followed.

Socialising is not altogether an SMC forte, nor mine. So I headed my vehicle westwards for the Lang Craigs and home. But . . . a glass of wine, a loaf of bread . . . it might prove to be an opportunity to enlist a climbing partner for Mount Aspiring. I had funds towards just one more research visit to the University of Auckland and a dozen or more Scots cousins throughout New Zealand. And, in February that year, with my wife, Ewa, we had been mountain trail-walking in the Southland Range. Who would not aspire to that summit, once having set eyes on it, standing some 300m above all its surrounding peaks and in such a superb mountain and fiordland setting? The Matterhorn of New Zealand, I mused, as I turned my vehicle about and headed for the cheese and wine.

'We must have been in New Zealand at about the same time as you,' said Ron, as I entered the bustle and searched for a non-empty bottle of wine. The Hockeys have a daughter in Perth, Western Australia. 'So whereabouts were you', said I, trying to direct the red into a glass with one hand and balance a large slice of blue on a tiny crust of French with the other.

'We toured the South Island mostly,' said Ron. They had been in New Zealand, in February of that same year, for a stay of two or three weeks only. 'Did you get to the Southland National Park,' I asked excitedly between and through mouthfuls of crumbling blue cheese and crusty French bread. 'Yes, I wish I'd had a climbing partner', said Ron. 'Isn't that a superb mountain?' We quickly established that one week apart we had both been there, in fine weather, thinking the same thoughts. 'Let's go next February,' I said, between more excited mouthfuls. Ron's eyes glazed; serious mental calculations showed on his brow. He disappeared to find Paddy, his wife, and to serve her more and stronger wine. I grabbed Donald and retrieved from him my *info pack* of maps and proposals for my hoped-for Mt. Aspiring Geriatric Expedition 1996. Donald, and Robin too, had eventually decided against. For both, Spitzbergen beckoned, in April/May; aspiring climbers for 1996 were looking thin on the ground.

Ewa and I had bought earlier that year, and still owned in NZ, *Regina,* an ancient (1968) Commer Campervan; it was currently garaged at Lake Hawea near Wanaka on the South Island's proud 45th parallel (they have a monument to that!), on the edge of the Mt. Aspiring Park. It would provide the four of us with transport; once reached by bus from Christchurch, where no less than six of our Scots cousins reside. December and January became peppered with decisions and snowy Munros. Time shrank, as it does, and global-circumnavigating departures from Glasgow, in opposite directions, were made before January was through; from temperatures of -13°C, to high summer down under.

We met up in Christchurch, among many Grigors (their ancestors were proscribed McGregors from Elgin), to the accompaniment of more excellent cheese and wine, this time of NZ origin. Midst this we were joined by Peter and Dorothy; the Reads from Motueka, near Nelson (friends from Canadian climbing days, and originally from the UK – they had met in Glen Coe 45 years ago). They too had a Campervan; and two of us travelled with them to Wanaka. At Lake Hawea, *Regina* purred proudly into life. But Greg our garage friend reported dejectedly that NZ 'warrant of fitness' regulations have, in just the past two months, tightened rigidly regarding rust – in particular, around door sills and similar areas where *Regina* regrettably suffered. She was without warrant for the road, and thus registration. Undeterred from the immediate plan, we headed into Mt. Aspiring Park and off the public road, but into cloud and rain. At least the latter kept down the dust as two huge low-loaders, carrying sections of a new Colin Todd Hut, roared past *Regina* in her slow and stately progression along the 35km of unmetalled track to Raspberry Creek. Here our walk-in to Aspiring Flats was to begin; an easy track, but for two could-be treacherous river-crossings.

We spent the evening of our first day out from Christchurch at the NZAC Aspiring Hut, where SMC reciprocal facilities and – more important – hut fees were enjoyed, making it a welcoming roof for two of us from the Glasgow contingent; while two, plus the non-NZAC-members from Motueka, set up a comfortable camp by Cascade Creek. This river, having descended in huge falls from the steep and wooded slopes surrounding us, meandered musically through the Aspiring Flats close by.

The weather forecast did not auger well for the morrow. Pete and Dorothy decided that the steep track to Cascade saddle might provide a view. Ron and I, however (all this way from Glasgow), felt the need to be in position, should the weather do the unlikely and provide a window of clear skies for the climb. Tomorrow, too, the chopper – they said – expected to be able to hoist the sections of the new Colin Todd Hut to the Bonar Glacier. Meanwhile, we learned also that on the previous day a helicopter hoisted 10 climbers to the old hut there, with 12 days' provisions. Climbers who reached the hut yesterday, after the two-day haul from Aspiring Hut, had to bivouac in the screes and snow outside.

Dispiriting news indeed. Nonetheless, we set off early; the track to Scott Bivvy leading through tiny-leafed NZ beech forest, across Shovel Flat, more forest (black and silver beech) to Pearl Flat and a breakfast stop. Low dark clouds switched our deliberations from Scott Bivvy and the then farther long day's haul to the Bonar Glacier, to the steep-looking wooded bluff rising from the far side of the West Matukituki River, and leading to the French Ridge Hut below Mt. Avalanche. A wire suspension bridge 1km up-river gave access to the well-named Gloomy Gully and eventually, we reached the upper shoulder of the steep bluff. Avalanche Glacier, alongside, remained hidden in thick mist.

By early afternoon, in gathering cloud and gloom we were spreading sleeping bags on bunks in the hut, deserted but for the part-time warden, a student and climber from Dunedin (New Zealand's Edinburgh). My crampons, I find, to my dismay, are at the breakfast spot. Without them, nothing can be done above the hut, so I retrace with self-deprecating curses, heading down Gloomy Gully for Pearl Flat, where some kind soul (descending from Scott Bivvy?) had lifted my abandoned crampons and thoughtfully carried them back to Aspiring Hut. It was there that I spent the night; rejoining Ron in the cloud and mist at French Ridge Hut by mid-morning. One sure way of getting fit, I mused. And I smiled too at what Robin might say; the crampons are borrowed ones – from him.

Ron has meanwhile made an ascent of the readily accessible snowy peak, Mt. French, at the edge of the Bonar Glacier; returning to the hut in thick mist which would have frustrated our planned attempt of Mt. Avalanche. Climbers arriving that afternoon down the heavily crevassed Bonar Glacier from the Colin Todd Hut had taken nearly eight hours; normally a three to four hour traverse. The next morning dawned with all the signs of pending storm, including lenticular clouds and rising wind. We retreated to Aspiring Hut and then, wading the now rapidly rising and would-be treacherous rivers, out by Campervan, to the Glen Dhu campsite beside enchanting Lake Wanaka.

All roads beyond there were public. *Regina* was unwarranted and unregistered. The weather and fresh snow in the mountains would need a week or 10 days to clear. Time was up for the Motueka contingent; the Reads took the road north, and we the road for Dunedin – along the Clutha (Clyde.) River. Before we reached Alexandra, almost at the 45th Parallel, a Police car signaled us to pull over. Ewa wonders aloud if our Commer is to become a 'full stop'.

We had a problem we explained, describing our predicament in full – but adding an intention to seek salvaged door sills for repair work in Dunedin. The NZ Police Officer pondered, scratched his head – and, far from unfriendly, searched for remote signs of sanity in the four geriatric faces within. 'Yes, you do have a problem,' he agreed. 'I'm going to have to give you a ticket. In fact, I think it will be better for you if I give you two, one for no warrant of fitness and one for no registration . . . then you can show them both when you are stopped again – which you will be, I'm sure . . . But I'll tell you how to get out of them,' he continued, as he wrote out tickets totalling NZ$450, and then the name and address of his 'boss', to whom we were to write, once warranted and registered.

There must be few police officers in the world who have been thanked and had their hand shaken warmly for giving out tickets totalling £200! But how, we wondered, were we to 'get warranted and registered'? A short time later we pulled off the road to have lunch, and found that we had stopped opposite a police station. We bundled back into *Regina,* gulping furtive mouthfuls, and moved on – all eyes on the mirror. Two hundred fugitive miles to Dunedin. However, at Portobello campsite, to the far side of this NZ Edinburgh, we (or I, not the 'royal' we, as Ewa rightly insists) procured fibreglass matting and other related materials from a derelict and decaying boat. We constructed a makeshift ramp for *Regina* and spent hours that stretched to days beneath her, de-rusting and rebuilding. Then, rejoined by the Hockeys – from visiting friends nearby – we presented her, with carefully concealed trepidation, for a warrant of fitness in Dunedin. She passed! And so she displayed with pride her two certificates for the remainder of our expedition.

The daily deluge at Portobello campsite gave way to days of dreich weather, and then to hot NZ sun. Could it last? We re-crossed the Southern Alps to Fiordland, and explored its scenic and ecological engineering (hydro-electrical) wonders; both deserving of a place among the world's Seven. Here, too, where the annual rainfall is nearly three times that of Glasgow, the skies began to clear. We worked north and 10 days from our rapid retreat were setting up camp by Wishbone Falls on a delightful bank of the West Matukituki River, 1km short of Raspberry Creek.

Was it dismay or resignation in the eyes of Paddy and Ewa? They would trail-walk, the Rob Roy track and others. For Ron and I an early start, with gear and tent, for the elusive Scott Bivvy. We lunched this time at Pearl Flat, treble-checking crampons as we moved off. A substantial part of the trail high above had disappeared in a tree avalanche. Ron got well ahead. Emerging from bush to the river, in a clearing below Matukituki Saddle, I explored for a crossing to the cairns on the far side. The river gravel here was soft; impossible not to leave tracks – but there were none to be seen. How could I have passed Ron? Mystified, I eventually continued, thigh deep for moments in the raging snow melt from above. At Scott

Bivvy, for the past 40 minutes or more, Ron was equally puzzled; he had scrambled a steep uncairned bluff to emerge at a higher crossing. He had settled in to the cramped two-person rock bivvy, with a walker descending from the Liverpool Bivouac on the flank of Mt. Barff above. After our meal, I set up the tent. I found in any case that the lack of flat area restricted its floor space to comfortable room for one only; and at first light we set out on the long haul to the Colin Todd Hut – a good Munro above us.

The flank of a high waterfall, beyond the saddle, lead into an awkward 500m-long slabby rock gully. We were overtaken by a young Swiss couple who had camped at Pearl Flat. They took the steep grassy and slippery (deer?) track that rose directly up from the waterfall. We elected to negotiate the gully. The glacier and rock scenery become superb. By afternoon we gained the Bonar Glacier and could see the hut now silhouetted at the foot of Mt. Aspiring's NW Ridge.

The glacier was heavily crevassed but dry. There was a clearly trodden track. An hour, says the guide, from here to the hut. Ron overtook the Swiss couple, who roped for the glacier. The new Colin Todd hut, now in position and habitable but with no stove or bunks, is the one silhouetted. Its floor was crowded with a party of Americans and Kiwis. Ron had led on down to the old hut; farther, but 50m lower. We shared it with only the Swiss couple, Juerg and Sabina, from Dunedin. I settled in; it was now nine hours since our Scott Bivvy departure. The ridge and summit above were enveloped in mist. A flock of inquisitive Keas (New Zealand mountain parrots!) held our attention. If they could only lift them, they would have flown off with our boots, left out to dry. Later the clouds lifted and swirled; then the alpen glow on peaks and glacier becomes stunning. Can it last? The summit (3030m) is the height of Ben Nevis above. Juerg and Sabina spent a week at this hut a year ago; cloud and mist had prevented their once seeing the glacier below, let alone the ridge and summit above.

The clouds rolled back in, and enveloped all. In the night, stars and then the ridge reappeared. At first light (6.00am on the 45th Parallel) we were heading up the ridge. A good gauge of its difficulty was a comparison with the Askival Pinnacle on Rum; but with 1200m of it to the summit. We roped and unroped as sections alternated in difficulty and exposure; with the latter sustained almost throughout. The now miniature Bonar Flats and Waiatoto River to north are 2000m below. Our Swiss friends could be seen far ahead. Parties from the new hut overtook us. We gained on them on the final snow dome and its spectacular ice and snow crest. Ron, the bit now between his teeth, gained the summit well ahead – catching up there with Juerg and Sabina – as I wrestled with a dislodged crampon on the steep wall below. A NZ party, on this wall, are cutting steps and belaying with snow stakes. My length of alloy Dexion with karabiner (old friend from the Andes; forerunner of the snow stake) was buried in my pack. I front-pointed the wall, as Ron did ahead of me. He retraced the surely spectacular crest, to straighten my crampon heel-bar with his axe, and we made the summit together.

We had it to ourselves; on a day that was still and cloudless. Mountains stretched to our horizon and beyond: we could make out Mt. Cook clearly, 130km north east, standing – as did our summit – 300m above its neighbours. And below, terrace upon terrace of the Therma and Volta Glaciers cascaded nearly 3000m to the Bonar Valley floor. Eight hours of toil, I counted, from the hut; and from there, the next day, we descended in gathering cloud and swirling mists, escaping another pending storm.

Morocco

HAMISH BROWN reports:– A season of wet and wildness such as Morocco has not known in my lifetime: great for crops, damaging to roads and buildings. In February, with Charles Knowles we had some good skiing at Oukaïmeden, based on the pleasant CAF chalet before heading off to try and ski on the western Tichka Plateau. A mule going head-over-heels and then days of deluge wiped out that effort and it was necessary to walk out from the hills to the Taroudant road. Various wanderings were made in the Da des and Todra Gorges, useful recces if snow denied the heights again.

An OHC gang couldn't penetrate the hills beyond Demnata's *pont naturel* because of floods but the four days' trekking to the Bou Willi and the Bou Goumez was a superb alternative. The Tessaout plateau approach for M'Goun was deep in snow (now into April). So 'no go' but Jbel Igoudamene 3519m was a magnificent traverse/viewpoint and the walk out by the Tizi n' Aït Ourit and Sremt to Aït M'hamid was a good journey completion. A week of car hire took in the dramatic cascades d'Ouzzoud and the far eastern High Atlas foothills – lots of potential walking/climbing areas. Roads rebuilt, it was back to the Western Atlas for treks/climbs based on Imoulas and Tagmont (Medlawa). Several wound-licking retreats were made to Essaouira.

A month in Scotland then, with a mainly F & RCC group, a June visit to the area east of the Tizi n' Tichka produced first great heat, then a week of storms, including a couple of scary flash floods. The party seemed to live a charmed life however, and Anhromher 3609m and Zarzemt 3113m were climbed and the southern limestone wilderness plateau of Thel Tafdjat followed from the *lacs* to Animiter. The historic Tizi n' Tebuet 2567m was crossed to Titoula and the Tezgi gorge taken to the meadows of the Tizi n' Telghist 2220m from which various peaks were climbed. All this region has an unusually rich alpine flora. From Oukaïmeden Attar (3246m) was climbed crossing to Timichchi and a descent of the Ourika valley to Setti Fadma, busy rebuilding after last year's devastating floods, and laying on a bridge-destroying spate for us. As Ali said: '1996 was different.'

An illustrated article on the 1995s 96-day, 900-mile end-to-end traverse of the Atlas appears in the 1997 *Alpine Journal* and I hope to produce a book about the Atlas ranges and peoples based on this trip. Meanwhile, several spring or autumn treks are planned for next year.

East Greenland

CHARLIE ORR reports: In April-May 1996 a short expedition was made to the Roscoe Berge-Liverpool Coast area of East Greenland. A Twin Otter was chartered from the northern seaport of Alurreyri in Iceland from the tour firm, Arcturus, which flew the party and equipment into the air strip at Constable Point on the Hurry Fjord (Lat. 71°N). A short helicopter hop then took all personnel, equipment and previously freighted food supplies into the interior, dropping us at the head of the Heks Glacier at 800m where a base was set up. The first week was spent making ski ascents of many of the peaks in the area which average around the 1200m mark. During that week one of our number, John Hay, left on his own on skis with a sledge and made a multi-day trip round the coast to the settlement at Scorsebysund where he spent time hunting and fishing with the Inuit there.

At the beginning of the second week, base camp was moved nearer the coast onto the Age Neilsens Glacier and again a number of ski ascents were made both there and farther north on the Pedersens Glacier. Many of the tops could be skied to the summit but more often than not, the last few hundred feet required rock climbing. Late in the second week a return was made to the original base camp and an ascent was made of the highest mountain in the area Twillingerne 1475m, the summit rocks yielding up a can of beans left by Malcolm Slesser's expedition who made the first ascent in 1971 (still *in situ,* in case of emergency pierce can, consume contents and send 50 pence cheque/PO to address as per membership list).

Two of the party, Alan Petit and Gerry Rooney, skied overland from the Heks Glacier base via the Grete Glacier to Scorsbeysund where they met up with John Hay, all returning to Constable Point by dog sled. The rest of the party skied out over two days via the Subbedal Valley re-crossing the Hurry Fjord to Constable Point.

The weather was excellent with sunshine every day apart from two on which snow and high winds kept us in the tents. Temperatures hovered around freezing during the day falling to about -20°C at night. The rock scenery is magnificent and is very reminiscent of a scaled-down Chamonix Aiguilles with boundless opportunities for technical rock climbing at all grades. Skiing conditions were excellent throughout.

Party: Malcolm Slesser, Jane King, Bill Wallace, John Hay, Charlie Orr, Stan Paterson, Alan Petit and Gerry Rooney (Starav MC.)

Svalbard, Spitzbergen

TIM PETTIFER reports:– A happy, successful and comfortable expedition with comic and potentially unhealthy consequences

We flew out of Aberdeen with the first warm flush of spring, and travelled north to the last land before the Pole. We flew the length of Norway, and as we slowly progressed to the North we studied the history of the land in reverse. The extensive pines of the south gradually gave way to birch – the first trees to colonise after the great glaciers receded – until we arrived in Spitzbergen, still in the grip of the ice age. We looked on a land as big as Holland and Denmark put together, with as much ice as Europe locked to the frozen shore and stretching from 70° north over the Pole to Canada and Russia. The archipelago of Svalbard has more than 1000 summits of 1000m, some unnamed, some possibly unclimbed; not because they are difficult but because there are so many, and there are so few climbers. The mountains are copies of the Mamores, younger and a little like Glencoe but the low sun strengthens their snowy buttresses and highlights the ridges with perpetual alpen glow.

While Scotland warmed to the lengthening evenings of the summer to come, the children of Longybearen travelled to school in constant sunshine. In the early hours of morning it still registered -30°C but Spitzbergen was vibrant now the polar night was over, and they were living 24 hours a day. There were a few other expeditions in the field and the foyers of the hotels were piled with pulks and skis.

Locals and visitors strolled around with rifles and pistols and we knew were in the land of the ice bear.

This is a land of space and stillness where even the quietest man-made sound is sacrilege. In the clear northern light you can see to eternity. Nonetheless, this did not prevent us hiring a ride on a 1000hp Weasel to transport our food and equipment half-a-day's travel to the south. This was a dual-headed caterpillar-driven hotel, equipped with radar, GPS, radio and heated. Designed for commercial exploitation of the Arctic and Antarctic wilderness it got us to Nathosrt Land far to the south quickly and comfortably. I regretted sitting there, but it was fascinating watching a week's man-hauling whiz by in four hours. The glaciers, valleys and cols we had slowly crossed four years before comically speeding by like a Charlie Chaplin film.

We made a base camp on the main polar bear highway that links the east and west coasts, in the lee of a beautifully-curved snow drift that covered an ancient and crumbling moraine. We shared a communal mess tent, that was cramped but warm, with just one stove going, and so we all shared the cooking and preparation which was occasionally lengthy. We had unwisely provisioned ourselves with a supply of fresh vegetables and meat from the Longybearen supermarket, on the basis that this would quickly be deep-frozen, but a home-based freezer is a poor performer compared to the arctic and spares nothing.

From our base camp we prospected into the hills, and each climb followed a pattern of long-level approach, progressively steeper skinning and eventually, reaching the summit using crampons and axe. Many hills and excursions were made, including a three or four-mile crossing of the sea ice to an excellent hotel. The team members were initially doubtful with regard to ruining the wilderness experience but soon realised that even the high Arctic is populated, and the welcome can match the arrival of guest with a Gold Card at a Highland hotel.

The camp was protected from bears using alarm trip wires, which proved their worth. While we were across the ice a crafty bear's dream of a free doss was rudely shattered. We measured the bear's footprints as a foot across and the length of his bound at 12ft. This had a remarkable effect on the party who double-checked the security devices, slept with a loaded gun or moved to a hut.

All good things, especially the best, have to end, so we were picked up and taken back to Longybearen. We arrived there at 3am had a meagre meal of reindeer, local queenie scallops, bacon, fried potatoes, salad and draft beer in Longybearen's best restaurant, which was making up for lost time and the polar night. So ended the most pleasant expedition I have been on – except for the finale.

At the last minute we discovered we were short of one bag which we had left in the back of the transporter. The team called at the garage to collect this and discovered a further parcel which contained two weeks' human waste for eight people, which had nicely thawed. This was securely packed in a strong plastic bag that had my address on it from a previous expedition. The driver was not aware of its contents but with helpful intentions in mind was going to post it back to Scotland.

Contents of the bag contained contributions from Donald Bennet, Mike Taylor, Bill Morrison, Robin Chalmers, Ian Angell, Tim Pettifer, Bob Barton and client, Simon.

Eire

JOHN STEELE reports on a fast trip around the Irish furth last September.

Just south of Dublin lie the Wicklow Mountains. The only mountain here though is Lugnoquilla (Log na Coille) which may be quite difficult to get at as the main approach traverses an army firing range! Round to the east though, an approach can be made up the Carrawaystick falls, a somewhat tedious route comparable say to crossing the western ramparts in Arran. The track leads to the bald summit and a timely reminder to greet you *sic* 'shell firing may be taking place in the vicinity.' No place to idle. (3 hours camping, Roundwood).

Heading away from the east coast and considerably more inland are found the Galtee Mountains, dead centre being Galteemore (Coille te Mhor), a kind of bigger version of Moel Hebog. Yet again the right access is a wee bit difficult to execute. It consists, however, of the usual drive along a high-banked winding farm lane (bohreen) which leads to a cart track which then climbs up beside the Shanbally River onto the high moor to veer off over a ridge, leaving a final steep boggy staircase to the summit. The descent though is a treat particularly if a diversion to the pretty Monabrook woods is made. (2.5 hours camping, Roundwood)

Having been told that the only real mountains in Ireland are to be found in Kerry in the deep south-west, a base was quickly established just outside Killarney. From here the view of the Reeks is a bit like looking south from Aviemore; dark silhouttes of distant hills with deep valley trenches between. The Reeks are a grand range and would provide for one long day's outing. I chose to make two good half-days of it, by setting up camp behind Loch Caltee, deep in the mountains. A route straight up the ice gouged nose of Cnoc am Chuilin, over grassy Cummeennpeasta and an airy scramble led to the mountain cairn of Cruach Mhor. Descent was made to the foot of the Bone where lies the loch named Caltee. This provided the most majestic of settings for an evening bathe as the autumn sun dropped quickly, cooling the mountain air. The powder for the all night salvo of cracks and booms that was to follow as the steep corrie walls contracted in the frosty night. (4 hours camping, Loch Caltee)

The three other mountains of the Reeks lay across the Hags glen from my camp. Stout sentinels the previous evening but obscured by thick mist during the morning of ascent. A bold line by the Eagle's Nest soon led to the stony top of Beenkeragh, a Brocken spectre led onto Carrauntoohil and brilliant sunshine onto the outlier of Cahir. Camp was soon reached via the Devil's ladder descent and a return made to the valley heat amid musk of sheep. Thirst was quenched in Tralee after a blinding drive into the setting Atlantic sun, seen finally as a huge orange orb setting behind the fishing boats moored in Dingle harbour. (5.5 hours camping Loch Caltee)

Brandon (St. Brendan's) Mountain is as impressive as Ben Sgriol, but with its own Corrie Ghrundda, hidden from the ocean. Seen from the west no more than a tourist path: from the east a wall of broken cliff and gullies, laced by a line of rockbound pools beneath. This particular mountain in Ireland typifies so many of our own with broad sea views in one eye while the other is filled by dark and dank recessed steepness. A worthy and memorable summit. The route I chose to descend from Brandon Peak to drafty Loch Cruttia was tricky and untrod. (5.5 hours/ camping Castlegregory)

So in four-and-a-half days the Irish round was completed which left several days to reflect and enjoy visits to the salty cliffs of Moher and rough leagues of Connemara at a more leisurely pace.

REVIEWS

ICE WORLD – Techniques and Experiences of Modern Ice Climbing:– Jeff
Lowe. (The Mountaineers. 1996. £19.95, 256 pages, more than 250 photographs.
ISBN 0-89886-446-1).

Hailed as the ultimate book on ice climbing, this is a thoroughly modern treatise
on the subject by American ice expert, Jeff Lowe. It starts with a brief history of the
sport, describes basic and advanced techniques and overviews equipment and
clothing. This is more than just an instructional book however, and the text is
peppered with stories and anecdotes from the author's vast experience. Without
doubt Lowe has written an important and authoritative work, which in many ways
reminded me of an ice climbing version of Doug Scott's *Big Wall Climbing*.

The technique section, which is well illustrated with copious photographs, will
undoubtedly raise a few eyebrows. There is a lifetime's experience here, and I
found the detail and variety of techniques described for tackling the harder routes
a little bewildering at first acquaintance. We don't have huge sweeps of vertical ice
in Scotland, and I must admit that just looking at photos of these routes makes my
biceps ache. Perhaps with techniques such as monkey hangs, diagonal crossover
pick placements and figure of fours, my grade may go up a notch! The mixed
climbing shots were particularly fascinating. In areas such as Vail in Colorado,
many of the routes have fixed protection which allows some really futuristic lines.
A good example is Lowe's own Octopussy, rumoured to be the hardest mixed climb
in the world, which breaks through a 3m horizontal roof to reach a vertical hanging
ice pillar. The dry continental weather results in a different set of ethical constraints
to our own. Climbing rock with tools and crampons is termed 'dry tooling'. There
is no concern that it is not covered with snow – it is just a means to an end to reach
the ice.

I must admit to be being a bit put off by the book's pompous title, but it is apt.
I found the most interesting chapter was the Hard Water Ice Guide which describes
16 of the World's classic ice routes. These have been chosen to demonstrate highly-
technical climbs on different types of ice, in a wide variety of geographical
locations. They range from the short technical routes such as Bridalveil Falls in
Colorado, through major alpine undertakings such as the Central Couloir on the
Jorasses, to major Himalayan climbs such as the Hungo Face on Kwangde. Lowe
has deliberately chosen routes that he has been on, although he does make the point
that he has not always succeeded. This allows him to give first-hand accounts and
make a consistent grading between climbs. For anyone interested in the world-wide
development of the sport, this all makes fascinating reading.

Even Scotland is featured in the top 16 routes, although Lowe does hedge a little
by plumping for several 'landmark routes' on Ben Nevis rather than one particular
climb. The landmark routes include the classic gullies such as Zero, Point Five and
Minus Two, and Lowe is clearly impressed by the achievements of the likes of
Marshall and Smith: 'These routes were 10 years ahead of their time and technically
more difficult than contemporaneous ice climbs in the Alps. To my mind, the most
classic, Orion Face Direct . . . is roughly comparable to routes done in the high
mountains during the 1970s such as the climbs on the Grand Pilier d'Angle, and the
Balfour Face of Mount Tasman in New Zealand'.

You must forgive me for being a little parochial, but I feel that Lowe is not fully
up to speed on the state of contemporary Scottish winter climbing. He sums up Ben
Nevis for example by stating that 'any ice climber interested in the history of the

sport should make pilgrimage there in the honour of the old masters.' There is no mention of the leap in standards in the late 1970s, and surely dream routes such as The Shield Direct or Gemini should be on any globetrotting ice climber's tick list? Lowe does include a Cairngorm mixed route though – Citadel with the Rouse-Hall Variation. To his credit he made the second ascent of the climb with Gordon Smith in 1976, but mixed climbing has moved on considerably in the intervening 20 years. The complete Citadel route may have been a more appropriate choice to illustrate the current state of play of the top end classic winter routes in Scotland.

On reflection however, I think that perhaps we ourselves are to blame for the lack of recognition of hard Scottish winter climbing. Having been fortunate enough to have done a handful of the climbs Lowe describes in the Alps and the Americas, it is clear to me that standards here are as high as elsewhere. Few of today's current Scottish winter activists seem prepared to write about their experiences however, and a complete history of Scottish mountaineering is well overdue. Are there any takers out there?

Simon Richardson.

May the fire be always lit – a biography of Jock Nimlin:– I. D. S. Thomson. (1995; The Ernest Press; 210 pp.; illus; £11.95; ISBN 0948153 39 3).

Mention Jock Nimlin and most climbers of recent generations will think of classic lines on the Cobbler, the Red Clydesiders, draughty howffs and perhaps the first ascent of Raven's Gully. Until I. D. S. Thomson produced this book, the standard sources revealed little about the man. Nimlin was clearly an important figure in the eyes of his contemporaries, but the works of Humble, Murray, Borthwick *et al* only mention him in dispatches. This biography therefore performs a service in gathering together what material there is, much of it obscure, and giving a fuller picture of Nimlin's exploits.

That he was a committed weekender, howffer, climber and walker was never in doubt. It will, however, surprise the reader to learn that Nimlin is on record as having contributed just 30 new lines, albeit some of these of the highest quality. This illustrates the low profile that Nimlin sought to maintain, and the diverse amounts of publicity given to the activities of the pre-World War Two working class climbers as against their more well-to-do brethren. Thomson's book is, however, that clichéd thing, a curate's egg. It is at its best where Nimlin's own writing is used, in which his love of the hills and his character really comes alive, albeit in somewhat purple terms at times. Thomson as a narrator is somewhat wooden, and you long for Nimlin's enthusiasm, for him to have written the whole thing, something his sense of modesty would not have allowed.

Thomson has not provided much detail of Nimlin's climbs other than in relation to what has already been credited to him. But there is quite a lot of material about the pre-war years which makes for engaging reading. It is disappointing to find that the last 40 years of his life is summarily dealt with in the last quarter of the book. We learn about his work for the NTS, his interest in gemstones, and his days as an instructor at Glenmore Lodge. But we hear little more about his climbing – why did he (we assume he did) give up? The In Memoriam section of the Journal (SMCJ 180, 1989, p334) provides answers, but Thomson does not. Surely, this should have been touched on? The result is therefore a bit patchy, but the good bits certainly justify the read. And it was always going to be difficult to pin down a man whose view on guidebooks was 'it seems to be the custom to open a guidebook, select

carefully a detailed route and follow the instructions as one might follow a recipe
. . . isn't there something missing? . . . Shouldn't the ideal climber's guide
emphasise the *possibilities* and let the established routes rest upon their cairns and
well-trodden ways?' Idealistic perhaps, but that seems to have been Nimlin's
nature. And the Journal would have been a lot slimmer too . . .

Alec Keith.

The Hewitts and Marilyns of Wales:– (TACit Press, compiled by Alan Dawson,
£2, ISBN 0-9522680-6-X).

Another booklet out of the TACit hothouse. I confess my ignorance right away
and am assuming that Marilyns are so-called due to some fancied resemblance to,
er, a physical feature once possessed by a legendary film star. Hewitts are more
readily analysed, being one of the Editors of the *Angry Corrie*. (OK he provides a
clever acronym, but it fools nobody.) This is, like its companion series, a listing of
hills, or two listings in this case. The Hewitts are the hills in England, Wales or
Ireland over 2000ft. The Marilyns are hills of any height with an all-round drop of
150m.

TACit Press have just flitted, and are now nestling in five minute's away by bike
from the origin of the SMC Journal. As one e-mail correspondent wrote recently:
'Do all mountain editors live in Menstrie?' Well not quite, but let's do them a
politeness by publishing their new address: TACit Press, 138 West Stirling Street,
Alva, Clackmannanshire, FK12 5EN.

This series of booklets have a major plus going for them; they can lead the
disgruntled walker onto the quieter hills. This may help explain the occasional
smug smile which flits across some Corbett-bashers' faces. (The peace and quiet
of the Ochils have certainly done in many an editor's productivity, he said from
personal experience.) The companion volume to the Irish hills is particularly
useful, as it draws on a recently-done updating of the Irish OS 1:50 000 sheets

Finally, in the booklet is a list of the Welsh Council Tops. I thought it was Tips
at first, which would have been odd even for TACit Press, but it is, in fact, the
highest points of the 22 unitary authorities in Wales. Like the earlier booklets, 10%
of sales goes to the John Muir Trust.

World Tops and Bottoms:– compiled by Grant Hutchison (TACit Press, 1996,
29pp., line illus., £2.00, ISBN 0 9522680 4 3).

A companion volume to The Marilyns & The Hewitts, The Grahams and the New
Donalds, and The Murdos. The last two were reviewed here last year. It takes a
special kind of enthusiasm to compile a list such as found here. Filthy politics
constantly interrupt one's orographical meanderings for example, such as the little-
thought-of point that a river may well change its name when it innocently crosses
some human defined dotted line on a map. Or that some countries share a summit,
such as happy Uganda/Zaire, or chucklefull Albania/Macedonia. The Vatican City
State has a highest point which does not lie at a summit, because the ground
continues to rise beyond the border. Another way of saying it lies on the side of a
hill I suppose, like Edinburgh. I won't even begin to discuss Antarctica.

If you want to collect countries via their highest points then this could be a good
buy. If you are bone idle and want to collect countries by their lowest points then
this could be a good buy. And if you are totally attached to your couch then buy it
anyway, as 10% of the cover price goes to the JMT.

Ken Crocket.

Over The Hills and Far Away:– Rob Collister. (The Ernest Press, 1996, 190pp., illus., £11.95, ISBN 0 948153 40 7).

That Rob Collister is a proficient and much travelled mountaineer is much in evidence in this collection of mountaineering essays which have as their varying backdrop the hills of Wales, the Antarctic, through the Alps to the greater ranges of the Himalaya. Unfortunately, his ability as a writer is not so strongly to the fore.

What we have here is a collection of essays, sometimes written years apart, presented as a whole, a book, with little or no attempt having been made to 'edit' them into their new role with the result that most readers, I feel, would find the repetition of detail boring if not irritating. Description of a trouser-filling struggle to reach the haven of a small ledge tends to involve the same detail whether it occurs in Wales or the Himalaya. And allowing for the fact that most of us are quite interested in the flowers we see on our mountain travels Collister's descriptions as per his *Collins Guide To Alpine Flowers* are just that, descriptions repeated and repeated and – Collister is no Jim Perrin and it is just that quality which is required for a collection of this type to succeed. The ability to see and feel more than merely what is happening around you, the ability to enter into the realm of the metaphysical and more importantly to transfer these 'travels' onto the page. Collister relies far too much on thin, two dimensional description of what he sees as 'reality.'

> On the top of the knoll, Netti took her pack and carried on
> while I went back for mine. *(The Hidden Valley).*

> Ian took off his pink and lilac rucksack with the rolled
> yellow karrimat strapped to its side and dumped it beside
> the path with a grunt. *(Alpine Guide).*

This is 'What I did in the Holidays' stuff and the fact that in one essay we are told the make of the author's running shoes reinforces my point about two-dimensional description.

The book is interspersed with poetry and in the last stanza of the poem *Wanganui River*, written about a canoe trip in New Zealand, I detect perhaps a hint of the quality of writing that would have been required to carry this book.

> – until movement without
> becomes stillness within, and we are,
> just for a moment, one,
> and we are not on the river
> but we are the river.

It may be that Collister does experience 'reality' in this way and that he simply has difficulty transferring it to the page, but I rather tend towards the theory that it was a flash of insight in a mind which sees things in a rather more straightforward and flat way.

The book will undoubtedly have some value to anyone planning expeditions to the areas concerned but, in the main, Collister fails to convey the delight, intensity of feeling and 'spark' commensurate with his vast experience as a mountaineer.

Charlie Orr.

Mountain Holidays:– Janet Adam Smith (1996. The Ernest Press. £12.50, paperback ISBN O 948153 45 8.).

Republication of Janet Adam Smith's *Mountain Holidays* by Ernest Press 50 years after its first publication by Dent in 1946 affords welcome access to this gem of mountaineering literature. It is one of three classics by lady alpinists recalling the climbing scene between the World Wars, the other two being Dorothy Pilley's *Climbing Days* and Miriam Underhill's *Give Me The Hills*. Together the books recall a bygone era of Alpine Mountaineering when climbers not infrequently stayed in hotels and climbed their harder routes with guides, with whom they formed enduring friendships. *Climbing Days* contains accounts of first ascents in Wales and of the formidable North Ridge of the Dent Blanche; *Give Me The Hills* describes the first ascents of the Diable Arête of Mont Blanc du Tacul and the life-threatening East Face of the Finsteraarhorn as well as several notable manless (ladies only) Alpine ascents.

Seemingly by contrast, the Foreword to *Mountain Holidays* states: 'It records no great feats of mountaineering, no striking new ascents . . . also attempts to recall the pleasures of inns and villages, glens and pastures, gossip and idleness – all the varied texture of holidays.'

But do not let this fool you, Janet Adam Smith was tough as well as being a perceptive and gifted writer. Perhaps in the first one-and-a-half chapters, when the writer was exposed to family climbing influences but had not yet fully caught the bug, I was not fully committed as a reader. But by the end of Chapter Two she is hooked on the Alps and I on the book. Chapter Three describes Cairngorm crossings by the four great passes. Nothing notable about that? Well, each one was in autumn, solo, straight after an overnight train journey from London, at a fair clip and whatever the weather. And remember how much longer the Cairngorm approaches were in those days – a chapter to savour. Thereafter the scene is the Alps. Beautiful descriptions of peaks and passes in the West and East Graians, places where even today you can escape the crowds, for example descending from the Gran Paradiso via the Tribulazione glacier.

Most of her Alpine climbs were with Michael Roberts, her fiancé and then husband, often starting also with a party of schoolboys, and proceeding later in the holiday to peaks in the High Alps with the guide, Ottone Bron, many of these big mountains being climbed at highly-respectable speeds. I will leave it to you to discover the details. But to convey the writer's perceptions, let me close with this passage on a place where I and perhaps many readers have found no time in their busy Alpine schedules for anything except planning the next peak or seeking out the fleshpots.

'Standing in the square at Aosta we could see the snows of the Combin shining far above, but had eyes too for the works of man – the fan-shaped pattern of the paving stones in the big square, the dignity of the colonnade, and, down the road, the great Triumphal Arch. Here, in Augusta Praetoria, were all the reasons that make the Western Alps the greatest mountains in the world. Beside Augustus's arch, or at the foot of the great pass, one felt the Alps, not as on the fringes of European civilization, but at the heart. Over the St. Bernard went one of the greatest roads in the world, the pilgrims road to Rome, linking the maize fields of Piedmont with the fells of Norway, Renaissance with Gothic, Giotto with Dürer, Dante with Ockham.'

Ted Maden.

Scotland's Mountains:– An Agenda for Sustainable Development. Andy Wightman. (Scottish Wildlife and Countryside Link, 1996, 24pp. £4, ISBN 0 9518582 5 4.)

This booklet was produced for an International Conference on Mountains held in Aviemore in 1996. The chairman was Bob Aitken and the booklet was published on their behalf by the Scottish Mountaineering Trust (Publications) Ltd. There are other areas of input by SMC members too, including the Foreword by Bill Murray, who died two weeks after his contribution. It is fitting that W.H.M. should have written the Foreword, as in a way much of the booklet is a miniaturised version of his *Scotland's Mountains,* published by the SMT a decade ago. It is well laid out, with many good colour photographs but is a bit pricey for the casual purchaser (for whom, of course, it is not intended).

Ken Crocket.

The High Andes – A guide for climbers:– John Biggar (Andes, 1996, £16. ISBN 1-871890-38-1).

I first met John Biggar at an SMC Eastern Section slide show where he gave a very informative talk about mountaineering in the Andes. A few months later I bumped into him again, this time at about 5000m on Aconcagua. He certainly has a deep passion for, and detailed knowledge of, these mountains and is well qualified to write this guide.

To quote from the rear cover 'this book is the first comprehensive climbing guide to the highest peaks of the Andes. Included are route descriptions for the normal routes on all 99 of the major 6000m summits and also 75 of the most popular and accessible 5000m peaks.' The guide therefore excludes Patagonia but still covers a lot of ground – seven countries, from Venezuela to Chile. Not only does it include the normal routes but other routes are also mentioned, albeit very briefly. In fact, compared to what we are used to in the Alps for instance, even the normal routes get rather brief descriptions. However, they seem to be adequate and appropriate for these mountains, especially as it is the first time most routes, and even some mountains, have been described in any detail. There are still a lot of unknowns about the more remote and rarely climbed peaks and the abbreviation, N/K, appears regularly throughout the text. There may even be a few 6000m peaks awaiting first ascents in the Puna de Atacama. Where information is lacking the author has honestly admitted this and often given his best guess.

The introduction and appendices to the book are packed full of helpful advice and information, ranging from acclimatisation to minefields. On the latter point the author comments that 'attempts to find out whether these are anti-vehicle mines or anti-personnel mines have not been successful'! There are lots of useful maps and diagrams but these lack sharpness. (They were perhaps drawn on computer?). There are also a few colour photos which visually spice up the book. The cover is rather flimsy and I suspect that anyone going to the Andes would photocopy the relevant pages, despite the dire copyright warning.

In short, an excellent guidebook, painstakingly assembled and packed full of the best available information and good advice. Highly recommended, especially to anyone making their first trip to the Andes. By the way, an appendix lists all the 6000ers in order of height – perhaps these will become known as the Biggars. Biggar Bagging? Just a thought.

Grahame Nicoll.

The Mountain Weeps, Thirteen Exercises:– Ian Mitchell (Stobcross Press, 1997 £7.99 ISEN 0 952974 07).

These short stories are almost all set in Scotland. Indeed some of the locations are recognisable to hill-goers. Fantasy is a common thread. But the big issues: guilt, temptation, sex, death, as trailed in the blurb? Well . . .

The author evokes our mountain landscape with easy familiarity. The people of these tales are a different matter. They are mostly without names and are introduced as the hillwalker, the traveller, the climber, the wife, the chemist, the Director etc. On occasion such stereotypes are described as 'the Skoda couple' or 'the man with the Aschenbrenner'.

Their actions and words are less than riveting. More effective are the word pictures of the backdrops of hill and corrie.

Don Green.

Midges in Scotland:– George Hendry. (The Mercat Press; 75pp.; illus.; 2nd edn.; paperback; ISBN 1873644 612. £4.99.)

This slim volume puts a little more flesh on the bones of the 1989 edition. Field tests conducted in Glen Brittle one muggy July evening were not a success as the book's instructions do not indicate whether it is to be worn, burned or rubbed on.

George Hendry deals with his topic informatively, mixing scientific observation with anecdote, and generally scotching myths. He bemoans the lack of recent research into midge control, and it is disappointing to learn that there are no miracle cures in the offing. There is some useful practical advice, but the main message is to keep slapping on the ointment. Hendry reveals that it is not possible to catch AIDS from midges, although he does not clarify if this applies in unprotected as well as protected situations.

Hendry's final word on the midge, that it is 'a diminutive guardian of the Highlands . . . a significant factor in limiting our grossest activities', will leave many readers scratching their heads. It also seems unkind to compare midges with SMC Hut Custodians.

Alec Keith.

Journals of Kindred Clubs

The Rucksack Club Journals, 1993 and 1994. Editor Inken Blunk.

The big article in the 1993 issue is *The Scottish Cardinals,* by Mike Cudahy. This guy is the sort of bionic walker/android my knees collapse at the sight of. The cardinals are the cardinal Munros of the mainland, i.e. the most west, east, north and southerly. He allowed 10 days, and if I indicate that Day 1 reads: Ben Lomond – Inveroran; 38mls, 5065ft, 9.25 hours then you will know what sort of iron walker we are talking of. The journey summary is some 521 miles, 384 of that on foot the remainder on bike. The daily average was 38.4 miles. Some 3-4 hours of sleep per night was allowed. I won't tell you whether they enjoyed themselves. The 1994 issue repeats what seems to be a peculiarity of southern journals; the cult of the photograph showing a recognisable face, sometimes several times. Just try that one up here! Photographic covers make a distinct difference from our more austere binding, but I still can't live with shiny paper.

Ken Crocket.

On The Veg:– Etchachan Climbing Club Journal 1996, No. 20. Editor John Wilson.

The first thing I did was check that the blue paper used for the cover of this 'small, but powerfully built' publication was not the same paper as that used by our very own thingy – but ours is a darker blue, so either the canny Aberdonians are bleaching left-over SMC paper stock in the perpetual sunshine of the North East Coast, or they are actually buying their own. I can say that getting a copy sent to the SMCJ for review was like getting blood out of granite.

Sadly missing are the cartoon covers of early editions, of which I treasure several early examples. At least the title remains punny. Its 26 pages of text are made up of nine articles. Our own Simon Richardson is one author, writing about *The Cardinal* on Beinn a' Bhuird. Mac Smith does the treatment on the naming of routes, which I found revealing. Jazz, it seems, has had a greater influence on route names than previously known.

Personally, I have had as much fun naming a route as climbing it, a pleasure doubled when some innocent name has annoyed the establishment. *Squareface*, for example, is from a well-loved 78 classic (vinyl youth, not year), in which 'a self-disgusted Wingy Manone intones this drunken soliliqy to a gin bottle: "Old squareface, old double-chin, what you hangin' round for me to sorrow and sigh?", and ends, "better bring in those pink elephants, squareface you got me again".' It's a classic article on classic names by a classic climber!

There is still energy in the far North East, energy visible in the writing which belies the distinct lack of energy in the limp tat carried by most Aberdonians. Waiting for gear to fall on your head at the foot of a big cliff does limit the choice somewhat. A nice wee read, but bring back the cartoon covers lads.

The Pinnacle Club Journal. No. 23, 1994-1996. Editor Chris Stretch.

The attractive cover sketch is from a design for the Club bookplate, by Miss J. Tebbutt, 1947. A nice collection, some 96pp worth, of stories, reports, poems etc. by the women of the Pinnacle Club, whose headed notepaper is subtitled 'for women rock climbers'. Nice to know your *raison d'être* I think! Quite a few of the names will be known to the mountaineering world; several are partners of SMC members. The text is pleasantly broken up by photographs and cartoons. We wish the PC well in their 76th year.

The Himalayan Journal. Vol. 52, 1996, 339pp. ISBN 0 19 564015 2. Editor Harish Kapadia.

Articles by John Hunt, Mick Fowler, Martin Moran, Kurt Diemberger etc., Expeditions and Notes, Panoramas (of the pull-out kind), more than 50 photographs, 15 colour plates and much more leave one exhausted before reading it. The Editor is now on e-mail incidentally (nawang.nkapadia@gems.vsnl.net.in). The adverts are interesting as well, especially the one titled 'Hair Fall?', of interest to the follicularly-challenged.

Cambridge Mountaineering 1996 Journal. Editor Martin Jackson.

Fifty-nine pages of student enthusiasm: 'I could not stop laughing as spindrift avalanches choked me in powder.' This in Scotland, as are several other articles. The usual stuff; late coming off the hoary old Ben etc, but fun nonetheless. Competently put together.

Ken Crocket.

OFFICE BEARERS 1996-97

Honorary President: W. D. Brooker

Honorary Vice-Presidents: James C. Donaldson, M.B.E., Douglas Scott

President: Robert T. Richardson

Vice-Presidents: John Mackenzie, Derek Pyper

Honorary Secretary: John R. R. Fowler, 4 Doune Terrace, Edinburgh, EH3 6DY **Honorary Treasurer:** T. B. Fleming, West Lynn, Dalry, Ayrshire, KA24 4LJ. **Honorary Editor:** K. V. Crocket, Glenisla, Long Row, Menstrie, Clackmannanshire FK11 7EA. **Assistant Editor:** I. H. M. Smart, Auchenleish, Bridge of Cally, by Blairgowrie, Perthshire. **Convener of the Publications Sub-Committee:** D. C. Anderson, Hillfoot House, Hillfoot, Dollar, SK14 7PL. **Honorary Librarian:** R. D. M. Chalmers, 14 Garrioch Drive, Glasgow G20 8RS. **Honorary Custodian of Slides:** G. N. Hunter, Netheraird, Woodlands Road, Rosemount, Blairgowrie, Perthshire, PH10 6JX. **Convener of the Huts Sub-Committee:** G. S. Peet, 6 Roman Way, Dunblane, Perthshire. **Custodian of the CIC Hut:** Robin Clothier, 35 Broompark Drive, Newton Mearns, Glasgow G77 5DZ. **Custodian of Lagangarbh Hut:** R. G. Ross, 16 Milton Court, Milton, Dunbartonshire. **Custodian of the Ling Hut:** D. J. Broadhead, Cul Beag, Blackwood, Urray, by Muir of Ord, IV6 7UL (01463 871274). **Custodian of the Raeburn Hut:** W. Duncan, Kirktoun, East End, Lochwinnoch, Renfrewshire, PA12 4ER. **Committee:** Phil Gribbon; Niall Ritchie; Roger Webb; Bill McKerrow; Simon Richardson; Matthew Shaw; Chris Cartwright; Oliver Turnbull; John Peden. SMC Internet Address – http://www.smc.org.uk/smc/

Journal Information

Editor:	K. V. Crocket, Glenisla, Long Row, Menstrie, Clacks. FK11 7EA (e-mail: kvc@dial.pipex.com).
New Routes Editor:	A. D. Nisbet, 20 Craigie Ave., Boat of Garten, Inverness-shire PH24 3BL. (e-mail: anisbe@globalnet.co.uk).
Editor of Photographs:	Niall Ritchie, 37 Lawsondale Terrace, Westhill, Skene, Aberdeen AB32 6SE.
Advertisements:	D. G. Pyper, 3 Keir Circle, Westhill, Skene, Aberdeen AB32 6RE. (e-mail: d.pyper@leopardmag.co.uk).
Distribution:	D. F. Lang, Hillfoot Hey, 580 Perth Road, Dundee DD2 1PZ.

INSTRUCTIONS TO CONTRIBUTORS

Articles for the Journal should be submitted before the end of January for consideration for the following issue. Lengthy contributions are preferably typed, double-spaced, on one side only, and with ample margins (minimum 30mm). Articles may be accepted on floppy disk, IBM compatible (contact Editor beforehand), or by e-mail. The Editor welcomes material from both members and non-members, with priority being given to articles of Scottish Mountaineering content. Photographs are also welcome, and should be good quality colour slides. All textual material should be sent to the Editor, address and e-mail as above. Photographic material should be sent direct to the Editor of Photographs, address as above.

Copyright. Textual matter appearing in the Miscellaneous section of the Journal, including New Climbs, is copyright of the publishers. Copyright of articles in the main section of the Journal is retained by individual authors.

SCOTTISH MOUNTAINEERING CLUB

SCOTTISH MOUNTAINEERING TRUST

DISTRICT GUIDES

Southern Uplands	£16.95
Southern Highlands	£16.95
Central Highlands	£17.95
The Cairngorms	£17.95
Islands of Scotland (including Skye)	£19.95
North-west Highlands	£17.95

SCRAMBLERS GUIDE

Black Cuillin Ridge	£4.95

CLIMBERS GUIDES (Rock and Ice Guides)

Scottish Winter Climbs	£16.95
Ben Nevis	£14.95
Northern Highlands Vol. 1	£13.95
Northern Highlands Vol. 2	£14.95
Glen Coe (including Glen Etive and Ardgour)	£13.95
The Cairngorms Vol. 1	£11.95
The Cairngorms Vol. 2	£11.95
Skye and the Hebrides Vols. 1 and 2 1997	£19.95
Arran, Arrochar and Southern Highlands 1997	£14.95

Outcrop Guides

North-east Outcrops	£13.95
Lowland Outcrops	£14.95

OTHER PUBLICATIONS

The Munros	£16.95
Munro's Tables	£9.95
The Corbetts and Other Scottish Hills	£16.95
A Chance in a Million – Scottish Avalanches	£4.95
A Century of Scottish Mountaineering	£15.95
Ski Mountaineering in Scotland	£12.95
Ben Nevis – Britain's Highest Mountain	£14.95
Scotland's Mountains	£17.95
The Cairngorms Scene – And Unseen	£6.95
Heading for the Scottish Hills (1996 Edition)	£6.95
Scottish Hill and Mountain Names	£9.95

MAPS

Black Cuillin of Skye (double-sided)	£3.95
Glen Coe	£2.95

Distributed by:
Cordee, 3a De Montfort Street, Leicester LE1 7HD
Telephone: Leicester 0116 254 3579 Fax: 0116 247 1176

These books and maps are available from many bookshops and mountain equipment suppliers

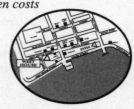

viii

ix

xii

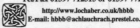

The Ernest Press

Publisher

BIOGRAPHY AND HISTORY

May the Fire be Always Lit: a biography of Jock Nimlin. By Ian Thomson. ISBN 0-948153-39-3. P/back. £11.95. H/back £16.

The First Munroist: a biography of A.E. Robertson. By Peter Drummond & Ian Mitchell. ISBN 0-948-153-19-9. H/back. £13.95.

Menlove: a biography of John Menlove Edwards. By Jim Perrin – Winner Boardman/Tasker Award 1985. ISBN 0-948153-28-8. P/back £9.95.

Hands of a Climber: a biography of Colin Kirkus. By Steve Dean. H/back £15.95. ISBN 0-948153-21-0.

Gary Hemming: the beatnik of the Alps. By Mirella Tenderini. P/back £11.95. ISBN 0-948153-38-5.

Whensoever: 50 years of the RAF Mountain Rescue Service; 1943-1993. By Frank Card. ISBN 0-948153-23-7. H/back £17.95.

ADVENTURE AND TRAVEL

Mountain Holidays. By Janet Adam Smith. ISBN 0 948153 45 8. P/back £12.50.

The Black Cloud: Mountain Misadventures 1928-1966. By Ian Thomson. ISBN 0-948153-20-2. P/back £9.99; H/back £16.

In Monte Viso's Horizon: climbing all the Alpine 4000m peaks. By Will McLewin – Winner Boardman/Tasker Award 1992. ISBN 0-948153-09-1. H/back £16.95.

The Undiscovered Country: the reason we climb. By Phil Bartlett. H/back £15.95. ISBN 0-948153-24-5.

Arka Tagh; the mysterious mountains. By Wm. Holgate. H/back £15.95. ISBN 0-948153-33-4.

Over the Hills & Far Away; essays by Rob Collister. P/back £11.95. ISBN 0-948153-40-7.

Tight Rope: the fun of climbing. By Dennis Gray. P/back £9.95; H/back £16.00. ISBN 0-948153-25-3.

Breaking Loose: a cycle/climbing journey from the UK to Australia. P/back £9.50; H/back £16.00. ISBN 0-948153-26-1.

MOUNTAINEERING ESSAYS

The Ordinary Route. By Harold Drasdo. ISBN 0 948153 46 6. P/back £12.50.

A View from the Ridge: essays by Dave Brown & Ian Mitchell – Winner Boardmen/Tasker Award 1991. P/back £6.50. ISBN 0-948153-11-3.

A Necklace of Slings: essays by Dave Gregory. H/back £15.00. ISBN 0-948153-37-7.

THE ERNEST PRESS, 8 Rehoboth Est., Llanfaelog, Anglesey, LL63 5TS. Tel/Fax 01407 811098.

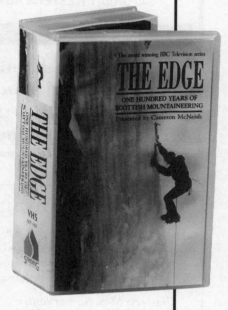